IN PURSUIT OF THE WHITE HOUSE

IN PURSUIT OF THE WHITE HOUSE
How We Choose Our Presidential Nominees

Edited by

William G. Mayer
Northeastern University

Chatham House Publishers, Inc.
Chatham, New Jersey

IN PURSUIT OF THE WHITE HOUSE
How We Choose Our Presidential Nominees

Chatham House Publishers, Inc.
Box One, Chatham, New Jersey 07928

Publisher: Edward Artinian
Editor: Christopher J. Kelaher
Production supervisor: Katharine F. Miller
Cover design: Lawrence Ratzkin
Composition: Bang, Motley, Olufsen
Printing and binding: R.R. Donnelley and Sons Company

LIBRARY OF CONGRESS CATALOGING-IN-PUBLICATION DATA

In pursuit of the White House : how we choose our
   presidential nominees / edited by William G. Mayer.
         p.   cm.
      Includes bibliographical references and index.
      ISBN 1-56643-027-5
      1. Presidents—United States—Nomination.
   I. Mayer, William G., 1956–   .
   JK 521.I5   1996
   324.6'3'0973—dc20   95-20995
                                                           CIP

Manufactured in the United States of America
10   9   8   7   6   5   4   3   2   1

To the memory of Joseph King
(1955–1995)

Now cracks a noble heart. Good night, sweet prince,
And flights of angels sing thee to thy rest!

And for Mary Beth and their children

Contents

Tables and Figures

Tables

Figures

Preface

Not so very long ago, American political science could justly be accused of a strange sort of tunnel vision when it came to the study of U.S. presidential elections. While a great deal of energy, money, and ink was devoted to the general election battle between the Democrats and Republicans, remarkably little attention was given to the presidential nomination process that preceded it and the question of how it was that, among the dozens or even hundreds of people who gave serious thought to running for the nation's highest office, two particular men were selected to be their party's standard-bearers. As recently as about 1974, one could master the academic literature on presidential nominations by reading about a half dozen books and perhaps ten or twelve significant articles. Today, studies of the presidential nomination process represent one of the most rapidly growing subfields in American political science.

The heightened attention to presidential nominations—not only from academics, but from journalists, party activists, and ordinary citizens—is a product of several interrelated developments. The wholesale rewriting of the delegate selection rules and campaign finance laws between 1969 and 1974—shaking up a system that had seen little formal change since the 1920s—reminded observers of the many and complex ways in which rules shape behavior, and provided a fascinating case study in the dynamics of political "reform." A number of controversial nominations—especially those conferred by the Republicans in 1964 and the Democrats in 1972—made it clear that what went on during the year or so before the party conventions could be at least as consequential as what occurred in the two or three months between the conventions and the November balloting.

Above all, the race for the nomination has simply become much more visible. Where presidential contenders once announced their candidacies at the beginning of the election year or in the final months of the preceding year, contemporary aspirants for the White House routinely launch their campaigns a year or a year-and-a-half before the national conventions. And where the ultimate power of decision on presidential nominations once rested with a relatively small number of party elites, who conducted their negotiations and made their choices behind closed doors, the current system is considerably more public, with almost all delegates selected in primaries and caucuses that are open to essentially any American citizen who wants to participate in them. Indeed, as several commentators have pointed out, while the United States is often criticized for its low level of voter participation in the general elections, there is no other democracy in the world where so many people take part in party nomination decisions.

Each presidential nomination race is, inevitably, a personal drama: a test of the candidates' strengths and abilities and sheer physical stamina; a high-stakes showdown between the rival campaign managers and consultants; a wild and exhausting ride for reporters. And if this were all there was to the process, there would be little to say about it in advance—except, perhaps to provide biographies of the principal candidates and their handlers. But in fact, there is a lot more to a presidential nomination race than personality and luck. Running for a presidential nomination is not like writing a novel, where a lone, creative individual confronts a blank page, limited only by his or her skill and imagination. Every nomination battle is fought within a highly constrained environment, where certain tasks are required, some forms of behavior are expected or frowned upon, and various strategies are favored or precluded. An imposing mix of party rules and federal and state laws closely regulates the selection of national convention delegates, the forms and opportunities for public participation, and the raising of campaign money. Such rules, along with past practices and the larger political culture, have given rise to various public expectations about how the candidates will conduct their campaigns. And the press has its own set of norms and routines that help structure the way the race will be reported and interpreted. Thus, while it may not be possible to predict the outcome of a nomination contest in advance (see, however, chapter 2), a great deal can be said about the inescapable realities and choices that every campaign will need to confront.

It is this set of rules, norms, and regularities—what Nelson W. Polsby and Aaron Wildavsky have called the "strategic environment" of presidential election politics—that provides the subject matter of this book. In brief, the book attempts to present a broad overview of the current nomination process through a detailed examination of some of its most significant components: money and media, super Tuesday and the invisible primary, caucuses, social movements, third parties, and nomination activists. Not surprisingly, most of the analysis in each chapter concerns how its subject has functioned in past nomination races. But each author also seeks to draw out some general lessons about the character of the nomination process, and thus to offer some guidance and perspective as to what lies ahead in 1996. In addition, this book tries to showcase some of the most interesting work now being done on the politics of presidential nominations, in order to make its insights and conclusions available to a wider audience.

Acknowledgments

Since most of the authors in this book have already acknowledged the many people who made substantial contributions to the individual chapters, I wish only to add a few words of appreciation and gratitude to those who assisted in bringing the book as a whole to completion. Particular thanks are due to Ed Artinian, the hardest-working man in political science publishing, for his early interest in this project and his advice and support in shaping the final product. Thanks also to the rest of the Chatham House staff, especially Katharine Miller, Chris Kelaher, and Cynthia Arbour, for their attentiveness to detail as the book moved through production.

On the academic side, anyone who does work in this field owes a substantial debt to Nelson W. Polsby and Gerald M. Pomper, two scholars who recognized that presidential nominations were important long before the rest of the profession caught on. In my case, the debt is personal as well as intellectual, and this book owes much to both men for their support and encouragement. I also benefited significantly from the advice and suggestions of Sandy Maisel and John Strahinich.

Finally, like my first book and everything else I shall ever write, I regard this volume ultimately as a triumph of family. A decade and a half of academic life has made me cynical about a lot of things—but not about my family. Lacking any real way to "repay" this debt, I can only offer my heartfelt love and appreciation to my mother and father; Joe, Rita, and Lauren; Mary Beth, Joe, and Allie; Jack; Tom; and Rosemary, Scott, Andy, and Steven. Most of all, for expressions of love and sacrifice too numerous to mention, I wish to thank Amy Logan, the newest member of my family, my best friend, my wife.

I

The Invisible Primary

Emmett H. Buell, Jr.

The afternoon of 1 July 1994 was typically hot and humid in Nashville when a predominantly white and middle-class crowd of Tennesseans began forming at the Davis Kidd bookstore in suburban Green Hills. By six o'clock —the hour of Dan Quayle's scheduled appearance to autograph copies of his best-selling memoir of political trials and triumphs[1]—the line extended from a parking lot into the spacious main floor. From there the queue ascended a long stairway to clog even more corridors on the next level until it reached the table where, amid the balloons and bunting, the former vice-president would autograph as many books as time permitted. (Nashville's Channel 5 later estimated the turnout at 800 to 1,000; the next morning's *Tennessean* guessed 1,200.[2]) An upbeat Quayle swept into the store with his entourage half an hour late from taping a segment of TNN's "Music City Tonight." Ringed by police and youthful aides, he obliged local reporters with a few sound bites before doffing his jacket and signing books at the "extremely rapid" pace promised by store management. It is unlikely that many witnessing this event regarded it merely as the marketing of another celebrity's book. A more likely view pronounced by pundits across the land was that of a probable presidential candidate working hard to entice friendly crowds and generate favorable publicity during the long run-up to the 1996 caucuses and primaries.

Hadley's "Invisible Primary"

If the pundits were right, private citizen Quayle had journeyed to Nashville (and to thirty-five other cities on the same book tour) for the latest iteration of what journalist Arthur T. Hadley described almost twenty years ago as the "invisible primary."[3] Probably the first to publicize, if not recognize, the importance of this lengthy interval between the last election of a president and the next cycle of presidential primaries,[4] Hadley wrote an erratic, often mistaken, but frequently insightful book about the preliminary campaigns of Senator Birch Bayh of Indiana, Senator Lloyd Bentsen of Texas, former governor Jimmy Carter of Georgia, former senator Fred Harris of Oklahoma, Senator Henry Jackson of Washington State, former governor Ronald Reagan of California, Congressman Morris Udall of Arizona, Governor George Wallace of Alabama, and several other aspirants, assessing their prospects for the upcoming nomination battles of 1976.

Hadley reckoned that the process of selecting the 1976 nominees had begun no later than the day of Richard Nixon's reelection in 1972. Though paralyzed by an assailant's bullet while campaigning for the 1972 Democratic nomination, Wallace still aspired to the White House and had not dismantled his organization. Similarly, according to Hadley, Jackson had "never stopped running" since 1972.[5] Ironically, given Hadley's dismissive treatment of Carter, the future president was one of the first out of either party's gate, having thought seriously about a 1976 race for five years and having actively campaigned since early 1973.[6] Hadley paid much greater attention to other long-shots, such as Bayh and Udall, perhaps because they responded more graciously to his inquiries. In any event, nine Democrats and two Republicans had formally entered the race when Hadley stopped following the candidates in late November of 1975.

His cast of characters also included hopefuls who tested the waters early and decided not to take the plunge. One case in point was Senator Walter Mondale of Minnesota, whose 1976 candidacy effectively began on election day of 1972, according to Hadley, when an effusive Hubert Humphrey endorsed him as a future Democratic nominee. "If it isn't being too sacrilegious," said a man who knew something about losing his head to presidential ambition, "I don't mind being John the Baptist for Walter Mondale."[7]

Yet, after spending $100,000 and stumping on behalf of seventy-odd Democratic candidates for congressional and statewide office in less than a year's time, Mondale dropped out of the race on 20 November 1974. Mondale, moreover, spent most of his time as a 1976 candidate overshadowed by Senator Edward M. Kennedy of Massachusetts. Early front-runner Kennedy decided against making the race, however, after pondering the legacy of Chappaquiddick, related polling negatives, unfavorable primary scheduling, and the recently amended Federal Election Campaign Act (FECA). Senator Charles Percy of Illinois gave up the Republican race after ten months of campaigning in twenty-six states and raising a paltry $215,000. Percy had taken a candidate's first steps right after Nixon's reelection but got lost in terrain suddenly altered by Watergate. Endeavoring to make the most of Watergate, former attorney general Elliot Richardson visited thirty-six states between February and November of 1974 before joining Percy on the Republican sidelines.[8]

Experience has confirmed Hadley's account of the invisible primary as a time of as many candidacies aborted as brought to term. Consider the run-up to 1988 when Governor Bill Clinton of Arkansas, Senator Dale Bumpers of Arkansas, Senator Sam Nunn of Georgia, Governor Mario Cuomo of New York, Senator Paul Laxalt of Nevada, Congresswoman Patricia Schroeder of Colorado, Governor Richard Celeste of Ohio, and former U.N. ambassador Jeane Kirkpatrick all hinted at getting into the race and agonized over their prospects before bowing out. (A former senator, Gary Hart of Colorado, made history, of course, by formally announcing his candidacy in mid-April of 1987, pulling out almost a month later, and then rejoining the race in December.[9]) Similarly, the 1992 invisible primary saw more Democratic aspirants declare themselves noncandidates than candidates. Among the most noteworthy no-shows were Cuomo, the Reverend Jesse Jackson, George McGovern, Senator John D. Rockefeller IV of West Virginia, Congressman Richard Gephardt of Missouri, and Senator Al Gore of Tennessee. As for the 1996 Republican race, Governor Carroll Campbell of South Carolina withdrew in June 1994, followed two months later by William Bennett, former education secretary and drug czar. Dick Cheney and Jack Kemp, both former members of the Bush cabinet, pulled out in January 1995. Quayle got out in February.

Of all the generalizations in Hadley's book, the one most validated by experience in presidential nominating races since 1976 is that the process begins long before Iowa and New Hampshire voters select the first delegates or, for that matter, well before the first aspirants formally announce their candidacies. However labeled, the notion of a long, largely unheralded, but important run-up is now part of the conventional wisdom about presidential nominating politics.[10] Indeed, some invisible primaries get under way long before the general election that officially ends the old cycle. Hart and Jackson effectively announced their 1988 intentions while conceding the 1984 nomination to Mondale at the Democratic convention in San Francisco. The "great mentioners" of the press began naming likely contestants for the 1996 Republican nomination more than a year before the New Hampshire primary of 18 February 1992.[11]

A more dubious proposition is that incumbent government officials operate at a distinct disadvantage during the invisible primary compared to former officeholders. According to Hadley, "the candidate who has time to travel and is reasonably appealing gets seen, while the candidate who elects to stay at his work as governor, mayor, or senator loses out. We have created a new American job classification: Running for President."[12]

The alleged advantage of ex-officialdom is examined at length later in this chapter. At present, it is enough to note that unemployed and employed aspirants alike travel extensively during the invisible primary. The same goes for front-runners, long-shots, and all others in between. Many, though hardly all, of the stops in this seemingly endless cycle of early campaigning are in Iowa, New Hampshire, and other key states in a front-loaded schedule.[13] As Hadley described it, continuous travel was the crucible in which potential candidacies either hardened or dissolved, where messages resonated or flopped, where money got raised or not. Table 1.1 illustrates the demands of invisible primary campaigning by listing Lamar Alexander's schedule of state party conventions, forums, dinners, and other political gatherings in 1993–94, including a dozen such appearances in Iowa and New Hampshire.

Bearing in mind that Hadley finished his manuscript months before the selection of a single delegate in the caucuses and primaries of 1976, one might empathize with him even while disputing his sweeping generalization that all subsequent stages of the nominating process are mere reflections of what already has been decided during the invisible primary. "The burden of this book," he avowed at the outset, "is that the critical battles for the presidency are fought long before the first state primaries. Far from being decisive politically, the primaries appear more as a ritual encounter, a symbolic show whose results reinforce a victory already decided."[14]

The Strategic Environment of Invisible Primaries

It is to Hadley's credit that he tempered the grandiose claim just quoted by acknowledging the importance of formal rules and other variables long familiar to political scientists as elements of the "strategic environment" of presidential nominating politics.[15] According to Hadley, success in the invisible primary depended on the right mix of character, message, money, staff, popular appeal, media coverage, and, hardly least important, luck.[16] Furthermore, a serious candidate had to develop a strategy applying these factors to political reality as generally understood. Such a plan, he insisted, meant more than "just yo-yoing around from invitation to invitation."[17]

Planning is indeed essential in today's strategic environment—that complicated framework of formal rules, generally accepted conventions, and myriad other circumstances within which the major parties nominate their presidential tickets. Every serious aspirant must plan to overcome the obstacles and exploit the opportunities created by formal regulations governing campaign finance, delegate selection, and the scheduling of state primaries and caucuses. Rather than treat all candidates alike, the rules help some and handicap others. The time to anticipate such consequences is before rather than after they come into play.

Anticipation begins with the calendar of presidential primaries and caucuses two or more years distant. A "strategic imperative" for every serious

TABLE 1.1
SCHEDULE OF LAMAR ALEXANDER'S INVISIBLE
PRIMARY CAMPAIGN, 6 FEBRUARY 1993
THROUGH 24 JUNE 1994

Date	Event
6 February 1993	Knox County, Tennessee, GOP dinner in Knoxville
8 February	Carter County, Tennessee, GOP dinner
19 February	Hudson Institute dinner in Indianapolis, Indiana
20 February	Shelby County, Tennessee, GOP dinner in Memphis
23 February	School visits in Akron, Ohio
6 March	Louisiana Women's GOP convention in New Orleans
8 March	GOP Lincoln Day dinner in Cleveland, Ohio
9 March	GOP Lincoln Day dinner in Albany, New York
12 March	President's dinner in Washington, D.C.
19 March	GOP national congressional campaign committee breakfast in Palm Springs, California
30 March	Tarrant County GOP dinner in Fort Worth, Texas
16 April	Arkansas GOP dinner in Little Rock
26 April	Free Congress Foundation anniversary in Washington, D.C.
7 May	Southern GOP Exchange Conference in Louisville, Kentucky
9 May	William Penn commencement in Des Moines, Iowa
1 June	Republican Neighborhood Meeting in Milwaukee, Wisconsin
12 June	Pachyderm dinner in St. Louis, Missouri
18 June	Iowa Association of Business and Industry in Spencer, Iowa
19 June	Utah State GOP convention in Salt Lake City
24 June	CNN interview in Washington, D.C.
26 June	Young Republican convention in Charleston, West Virginia
26 June	*National Review* conference in Washington, D.C.
6 July	Republican Neighborhood Meeting in San Antonio, Texas
16 July	College Republican conference in Washington, D.C.
21 July	President's dinner, honoring Reagan, in Los Angeles
22 July	Republican National Committee dinner in Los Angeles
28 July	National Conference of State Legislators convention in San Diego
3 August	Republican Neighborhood Meeting in Orlando, Florida
10 August	Rochester-Buffalo tour with Congressman Bill Paxon of New York
18 August	Bull Moose Club of Des Moines, Iowa
21 August	Louisiana State GOP convention in New Orleans
28 August	Rhode Island GOP dinner in Newport
7 September	Republican Neighborhood Meeting in Springfield, Illinois
10 September	Campaigning for Republicans in Virginia
17 September	Ashbrook Center dinner in Ashland, Ohio
20 September	School Choice Initiative events in San Diego
25 September	National Federation of Republican Women conference in Las Vegas, Nevada
1 October	Southern GOP Exchange in New Orleans
7 October	Alliance for Better Schools in Washington, D.C.
15 October	Western States Leadership Conference in Santa Fe, New Mexico

20 October	Board of Home Builders and Realtors in Akron, Ohio
22 October	Alabama GOP Women's dinner in Birmingham
23 October	Tennessee GOP Women's lunch in Chattanooga
26 October	Sioux County GOP dinner in Sioux Center, Iowa
28 October	Public forum in Springfield, Massachusetts
2 November	Republican Neighborhood Meeting in Des Moines, Iowa
3 November	School Choice Roundtable in Lansing, Michigan
5 November	New Hampshire State GOP dinner in Bedford
6 November	New Hampshire GOP town meetings in Derry, Rochester, and Dover; meetings with students and faculty at University of New Hampshire
9 November	Dallas GOP Forum in Dallas, Texas
20 November	Richmond Forum in Richmond, Virginia
20 January 1994	Nixon inaugural anniversary in Yorba Linda, California
3 February	Team 100 dinner in Washington, D.C.
8 February	Republican Neighborhood Meeting in San Francisco
11 February	Lincoln Day lunch in Springfield, Illinois
12 February	C-PAC meeting in Washington, D.C.
15 February	Lincoln Day dinner in Lake View, Iowa
16 February	"Larry King Live" interview in Washington, D.C.
5 March	Cobb County GOP breakfast in Atlanta, Georgia
8 March	Republican Neighborhood Meeting in Atlanta
16 March	New Hampshire Board of Education in Durham
21 March	New Castle Chamber dinner in Wilmington, Delaware
22 March	Don Sundquist campaign dinner in Memphis, Tennessee
29 March	Taft lunch in Cleveland, Ohio
29 March	Hudson dinner in Indianapolis, Indiana
30 March	Citizen's Insurance Symposium in Lansing, Michigan
6 April	Education forum in Augusta, Maine
7 April	WMUR-TV interview in Manchester, New Hampshire
11 April	Catholic Archdiocese in Louisville, Kentucky
12 April	Republican Neighborhood Meeting in Bedford, New Hampshire
16 April	Lincoln Day dinner in Portsmouth, New Hampshire
28 April	Lincoln Day dinner in Murfreesboro, Tennessee
30 April	Southern GOP leadership conference in Atlanta
4 May	Middlesex GOP Club dinner in Boston
10 May	Republican Neighborhood Meeting in Grand Rapids, Michigan
18 May	McKinley Day dinner in Akron, Ohio
21 May	Warren County GOP dinner in Carlisle, Iowa
24 June	Iowa State GOP convention and straw poll in Des Moines

SOURCES: Alexander's schedule provided by Kevin Phillips of the Republican Exchange Satellite Network, with additional information supplied by James McKay and Jeff Lucey of the New Hampshire Republican State Committee.

candidate is making the most of the sequence of early caucuses and primaries. Leading contenders must satisfy the pundits in these early contests, and doing "better than expected" is the only hope of most long-shots. However calibrated by the press, success in such events generally aids poll standings, attracts more coverage, and swells campaign coffers. The combined effect in some cases is enough to gain "momentum" for overcoming adversity later in the season.[18] Serious campaigns spend much of the invisible primary planning for these contingencies, and nothing matters more to their calculations than the scheduling of actual primaries and caucuses. When will Iowa and New Hampshire start the process? Which states vote in the next six weeks and in what sequence? How many delegates will these early contests select?

"Front-loading" is the scheduling of primaries early in an election year to enhance the importance of particular states or regions in the overall process. Many officials in the national parties welcome this trend as a way of swiftly concluding a divisive process. In 1972, the first race of the contemporary nominating system, the Democrats held no primaries in February, only three in March, and no fewer than fifteen in May and June. In 1976, however, the number of Democratic primaries held before 1 April doubled to six (of twenty-seven total). This figure increased again in 1980 to ten (of thirty-five total) and remained at ten in 1984 (of thirty total). The quantum leap came in 1988, when twenty-two of thirty-seven Democratic primaries took place in February and March, sixteen on a single "Super Tuesday." Of forty Democratic primaries in 1992, seventeen occurred before the end of March. Republicans were obliged to emulate the Democratic calendar in every instance.[19]

Increased front-loading, of course, meant earlier harvests of delegates, with obvious consequences for the nominating process. According to Elaine Kamarck and Kenneth Goldstein, the proportion of Democratic delegates chosen in caucuses and primaries before 1 April increased from 21 percent in 1972 to 26 percent in 1976, 40 percent in 1980, 42 percent in 1984, and 52 percent in 1988, before falling back to 41 percent in 1992. By 1980 the Republicans were selecting 40 percent of all their delegates over the same span of eight weeks. This figure jumped to 61 percent in 1988, before settling at 48 percent in 1992.[20]

Front-loading in 1996 promises to set new records for both parties, and, at this writing, at least twenty-four Republican and as many Democratic primaries are scheduled for February and March. Moreover, the first stage of precinct caucuses will occur before 1 April in twelve of the fourteen states where Democrats plan to select delegates in a caucus-convention process. Table 1.2 lists these and all other 1996 nominating contests in chronological order according to tentative calendars released by the national committees of both major parties. Overall, pundits estimate, the emerging lineup of February and March contests could select more than 70 percent of all Republican convention delegates.[21] Most Democratic delegates also will have been chosen at this point.

The prospect of selecting so many delegates so early in the process reflects the early primary plans of the biggest states. At least seven of the ten most populous states have scheduled 1996 primaries before the end of

TABLE 1.2

FRONT-LOADING OF 1996 PRESIDENTIAL PRIMARIES AND CAUCUSES

State	Republican timetable	Type of contest	Number of delegates	Democratic timetable	Type of contest	Number of delegates
Iowa	12 February	caucuses	25	12 February	caucuses	48
New Hampshire	20 February	primary	16	20 February	primary	20
Delaware	24 February	primary	12	24 February	primary	14
Arizona	27 February	primary	39	27 February	primary	44
South Dakota	27 February	primary	18	27 February	primary	15
South Carolina	2 March	primary	37	9 March	primary	49
American Samoa	date not set	undecided	4	5 March	caucuses	3
Colorado	5 March	primary	26	5 March	primary	49
Georgia	5 March	primary	42	5 March	primary	76
Maryland	5 March	primary	32	5 March	primary	68
Utah	date not set	convention	28	5 March	caucuses	24
Vermont	5 March	primary	12	26 March	caucuses	15
Minnesota	5 March/2 April	caucuses/primary	33	5 March/2 April	caucuses/primary	76
New York	7 March	primary	102	7 March	primary	244
Nevada	date not set	caucuses	14	10 March	caucuses	18
Florida	12 March	primary	98	12 March	primary	152
Hawaii	date not set	caucuses	14	12 March	caucuses	20
Louisiana	12 March	primary	27	12 March	primary	59
Massachusetts	12 March	primary	37	5 March	primary	93
Mississippi	12 March	primary	32	12 March	primary	38
Missouri	date not set	caucuses	35	12 March	caucuses	76
Oklahoma	12 March	primary	38	12 March	primary	44
Rhode Island	12 March	primary	16	12 March	primary	22
Tennessee	12 March	primary	37	12 March	primary	68

State	Date	Type	Delegates	Date	Type	Delegates
Texas	12 March	primary	123	12 March	primary/caucuses	194
Puerto Rico	17 March	primary	14	7 April	primary	51
Illinois	19 March	primary	69	19 March	primary	164
Michigan	19 March	primary	57	19 March	primary	128
Ohio	19 March	primary	67	19 March	primary	147
California	26 March	primary	163	26 March	primary	363
Connecticut	26 March	primary	27	26 March	primary	53
Virgin Islands	date not set	caucuses	4	30 March	caucuses	3
Kansas	2 April	primary	31	2 April	caucuses	36
Wisconsin	2 April	primary	36	2 April	primary	79
Virginia	date not set	undecided	53	13 April	caucuses	79
Pennsylvania	23 April	primary	73	23 April	primary	167
Alaska	26–27 April	convention	19	4 April	caucuses	13
Maine	3 May	caucuses	15	5 March	primary	23
Wyoming	4 May	caucuses	20	9 March	caucuses	13
Guam	date not set	undecided	4	5 May	caucuses	3
District of Columbia	7 May	primary	14	7 May	primary	17
Indiana	7 May	primary	52	7 May	primary	74
North Carolina	7 May	primary	58	7 May	primary	84
Nebraska	14 May	primary	24	14 May	primary	25
West Virginia	14 May	primary	18	14 May	primary	30
Arkansas	21 May	primary	20	28 May	primary	36
Oregon	21 May	primary	23	21 May	primary	47
Idaho	28 May	primary	23	5 March	caucuses	18
Kentucky	28 May	primary	26	28 May	primary	51
Washington	28 May	primary	36	5 March	caucuses	74
Alabama	4 June	primary	39	4 June	primary	54
Montana	4 June	primary	14	4 June	primary	16
New Jersey	4 June	primary	48	4 June	primary	104

Continued . . .

State	Republican timetable	Type of contest	Number of delegates	Democratic timetable	Type of contest	Number of delegates
New Mexico	4 June	primary	18	4 June	primary	25
North Dakota	11 June	primary	18	7–21 March	caucuses	14

SOURCES: Republican data provided by Mark Acton of the Republican National Committee; Democratic data supplied by Hemal K. Vaidya of the Democratic National Committee. Both schedules were updated with information reported in "The Primary Trail 1996," *Time*, 13 March 1995. Democrats Abroad caucuses of 9–11 March omitted. At this writing Connecticut, Rhode Island, and Massachusetts were expected to move their primaries up to 5 March, possibly joining Vermont and Maine in an effort to enhance New England's role in the nomination process.

March. In addition to Texas, Florida, Illinois, and Michigan, with their recent history of early primaries, the list now includes California, New York, Ohio, and possibly Pennsylvania. In previous cycles of the contemporary nominating process, Californians voted on the first Tuesday in June, New York Democrats in April, Ohioans in May or June, and Pennsylvanians in April.

So lopsided a calendar dictates the invisible primary strategy of every serious candidate. Front-runners and long-shots alike must raise enormous sums to compete in so many primaries in so little time. Candidates must also know that the media will judge their early efforts in the front-loaded states and help or hinder their campaigns accordingly. News organizations typically base such preliminary evaluations on poll standings, straw votes at party gatherings, noteworthy endorsements, and fund-raising prowess. The sheer volume of news coverage generally interacts with poll ratings in so reciprocal a fashion that cause and effect are difficult to disentangle.[22] Notable success (or failure) in raising money also attracts coverage.[23]

No less a part of the strategic environment is the *fortuna* factor mentioned by Hadley. Candidates cannot escape the winds of circumstance. Unforeseen developments dash some candidacies into oblivion and loft others to premature heights. Watergate elevated Gerald Ford on the ruins of Nixon's second term in 1974. Scandal destroyed front-runner Hart's credibility in 1987 and likewise drove Senator Joseph Biden from the race. In the aftermath of Desert Storm, one Democratic heavyweight after another shrank from entering the fray against George Bush.

Clearly, the invisible primary is now a fundamental part of the strategic environment, for the strategic environment of today's nominating process requires all serious aspirants to compete in the invisible primary. Only a Croesus of continental fame and uncommon readiness to spend his own millions can forgo this preliminary phase and still pursue a major-party nomination with any prospect of success. Lesser mortals must make the most of these early days to refine their messages, enlist staff, appeal to activists, and, perhaps most important, raise sufficient sums to support an actual primary campaign. And, as we have seen, the invisible primary eliminates as many potential presidents as the New Hampshire primary.

Anticlimax after the Invisible Primary?

What, then, are we to make of Hadley's argument of invisible rather than actual primaries determining presidential nominations? Importance is one thing, finality another. No one need deny the importance of the invisible primary in setting the stage and auditioning everyone who wants to play the lead part. Whether the invisible primary determines who gets which parts is another matter. Let us explore some of the reasons why all is not anticlimax after this preliminary period, beginning with money.

EARLY CAMPAIGN FINANCES

Since front-loading is so powerful a fillip to early fund raising, the projected 1996 calendar demands nothing less than a prodigious effort by every Republican aspirant (and any Democrat willing to contest Clinton's renomination). Republican operative Ed Rollins stated the point with characteristic bluntness: "From Super Bowl 1995 through Super Bowl 1996 a candidate has to raise between $20 million and $30 million in bites of $1,000 maximum. That takes a lot of time and organization."[24]

Rollins has a point, even if his admonition pertains only to those aspects of prenomination finances closely regulated by the FECA.[25] This law provides matching funds for qualified candidates seeking a major-party nomination, with the first payments issued on 1 January of each presidential election year. To qualify, each aspirant first must raise at least $100,000 from individual contributors in no fewer than twenty states, where the minimum per state is $5,000 and the maximum per individual is $250. (Of all candidates seeking major-party nominations since matching funds became part of the FECA, only Republican John Connally declined to take the taxpayers' money and thereby consent to government limits on campaign spending.) Thereafter individuals may give no more than $1,000 to a campaign committee, up to $250 of which the Federal Election Commission (FEC) matches when contributions are by check. Political action committee (PAC) donations cannot exceed $5,000 per committee and are not matched. The more a campaign raises in individual contributions, then, the more it earns in matching funds, at least up to a cap seldom if ever reached. The good news for long-shots unable to raise huge sums is that even modest success with individual contributors will yield enough in matching funds to run a respectable race, at least in the first few states to vote. The bad news, of course, is that modest success begets less government money than huge success, hence the perpetuation of inequality among campaigns.

If the invisible primary decides most nominations, as Hadley maintains, one would expect a rather strong correlation between money raised during this preliminary period and success in subsequent primaries and caucuses. Table 1.3 compares the finances of Democratic candidates in every invisible primary from the 1974 enactment of matching funds through 1992.

The table offers several instructive, if incomplete, indicators of each Democrat's finances right up to the beginning of each election year.[26] A critical sign, of course, is how much each campaign officially raised from individual and group contributors. This information appears under the receipts column and illuminates the inequality of resources in one important respect. Expenditure data also clarifies the picture, since successful candidates must spend as well as raise money. Still other considerations are cash on hand and debts owed to vendors of essential services. Other things being equal, rich is better than poor and surplus is better than deficit.

TABLE 1.3
DEMOCRATIC CANDIDATE FINANCES THROUGH
DECEMBER OF YEAR PRECEDING
PRESIDENTIAL ELECTION

Candidates	Receipts	Expenditures	Cash on hand	Campaign debts
1976 candidates				
Birch Bayh	$337,347	$294,085	$9,389	N.A.
Lloyd Bentsen	2,107,026	2,058,873	N.A.	N.A.
Jimmy Carter	1,035,949	977,917	N.A.	N.A.
Frank Church	26,832	13,538	13,294	N.A.
Fred Harris	436,075	395,613	N.A.	N.A.
Henry Jackson	3,358,649	2,448,061	N.A.	N.A.
Terry Sanford	373,144	369,274	N.A.	N.A.
Milton Shapp	283,878	280,369	−28,535	N.A.
Sargent Shriver	388,956	377,163	−17,126	N.A.
Morris Udall	964,183	960,237	N.A.	N.A.
George Wallace	5,951,923	5,563,735	N.A.	N.A.
1980 candidates				
Jerry Brown	$1,216,714	$1,143,836	$223,538	0
Jimmy Carter	5,751,579	4,854,219	911,000	0
Edward Kennedy	3,884,375	3,475,206	418,832	$905,973
1984 candidates				
Reubin Askew	$2,191,786	$2,084,758	$107,025	$608,417
Alan Cranston	4,715,995	4,742,997	27,001	840,164
John Glenn	6,417,718	6,322,862	99,674	1,029,841
Gary Hart	1,874,083	1,876,315	−2,231	1,046,514
Ernest Hollings	1,627,605	1,564,155	62,611	338,152
Jesse Jackson	309,077	193,932	98,547	0
George McGovern	249,827	159,295	90,532	44,857
Walter Mondale	11,448,262	11,102,680	345,581	775,301
1988 candidates				
Bruce Babbitt	$2,446,219	$2,342,291	$103,928	$163,000
Joseph Biden	3,915,213	3,893,498	21,715	86,317
Michael Dukakis	10,765,529	8,584,801	2,180,728	625,224
Richard Gephardt	5,905,763	5,120,921	781,841	1,909,363
Al Gore	3,941,887	3,047,814	894,073	106,315
Gary Hart	2,301,247	2,177,722	123,524	92,522
Jesse Jackson	2,017,765	2,003,186	14,580	364,245
Paul Simon	6,056,829	5,996,339	60,490	1,187,257
1992 candidates				
Jerry Brown	$514,817	$456,132	$57,684	0
Bill Clinton	3,304,020	1,414,591	1,889,429	$424,698
Tom Harkin	2,182,070	1,979,548	202,522	0

Continued ...

EMMETT H. BUELL, JR.

TABLE 1.3 — CONTINUED

	Receipts	Expenditures	Cash on hand	Campaign debts
Bob Kerrey	$1,945,313	$1,360,493	$584,819	0
Paul Tsongas	1,313,189	1,200,390	112,798	$245,935
Douglas Wilder	512,694	356,074	156,620	118,265

SOURCES: "Presidential Campaign Financing 1973–75," *Congressional Quarterly Weekly Report* 347 (2 February 1976): 319; 1980–92 data kindly supplied by Robert Biersack of the Federal Election Commission.

A simple test of the Hadley thesis is to determine how many eventual nominees surpassed their rivals on the measures reported in table 1.3. Although early debt had little bearing on later success, the other indicators proved more illuminating. After 1976, the candidate who had raised the most money at the end of the invisible primary went on to capture the Democratic nomination. The eventual nominee also had the most cash on hand in at least four of these races and outspent his rivals in three of the five.

It is another matter, however, to conjure the chief rivals of future nominees out of these early finances. Only in 1980 did the hierarchy of financial advantage faithfully manifest itself in primary and caucus outcomes. Looking solely at 1983 campaign finances, no one would have projected Hart as Mondale's most serious rival in 1984. As the invisible primary neared an end, Hart ranked fifth among the eight Democrats in receipts and expenditures, dead last in cash on hand, and first in debt. The financial picture in 1987 gave little basis for picking Gore and Jackson as Dukakis's main foes in 1988, since the two of them together had raised less than Senator Paul Simon and scarcely more than Gephardt. Gore looked comparatively strong only with respect to cash on hand, while in this regard, as in receipts and spending, Jackson lagged well behind everyone else. As for 1991, Senator Tom Harkin's finances looked significantly better than those of Paul Tsongas or Jerry Brown. First of the 1992 pack to form a campaign committee, Tsongas nonetheless trailed all other major Democratic candidates in fund raising except Brown, and Brown, of course, made an issue of not accepting contributions of more than $100. Tsongas and Brown also reported the smallest amounts of cash on hand.

Table 1.4 extends the comparison to Republican finances. According to the same criteria applied to the Democrats, Reagan should have won in 1976 and Connally in 1980. Reagan led Ford, the 1976 nominee, in every category of financial activity, and Connally likewise surpassed Reagan, the 1980 nominee. Prediction of Bush's main adversary in 1988 would have

TABLE 1.4

REPUBLICAN CANDIDATE FINANCES THROUGH DECEMBER
OF YEAR PRECEDING PRESIDENTIAL ELECTION

Candidates	Receipts	Expenditures	Cash on hand	Campaign debts
1976 candidates				
Gerald Ford	$1,688,256	$1,473,450	$185,845	N.A.
Ronald Reagan	1,925,571	1,508,846	200,249	N.A.
1980 candidates				
John Anderson	$505,989	$476,421	$29,568	$50,000
Howard Baker	3,084,617	2,944,783	139,716	1,001,122
George Bush	4,455,095	4,379,788	75,307	0
John Connally	9,159,737	8,202,299	957,437	150,225
Philip Crane	3,271,391	3,255,910	23,715	879,126
Robert Dole	790,439	764,478	25,958	211,242
Ronald Reagan	7,210,951	6,656,376	554,574	1,475,378
1988 candidates				
George Bush	$19,058,415	$13,358,397	$5,700,018	$1,041,043
Robert Dole	14,309,120	12,100,437	2,208,682	973,371
Pierre du Pont	5,537,436	5,767,104	−208,887	744,344
Alexander Haig	1,627,987	1,548,703	79,284	143,771
Jack Kemp	10,206,670	10,078,690	127,982	3,518,951
Pat Robertson	16,406,968	16,301,928	105,038	2,091,908
1992 candidates				
George Bush	$10,092,532	$3,138,221	$6,954,311	$425,720
Pat Buchanan	707,106	230,466	476,640	23,987

SOURCES: See table 1.3.

been complicated by Pat Robertson's 1987 receipts, though the other clues pointed to Bob Dole.

The fact that the best fund raisers and biggest spenders do not always win in the end is hardly proof of money's unimportance. Money alone may not decide a nominating race,[27] but it does make possible all manner of things conducive to victory. A huge war chest raised mostly during the invisible primary allowed Governor Michael Dukakis alone among the 1988 Democratic candidates to poll continuously in key states voting on Super Tuesday. When these soundings disclosed that Dukakis television and radio spots had accomplished their purpose in Florida, the campaign shifted its limited resources elsewhere. Similarly, when tracking polls uncovered problems in Texas, the Dukakis campaign spent more than initially planned in some of the state's media markets and less in others.[28] By contrast, Gephardt, who had depleted his resources in Iowa and New Hampshire, could not afford the kind of polling intelligence available to Dukakis. Lacking a clear base such as Jackson's or Gore's and a strategy for investment of his remaining funds, Gephardt spent almost everywhere on Super Tuesday and won almost nowhere.[29]

NATIONAL POLL STANDINGS

The most visible traces of candidate viability during the invisible primary are national poll ratings. It is no accident that Hadley turned to the Gallup poll for his only evidence of nominations decided by invisible rather than actual primaries. Polls taken one month before the New Hampshire primary proved almost infallible in his account. Whoever got the support of most party followers went on to win that party's nomination in seventeen of the twenty Democratic and Republican races from 1936 through 1972. Only Wendell Willkie in 1940, Adlai Stevenson in 1952, and George McGovern in 1972 defied this trend, according to Hadley. In other words, he concluded, "the race was over before we paid our money to watch, or reporters and TV crews pulled on their galoshes and headed for the New Hampshire snows."[30]

Hadley was mistaken in several respects. First, owing to selection of uncommitted delegates and lack of a presidential preference vote, candidates and pundits took little notice of the nation's first primary until 1952. Second, though the Eisenhower-Taft and Truman-Kefauver battles focused national attention on New Hampshire in 1952, the traditional flocking of journalists to the Granite State did not begin until later. In 1956, for example, the late Theodore H. White recalled being one of only seven reporters accompanying Senator Estes Kefauver on his New Hampshire rounds.[31] Third and most important, Gallup's crystal ball clouded over more often than Hadley reported. In addition to the several anomalies he acknowledged, the final polls of party faithful before New Hampshire named Senator Robert Taft of Ohio as the Republican favorite for 1948, Nixon as the Republican preference for 1964, and Lyndon Johnson as the Democratic choice for 1968.[32]

At first glance, Hadley's rule has enjoyed greater success in the most recent series of invisible primaries. If we substitute Iowa for New Hampshire as the end of the invisible primary, nine of ten front-runners in Gallup's last polls of candidate preferences nationwide have won nomination or renomination since 1976. So blinkered a view of polling, however, is no boon to understanding the dynamics of invisible primaries.

Table 1.5 offers a more dynamic perspective on polling trends for every invisible primary of the contemporary system except the uncontested Republican races of 1972 and 1984. The data consist of preferences of party followers responding to lists of possible candidates. Gallup begins asking such questions two and sometimes three years before the next round of presidential caucuses and primaries.[33] The results point up important differences in the recent invisible primaries of Democrats and Republicans.

TABLE 1.5
INVISIBLE PRIMARY POLL STANDINGS OF EVENTUAL NOMINEES, 1972–92

Election year	Eventual nominee (by party)	Pre-Iowa standing of eventual nominee in national polls
1972	McGovern (Democrat)	Never better than 6 percent or fourth in polls taken from 3 May 1970 through 10 January 1972
1976	Carter (Democrat)	1 percent or less in polls taken from 23 June 1973 to 5 May 1975, less than 4 percent in subsequent polls through 5 January 1976
1976	Ford (GOP)	Led Reagan in six of nine polls from 7 January 1974 through 2 January 1976
1980	Carter (Democrat)	Trailed Kennedy in 1978 and 1979 polls until passing him in the final poll of 9 December 1979
1980	Reagan (GOP)	Front-runner in eight of ten polls from 3 April 1978 through 10 December 1979, albeit by only 1 percent over Ford in May and July; led with 40 percent at end of 1979
1984	Mondale (Democrat)	Trailed Kennedy in all 1982 polls except the last, became front-runner in poll of 13 December 1982 after Kennedy's withdrawal and maintained his lead thereafter through 13 February 1984
1988	Dukakis (Democrat)	Evidently not mentioned in 1985–86 polls, rose rapidly in 1987 polls from less than 1 percent to 14 percent, yet lagged behind Jackson until the final poll of 24 January 1988 when he gained a 1 percent lead
1988	Bush (GOP)	Always the front-runner by a wide margin in polls dating from 10 June 1985 through 22 January 1988
1992	Clinton (Democrat)	Evidently not listed in 1990 polls, less than 10 percent in 1991 polls, took the lead in last poll of 2 February 1992
1992	Bush (GOP)	Lead declined from 86 percent in poll of 5 December 1991 to 84 percent in poll of 2 February 1992

SOURCES: George Gallup, Jr., *The Gallup Poll: Public Opinion 1935–1971* (New York: Random House, 1972), vol. 3, 2249, 2273, 2307, 2318, 2324, 2335. *The Gallup Poll: Public Opinion 1972–1977* (Wilmington, Del.: Scholarly Resources, 1978), vols. 1–2, 5, 15, 137, 173, 197, 213, 230, 242, 292, 361, 385, 442–43, 499–500, 534–35, 542, 591, 601–2, 649. Subsequent volumes under the same title were also published by Scholarly Resources and are cited here by *year* and year of publication: *1978* (1979), 140–41, 209, 211, 254; *1979* (1980), 13, 87–88, 175–76, 187, 196, 216–17, 262, 280, 285–86; *1982* (1983), 104–5, 207; *1983* (1984), 66–69, 93, 122, 147, 177, 212, 239, 250, 264; *1984* (1985), 10, 52; *1985* (1986), 159–60, 161; *1986* (1987), 41, 89, 91, 154–55, 156–57, 240, 242; *1987* (1988), 31, 33, 37, 84, 156, 158, 186–87, 221, 256, 258; *1988* (1989), 45; *1990* (1991), 50–51; *1991* (1992), 62, 97, 186, 196, 226, 248; *1992* (1993), 6, 16, 25–26.

The most dramatic revelation in this table is the long time so many Democratic nominees take before becoming front-runners. Only Mondale managed the ascent more than a year before the Iowa caucuses. Neither McGovern in 1972 nor Carter in 1976 ended the invisible primary as national party favorites; President Carter finally overtook Kennedy at the end of 1979; Dukakis tied with Jackson in January 1988; and Clinton never topped the list until February 1992. The contrast with Republicans is striking. Even the embattled Ford led Reagan in most polls of the 1976 invisible primary. Reagan consistently eclipsed every competitor from December 1978 though December 1979.[34] Bush similarly dominated his 1988 rivals and was the first, if not always enthusiastic, choice of more than 80 percent in every Gallup poll of Republicans nationwide when matched against 1992 rivals Pat Buchanan and David Duke.

The invisible primaries of the Democrats have been multicandidate affairs owing to the party's inability to win presidential elections. Only one Democrat occupied the Oval Office during the two decades at issue, and not even he escaped a bruising battle for renomination.

Thus, while Nixon faced only token opposition in 1972, the lowly McGovern had to compete against Edmund Muskie, Hubert Humphrey, and Ted Kennedy. And while Ford and Reagan squared off as near equals in the 1976 invisible primary, Carter struggled to make himself noteworthy in a throng initially overshadowed by Kennedy, Humphrey, and Wallace. After Ford's defeat, it was the turn of the GOP to field the larger crop of candidates in the invisible primary of 1980. Seven Republicans eventually emerged as formal candidates, compared to Carter and two rivals on the Democratic side. Carter's loss to Reagan in 1980 set the stage for another protracted struggle among eight Democrats in 1984. Meanwhile, President Reagan faced no challenger more prominent than Harold Stassen. Mondale's overwhelming defeat in the 1984 election led Gallup to list at least a dozen possibilities for the 1988 Democratic nomination. Leading contenders in his early polls included Chrysler's Lee Iacocca (26 percent in October 1986 and 29 percent in January 1987), Governor Cuomo (27 percent in October 1986 and 23 percent in January 1987), and New Jersey's Senator Bill Bradley (11 percent in January 1987). Another Democratic defeat in the 1988 presidential election promised yet another bumper crop of candidates for the invisible primary of 1992. Many heard the call but remarkably few committed themselves until late in the season. Of the eighteen-plus names given Democrats and Democratic-leaning independents in Gallup's March 1990 poll, only one of the six eventual candidates (Senator Bob Kerrey of Nebraska) elicited enough support (1 percent) to warrant mention in the published results. None of the six broke the single-digit barrier in any of Gallup's 1991 samplings except the controversial Jerry Brown.

Polling about future Democratic nominees would have helped Hadley even less in casting the chief rivals and also-rans. True, the early polls of 1978–79 correctly projected a Carter-Kennedy battle with Brown as third man out, but, as previously noted, Hadley and many others might well have picked Kennedy to win. Would Hadley (or anyone else) have predicted Hart over Senator John Glenn of Ohio to be Mondale's nemesis in 1984? Glenn took second but solid billing in all of Gallup's nationwide surveys from 13 December 1982 until 13 February 1984, when Jackson finally tied him at 13 percent. Even at this late date Hart could not rise above 3 percent. The Democratic demolition derby of 1988 transformed Dukakis and Jackson into front-runners by default, but no Gallup poll of that invisible primary indicated a major role for Gore. Late polls of the 1992 invisible primary chronicled the rapid ascent first of Clinton and then of Tsongas, but they also recorded Brown's plummet from 21 to 7 percent in the final five weeks. (Brown, of course, went on to win two primaries and the precinct caucuses in several states before losing to Clinton in New York's critical primary.)

Early polls proved more predictive in Republican races, but, as already noted, for good reason. The 1976 invisible primary quickly narrowed to Ford and Reagan, and neither Reagan in 1980 nor Bush in 1988 made any secret of his intentions in a well-defined race. In the 1980 invisible primary, however, it was difficult to divine the main rival to an eventual nominee. Bush hardly looked the part in pre-Iowa polls, posting only 8 percent (against 47 percent for Reagan, 12 percent for Howard Baker, and 12 percent for Connally) in the final survey of Republicans nationwide on 10 December 1979.[35]

In general, however, the polls of invisible primaries are taken at that point in the process when respondents know and care least about presidential nominating politics. Early surveys take a "round up the usual suspects" approach in which pollsters list familiar faces, victims of past defeats, and even such improbable celebrities as Iacocca (in 1985–86 polls of Democrats) and Ross Perot (in 1993–94 polls of Republicans). Less notorious but ultimately more serious aspirants require time to build public awareness of their candidacies, yet the earliest polls typically reflect shallow recognition more than information or conviction.

When Gallup polled Republicans and GOP-leaning independents in March 1994, for example, 59 percent said they had never heard of Governor Campbell of South Carolina. Another 51 percent had no clue about the identity of Lynn Martin, the former labor secretary; 49 percent were at a similar loss in the case of Lamar Alexander, a former education secretary and governor of Tennessee. Senator Phil Gramm of Texas was unfamiliar to 38 percent. Conversely, less than 1 percent had not heard of Dan Quayle; only 5 percent did not recognize Senate Republican leader Dole; 11 percent knew nothing of Pat Buchanan, the columnist and chief rival to Bush's renomination in 1992; and 14 percent blanked on General Colin Powell. Dole led in this poll as the first choice of 20 percent, followed by Powell (13 percent), Perot (12 percent), and Quayle (11 percent). Neither Alexander nor Martin got so much as 1 percent and Gramm registered only 2 percent.[36] (The correlation of name recognition with preference in this poll was a robust .713.) Uninformed or inchoate choice, in sum, is not a trustworthy guide to a process driven by money, media, and momentum.[37]

STRAW POLLS

Iowa Republicans hosted the first straw poll of the 1996 invisible primary on 24 June 1994 at their state party convention. To no one's surprise, Dole won with 27 percent of the 1,349 votes cast. He received some publicity for this feat, but would have gotten much more by finishing second or worse. Doubtless aware of this risk, he pleaded Senate business and stayed in Washington while a redoubtable organization mobilized supporters in Iowa. Hoping to cause the very upset Dole feared, five of his putative rivals showed up at the Des Moines convention center to address the delegates formally. Alexander surprised many by finishing a strong second with 15 percent. "Alexander and his supporters worked hard in recent days to encourage supporters to come in and vote," the *Des Moines Register* reported. "His backers said his second-place showing will improve his stature as a candidate and his ability to raise money."[38] Senator Gramm proclaimed his satisfaction with third place, since it put him ahead of Kemp, Cheney, and Quayle.[39] Kemp, the former secretary of housing and urban development, and Cheney, much respected for his Pentagon leadership during Desert Storm, rounded out the top five.

Whatever a straw poll represents, it is not randomly sampled choice. Many contests like the one just described are principally fund raisers with voting restricted to ticket holders. In 1979, after several straw polls of $50 ticket holders, one campaign operative complained that her party had "reinvented the poll tax."[40] Bush won a Maryland straw poll in 1987 by distributing more $30 tickets than Robertson. Each vote at the 1994 Iowa affair cost someone $25 with proceeds going to the state party. At a "unity" gathering afterward, leaders of the Iowa GOP assured the author that even a visiting professor from Ohio could have participated for the price of a ticket.

Not surprisingly, the cost of straw-poll competition has sometimes wrecked the already precarious finances of long-shot campaigns. In 1983, for example, former governor Reubin Askew avoided as many straw polls as possible, partly because of money and partly because most of those likely to participate would find his conservatism objectionable. That strategy ended, however, when the Democrats in his home state forced him into a showdown against Mondale. "Our undoing was the Florida straw poll, which we could not avoid," James T. Bacchus, Askew's campaign manager, said later. "While we won the straw poll, Mondale was able to hurt our finances terribly, and this in the end proved to be our undoing because we didn't have the money for media in Iowa and New Hampshire." His lamentations prompted the following exchange with journalist Ken Bode:

> *Mr. Bode:* You knew you were finished then?
>
> *Mr. Bacchus:* We knew we were close to finished, yes.
>
> *Mr. Bode:* You were one of the candidates knocked out by a straw poll in your own state?
>
> *Mr. Bacchus:* I would say effectively, yes.[41]

National party leaders have generally taken a dim view of straw polls despite their obvious utility to state and local party organizations and to some candidates some of the time. Charles T. Manatt, then chairman of the Democratic National Committee (DNC), denounced them as "divisive, non-useful, expensive, and extraordinarily irritating" in 1983.[42] He doubtless played a major role in getting the party to ban straw polls in the 1988 invisible primary. In 1991, however, Florida Democrats broke the fast to stage a widely publicized showdown between Clinton and Harkin.[43]

Straw polls differ in several noteworthy respects. Some, as already noted, double as fund raisers, while others do not. Some, like the Florida Democratic poll, restrict participation to party stalwarts, while others do not. State parties sponsor some, while others are impromptu or unofficial. An example of the latter type took place in 1979 at a Republican leadership conference in Indianapolis. Evidently bent on wringing some news out of this assembly, CBS distributed ballots only moments after a "characteristically forceful" speech by Connally and then reported the story of Connally's resounding victory.[44]

Neither the number of participants nor the degree of contrivance is a sure guide to coverage of straw polls in the national news media. Two equally synthetic victories in 1983 serve to illustrate the inconsistency of television news reporting. Consider first the June poll of 124 Alabama Young Democrats in which Cranston won 65 votes after spending $2,000 (or nearly $31 per vote) to entertain the delegates on the eve of their convention.[45] All three networks reported the outcome on their nightly news programs, with ABC proclaiming that it had lent "an added touch of credibility" to Cranston's candidacy.[46] Four weeks later, however, no network version of the nightly news recounted Askew's lopsided win at a local party gathering in New Hampshire where more than a thousand voted.[47] Perhaps there is a point of diminishing returns after which credibility evaporates with every increase in the winner's percentage.

In any event, other things being equal, a big straw poll is more likely than a small one to impress the national press corps as a meaningful clash of campaign organizations. When the news media take a straw poll seriously, so do most of the major candidates, and vice versa.

Thus, for example, after narrowly losing the Maine straw vote to Bush in 1979, Senator Howard Baker of Tennessee reportedly confided to his wife and a top aide that "it may not be possible to recover from this."[48] Like so many intrinsically trivial episodes in presidential politics, Jack Germond and Jules Witcover concluded, the Maine results got disproportionate notice because they affected perceptions of the candidates, first by affirming the rumored ineptitude of Baker's campaign and, second, by upholding Bush's claim to moderate Republican support.[49] Another case in point was the April 1983 Massachusetts straw poll for which Mondale's operatives mounted an effort suitable for a national nominating convention with floor whips, fancy communications, and a trailer command post.[50] His 939 votes in Maine's "Super Bowl of straw polls" reportedly cost Mondale at least $100 apiece and required the efforts of "more than fifty" campaign workers to round up.[51] Bush waged a similar blitzkrieg against Robertson in 1987 at the Florida GOP convention.[52]

Despite every reason to doubt its validity, a straw poll still might win some respect if its record exhibits some degree of reliability, however coincidental. A straw vote frequently "right" usually commands more respect than one almost invariably wrong. Several crude measures of reliability can be formulated for the results listed in table 1.6: First, how many straw polls did eventual nominees win? Second, how frequently did the winner of a state's straw poll go on to victory in its precinct caucuses or primary? And, third, which state had the most prophetic straw poll in either respect? The table lists every straw poll from 1975 through the present in which a thousand or more participated.[53]

The answer to question one is that eventual nominees won only nine of eighteen straw votes prior to 1994. Carter, the Democratic nominee in 1976 and 1980, won both Iowa polls as well as the 1979 Florida tally. Reagan, the 1980 Republican nominee, triumphed in Florida's straw vote. He needed a victory, however, after running a distant fourth in both the Iowa and Maine polls. Mondale, the 1984 Democratic nominee, came out on top in only three of seven 1983 straw votes. Bush prevailed in only one of three such polls in 1987, while eventual nominee Clinton ran up a big victory in the one straw poll of 1991.

The odds look only slightly better when we examine the match of straw poll and primary or caucus outcomes in the same state. Victory in the primary or precinct caucuses followed victory in straw votes in ten of eighteen pairwise comparisons. Carter won the 1975 straw vote in Iowa and the state's precinct caucuses some months later and repeated this feat in Iowa and Florida four years later. Kennedy won the Golden State's straw poll in January and its primary in June of 1980. In 1983, however, only the Iowa straw vote correctly forecast the winner of a state's precinct caucuses or primary. Similarly, of the three 1987 straw polls, only Florida's projected the primary winner some months later. Clinton prevailed not only against

TABLE 1.6

DEMOCRATIC AND REPUBLICAN STRAW POLLS, 1975–95

State (party)	Date	Total vote	Winner (vote %)
Iowa (D) + #	26 October 1975	1,094	Carter (23)
Iowa (D) + #	5 November 1979	2,320	Carter (71)
Florida (D) + #	18 November 1979	1,465	Carter (76)
California (D) #	20 January 1980	1,471	Kennedy (42)
Iowa (R) #	13 October 1979	1,454	Bush (36)
Maine (R) #	3 November 1979	1,336	Bush (35)
Florida (R) + #	17 November 1979	1,326	Reagan (36)
California (D)	15 January 1983	1,332	Cranston (59)
Massachusetts (D) +	9 April 1983	3,453	Mondale (29)
Wisconsin (D)	11 June 1983	2,035	Cranston (39)
New Jersey (D)	13 July 1983	1,125	Glenn (38)
Maine (D) +	1 October 1983	1,849	Mondale (51)
Iowa (D) + #	8 October 1983	4,143	Mondale (47)
Florida (D)	23 October 1983	2,325	Askew (45)
Iowa (R)	12 September 1987	3,800	Robertson (34)
Florida (R) + #	14 November 1987	2,313	Bush (57)
Virginia (R)	7 December 1987	1,325	Robertson (83)
Florida (D) + #	12 September 1991	1,800	Clinton (54)
Iowa (R)	24 June 1994	1,349	Dole (26)
Louisiana (R)	7 January 1995	1,253	Gramm (72)

SOURCES: For Iowa Democratic and Republican straw polls, 1975–83, Hugh Winebrenner, *The Iowa Precinct Caucuses* (Ames: Iowa State University Press, 1987), 73, 98, 134; 1979 Florida Democratic poll, "What's News" in the *Wall Street Journal,* 19 November 1983, A1; 1979 California Democratic poll, "Kennedy Wins Poll of Coast Democrats," *New York Times,* 21 January 1979, A1; 1979 Maine Republican poll, "Maine Republicans in Informal Ballot Give Bush a Victory," *New York Times,* 4 November 1979, A1; 1979 Florida Republican poll, "Reagan Wins a Poll of G.O.P. in Florida," *New York Times,* 18 November 1979, A1; all 1983 Democratic polls, "Straw Polls Shed Dim Light on Race," *Congressional Quarterly Weekly Report,* 41 (22 October 1983), 2184; 1987 Iowa Republican poll, Jack W. Germond and Jules Witcover, *Whose Broad Stripes and Bright Stars?* (New York: Warner Books, 1989), 108; 1987 Florida Republican poll, "Bush Wins Florida Straw Poll, Robertson Places Second," *Los Angeles Times,* 15 November 1987, A16; 1979 Virginia Republican poll, "Robertson Victor in a Straw Poll," *New York Times,* 7 December 1987, A15; 1991 Florida Democratic poll, "Clinton Wins Straw Poll at Florida Convention," *Washington Post,* 16 December 1991, A14; 1994 Iowa Republican poll, "Dole Wins Early Nod in Race for President," *Des Moines Register,* 25 June 1994, A1; 1995 Louisiana Republican poll, "Texas Senator Has a Victory in Louisiana," *New York Times,* 8 January 1995, A12.
NOTES:
+ : straw poll won by eventual nominee
# : same winner in straw poll and subsequent caucus or primary

Harkin in the Florida straw vote of September 1991 but also against Tsongas in the Florida primary of March 1992.

Of all the states listed in the table, Florida has amassed the best record of straw-vote victors going on to capture their party's nomination, however big the role of sheer coincidence. Florida and Iowa split the honors for projecting victory in a primary or first round of caucuses from straw-poll outcomes. Overall, however, the straw-poll record of successful prediction has not been much better than what one would have expected from chance.

NEWS MEDIA EXPOSURE

Hadley's book frequently mentioned, yet never systematically assessed, the role of campaign journalism in the invisible primary. Mostly he wrote about the numbing repetition imposed on candidates and reporters as they made the rounds of party dinners and forums together. In one place, ruminating about widespread mistrust of the press, Hadley wrote, "we help create the image that makes the candidate stand out and which often divides him from the people."[54]

One wonders whether Hadley would have agreed with contemporary charges of the news media usurping the nominating function of political parties. This supplanting of party leaders by news executives supposedly has forced fundamental changes in judging the candidates. Now presidential aspirants reportedly rise and fall according to the selfish and short-term priorities of news bureaucracies rather than the long-term interests of political parties.[55]

This chapter is not the place for an examination of every particular in so searing an indictment of the press as president maker. Still, if the news media exert the kind of control alleged, some of this power should be obvious during the invisible primary. Aside from damaging stories about an aspirant's character,[56] one way the news media may influence the invisible primary is by lavishing coverage on some candidates while virtually ignoring others. Another is by featuring the ideas of some aspirants while slighting others.

However favorable or substantive, sheer amount of news coverage is the most general indicator of media influence in the nominating process. Some candidates invariably get more press than others. Every invisible primary is a time of long-shots struggling to interest reporters, often to no avail, in hopes of boosting poll standings and contributions. Pseudo events such as straw polls notwithstanding, editors and correspondents pay most attention to aspirants they take seriously. At this point, when harder evidence is unavailable, coverage generally corresponds to standings in national polls. Statewide polls in Iowa, New Hampshire, and perhaps a few other places also figure in a candidate's coverage as the invisible primary draws to a close.

Journalists and academics alike have frequently noted the correlation of media coverage to national poll standings. According to television reporter Bill Plante, "the degree of scrutiny a candidate receives increases in direct proportion to his standing in the polls."[57] Political scientist William C. Adams likewise reported a close relationship in the invisible primary of 1984 between national poll standings and the amount of a candidate's coverage in newspapers and on the nightly news.[58] Similarly, the author's own research on coverage of the 1988 invisible primary uncovered a close relationship between poll standings and coverage accorded candidates by major newspapers.[59]

Let us first consider the Republicans, whose polls generally have been consistent in identifying leading and lesser contenders. Vice-President Bush's unbroken domination of the polls throughout the 1988 invisible primary should have meant more network coverage of him than any other rival in 1985–86. Dole should have appeared on the nightly news more often than any other Republican aspirant except Bush, and so on down the polling order. Similarly, Dole enjoyed a sizable lead over all likely rivals in early polling of the 1996 invisible primary. According to the literature, he should have led in television coverage as well. Powell should have been second in coverage because he ranked second in the poll, Perot third, and so on. Table 1.7 permits a test of the polling-coverage proposition by comparing the number of stories featuring one or more Republican aspirants listed in the Gallup polls of April 1986 and March 1994. The unit of analysis in both arrays is the television news story in which a potential candidate commented or responded to questions on camera, was mentioned or quoted without being shown, or was mentioned and shown at the same time.[60] For the sake of comparison with the early days of the 1996 invisible primary (1 October 1993 to 30 June 1994), the time frame for the 1988 cycle was 1 October 1985 to 30 June 1986.

This table resoundingly affirms the literature's finding of a strong relationship between poll standings and news coverage. (The simple correlation between poll standings and exposure on all three networks was .871 in 1985–86 and .693 in 1993–94). Howard Baker was the only anomaly of the earlier period (second in the polls and fifth in overall frequency of appearances). In 1993–94 the most noteworthy anomalies were Powell (second in the poll yet ninth in appearances on all three networks), Kemp (fifth in the poll while tenth in total coverage), and Gramm (ninth in the poll yet fourth in coverage). Dole reaped a bonanza of television coverage in 1993–94 by appearing in more than half of every network's stories mentioning likely Republican candidates. Bush had enjoyed no comparable media advantage over Dole, the runner-up in 1985–86.

This relationship between poll standings and frequency of coverage—at least for Republican aspirants—is as good a place as any to revisit Hadley's claim of the disadvantaged incumbent. Recall his argument that former public servants enjoyed a distinct advantage over incumbent governors and senators during the invisible primary because only the former had the time for continuous campaigning. Even in Hadley's day, however, presidential aspi-

TABLE 1.7
EARLY EVENING NEWS APPEARANCES
OF 1988 AND 1996 REPUBLICAN
PRESIDENTIAL ASPIRANTS
(IN PERCENTAGES)

	ABC	CBS	NBC	All 3	April 1986 Gallup poll
1988 Republicans	N = 65	N = 40	N = 65	N = 170	N.A.
Howard Baker	1.5	2.5	3.1	2.4	17.0
George Bush	49.2	47.5	41.5	45.9	51.0
Robert Dole	30.8	30.0	41.5	34.7	21.0
Pierre du Pont	1.5	0	1.5	1.2	N.A.
Alexander Haig	3.1	2.5	1.5	2.3	8.0
Jack Kemp	6.2	12.5	6.2	7.6	10.0
Pat Robertson	7.7	5.0	4.6	5.9	6.0
Other or Don't know					9.0
Total	100.0	100.0	99.9	100.0	>100.0
					March 1994 Gallup poll
1996 Republicans	N = 87	N = 126	N = 117	N = 330	N = 468
Lamar Alexander	0	.8	0	.3	<0.5
James Baker	1.2	2.4	2.6	2.1	4.0
William Bennett	1.2	1.6	4.3	2.4	3.0
Pat Buchanan	1.2	0	.8	.6	1.0
Dick Cheney	0	3.2	3.4	2.4	7.0
Robert Dole	58.6	50.8	55.6	54.5	20.0
Phil Gramm	9.2	8.7	4.3	7.3	2.0
Jack Kemp	0	1.6	.8	.9	9.0
Lynn Martin	0	.8	0	.3	<0.5
Ross Perot	21.8	13.5	12.8	15.7	12.0
Colin Powell	0	3.2	1.7	1.8	13.0
Dan Quayle	2.3	3.2	2.6	2.7	11.0
William Weld	1.2	0	1.7	.9	N.A.
Pete Wilson	3.4	10.3	9.4	8.2	1.0
Other or Don't know					16.0
Total	100.1	100.1	100.0	100.1	99.9

SOURCES: Vanderbilt Television News Archive; *The Gallup Poll Monthly* 343 (April 1994): 25; *The Gallup Poll: Public Opinion 1987* (Wilmington, Del.: Scholarly Resources, 1987), 89.

NOTE: Du Pont not listed in 1986 Gallup summary; Weld not listed in 1994. Some columns do not total to 100 percent due to rounding. Gallup percentages for 1986 are first and second choices combined, thus exceeding 100 percent. Gallup did not report subsample Ns for Republicans and Republican leaners in 1986 poll. The observation period for 1993–94 and 1985–86 television coverage in both invisible primaries is 1 October through 30 June.

N = number of stories.

rants generally preferred national television exposure to locally reported "cattle shows" and banquets. Table 1.7 reveals that incumbents appeared much more often on the evening news than former officeholders during both invisible primaries.

This pattern clearly appears in the 1985–86 data. Here the contrast between Howard Baker, who retired in 1984 as Senate GOP leader, and Dole, who immediately followed him in that position, is instructive. One might even conjecture that Dole owed a slim polling lead over his former leader to twenty times as much exposure on the evening news. Bush, of course, made the most of a highly visible but not overly taxing vice-presidency, while Alexander Haig, a former secretary of state, languished in the shadows of ex-officialdom (as would James Baker in 1994). Similarly, compare the coverage of Kemp, then an incumbent congressman, and Pierre "Pete" du Pont, an ex-congressman and former governor. As for 1993–94, Dole's Senate responsibilities placed him before the cameras more often than all his rivals combined and unquestionably nourished his lead in the early polls. Most of his likely opponents lost the capacity to interest the press on a regular basis when they departed government service with the change of administrations.

An attentive reader at this point might protest that the table shows the never-elected Perot leading many 1994 officeholders both in the poll and in television coverage. The monthly breakdown in figure 1.1, however, discloses that not even great wealth and notoriety could make Perot a regular presence on the evening news. True, he eclipsed Dole in November 1993 by debating the North American Free Trade Agreement (NAFTA) with Vice-President Gore. Dole, however, was on the nightly news before and after NAFTA, while Perot clearly was not. Perhaps a fairer comparison is Perot against those incumbents in table 1.7 who got half or less of his total coverage. Although Governor Pete Wilson of California appeared in only 8.2 percent of the stories, he got more coverage than Perot in every month observed except November and December. Likewise, Senator Gramm topped Perot in six of the nine months of nightly news coverage.

Table 1.8 shows a predictable inconsistency of coverage when nobody leads consistently in the polls. This muddle was most obvious in 1985–86 when Hart appeared most often on ABC, Cuomo led in CBS appearances, and Gore turned up most often on NBC. Biden, Bradley, and Kennedy tied for second on ABC's *World News Tonight;* Biden, Dukakis, and Gore all placed second on the CBS *Evening News;* both Iacocca and Jackson came in second on the NBC *Nightly News.* A similar lack of consistency marked early coverage of the 1992 Democratic aspirants. Jackson appeared in more ABC and NBC stories than any other Democratic hopeful and in enough CBS stories to top all rivals in total network news coverage. Gephardt turned up in one more CBS story than Jackson and thus shared a slim

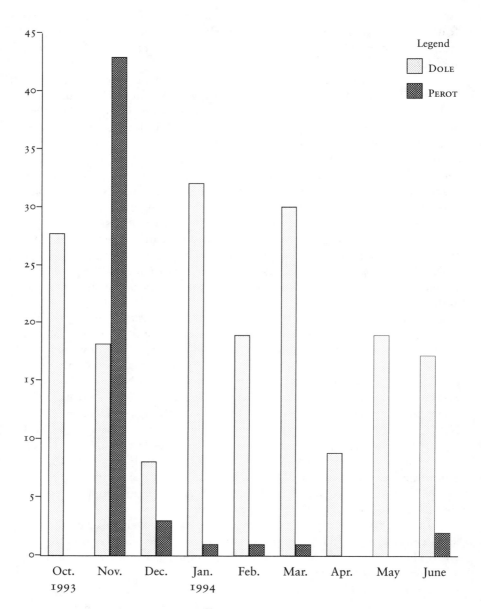

FIGURE 1.1
MONTHLY EXPOSURE OF DOLE AND PEROT ON EVENING
NEWS PROGRAMS OF ALL THREE NETWORKS
(NUMBER OF STORIES)

TABLE 1.8
EARLY EVENING NEWS APPEARANCES
OF 1988 AND 1992 DEMOCRATIC
PRESIDENTIAL ASPIRANTS
(IN PERCENTAGES)

	ABC	CBS	NBC	All 3
1988 Democrats				
No. of stories:	N = 46	N = 36	N = 49	N = 131
Bruce Babbitt	2.2	2.8	8.2	4.6
Joseph Biden	10.9	11.1	6.1	9.2
Bill Bradley	10.9	8.3	4.1	7.6
Mario Cuomo	8.7	13.9	10.2	10.7
Michael Dukakis	2.2	11.1	4.1	5.3
Richard Gephardt	4.3	5.6	2.0	3.8
Al Gore	6.5	11.1	16.3	11.5
Gary Hart	13.0	8.3	8.2	9.9
Lee Iacocca	8.7	8.3	12.2	9.9
Jesse Jackson	6.5	8.3	12.2	9.2
Edward Kennedy	10.9	5.6	6.1	7.6
Sam Nunn	8.7	2.8	4.1	5.3
Patricia Schroeder	6.5	2.8	6.1	5.3
Total	100.0	100.0	99.9	99.9
1992 Democrats				
No. of stories:	N = 34	N = 41	N = 53	N = 128
Bill Clinton	.0	4.9	3.8	3.1
Mario Cuomo	20.6	17.1	11.3	15.6
Richard Gephardt	11.8	21.9	13.2	15.6
Al Gore	8.8	7.3	3.8	6.3
Jesse Jackson	29.4	19.5	54.7	36.7
Bob Kerrey	8.8	4.9	3.8	5.5
John D. Rockefeller IV	2.9	2.4	1.9	2.3
Douglas Wilder	17.6	21.9	7.5	14.8
Total	99.9	99.9	100.0	99.9

SOURCE: Vanderbilt Television News Archive.

NOTES: The observation period for 1988 candidates was 1 October 1985 to 30 June 1986; for 1992 candidates: 1 October 1989 to 30 June 1990. No evening news program mentioned Harkin or Tsongas during the 1989–90 observation period. Some columns do not total to 100 percent due to rounding.

lead on that network with Governor Douglas Wilder of Virginia. More ABC stories mentioned Cuomo than Gephardt or Wilder.

More coverage need not mean more coverage of an aspirant's ideas during the invisible primary. In the final weeks leading up to the 1988 Iowa caucuses, for example, the *New York Times* and four other major newspapers mentioned Bush in more news stories and gave him more print lines than any Republican rival. A smaller proportion of these items cited Bush's specific issue stands, however, than those mentioning du Pont, Kemp, or Dole. Bush also suffered in comparison to Dole, Kemp, and Robertson in the proportionate coverage of campaign themes.[61]

Television news sometimes casts up similar anomalies, as table 1.9 reveals. Here the combined stories of all three evening news shows are broken down into domestic, foreign-military, "intermestic," and special-ceremonial categories. "Domestic" and "foreign-military" matters require no elaboration. "Intermestic" pertains to trade and environmental issues with domestic as well as international ramifications, NAFTA being a prime example. The "special-ceremonial" category combines a few reports of natural disasters in Clinton's Arkansas and Wilson's California with stories about state funerals, commencement speeches, and other rituals.

On the one hand, the table highlights Dole's extraordinary domination of network news coverage in the early days of the 1996 invisible primary. The Senate Republican leader appeared in 64 percent of all the stories about domestic politics and an astounding 77 percent of all stories about military and foreign policy. Jackson enjoyed a similar albeit less overwhelming advantage among Democrats early in the 1988 invisible primary.

Noteworthy anomalies also stand out in the table. Looking first at the 1988 invisible primary, Bush appeared in more network news stories than Dole or any other Republican rival in 1985–86, yet Dole's coverage on domestic issues exceeded Bush's by more than two to one. In 1993–94 Dole's extraordinary domination of the evening news did not extend to the NAFTA issue. Perot reigned as the king of news in that domain on all three networks. Still other anomalies emerge from the Democrats' 1988 invisible primary coverage: Although Senator Sam Nunn of Georgia seldom got on the evening news in 1985–86, he appeared in more stories about military and foreign policy matters than any of his likely rivals. And, owing to controversy over his leadership in refurbishing the Statue of Liberty, Iacocca appeared in the most stories about ceremonies and special events.

Getting on the nightly news, of course, is not the only way of getting on national television. Scarcely a trace of Buchanan turned up in the 1993–94 data, but this hardly mattered to the millions who recognized him as a regular advocate of right-wing views on CNN. Though his anti-NAFTA activities got the attention of news executives on all three traditional networks, Perot elected to debate Gore on CNN's *Larry King Live,* a familiar forum for his views. In all of the nine months of 1993–94 network news stories analyzed above, Lamar Alexander's coverage consisted of a single mention in a twenty-second story on CBS about the Iowa Republican straw poll. A newly established Republican Exchange Satellite Network, however, may become the means of regularly projecting his message to millions by way of cable and satellite.[62] Alexander has also appeared as a political commentator on TNN.

TABLE 1.9
EVENING NEWS APPEARANCES BY TOPIC

	Domestic	Foreign-military	Intermestic	Special-Ceremonial
1988 Republicans	*N = 74*	*N = 79*	*N = 1*	*N = 16*
H. Baker	5.4%	.0%	.0%	.0%
Bush	18.9	63.3	100.0	81.3
Dole	41.9	31.6	.0	18.7
Du Pont	2.7	.0	.0	.0
Haig	4.0	1.3	.0	.0
Kemp	14.9	2.5	.0	.0
Robertson	12.2	1.3	.0	.0
Total	100.0	100.0	100.0	100.0
1996 Republicans	*N = 178*	*N = 74*	*N = 57*	*N = 20*
Alexander	.6%	.0%	.0%	.0%
J. Baker	.6	4.0	3.5	.0
Bennett	4.5	.0	.0	.0
Buchanan	.6	.0	1.7	.0
Cheney	1.1	6.8	.0	5.0
Dole	64.0	77.0	5.3	30.0
Gramm	11.2	2.7	3.5	.0
Kemp	1.1	.0	.0	5.0
Martin	.6	.0	.0	.0
Perot	1.7	1.4	80.7	5.0
Powell	.0	5.4	1.7	5.0
Quayle	1.7	2.7	.0	20.0
Weld	1.7	.0	.0	.0
Wilson	10.7	.0	3.5	30.0
Total	100.1	100.0	99.9	100.0
1988 Democrats	*N = 100*	*N = 22*	*N = 1*	*N = 8*
Babbitt	3.0%	4.5%	100.0%	12.5%
Biden	10.0	9.1	.0	.0
Bradley	8.0	9.1	.0	.0
Cuomo	14.0	.0	.0	.0
Dukakis	6.0	4.5	.0	.0
Gephardt	5.0	.0	.0	.0
Gore	10.0	18.2	.0	12.5
Hart	11.0	9.1	.0	.0
Iacocca	8.0	.0	.0	62.5
Jackson	8.0	13.6	.0	12.5
Kennedy	10.0	.0	.0	.0
Nunn	2.0	22.7	.0	.0
Schroeder	5.0	9.1	.0	.0
Total	100.0	99.9	100.0	100.0

Continued ...

TABLE 1.9 — CONTINUED

	Domestic	Foreign-military	Intermestic	Special-Ceremonial
1992 Democrats	N = 85	N = 31	N = 2	N = 9
Clinton	1.2%	.0%	.0%	33.3%
Cuomo	15.3	9.7	.0	44.4
Gephardt	10.6	35.5	.0	.0
Gore	7.1	.0	100.0	.0
Jackson	31.8	54.8	.0	22.2
Kerrey	8.2	.0	.0	.0
Rockefeller	3.5	.0	.0	.0
Wilder	22.3	.0	.0	.0
Total	100.0	100.0	100.0	99.9

SOURCE: Vanderbilt Television News Archive.

NOTE: Some columns do not total to 100 percent due to rounding.
N = number of stories.

In fine, the news media obviously influence what happens in the invisible primary by selectively informing the public. Much of this reporting, however, reinforces inequalities among candidates apparent in the national polls. Still, even a big lead in coverage is no guarantee of dominating the news on every subject. Among Republican aspirants at least, however much free time former officeholders may have to campaign, incumbent officeholders seem to interest the press more.

Whither the Invisible Primary?

Writing his penultimate chapter a few days before Christmas 1975, Hadley asked himself the obvious question: who had won the 1976 invisible primary? It was impossible to say, he answered, partly because of the unsettled times and partly because Gallup had not yet taken his final poll before New Hampshire. What, then, of the six "tracks" so confidently offered in his first chapter not only as measures of success in the invisible primary but as determinants of "ritual" voting in the primaries and precinct caucuses to follow—the candidate's ego and drive, quality of campaign staff, soundness of strategy, fund-raising success, news media reaction, and popular support? Not all the data had come in, he pleaded, especially on popular support. Though well aware that he risked the scorn of future readers, Hadley acknowledged an obligation to them and himself to name the likely nominees of both parties in 1976.

"I see no walkaway for either man," he wrote of the struggle between Ford and Reagan for the Republican nomination. Still, because of greater strengths on the six tracks, Hadley concluded, "President Ford now seems to me to have an edge that will carve out his final victory." He arrived at this conclusion after selectively recounting candidate strengths and voter loyalties in upcoming state contests. In Florida, for example, Wallace might lure away enough conservative Republicans and independents to weaken Reagan's base in the Republican primary. Ford, meanwhile, would enjoy "all the power of the electronic presidency" assuming that he and his "inept" staff learned how to make effective use of that opportunity.[63] And so on with still more scenarios dependent on late-breaking developments. Somehow in all this guesswork a switch occurred: now actual primaries and caucuses would determine the meaning of the invisible primary, rather than the other way around.

Taking the same approach to the Democrats, Hadley predicted a battle for liberal votes between Udall and Bayh. Whoever won that struggle would find Jackson well positioned by dint of superior fund raising, time on the campaign trail, better organization, the allocation of many delegates on a proportional basis, Henry Kissinger's diplomacy, and still other factors. "So, on the strength of the tangibles," a hesitant Hadley concluded, "it should be Jackson."

Having already written Carter off as "the minor candidate who almost made it out of the ruck," Hadley concluded that the Georgia governor might stake a claim to the vice-presidential nomination by winning the otherwise inconsequential Iowa caucuses and by besting Wallace in the Florida primary. "Believe me," he summed up, "printed prophecy, like being hanged, concentrates a man's mind wonderfully."[64]

Waiting for the final poll before New Hampshire, as we now know, would not have helped Hadley predict the Democratic outcome more accurately: The unannounced Humphrey led with 29 percent support nationwide, Wallace got 20 percent, McGovern 10 percent, Jackson 10 percent, Shriver and Bayh 5 percent each. Gallup estimated Carter's support at less than 4 percent.[65] Carter might have looked stronger had Hadley gotten his hands on the 1975 financial reports of all candidates, but, as previously noted, Carter's fund raising lagged behind that of several rivals at year's end. Indeed the only outward sign of Carter's impending success was his victory in the Iowa straw poll, not the best of indicators. Hadley, in short, had ample basis to anguish over his predictions.

No invisible primary since Hadley's writing has so confounded the arts of prediction, but in remarkably few have the available indicators unequivocally identified the same man as his party's next nominee. The foregoing discussions of campaign finances, Gallup polling, straw votes, and media coverage should have supplied ample reason to reject simplistic notions of invisible primaries dictating actual primary results. Table 1.10 summarizes this evidence for every contested run-up of the last twenty years.

TABLE 1.10
SUMMARY OF INVISIBLE PRIMARY INDICATORS

Party (invisible primary)	Campaign finances	Gallup poll standings	Straw polls	News media coverage	Summary prediction
Democrats (1976)	Carter fourth in receipts and spending	Carter never broke out of the pack	Carter won Iowa straw poll	N.A.	Mostly wrong
Republicans (1976)	Reagan first in receipts, spending, and cash on hand	Ford ahead in most polls, led Reagan in January 1976 poll	No Republican straw polls	N.A.	Partly right
Democrats (1980)	Carter first in receipts, spending, and cash on hand	Carter trailed Kennedy until December 1979 poll	Carter won two of three straw polls	N.A.	Mostly right
Republicans (1980)	Connally first in receipts, spending, and cash on hand	Reagan first in eight of ten polls, big lead by end of 1979	Reagan lost two of three major straw polls	N.A.	Partly right
Democrats (1984)	Mondale first in receipts, spending, and cash on hand	Mondale clear front-runner in 1983	Mondale lost four of seven major straw polls	Television and major newspaper coverage closely correlated with polls	Mostly right

	Money	Polls	Straw polls	Media coverage	Assessment
Democrats (1988)	Dukakis first in receipts, spending, and cash on hand	Dukakis and Jackson led after Hart and Biden were driven from the race; Dukakis ahead of Jackson by 1 percent in final poll	No Democratic straw polls	No clear pattern of dominance in major newspaper or evening news coverage for any candidate, thus reflecting lack of poll hierarchy	Partly right
Republicans (1988)	Bush first in receipts and cash on hand; Robertson first in spending	Bush first in every poll	Bush lost two of three major straw polls	Bush's front-runner status reflected in television and major newspaper coverage	Mostly right
Democrats (1992)	Clinton first in receipts and cash on hand at end of 1991	Clinton finally first at end of the invisible primary after trailing in early polls	Clinton won Florida straw poll	Clinton rarely seen on evening news in 1989–90	Partly right
Republicans (1992)	Bush first in receipts, spending, and cash on hand	Bush first in every poll	No Republican straw polls	N.A.	Right
Republicans (1996)	N.A.	Dole first in early polls	Dole won Iowa straw poll; Gramm won Louisiana poll	Dole got disproportionate coverage on 1993–94 evening news programs	?

A review of each indicator's performance over time is helpful to understanding its limits during the invisible primary. Campaign finances, for example, correctly pointed to six of the nine eventual nominees in contested run-ups prior to 1996. Raising the most money and having the most cash on hand rightly designated Carter as the likely pick of the Democrats in 1980, Mondale as the Democratic choice for 1984, Dukakis for 1988, Bush as the Republican nominee in 1988 and 1992, and Clinton as the Democratic nominee in 1992. The same measures wrongly implied a Wallace victory in 1976, a Reagan nomination in 1976, and a Connally win in 1980.

Similarly, when considered over the course of an entire invisible primary, Gallup's nationwide polls correctly designated five of nine eventual nominees from 1976 to 1992. The preponderance of polling evidence favored Ford for 1976, Reagan for 1980, Mondale for 1984, and Bush for 1988 and 1992. In 1980, as noted earlier, most polls indicated more support for Kennedy than for Carter as the Democratic nominee. Clinton did not take the lead in Democratic polls until the end of the 1992 invisible primary. As already noted, Democratic polls of the 1988 invisible primary mirrored the chaos wrought by events. Finally, the polls of the 1976 invisible primary betrayed no signs of Carter's astounding breakthrough.

Given the caveats offered earlier about the validity of straw votes, readers will find no surprises in this table. State parties held at least one noteworthy straw poll in six of the nine invisible primaries from 1976 to 1992, and, as previously noted, eventual nominees won half of the most publicized straw votes taken during these invisible primaries.

News media coverage faithfully reflected national poll standings. Clear inequalities in the polls correlated with unequal coverage of Democratic aspirants in the 1984 invisible primary and of Republican contenders in the 1988 invisible primary. Likewise, unclear polls foretold inconsistent coverage of Democratic aspirants during the early days of the 1988 and 1992 races.

The final column of table 1.10 offers a general summary of all available indicators for each invisible primary since Hadley's writing. Only once did all signs point unequivocally to the same man: when Bush sought renomination for the 1992 election and escaped the embarrassment of straw votes. Most but not all indicators correctly designated eventual nominees in three other cycles: in the run-up to 1980, when Carter led in campaign finances and straw-poll wins but trailed Kennedy in most early polls; in the early days of the 1984 race, when Mondale led in finances and poll standings but lost most of his party's straw votes; and during the preliminaries of the 1988 Republican process, when Bush led the pack in fund raising, cash on hand, and poll ratings but lost two of the three most heralded straw votes. Less clarity obtained in the 1976 and 1980 invisible primaries of the GOP and the 1988 and 1992 invisible primaries of the Democrats. In the early days of the 1976 Republican race Reagan topped Ford in fund raising and other financial indicators, while Ford led Reagan in most Gallup polls. Similarly, in the invisible primary of 1980, Connally led the pack in finances, Reagan built up a big lead in the national polls, and Bush won two of the three most publicized straw polls. Dukakis dominated the finances but nothing else during the Democrats' invisible primary of 1988. And, as previously noted, Clinton became the front-runner in finances and polls at the end of the 1992 invisible primary. He also won the Florida straw poll. Previously, however, he had lagged behind Harkin in fund raising, had trailed several others in the polls, and had gotten almost no notice on the evening news. Finally, as Hadley effectively conceded, the 1976 invisible primary of the Democrats defied prediction.

In sum, what happens in an invisible primary is important to the rest of the nominating process but not to the point that actual primaries become mere affirmations of what the invisible primary has already decided. The available indicators, moreover, are even less helpful in identifying the main rivals of eventual nominees. They helped little or not at all in forecasting how the field would narrow for the Democrats in 1976, 1984, 1988, and 1992 or for the Republicans in 1980. Fund raising and straw votes (but not poll standings) proved equally misleading in the Republican run-up to 1988.

Moreover, one must regard these measures of success in the invisible primary with due caution. Though essential to waging a protracted nominating campaign, the raising and spending of "hard" money in accordance with present law is increasingly less reliable as an indicator owing to the rise of prepresidential PACs and other circumventions of the FECA. Early polls often omit several if not most of the eventual candidates, and, in any case, reflect a superficial recognition of names more than informed judgment or serious commitment. The amount of news coverage a candidate receives at this early juncture is largely a function of such poll standings. Straw polls are more tests of organizational prowess than popular support.

Clearly, as so many examples in this chapter attest, the voters in actual primaries are quite capable of defying whatever conventional wisdom has arisen from apparent success in the invisible primary. "Winning" the invisible primary, as Hadley had to acknowledge, hardly guarantees victory in what follows. Meager fund raising or some other shortcoming during the invisible primary, however, handicaps the dark horse suddenly favored by momentum, as Hart discovered in 1984. And, of course, abysmal failure during the invisible primary often spells the end of presidential aspirations. Necessary but not sufficient, then, this initial phase has become as much a part of the presidential nominating process as the Iowa caucuses or the national conventions. Nothing in the strategic environment of presidential nominating politics is likely to diminish its future importance.

Acknowledgments

In addition to Mark Acton, Robert Biersack, Kevin Phillips, and Hemal Vaidya, who kindly provided the data for several tables as noted, the author gratefully acknowledges the assistance of Emily Hoffmire of the Denison Library, John Lynch of the Vanderbilt Television News Archive, Charles Reitsma of the Denison Computer Center, and Hugh Winebrenner of Drake University.

Notes

1. *Standing Firm* (New York: HarperCollins, 1994).

2. Mark Ippolito, "Can You Spell Stampede?" *Nashville Tennessean,* 2 July 1994, A1.

3. Arthur T. Hadley, *The Invisible Primary* (Englewood Cliffs, N.J.: Prentice Hall, 1976).

4. Although Hadley deserves credit for first calling attention to this initial phase of the contemporary nominating process, nineteenth-century Americans were hardly unaccustomed to lengthy, complex, and largely invisible run-ups to presidential nominating conventions. The protracted fight over an ultimately unsuccessful effort to renominate former President Ulysses S. Grant for a third term in 1880 is a case in point. For a good account of this episode, see Charles W. Stein, *The Third Term Tradition: Its Rise and Collapse in American Politics* (New York: Columbia University Press, 1943), 71–116.

5. Hadley, *Invisible Primary,* 3.

6. For a good account of how Carter made up his mind to run, see Jules Witcover, *Marathon* (New York: Viking Press, 1977), 105–18.

7. Hadley, *Invisible Primary,* 29.

8. Ibid., 20–29 and 302–3.

9. Another historic instance of mind changing in response to events was then Vice-President Gerald Ford's disavowal of a 1976 candidacy on 17 December 1973. On 21 August 1974 he decided to make the race. See Hadley, *Invisible Primary,* 301–2.

10. John Kessel prefers "early days" to describe that period in the nominating process "prior to the beginning of delegate selection" in *Presidential Campaign Politics,* 4th ed. (Pacific Grove, Calif.: Brooks/Cole, 1992), 6. Rhodes Cook's "exhibition season" lasts from "the day after a general election to the start of primary and caucus action more than three years later. The exhibition season is a time for potential candidates to test the political waters, raise money, and begin to organize their campaigns around the country, wooing important individuals and interest groups and honing their basic campaign themes." See his chapter, "The Nominating Process," in *The Elections of 1988,* ed. Michael Nelson (Washington, D.C.: CQ Press, 1989), 31.

11. Maureen Dowd, "Stars of War Room Are Auditioning for the Presidential Battles to Come," *New York Times,* 11 February 1991, B7.

12. Hadley, *Invisible Primary,* 44.

13. In 1983, for example, Hart campaigned the better part of twenty-eight days in New Hampshire. Senator John Glenn visited the state fourteen times in

1983, Mondale thirteen times, according to the respective New Hampshire campaigns, which supplied the author with this information after the 1984 primary. More recently, almost every 1996 GOP hopeful visited New Hampshire in 1993–94. Early front-runner Dole even returned after April and May 1993 appearances to spend a week of his August "vacation" in the state. The state GOP informed the author that Senator Gramm's 1993–94 visits had been "too numerous to recall."

14. Hadley, *Invisible Primary*, 2. Later he repeats the claim as follows: "In summary, the way the system works today, the candidate who wins the state primaries is assured the nomination, and victory in the state primaries comes from placing first in the invisible primary." Ibid., 14.

15. We are all indebted to Nelson W. Polsby and the late Aaron Wildavsky for developing the concept of a strategic environment in their classic text *Presidential Elections*, now in its eighth edition (New York: Free Press, 1992).

16. Hadley's initial approach, alas never systematically applied, was to compare candidates on six "tracks": psychology, staff, strategy, money, media, and constituency. Hadley, *Invisible Primary*, 14–20.

17. Ibid., 16.

18. Elaine C. Kamarck and Kenneth M. Goldstein cover these points cogently in "The Rules Do Matter: Post-Reform Presidential Nominating Politics," in *The Parties Respond*, 2d ed., ed. L. Sandy Maisel (Boulder, Colo.: Westview Press, 1994), 169–95, esp. 179–80. For the definitive account of momentum, see Larry M. Bartels, *Presidential Primaries and the Dynamics of Public Choice* (Princeton: Princeton University Press, 1988).

19. See *Congressional Quarterly's Guide to U.S. Elections*, 2d ed. (Washington, D.C.: CQ Press, 1985), 420–41 for the primaries of 1972–84. The 1988 data are from *Congressional Quarterly Weekly Report* 46 (19 July 1988): 1894–95. See the national convention supplements to *Congressional Quarterly Weekly Report* 50 (4 July and 19 August 1992) for 1992 primary schedules. Primary totals include beauty contests in Vermont and a few other states.

20. "The Rules Do Matter," table 8.4, 183. The Democratic trend would have been even more dramatic had Kamarck and Goldstein omitted superdelegates from their totals.

21. Albert R. Hunt estimated that more than 80 percent of all GOP delegates would be allocated by the end of March 1996 in "Making Book on the GOP Race in 1996," *Wall Street Journal*, 10 March 1994, A19. George F. Will guessed about 70 percent "and probably the nominee" by the third week of March. See "From Nashville to the White House?" *Washington Post*, 10 April 1994, C7. In the immediate aftermath of the 1994 midterm elections, the Democratic nominating process could not be foretold. One early sign of difficulty for President Clinton, however, was a 1994 *Times-Mirror* poll in which 66 percent of the self-identified Democrats indicated that they would like to see him challenged in the primaries. "Democrats Support Challenge to Clinton," *Columbus Dispatch*, 8 December 1994, 4A.

22. See my chapter, "Meeting Expectations? Major Newspaper Coverage of Candidates During the 1988 Exhibition Season," in *Nominating the President*, ed. Emmett H. Buell, Jr., and Lee Sigelman (Knoxville: University of Tennessee Press, 1991), 150–95.

23. Elizabeth Kolbert, "Fighting Obscurity on Tight Primary Budgets," *New*

York Times, 24 November 1991, A1.

24. Quoted in Morton M. Kondracke, "Powell for President Effort Kicks Off, but Does He Want to Run?" *Roll Call,* 11 August 1994, 6. The Dole campaign began lining up fund raisers and campaign strategists as early as mid-June of 1994 according to Richard L. Berke, "Dole Takes First Real Steps toward '96 Presidential Race," *New York Times,* 15 June 1994, A1.

25. There is much more to campaign finances than the activity closely monitored by the FEC. For the most extensive account of prepresidential PACs and other means of circumventing the FECA in prenomination campaigns, see Anthony Corrado, *Creative Campaigning* (Boulder, Colo.: Westview Press, 1992).

26. Although the stop date for this activity was the same for every campaign (31 December), the starting date varied by campaign. The Bentsen and Wallace committees began raising money in 1973; Carter, Harris, Henry Jackson, Udall, and Sanford got going at various points in 1974. Bayh, Shapp, and Shriver committees opened their books in 1975. Carter's 1980 committee began raising money on 1 January 1979, about six months before Brown and nearly ten months before Kennedy. Askew started on 1 August 1981. Jackson was the last of the 1984 Democrats to take this step, on 1 October 1983. Gephardt opened the money part of the 1988 invisible primary on 17 November 1986. Gore was the last to form a committee on 20 April 1987. Tsongas formed his committee on 7 March 1991; Brown waited until 2 September 1991. Sources cited in table 1.3.

27. See Gary R. Orren, "The Nomination Process: Vicissitudes of Candidate Selection," in *The Elections of 1984,* ed. Michael Nelson (Washington, D.C.: CQ Press, 1985), 42–51. The winner outspent the loser in twenty-six Democratic primaries and caucuses, Orren notes, and in twenty-six others the loser outspent the winner.

28. See Linda Wertheimer, "Dukakis's Secret to Success: He Wouldn't Budge," *Washington Post National Weekly Edition,* 20–26 June 1988, 23–24.

29. In the words of William Carrick, his campaign manager, Gephardt attempted to compete almost everywhere in the South, however good his chances. The result was a $4 million strategy funded with a $1 million bank account. See David R. Runkel, ed., *Campaign for President: The Managers Look at '88* (Dover, Mass.: Auburn House, 1989), 177–78.

30. Hadley, *Invisible Primary,* 2.

31. Theodore H. White, *America in Search of Itself: The Making of the President, 1956–1980* (New York: Harper & Row, 1982), 30.

32. See the three volumes of George Gallup's *The Gallup Poll: Public Opinion, 1935–1971* (New York: Random House, 1972), for 1936–68 data. The last 1972 poll before New Hampshire is found in *The Gallup Poll: Public Opinion 1972–1977,* vol. 1 (Wilmington, Del.: Scholarly Resources, 1978). Yet another problem with Hadley's claim is that Gallup seldom polled precisely one month before the New Hampshire primary. In 1952, for example, Dwight Eisenhower led Taft in a poll taken on 20–25 January, while Taft led Eisenhower in the final survey of Republicans one week before the New Hampshire primary of 11 March.

33. These data are not without problems. Although all questions in table 1.4 asked respondents to choose from a list of likely (or actual) candidates, Gallup reported first choices in some published summaries and combined first and second choices in others. Question wording also varied, sometimes significantly. Comparison of these preferences suffers further because Gallup separated party identifiers

and independents in some polls while combining partisans and independents lean-ing toward the same party in others. The firm also substituted registered Demo-crats and Republicans for party identifiers in some polls. Interviewers occasionally asked two versions of the same question, the first with a prominent but unlikely candidate included and the second with this candidate absent and his support real-located. I chose the reallocated version only if the missing person had pulled out.

34. Ford led Reagan in April and July of 1978 but trailed him in all subse-quent polls. Gallup began reallocating the diffident Ford's support in June 1979, much to Reagan's benefit. Even with Ford in the lineup, however, Reagan still led, albeit by less. See *The Gallup Poll: Public Opinion 1979* (Wilmington, Del.: Schol-arly Resources, 1980), 13, 87–88, 175–76, 193, 216, 262, 280.

35. *The Gallup Poll: Public Opinion 1979*, 3.

36. David Moore, "Dole Leads GOP Presidential Hopefuls," *Gallup Poll Monthly*, 343 (April 1994), 24–25.

37. This is not the place for an extended discussion of sampling and nonsam-pling errors in prenomination polls. For good discussions of these issues, see Irving Crespi, *Pre-Election Polling* (New York: Russell Sage, 1988); and Thomas E. Mann and Gary R. Orren, eds., *Media Polls in American Politics* (Washington, D.C.: Brookings Institution, 1992).

38. David Yepsen and Phoebe Wall Howard, "Dole Wins Early Nod in Race for President," *Des Moines Register,* 25 June 1994, A1.

39. Gramm won the next straw poll on 7 January 1995 with 72 percent of 1,253 voting at the Louisiana Republican convention in Baton Rouge, but only af-ter the major effort Richard L. Berke described in "Texas Senator Has a Victory in Louisiana," *New York Times,* 8 January 1995, A12. Buchanan ran second with 12 percent, while Alexander, Dole, and Quayle trailed at 5, 2, and 1 percent, respec-tively. Even some Gramm supporters discounted this lopsided outcome. "Come on," said one, "Louisiana Republicans? To use this as a compass to point the country? It's a media gimmick." The *Wall Street Journal* of 3 March 1995 re-ported Republican schemes to raise money with straw polls in South Carolina, Wisconsin, Virginia, Iowa (again), Nevada, Maine, and Florida. See John Har-wood, "As South Carolina GOP Uses 'Straw Poll' Dinner to Raise Cash, Hungry '96 Hopefuls Crowd Table," A12.

40. Adam Clymer, "Bumper Crop of Straw Polls," *New York Times,* 12 No-vember 1979, A17.

41. Quoted in Jonathan Moore, ed., *Campaign for President: The Managers Look at '84* (Dover, Mass.: Auburn House, 1986), 15–16. Bode similarly ques-tioned John M. Russonello, Cranston's press secretary. Unlike Askew, Cranston sought out straw polls as opportunities to establish credibility with the press. Russonello recounted that the campaign "spent a lot more money than we thought we were going to" in waging these pseudo events. Ironically, reporters began ask-ing about Cranston's high level of spending relative to receipts. Bode asked Russonello: "Are you saying these straw polls, rather than present an opportunity for long-shot candidates, can be precisely the kind of thing that drained them, forced them out of their strategies?" Russonello replied, "A series of them obvi-ously will drain you." Ibid., 34.

42. Kathy Sawyer, "Democrats' Straw Polls Are Called Divisive," *Washing-ton Post,* 19 July 1983, A1.

43. Thomas B. Edsall, "Clinton Wins Straw Poll at Florida Convention,"

Washington Post, 16 December 1991, A14.

44. Jack W. Germond and Jules Witcover, *Blue Smoke and Mirrors: How Reagan Won and Carter Lost the Election of 1980* (New York: Viking Press, 1981), 101.

45. Robert Shogan, "Straw Polls Stir Enthusiasm but Generate Fears," *Los Angeles Times,* 20 June 1983, A1.

46. Sawyer, "Democrats' Straw Polls," A4.

47. Askew owed many of his 1,066 votes to visiting Amway conventioneers, according to Charles Brereton in *First in the Nation: New Hampshire and the Premier Presidential Primary* (Portsmouth, N.H.: Peter E. Randall, 1987), 225. In any event, as Brereton also noted, Askew won only 1,025 votes in the 1984 primary, or 41 less than in the straw poll.

48. Germond and Witcover, *Blue Smoke and Mirrors,* 105.

49. Ibid. See also Adam Clymer's lead story, "Maine Republicans in Informal Ballot Give Bush a Victory," *New York Times,* 4 November 1979, A1.

50. Shogan, "Straw Polls Stir Enthusiasm," 15.

51. David Broder, "Mondale Captures Maine Straw Poll, AFL-CIO Backing," *Washington Post,* 2 October 1983, A1; Chris Black, "Mondale Favored in Maine," *Boston Globe,* 1 October 1983, A5; Rowland Evans and Robert Novak, "Mondale: Uneasy in Maine," 19 September 1983, *Washington Post,* A13.

52. Cathleen Decker, "Bush Wins Straw Poll, Robertson Places Second," *Los Angeles Times,* 15 November 1987, A16.

53. Omitted are the 1983 poll of Alabama YDs and Askew's victory at the Manchester CDC picnic already discussed. The 1987 Maryland poll won by Bush after distributing more $30 tickets was also omitted owing to unavailable vote totals.

54. Hadley, *Invisible Primary,* 257.

55. See especially Thomas E. Patterson, *Out of Order* (New York: Knopf, 1993).

56. See Buell, "Meeting Expectations," 158–67, for a detailed account of character coverage during the 1988 invisible primary.

57. Quoted in Michael J. Robinson and Margaret Sheehan, *Over the Wire and on TV: CBS and UPI in Campaign '80* (New York: Russell Sage, 1983), 116.

58. William C. Adams, "Media Coverage of Campaign '84: A Preliminary Report," in *The Mass Media in Campaign '84,* ed. Michael J. Robinson and Austin Ranney (Washington, D.C.: American Enterprise Institute, 1985), 10.

59. Buell, "Meeting Expectations," 154–56. In sharp contrast to the clear and consistent ratings of Republican aspirants, Democratic polls in 1987 pointed up the lack of a distinct front-runner. Republican and Democratic coverage in five major newspapers reflected these differences with Bush getting much more coverage than Dole in all five, Dole surpassing Robertson in every newspaper except the *Atlanta Constitution,* Robertson leading Kemp in all five, and Kemp surpassing Haig and du Pont in all five. With newspaper coverage defined as print lines about each candidate, the Democratic pattern of coverage—or lack thereof—faithfully reflected the polling muddle. No Democratic candidate consistently led his rivals in every newspaper. Jackson, the nominal front-runner after Hart's withdrawal, got more coverage than any rival only in the *Constitution.* His print-line total was second in the *Chicago Tribune* and *New York Times,* third in the *Los Angeles Times,* and fourth in the *Boston Globe.*

60. Note that these data do not pertain to exposure as measured in news seconds because this would have required the viewing of every story about more than one candidate and the timing of each candidate's appearance.

61. Buell, "Meeting Expectations," 168–70.

62. According to his literature, Alexander was the moderator of Republican Neighborhood Meetings held on the first Tuesday of every month at 8:00 P.M. EDT. Broadcasting from a different state every month, this "outside-the-beltway, grassroots idea network of neighborhood meetings" afforded him an opportunity to discuss education and other issues, criticize Clinton, and otherwise hone political skills. See "First Tuesday: The Republican Neighborhood Meeting," (Nashville, Tenn.: Republican Exchange Satellite Network, n.d.).

63. Hadley, *Invisible Primary*, 268. "What I really have wanted to do," he wrote on the next page, "is indicate the nature and location of key early battles, the state primaries and caucuses which, read correctly, will show *how* the invisible primary was fought and won." Emphasis in original.

64. Ibid., 214–15, 268–69, 275.

65. *The Gallup Poll: Public Opinion 1972–77*, vol. 2, 649.

2

Forecasting Presidential Nominations

William G. Mayer

> Madame Sosostris, famous clairvoyante,
> Had a bad cold, nevertheless
> Is known to be the wisest woman in Europe,
> With a wicked pack of cards.
> — Eliot, "The Waste Land"

One of the latest vogues in academic political science has been the development of "forecasting models" that try to predict the outcome of an election months before the actual voting takes place. Using a few basic variables such as the president's job-approval rating in the midsummer polls or the recent growth rate of the national economy, these models generate forecasts as to which party will win the presidency or how many seats a given party will win or lose in the House of Representatives.[1]

To date, such models have been developed exclusively for predicting how the two major parties will do relative to one another in the general elections held every second or fourth November. No one (until now) has been foolhardy enough to try to apply them to the presidential nominating process. Indeed, to all outward appearances, presidential nominations are exactly the sort of event one *would not* want to try to forecast, a realm of vast uncertainty, unpredictability, and chaos. Unknown candidates rise out of nowhere to become front-runners; "can't miss" candidates suddenly see their best-laid plans come undone; primary voters, with no partisan signposts to guide them, must choose among a cast of characters about whom they possess very little in the way of firm impressions or solid information.

As Gelman and King argue, in an article that is quite confident about political scientists' ability to predict the outcome of the presidential vote in *general* elections:

> ... in primaries, low-visibility elections, and uneven campaigns, we would not expect forecasting based on fundamental variables measured before the campaign to work. The fast-paced events during a primary campaign (such as verbal slips, gaffes, debates, particularly good photo opportunities, rhetorical victories, specific policy proposals, previous primary results, etc.) can make an important difference because they can affect voters' perceptions of the candidates' positions on fundamental issues. Also, primary election candidates often stand so close on fundamental issues that voters are more likely to base their decision on the minor issues that do separate the candidates. In addition, the inherent instability of a multi-candidate race heightens the importance of concerns such as electability that have little to do with positions on fundamental issues.[2]

Such appearances notwithstanding, the purpose of this chapter is to argue that recent presidential nomination contests have, in fact, been less chaotic than they might appear at first glance; that nomination races are actually conducted under a system of rules and norms that give considerable structure and regularity to the process; and that one can, for that reason, make at least reasonably reliable forecasts as to how they will turn out.

Two Predictors

For reasons to be explained more fully later in this chapter, my focus here is restricted to a rather small number of nomination contests—specifically, those that have taken place from 1980 to the present. During that time, eight distinct presidential nominations were conferred by the Democratic and Republican parties; but one of them was a foregone conclusion (Reagan was entirely unopposed when he sought renomination in 1984), and a second incumbent, George Bush in 1992, faced no more than token opposition. In six other cases, however, there was a serious battle for the party designation, with considerable uncertainty as to how it would turn out and a large number of commentators picking the wrong candidate to win. The question I wish to pose is: were there any reliable indicators that might have enabled us to guess in advance who the winning candidate would be? As it turns out, there are two such indicators, both available in January or early February of the election year, and both of which pointed out the winner in five of the six contested nomination races.

The first of these indicators is the candidates' relative standing in polls of the national party electorate. For at least a year before the first actual delegate selection event, pollsters ask national samples of Democrats and Republicans whom they would like to see nominated as their party's candidate for president. The Gallup poll results from these inquiries are shown in table 2.1.

TABLE 2.1

PRESIDENTIAL NOMINATION PREFERENCES
OF NATIONAL PARTY IDENTIFIERS, 1980–92
(IN PERCENTAGES)

1980 REPUBLICAN NOMINATION RACE

	22–25 June 1979	13–16 July 1979	2–5 Nov. 1979	7–10 Dec. 1979	4–6 Jan. 1980
Reagan	50	38	41	47	41
Baker	13	14	18	12	14
Connally	11	15	13	12	13
Bush	2	*	2	8	9
Dole	2	7	3	6	*
Anderson	*	2	*	*	4
Crane	*	1	*	*	*

1980 DEMOCRATIC NOMINATION RACE

	22–25 June 1979	13–16 July 1979	2–5 Nov. 1979	16–19 Nov. 1979	7–10 Dec. 1979	4–6 Jan. 1980
Carter	26	30	32	36	46	51
Kennedy	68	66	54	55	42	37

1984 DEMOCRATIC NOMINATION RACE

	7–10 Oct. 1983	18–21 Nov. 1983	9–12 Dec. 1983	13–16 Jan. 1984	27–30 Jan. 1984	10–13 Feb. 1984
Mondale	40	47	40	47	47	49
Glenn	21	19	24	16	15	13
Jackson	10	7	9	9	11	13
McGovern	8	7	8	4	7	5
Cranston	6	3	3	4	3	3
Hart	3	2	3	3	2	3
Askew	1	3	1	1	2	2
Hollings	1	1	1	1	1	1

SOURCE: Gallup poll.
* Candidate was favored by less than 1 percent of the survey respondents.

TABLE 2.1 — CONTINUED

1988 REPUBLICAN NOMINATION RACE

	8–14 June 1987	10–13 July 1987	24 Aug.– 2 Sept. 1987	23–26 Oct. 1987	22–24 Jan. 1988
Bush	39	40	40	47	45
Dole	21	18	19	22	30
Kemp	8	10	9	4	5
Haig	6	7	4	4	2
Robertson	5	5	8	7	8
Du Pont	2	3	2	1	2

1988 DEMOCRATIC NOMINATION RACE

	8–14 June 1987	10–13 July 1987	24 Aug.– 2 Sept. 1987	23–26 Oct. 1987	22–24 Jan. 1988
Hart	—	—	—	—	23
Jackson	18	17	19	22	15
Dukakis	11	13	13	14	16
Biden	7	4	3	—	—
Gephardt	7	3	6	5	9
Simon	7	7	7	8	9
Gore	5	8	8	7	6
Babbitt	2	2	2	1	4

1992 REPUBLICAN NOMINATION RACE

	5–8 Dec. 1991	3–6 Jan. 1992	31 Jan.– 2 Feb. 1992
Bush	86	85	84
Buchanan	5	10	11
Duke	6	3	4

1992 DEMOCRATIC NOMINATION RACE

	13-15 Sept. 1991	31 Oct.– 3 Nov. 1991	3–6 Jan. 1992	31 Jan.– 2 Feb. 1992
Clinton	6	9	17	42
Brown	21	21	21	16
Harkin	6	10	9	9
Kerrey	5	10	11	10
Tsongas	5	7	6	9
Wilder	10	12	9	—

"—" Not a candidate at the time of the survey, so was not included in the list of candidates read to respondents.

There is some tendency, in media reports, to dismiss such figures as reflecting little more than name recognition, but a closer look at these data suggests that they may actually have more solidity and meaning than that. To begin with, many of the men listed in table 2.1 had been prominent national media figures for a number of years before announcing their candidacies, and many voters probably knew a good deal more about them than just their names. Ronald Reagan, for example, was not just the country's most prominent conservative spokesperson in 1980; he had also come close to being his party's nominee four years earlier. Jimmy Carter was an incumbent president in the same year; Walter Mondale in 1984 and George Bush in 1988 had both served as vice-president. Edward Kennedy, John Glenn, Jesse Jackson, and John Connally were also, for various reasons, likely to have had reasonably well-developed reputations even with many Americans who were not especially interested in politics.

Equally important, there is enough movement in these figures to indicate that *something* is going on during the half year or so before the states start selecting their convention delegates. This period—often called "the invisible primary"—has not received much attention from academic students of the nomination process, but the data in table 2.1 suggest that it is worthy of closer scrutiny. While the average voter may not yet be giving much attention to the nomination races at this stage, the press and party activists clearly are—and some of their impressions and judgments are apparently filtering through to the voters.

In 1980, for example, one can see signs of George Bush's emergence from the pack of Republican also-rans, as his support among GOP voters rose from an asterisk in July 1979 to 9 percent in early January. The 1984 results, by contrast, provide early evidence of John Glenn's weakness, as his standing with self-identified Democrats fell from 24 percent in December 1983 to 13 percent in mid-February 1984. Especially dramatic is the rise of Bill Clinton in 1992, who went from 6 percent in a September 1991 survey to 17 percent in early January 1992 and then to 42 percent in early February.

For our present purposes, however, the most important point to be gleaned from table 2.1 is that these prerace polls prove to be a quite accurate predictor of who will eventually win the nomination. As shown in table 2.2, if we focus on the last poll taken before the start of delegate selection activities[3]—that is to say, the last poll before the Iowa caucuses—the person leading in the poll went on to win the nomination in five of six cases (six of seven if one includes the Bush-Buchanan race in 1992).

The second indicator is the candidates' relative success in raising money. Under the campaign finance laws that have been in effect since 1974, every active candidate for the presidential nomination is required to turn in periodic reports indicating how much money he or she has raised and spent.

TABLE 2.2
NATIONAL POLL STANDINGS AS A PREDICTOR
OF PRESIDENTIAL NOMINATIONS

Year	Party	Candidate leading in the last poll before the Iowa caucuses	Eventual nominee
1980	Republican	Reagan	Reagan
1980	Democratic	Carter	Carter
1984	Democratic	Mondale	Mondale
1988	Republican	Bush	Bush
1988	Democratic	Hart	Dukakis
1992	Republican	Bush	Bush
1992	Democratic	Clinton	Clinton

Table 2.3 lists the total amount of money that each candidate had raised as of 31 December of the year before the election. Again, in five of six cases, the leading money raiser went on to win the nomination (see table 2.4). The money-raising totals also predict the 1992 Republican race accurately.

Obviously, there is a substantial degree of overlap between these two indicators. As a comparison of tables 2.2 and 2.4 will show, there were four nomination races between 1980 and 1992 in which both predictors pointed in the same direction: four cases, that is, where one candidate was leading in the final poll taken before the Iowa caucuses *and* had raised more money than any of his rivals. And in all four instances, that candidate was the eventual nominee.

Forecasting Primary Vote Shares

Since many political scientists appear to believe that a forecast is not really a forecast unless it involves a regression equation, I have decided—principally for comparison purposes—to combine these two indicators into a single model that generates a numerical prediction of each candidate's relative success in the presidential nomination race.

The dependent variable, selected from a number of possible alternatives, is the percentage of the total vote won by each candidate in all presidential primaries held by that candidate's party during the nomination season. In the 1992 Democratic nomination contest, for example, thirty-nine distinct primaries were held, at which a total of 20,239,385 presidential preference votes were cast. Bill Clinton received 10,482,411 of these votes, or 51.8 percent; Jerry Brown had 4,071,232 votes, or 20.1 percent; Paul Tsongas received 18.1 percent; and so on.

Two independent variables are used to predict these primary vote shares. The first is the percentage of party identifiers who supported each candidate in the last national Gallup poll taken before the start of delegate selection activities, as reported in table 2.1. The second is the total amount of money each candidate raised before the election year, divided by the largest amount of money raised by any candidate in that party's nomination race. In the 1992 Democratic nomination contest, for example, the largest fund raiser during 1991 was Bill Clinton, who raised $3,304,000. Clinton himself thus receives a score of 100 on this variable. Paul Tsongas, who raised $2,630,000, receives a score of 79.6; Jerry Brown is given a value of 31.3; and so on.

TABLE 2.3

TOTAL NET RECEIPTS FOR PRESIDENTIAL CANDIDATES
PRIOR TO THE YEAR OF ELECTION, 1980–92

	Republicans		Democrats	
	Candidate	Amount raised	Candidate	Amount raised
1980	Connally	$9,159,737	Carter	$5,751,579
	Reagan	7,210,951	Kennedy	3,893,375
	Bush	4,455,095	Brown	1,216,714
	Crane	3,271,391		
	Baker	3,084,617		
	Dole	790,439		
	Anderson	505,989		
1984			Mondale	$11,448,262
			Glenn	6,417,718
			Cranston	4,715,995
			Askew	2,191,786
			Hart	1,874,083
			Hollings	1,626,384
			Jackson	358,415
			McGovern	249,827
1988	Bush	$19,058,415	Dukakis	$10,371,229
	Robertson	16,406,966	Simon	6,056,829
	Dole	14,314,121	Gephardt	5,902,763
	Kemp	10,206,670	Gore	3,941,887
	Du Pont	5,537,436	Babbitt	2,446,219
	Haig	1,655,058	Hart	2,301,247
			Jackson	1,403,094
1992	Bush	$10,092,532	Clinton	$3,304,020
	Buchanan	707,106	Tsongas	2,629,892
	Duke	8,764	Harkin	2,182,070
			Kerrey	1,945,313
			Brown	1,034,474

SOURCE: Computed from FEC reports.

TABLE 2.4

NET RECEIPTS AS A PREDICTOR
OF PRESIDENTIAL NOMINATIONS

Year	Party	Candidate raising the most money prior to the year of election	Eventual nominee
1980	Republican	Connally	Reagan
1980	Democratic	Carter	Carter
1984	Democratic	Mondale	Mondale
1988	Republican	Bush	Bush
1988	Democratic	Dukakis	Dukakis
1992	Republican	Bush	Bush
1992	Democratic	Clinton	Clinton

The equation that results, shown in table 2.5, is obviously not intended as a fully developed causal model, but rather as a tool for drawing some general lessons about the predictability of presidential nomination races.[4] From this vantage point, forecasting models can be assessed in a variety of ways; probably the three most commonly used indicators are the R^2 statistic, the standard error of estimate (SEE), and the model's record in making out-of-sample forecasts. All have their pluses and minuses, their critics and defenders.[5] But in this case, all three point to the same general conclusion: that presidential nomination races can be forecast to some extent, but with considerably less precision or certainty than general election races. The R^2 statistic in table 2.5, for example, indicates that the two variables in this model can explain about 70 percent of the variance in primary vote shares.

TABLE 2.5

REGRESSION EQUATION FOR PREDICTING
PRIMARY VOTE SHARES

Dependent variable is the percentage of the total primary vote won by a candidate in all presidential primaries held by that candidate's party during the nomination season.

Independent variables	Regression coefficients	Standard errors
National poll standings	.94	.14
Total funds raised	.02	.08
Constant	1.31	3.37

$R^2 = .70$
Adjusted $R^2 = .69$
$SEE = 11.93$
$N = 38$

Especially when weighed against the claim that presidential nomination races are entirely too capricious to be forecast in advance, this is an impressive result. On the other hand, it is somewhat smaller than the percentage of the variation explained by most general election forecasting models, which typically have an R^2 of around .90.[6]

Particularly worth examining is the model's record in predicting the nomination outcome, using a technique known as out-of-sample forecasting.[7] These predictions are shown in table 2.6. Obviously, some of these forecasts are rather wide of the mark. Nothing in the model can account for why George Bush emerged from the Republican pack in 1980, or why Gary Hart came to be Walter Mondale's principal opponent in 1984. Nor does it help us understand why John Connally in 1980 and John Glenn in 1984 did so poorly. But it *does* correctly forecast the winning candidate in five of the six contested nomination races.

Why Nomination Races Are at Least Partially Predictable

As the forecasting of general election (especially presidential) results has developed over the past several years, two distinct trends in the academic literature are visible. On the one hand, the predictions generated by these models have become (perhaps) a bit more accurate. On the other hand, the forecasting enterprise has become less and less useful for helping us understand anything interesting or valuable about electoral politics.[8] In contrast, I regard the predictions generated by my own model as of distinctly less significance than what they tell us about the current state of the presidential selection process.

To say that a political process produces predictable results means, in general, that the outcome of that process is largely determined by certain major underlying regularities; and that these regularities (or their surrogates) can be measured with some precision before the process actually gets under way. If the presidential nomination process truly were as unsystematic and chaotic as it is sometimes portrayed to be, if the final result really did hinge on such unpredictable occurrences as verbal gaffes, good debate performances, and brilliant strategic maneuvers, then its outcome would not be forecastable to any significant degree. But if the evidence and analysis just presented are accurate, then we must conclude that these unpredictable campaign events are less important than they might initially appear to be, and that the presidential nomination process actually operates with a considerable measure of structure and regularity. More specifically, I see the nomination outcome as heavily shaped by four important regularities.

TABLE 2.6
OUT-OF-SAMPLE FORECASTS OF PRIMARY VOTE SHARES

Year	Candidate	*Actual primary vote*	*Predicted vote*	*Error (actual – pred.)*
1980	Reagan	60.8	40.5	20.3
	Bush	23.3	11.3	12.0
	Anderson	12.4	4.4	8.0
	Baker	0.9	14.7	−13.8
	Crane	0.8	2.9	−2.1
	Connally	0.6	17.9	−17.3
	Dole	0.1	1.2	−1.1
1980	Carter	51.2	51.6	−0.4
	Kennedy	37.1	37.7	−0.6
1984	Mondale	37.8	51.9	−14.1
	Hart	36.1	2.9	33.2
	Jackson	18.2	11.5	6.7
	Glenn	3.4	15.0	−11.6
	McGovern	1.9	3.8	−1.9
	Cranston	0.3	4.5	−4.2
	Askew	0.3	2.1	−1.8
	Hollings	0.2	0.8	−0.6
1988	Bush	67.9	44.2	23.7
	Dole	19.2	30.4	−11.2
	Robertson	9.0	11.1	−2.1
	Kemp	2.7	7.9	−5.2
	Du Pont	0.4	4.8	−4.4
	Haig	0.2	4.5	−4.3
1988	Dukakis	42.8	14.6	28.2
	Jackson	29.1	18.0	11.1
	Gore	13.7	7.4	6.3
	Gephardt	6.0	9.5	−3.5
	Simon	4.4	9.4	−5.0
	Hart	1.7	25.9	−24.2
	Babbitt	0.3	6.0	−5.7
1992	Clinton	51.8	42.6	9.2
	Brown	20.1	17.1	3.0
	Tsongas	18.1	12.1	6.0
	Kerrey	1.6	12.4	−10.8
	Harkin	1.4	11.7	−10.3
1992	Bush	72.5	89.2	−16.7
	Buchanan	22.8	12.0	10.8
	Duke	0.9	4.6	−3.7

1. *The need to seek the office.* The first of these regularities is the simple fact that any person who wants the nomination must actively pursue it: that is, he must actually announce his candidacy, organize a campaign, and enter a substantial number of primaries and caucuses in an active quest for delegates. This regularity is easily overlooked when scrutinizing tables 2.1–2.6, which focus on the relative success of *announced* presidential candidates. But the model developed here also contains a second, implicit prediction: that only announced presidential candidates have a serious chance to be nominated; that any presidential wanna-be who does not actually get into the race should not count on getting to the White House except as a dinner guest. If, by the time of the Iowa caucuses, six people have announced their candidacies for a given party's nomination, the eventual nominee will, almost certainly, be one of those six.

This point is worth emphasizing because, in many recent presidential election cycles, there has been a major figure in one party or the other—Gerald Ford in 1980, Mario Cuomo in 1988 and 1992—who seemed to want the nomination but did not want to campaign actively for it. And especially in the Democratic races of 1988 and 1992, when no one candidate emerged to dominate the early primaries and caucuses, a spate of articles appeared suggesting that perhaps none of the active candidates would accumulate a majority of the delegates; that, instead, a long-awaited, much-fabled "brokered convention" would take place and confer the nomination on one of the major unannounced figures sitting on the sidelines.[9]

In fact, nothing even remotely resembling this scenario has ever come close to occurring. In every one of these races, one candidate did eventually emerge with a clear lead in the delegate hunt, who finally gained enough delegate pledges so that, by the end of the primary season, he was declared by all the major media organizations as having ensured himself a first-ballot nomination. The fate of unannounced candidates in recent nomination contests is eloquently summarized by one simple fact: in the eight major-party conventions held between 1980 and 1992, no unannounced candidate has ever received even 1 *percent* of the votes on *any* presidential roll-call ballot.

The regularity with which this happens suggests that it is hardly an accident. To the contrary, many important features of the current selection system have a clear tendency to push nomination races toward a convergence around one or two leading candidates. Competitive pressures within the media lead them to overcover and overinterpret early results; these interpretations then send important signals to voters as to which candidates are still viable and which are not; nonviable candidates receive substantially less press coverage, further diminishing their ability to communicate their message to the voters; and even though many such candidates would still love to "fight it out all the way to the convention," the campaign finance laws usually force them to run skeletal campaigns and finally to withdraw from the race altogether.[10] While there may be some dispute as to which of these factors are most important, the end result is clear: candidates do drop out, convergence does occur, and one of the announced candidates does win the nomination. Those who do not actively seek the nomination, under the current rules of the game, have essentially no chance of getting it.

2. *The resilience of front-runners.* Anyone who follows the day-by-day, minute-to-minute twists and turns in a contested nomination race usually comes away impressed by how precarious life is for a presidential front-runner, how fragile his or her hold is on the party's voters, how readily well-crafted plans can be upset by gaffes and small miscalculations and simple bad luck. But if we take a somewhat longer view of the process, what impresses one is how resilient front-runners actually are. To be sure, almost every one of the front-running candidates listed in table 2.2 suffered some major setback once the delegate selection season began. Ronald Reagan lost the Iowa caucuses in 1980; Walter Mondale saw an apparently insurmountable lead disappear in eight days and was upset by Gary Hart in New Hampshire; George Bush came in third in Iowa in 1988; Clinton's private life suddenly became a topic of public discussion, causing him to lose a large early advantage in New Hampshire.

Moreover, whenever such a mishap does occur, one can count on a huge flood of reporting and commentary that declares the erstwhile front-runner politically dead and wonders whether the new favorite will run for a second term or not. The most remarkable example of this "one strike and you're out" reporting came in the 1980 Republican nomination race, after George Bush's upset victory in the Iowa caucuses. Even though Reagan clearly had a large and loyal following among Republican voters and activists, and even though he had rebounded from a far more serious string of losses in the 1976 nomination contest (against a considerably more formidable opponent), an extraordinary number of pundits and commentators wrote their "first rough drafts" of Ronald Reagan's obituary. (Some examples are shown in table 2.7.)

TABLE 2.7
REPORTING AND COMMENTARY ON RONALD REAGAN'S
POLITICAL FUTURE AFTER HE LOST
THE 1980 IOWA CAUCUSES

Bruce Morton, CBS News, 21 Jan. 1980:
"A lot of people in the politics business have said for a long time that if Ronald Reagan loses once, or maybe even just gets tested once, then the magic is gone, and all of a sudden he's an elderly candidate instead of a sure winner."   *Continued . . .*

Tom Brokaw, *Today* show, 22 Jan. 1980:
"I guess we now refer to him [Reagan] as the former front-runner."

Tom Pettit, NBC News, 22 Jan. 1980:
"I would like to suggest that Ronald Reagan is politically dead."

Time, 11 Feb. 1980:
"Reagan, however, may be getting tough too late. A *Boston Globe* poll showed that in late January, he was trailing Bush in New Hampshire by 36% to 45% among Republicans and independents. Reagan is also having trouble adjusting to a busier schedule. His organization is so large that shifting it is much like maneuvering an ocean liner in a lake. . . .

"On top of being considered the favorite in New Hampshire, Bush is expected to win the 4 March Massachusetts primary . . . and he is picking up support in the South. . . ."

Jack Germond and Jules Witcover, syndicated columnists, 22 Feb. 1980:
"A rough consensus is taking shape among moderate Republican politicians that George Bush may achieve a commanding position within the next three weeks in the contest for the 1980 presidential nomination. And those with unresolved reservations about Bush are beginning to wonder privately if it is even possible to keep an alternative politically alive for the later primaries.

"Barring some unforeseen developments, Republican professionals now expect Bush to sweep the New England primaries here [in New Hampshire] next Tuesday and the following week in Massachusetts and Vermont. . . . What the professionals also foresee is the strong possibility that, riding the New England momentum, Bush could defeat Ronald Reagan in Florida 11 March and then stand alone as king of the Republican hill."

Robert Healy, columnist, 22 Feb. 1980:
"George Bush is a Republican golden boy. It is possible that he will go through 1980 without a scratch on his gilt, without losing an important presidential primary. . . .

"Reagan is being chipped away in New Hampshire not for a major blunder but for scrambling a series of lines. . . . Even though he is still called the leading candidate in some places, Reagan does not look like he'll be on the presidential stage much longer."

Time, 25 Feb. 1980:
"Nobody is campaigning harder [in New Hampshire], or more exuberantly, than the newly established Republican front-runner, George

Bush.... If [Reagan] comes in second and then loses to Bush in Massachusetts, as expected, he cannot count on his support in the South and West holding up. Already there are signs of erosion to Bush in Reagan territory."

SOURCES: Quotations from Morton, Brokaw, and Pettit were taken from Jeff Greenfield, *The Real Campaign: How the Media Missed the Story of the 1980 Campaign* (New York: Summit Books, 1982), 39. The columns by Germond and Witcover and Healy appeared in the *Boston Globe*, 22 Feb. 1980, 15.

NOTE: The Iowa caucuses took place on 21 January 1980. The New Hampshire primary was held on 26 February.

For the benefit of those readers who slept through the 1980s, Reagan did recover (rather quickly, in fact) and went on to win the nomination for which he had been the early favorite. So, too, did Walter Mondale in 1984, George Bush in 1988, and Bill Clinton in 1992. All of which suggests that nomination front-runners are a good deal more resilient than they are frequently portrayed to be in the mass media. A front-runner who loses early can—and usually does—come back. Any candidate who maintains a front-runner's status after a year or more of screening by the press and party activists, or who emerges as a front-runner during the same period, does have some important resources to fall back on. Four of the front-runners in table 2.1, for example, were well-known national figures when the nomination race commenced (Reagan and Carter in 1980, Mondale in 1984, Bush in 1988), with established, generally positive reputations with their own party's voters. Contrary to what Samuel Popkin has suggested, this reservoir of good feeling is not entirely obliterated by a few campaign setbacks.[11] A candidate who has successfully endured a vigorous "invisible primary" campaign is also likely to have a reasonably appealing message, a good campaign organization, and substantial campaigning skills of his own. Again, none of these disappears just because a candidate loses a few early primaries or caucuses.

3. *The power of money.* Of the resources that a front-runner possesses to help withstand an early gaffe or setback, perhaps none is more crucial than money. If this seems like an obvious statement, it is one that has generally eluded most recent academic students of the presidential nomination process. Over the past decade or so, a number of political scientists have tried to construct models that explain how the nomination process works, how it generates that elusive quality known as momentum, and how one candidate finally emerges victorious. With very few exceptions, these models completely ignore the role of money.[12] By contrast, I see money as having a central, crucial role in the dynamics of the entire process.

Under the campaign finance system that existed prior to 1974, a candidate who struggled in the early stages of the nomination race might still hang on financially if he could convince a few very wealthy supporters to give or lend him the necessary funds. But in 1974, in reaction to Watergate, Congress initiated a sweeping change in federal campaign finance laws and thus ushered in a very different regime. With any one individual now prohibited from contributing more than $1,000, a candidate's financial health depended on mass marketing his candidacy to a large number of contributors. And contributors, like voters, were reluctant to support a candidate whose viability was in serious doubt.

For candidates who were unable to raise a great deal of money in the first place, then, early losses inevitably confronted them with a set of highly disagreeable choices. They could continue to campaign in the hopes of doing better—but, of course, they had almost no money available to wage the kind of active and vigorous campaign that would make a better showing likely. They could borrow money—but the campaign finance laws also made borrowing difficult, and if the candidate's fortunes did not revive, the laws made it all but impossible to pay off large campaign debts. (As of early 1994, for example, both John Glenn and Gary Hart were still trying to pay off the debts they had accumulated during the nomination race of 1984.)

The only other option was to withdraw—an option that, not surprisingly, most candidates quickly realized they had to take. As a number of commentators have noted, one of the most prominent features of the current nomination process is its tendency to "winnow out" candidates who do poorly in the early primaries and caucuses, forcing them to end their candidacies only days or weeks after the first delegates are selected.[13] In the 1984 Democratic nomination race, for example, five of the eight announced candidates had withdrawn from the contest within two and a half weeks of the first primary. In 1992, three of five candidates dropped out just thirty days after New Hampshire. By and large, it is money that provides the immediate explanation for most of these withdrawals.[14]

But a front-running candidate who had been more successful at fund raising—and all of the leading candidates in table 2.1 except Jesse Jackson and Gary Hart in 1988 were also good at fund raising—had a significantly greater capacity to withstand an early reversal. Having a substantial campaign war chest helps front-runners in two major ways. First, a candidate who suffers an early setback must do something to overcome the unfavorable publicity that invariably accompanies such events and to reestablish a positive image with the voters. Such a candidate has little control, of course, over what the media are reporting, but with an adequate supply of funds, he can work to get *his own* message out to the voters. He can purchase large blocks of time on television and radio, organize rallies, and get his field organization to contact and mobilize potential voters. The candidate who lacks money, by contrast, is even more dependent on whatever the media decide to report about him.

Second, and perhaps more important, money simply allows a candidate to survive: to stay in the race long enough for his luck to change, for the press to get over its feeding frenzy, for his opponents to make their mistakes, for a new "fresh face" to acquire its share of blemishes.[15] Perhaps the best example of this was Bill Clinton's experience in 1992. Contrary to the usual accounts of the nomination process, which stress how absolutely crucial the early primaries and caucuses are, Clinton's early record in these events was marked by one loss after another. In fact, Clinton did not win a single caucus or primary until 3 March, nearly a month after the Iowa caucuses. Because he had a sufficient financial base, however, Clinton was able to withstand these early setbacks until the nomination race finally moved to the South, his home region, where he quickly racked up a series of huge victories. A less well-heeled candidate might have had to withdraw before the first southern state cast its vote.[16]

4. *The perils of the long-shot candidate.* If front-runners have ample resources to fall back on, what also comes through in tables 2.1–2.6 is how strongly the odds are stacked against the less well-known and well-financed candidates. Every four years, a number of little-known, long-shot candidates enter the presidential sweepstakes, hoping that an early victory or two and a lot of luck will propel them to their party's nomination. But, in fact, no one has done this successfully since Jimmy Carter in 1976.

To be sure, a number of other candidates have come close: George Bush in 1980, Gary Hart in 1984, perhaps Paul Tsongas in 1992. And, those who follow nomination races closely might insist, were it not for one or two crucial missteps, each of these races might have turned out very differently. If George Bush had not messed up that debate in Nashua, if Walter Mondale had not come up with his "Where's the Beef?" line, if Gary Hart had been able to get his commercials off the air in Illinois. . . .

Playing the "What If" game is a wonderful source of amusement for hard-core political junkies, and I have surely spent many a pleasant hour doing it myself. But two general points should be made about this kind of speculation. First, precisely because such conjectures usually cannot be conclusively proved or disproved, there is a strong tendency among many "What If" players to treat each small gaffe or mishap as if it were a decisive turning point in American political history. A closer and more dispassionate scrutiny of these races, however, suggests that many celebrated campaign blunders were not as significant as they are often alleged to be and that the candidate committing the error probably would have lost anyway. In the 1980 Republican nomination race, for example, there is considerable evidence that Ronald Reagan would have won New Hampshire even without Bush's strange and stony silence during the Nashua debate;[17] and that Reagan had a huge and quite loyal following of conservative Republicans in southern and western states who would have stuck by him even if he had lost the Granite State primary. Indeed, of the candidates listed above, I think Gary Hart was the only one who had a realistic shot at winning his party's nomination.

But even if one thinks these campaign miscues were more important than I do, this only emphasizes the fragile position of the long-shot candidate. *All* candidates make a few mistakes somewhere along the line: the perfect campaign has yet to be run. The difference is that front-running candidates can survive these mistakes because, as I have stressed, they have considerable resources to fall back on. Long-shot candidates have such a tenuous hold on the voters' loyalties, and so few other resources at their disposal, that they have to hope that everything will go exactly according to plan—which, in the end, it never does.

Structural Regularities, Rules Changes, and Strategic Convergence

This focus on the underlying regularities that make prediction possible also helps explain why I have applied this model only to the elections held since 1980. Prediction of this kind is possible only when these regularities remain undisturbed: that is to say, only when the basic system of rules, procedures, and norms governing a particular process has not been decisively changed. For example, several forecasting models have been developed to predict the number of House seats won or lost by the party of the incumbent president. But no one argues that these same models would continue to generate accurate forecasts if the United States were to adopt a parliamentary form of government or if the Constitution were changed so that members of Congress were elected through a proportional representation system.

Any forecasting model of this kind, then, assumes a substantial measure of stability in electoral rules and institutions. And while this assumption is quite valid when applied to American general elections, the presidential nomination process, as is well known, has been decisively altered in recent years. In fact, *two* enormous changes have taken place in the basic rules of the nomination process.

The first and more celebrated of these changes took place between 1969 and 1972, when the Democratic Party completely rewrote its rules governing the selection of national convention delegates, which in turn compelled substantial changes in state primary laws and caucus procedures. The major effects of this reform movement have, by now, been amply chronicled. The number of states holding primaries doubled between 1968 and 1980; state laws were also changed to provide a much closer linkage between the presidential preferences of the primary voters and the actual selection of convention delegates. Several distinct types of delegate selection procedures were entirely banned. Those states that continued to use caucuses were now required to publicize them well in advance; to adopt formal, written rules of procedure; and to open them up to any party member who wanted to participate.[18]

The result was a radical transformation of the entire presidential selection process, such that it is extremely problematic whether many of the generalizations one could make about the nomination races of the 1950s and 1960s would apply to the contests held since then. To take just one example: Before 1972, it was *not* always necessary for a presidential hopeful to announce his candidacy well before the first delegates were selected, organize an active campaign, and then enter as many primaries as possible. Of the eight major-party nominations between 1952 and 1968 in which an incumbent president was not a candidate for reelection, two were won by men who did not enter a single primary (Stevenson in 1952 and Humphrey in 1968), and a third nominee did not begin to campaign actively until all the primaries were over (Eisenhower in 1952). Even those candidates who did pursue the "primary route" to nomination generally used primaries more for their demonstration effect than for the number of delegates they provided. In 1960, for example, John F. Kennedy entered and won a total of only seven primaries. In 1964, Barry Goldwater faced serious opposition in only three primaries, and won only one of them.

According to many accounts, then, 1972 is the first nomination race of the "new era."[19] As I have suggested earlier, however, this characterization ignores the existence of a second major change in nomination rules and procedures, which was not instituted until 1974: the wholesale revision of the campaign finance laws passed by Congress in the wake of Watergate. The Democratic nomination contest of 1972 was played out under the old campaign finance rules, in which both McGovern and Humphrey's ability to stay in the race depended, at crucial times, on large loans and contributions from a very small number of wealthy benefactors.[20]

But I have also excluded 1972—and 1976—from this model for a different and more important reason: in my view, the nomination races held in these years are best seen as "transitional elections." Any system of rules and procedures rewards certain kinds of strategies and behaviors and punishes others. But especially in the complex environment of a presidential nomination race, the strategies that will succeed or fail may not be immediately clear to all the participants. Indeed, most accounts of the new selection process stress that the changes in party rules and finance laws both spawned a host of *"unanticipated* consequences."

Against this background, we should not be surprised that it took the candidates, the media, and the voters some time to learn how the new system operated—and that it was during the elections of 1972 and 1976 that most of this learning took place.

Consider two examples:

1. One clear tendency of the new selection process has been to lengthen

the active nomination campaign quite substantially, forcing candidates to enter the race much earlier than they did during the campaigns held between 1952 and 1968.[21] But this need to run a longer campaign was not apparent to many candidates in 1972 and 1976. In 1972, for example, George McGovern announced his candidacy in January 1971, but the three other leading contenders for the Democratic nomination—Hubert Humphrey, George Wallace, and Edmund Muskie—did not enter the race until almost a year later, in January 1972. Even in 1976, two major candidates, Birch Bayh and Sargent Shriver, did not launch their candidacies until the fall of 1975; and two others, Jerry Brown and Frank Church, joined the race in March of the election year, almost two months *after* the Iowa caucuses.

2. Another leading cliché about the current nomination process concerns the importance of early delegate selection events, especially the Iowa caucuses and the New Hampshire primary, which receive substantially more coverage than any other states and therefore help provide successful candidates with the "momentum" to carry them on to subsequent victories.[22] Again, however common this insight has now become, it was not apparent to many candidates in these transitional elections. In 1972, only two serious candidates bothered to enter the New Hampshire primary (Muskie and McGovern).[23] As late as 1976, two contenders for the Democratic nomination (Brown and Church) got into the race almost a month after New Hampshire, and two other candidates who had already announced (George Wallace and Henry Jackson) simply decided to bypass Iowa and New Hampshire.

In this sort of murky strategic environment, a major payoff would come to the candidates who could best sense the incentives and consequences of the new rules. Those candidates were George McGovern and Jimmy Carter, and both won the nomination as a result. The essential point for the present, however, is that this kind of decisive strategic advantage was bound to be temporary. It might hold up for one or two runs through the cycle, but after a while, the effects of the new rules would start to become clearer, the strategy that worked the last time would be carefully studied and copied, and a "conventional wisdom" about the nature of the process would gradually begin to emerge.

There has been, in short, a perceptible convergence in candidate strategies. By 1980, almost all candidates were doing the same things: announcing early; targeting Iowa and New Hampshire; recognizing that if they wanted to be nominated, they would have to enter and win a substantial number of primaries and caucuses rather than just a select few in carefully chosen states. Since 1976, no serious candidate has tried to enter the race after it was about half over; nor has any major candidate tried to bypass Iowa and New Hampshire.[24] As Elaine Kamarck, an adviser to Walter Mondale in 1984 and Bruce Babbitt in 1988, has commented: "The difference between now and the past is that now there is only one strategy. It doesn't matter whether you are Walter Mondale with deep ties to the party or whether you are a newcomer—you both do the same things."[25]

The Transformation of Iowa and New Hampshire

This convergence in candidate strategies had a particularly important effect on the character of the campaign waged in the crucial early battleground states of Iowa and New Hampshire. In so doing, it helped neutralize one final resource that might otherwise have been available to the underfinanced, long-shot candidate.

As soon as the dust had settled from the 1976 election, Jimmy Carter's campaign became the paradigm for how a little-known, underdog candidate could make his way to the White House. Such candidates could not hope to match the fund-raising capacity or national media exposure of the front-runners, but (or so the theory went) they could compensate for these disadvantages by spending more of their own time out on the campaign trail. The Iowa caucuses and the New Hampshire primary, both of which typically involved a total turnout of less than 100,000 party members, seemed especially well suited to this strategy, holding out the possibility that, with a year or so of sustained effort, an ambitious candidate could personally meet and talk to a substantial percentage of the eventual voters or caucus attenders.

In fact, Carter *had* spent much of 1975 and early 1976 meeting the voters in Iowa and New Hampshire, speaking in front of small groups, seeking coverage in local newspapers—and then went on to win both states. What is all too rarely mentioned about the 1976 campaign, however, is that Carter's efforts in Iowa had received a huge boost from one other special circumstance: *through most of 1975, he was the only major candidate campaigning there.* As Jules Witcover has pointed out, Iowa snuck up on the national media and the field of Democratic candidates in 1976; until rather late in the game, nobody but Carter expected it to be a significant milestone in the nomination race. Henry Jackson and George Wallace bypassed Iowa to concentrate on later, big-state primaries. Sargent Shriver did not announce his candidacy until September 1975, nine months after Carter's announcement, and then made only a token effort in a few heavily Catholic areas of the Hawkeye State. Birch Bayh (who eventually came in second in Iowa) did not announce until October. Morris Udall, who did announce early, concentrated his initial campaign efforts in New Hampshire, and did not come to realize the potential importance of Iowa until quite late in the "invisible primary" period. For most of 1975, then, Carter's only competition for the attentions and affections of Iowa's caucus attenders was Fred Harris, whose message, style, and electability problems made him unacceptable to all but a very small segment of the Democratic electorate.[26]

Carter faced a bit more competition in New Hampshire, especially from Udall. But as it so happened, all the other candidates in the Granite State were competing for the support of the liberal wing of the party. Wallace and Jackson, the two candidates who might have given Carter some competition for the moderate-to-conservative vote, had once again decided to skip the state.

But if it was possible to surprise everybody once—to win an important delegate selection event because the other candidates did not appreciate its significance—such a feat would obviously become more difficult the next time around. By 1980, there was nothing especially surprising about Iowa: everyone understood that it would be the first big test of strength on the road to the nomination. The only person who did not entirely get the message was Ronald Reagan's campaign manager, who recognized that Iowa would be important, but thought he could win the state by sitting back on an early lead in the polls, keeping Reagan "above the fray," and staying out of a nationally televised debate. This greatly misconceived strategy enabled George Bush to pull off a narrow upset victory—and ultimately led Reagan to fire his campaign manager.

By 1984, Walter Mondale, another early front-runner, recognized that particular pitfall and avoided it. If Hart, Cranston, Glenn, and Askew were going to spend lots of time personally campaigning in Iowa and New Hampshire, well, so was Mondale. According to one report on the Granite State campaign, for example, by December 1983, Alan Cranston had already spent twenty-one days in New Hampshire, John Glenn sixteen days, Gary Hart and Ernest Hollings thirty days. But Walter Mondale matched them all, spending twenty-five days in New Hampshire.[27] Similarly, when Republican candidate Pierre "Pete" du Pont spent most of 1987 organizing and proselytizing in Iowa and New Hampshire, he kept bumping into George Bush, Bob Dole, Jack Kemp, and Pat Robertson. It was, in other words, no longer just the long-shot candidates who counted on devoting almost two full years of their lives to a run at the White House. The better-known and better-financed candidates understood that they had to do the same thing. Those who found such activity distasteful, or who felt they could not spare the time because of the press of governing responsibilities, simply did not get into the race in the first place.

Thus, the convergence in candidate strategies neutralized what had once been thought to be the one clear advantage of an underdog, long-shot candidate. Iowa and New Hampshire have become, in effect, national battlegrounds, where all the candidates are actively seeking support, with the national media there in full force to cover their every move. All of which only makes it that much more unlikely that another Jimmy Carter could win a string of early primaries and caucuses while still trailing badly in the national polls.

Conclusion

Presidential nomination races, as I have noted earlier in this chapter, are not as predictable as general elections. The skills of the individual candidates and campaign managers, the behavior of the media, the inherent instabilities of a multicandidate race, the importance of particular events and mistakes —all seem to count for more than they do in the fall campaign. In addition, small changes in nomination rules and procedures are constantly being made—the establishment of a southern regional primary in 1988, California's decision to move up the date of its primary in 1996—some of which may alter the dynamics of future races in ways that are difficult to anticipate. And perhaps, for one or both reasons, the 1996 nomination races may turn out quite differently from the pattern outlined here.

Regardless of what happens in the future, however, it is striking that, after a remarkable series of institutional innovations carried out between 1969 and 1974, a clear system of norms and behaviors had emerged by at least 1980, and that over the last four election cycles, that system has produced fairly predictable final results. To say that a system is now stable and predictable, of course, is not to say that it is desirable. A number of telling criticisms clearly can be made about the current presidential selection process. As political scientists are wont to stress, however, any further attempts to reform the nomination process ought to begin with an accurate understanding of how the current system functions; and if the account presented here is accurate, many criticisms of that process may be off the mark. More specifically, the analysis in this chapter has at least three significant implications for our understanding of presidential nomination politics.

First, *the importance of momentum has probably been overstated.* If there is one thing that academic and journalistic accounts of the nomination process agree on, it is the central role of momentum in explaining how the system works and how a nominee is finally selected. And, to be sure, momentum *is* important if you want to explain the day-to-day, week-by-week changes in primary and caucus outcomes. Only momentum, for example, can provide a plausible explanation as to how Gary Hart's support among New Hampshire voters jumped from about 12 percent in a poll taken just before the Iowa caucuses to 37 percent of the votes that were cast just eight days later.[28]

But if we turn our attention from the trees to the forest, the results of the last four nomination cycles suggest that the forces of momentum actually operate within very distinct limits. In the end, after all the ebbs and flows of momentum have run their course, the process usually winds up just about where it started out. In five of the last six contested nomination races, the pre-Iowa front-runner ultimately won the nomination. To be sure, one could make an argument that Reagan, Mondale, Bush, and Clinton all established a momentum of their own later on in the primary season and that

' momentum explains their eventual triumph. But given
 ndidates was at least 15 percentage points ahead of his
 st poll *before* Iowa, it seems highly misleading to claim
 . won the nomination because of the momentum they sup-
 ..quired *after* Iowa.

Momentum has other effects on the process, but these, too, seem to be
of distinctly secondary importance. Almost every four years, momentum
does give a short, exhilarating ride to one or two lucky candidates: Bush and
Anderson in 1980, Gary Hart in 1984, Paul Tsongas in 1992. Since 1976,
however, none of these "momentum-driven" candidates has actually managed to win the nomination. From the perspective of long-term effects, the
most one can say is that such candidates become major celebrities, who may
then play an important role in future political events.

The most significant and lamentable effect that momentum does have,
in my view, is that it accelerates the *ending* of so many presidential campaigns. Some of these early withdrawals—such as Philip Crane in 1980,
Alan Cranston in 1984, Alexander Haig, Pierre du Pont, and Bruce Babbitt
in 1988—probably never had much chance of being nominated in the first
place. But others, like Baker and Connally in 1980, Glenn in 1984, and Dole
in 1988, were generally regarded as significant national leaders of their parties. Such candidates did not, of course, derive automatic title to the nomination on that basis. But they *did* deserve, I would argue, to have their candidacies assessed by more than just the voters in a few unrepresentative
states like Iowa and New Hampshire.[29]

Second, *the chances of nominating a little-known, long-shot candidate
have also been exaggerated.* After Jimmy Carter's remarkable victory in
1976—and especially after he had such difficulties governing the country between 1977 and 1980—one major criticism of the nomination process was
that it gave too much of an advantage to long-shot, outsider candidates,
who lacked the experience essential for effective performance in the White
House, whose ideological views and personal abilities were unknown to
large parts of the national electorate. As I have noted, however, nothing
quite like the Carter phenomenon of 1976 has occurred in any of the nomination races since then. Of the eight nomination races that have been held
since 1980, three were won by the incumbent president—two of whom, it
might be added, were renominated with little or no trouble. In the other five
cases, where no incumbent was running, three were won by major national
leaders of their party (Reagan in 1980, Mondale in 1984, Bush in 1988),
who almost certainly would have been leading contenders under any plausible nomination system—including the system that existed up through
1968.[30] The two remaining nominees—Dukakis in 1988 and Clinton in
1992—were not as well known nationally as Reagan, Mondale, and Bush.
But they were men of considerable experience, well regarded by other

elected officials and party leaders, clearly well within the ideological mainstream of their party.

Finally, this analysis also lends support to a number of important criticisms of the current nomination process. In particular, it raises some troubling questions about *the set of rewards and incentives that process presents to any politician who may be contemplating a race for the White House.* Running for president has now become an extraordinarily lengthy and time-consuming marathon. Since at least 1976, the conventional wisdom has claimed that any politician who seriously wants to be president should start planning his or her campaign about two or three years in advance and then devote at least a year and a half to heavy-duty campaigning. And nothing in this chapter indicates that this counsel is misadvised. Indeed, if anything, the forecasting model developed here suggests that the invisible primary period, the year or two before the start of delegate selection activities, may be even *more* important than previous accounts have suggested.

The problem with this marathon, of course, is not that presidential campaigning is an inherently distasteful activity but that the norms and incentives that structure this process do not, in any obvious way, contribute to the ongoing business of governing. To the contrary, a lengthy invisible primary culls out a number of our most talented political leaders, removes or diverts them from their principal governing responsibilities, and requires them to spend month after month raising money, cultivating the press, and soliciting the support of individual primary and caucus participants. Nor is there any reason to believe that one's presidential prospects are improved during the invisible primary by passing legislation or solving problems. Instead, the lengthening presidential campaign probably contributes to a premature polarization of partisan and ideological positions (there are, of course, a number of other factors that also work in this direction), making cooperation and compromise that much more difficult.

As James Ceaser has noted, one important concern of those who designed and shaped America's political institutions was to "minimize the harmful effects of the pursuit of office by highly ambitious contenders."[31] Judged by this criterion, it is difficult to argue that the current system performs very effectively.

Acknowledgments

The author would like to thank Joseph Cooper, Timothy Prinz, Lois Timms Ferrara, Amy Logan, Michael Dukakis, Michael Nickerson, Robert Biersack, and Anthony Corrado for their generous assistance with this article.

Notes

1. For those seeking an introduction to the forecasting literature, probably

the best place to begin is Michael S. Lewis-Beck and Tom W. Rice, *Forecasting Elections* (Washington, D.C.: CQ Press, 1992). Other major items in the canon include Steven J. Rosenstone, *Forecasting Presidential Elections* (New Haven: Yale University Press, 1983); Alan I. Abramowitz, "An Improved Model for Predicting Presidential Election Outcomes," *PS* 21 (Fall 1988): 843–47; and James E. Campbell and Kenneth A. Wink, "Trial-Heat Forecasts of the Presidential Vote," *American Politics Quarterly* 18 (July 1990): 251–69. For an excellent critique of these models, see Jay P. Greene, "Forewarned before Forecast: Presidential Election Forecasting Models and the 1992 Election," *PS* 26 (March 1993): 17–21.

2. Andrew Gelman and Gary King, "Why Are American Presidential Election Campaign Polls So Variable When Votes Are So Predictable?" *British Journal of Political Science* 23 (October 1993): 419–20.

3. It is important to emphasize that I am claiming predictive accuracy only for the *last* poll before the start of delegate selection activities. As the data in table 2.1 also indicate, polls taken during the summer or early fall of the preceding year are not an especially good predictor of how the race will turn out, being wrong in three of seven cases.

4. This also explains why I have not made a greater effort in table 2.5 to disentangle the influences of poll standings and fund raising, which almost certainly exert reciprocal effects on one another. As will become clear in the next section, the general position taken here is that *both* are essential: a wealthy candidate without a significant base of popular support will come to naught (witness John Connally); but even a very popular candidate needs a hefty supply of campaign funds. An interesting test case would be to observe the performance of a candidate with a large lead in the national polls who was a poor or mediocre fund raiser—but as a comparison of tables 2.1 and 2.3 will indicate, there has been no such candidate in any of the nomination races since 1980 (which probably explains why the coefficient for total funds raised in table 2.5 is so small and statistically insignificant). That is to say, every candidate who registered at least 30 percent in the preprimary polls also turned out to be one of his party's most successful fund raisers. A more definitive resolution of the linkage between money, popularity, and success in the primaries is obviously an important question for future research, but will probably require one to go beyond the data presented in tables 2.1–2.6.

5. For an exchange of views on the relative strengths and weaknesses of R^2 and *SEE,* see Michael S. Lewis-Beck and Andrew Skalaban, "The *R*-Squared: Some Straight Talk," *Political Analysis* 2 (1990): 153–71; Christopher H. Achen, "What Does 'Explained Variance' Explain?: A Reply," *Political Analysis* 2 (1990): 173–84; and Gary King, "Stochastic Variation: A Comment on Lewis-Beck and Skalaban's 'The *R*-Squared,'" *Political Analysis* 2 (1990): 185–200.

6. For a useful compilation of data about general election forecasting models, see Lewis-Beck and Rice, *Forecasting Elections,* 91–96.

7. One could produce a prediction for each candidate on the basis of the equation shown in table 2.5. But, as is widely recognized, this is kind of cheating, since the same observations supposedly being "predicted" have already been used to estimate the equation. A better technique, therefore, is to make "out-of-sample" forecasts. This involves dropping all the candidates from a particular nomination contest, reestimating the equation, and then seeing how well this new equation would have predicted the candidates that were excluded. These results, done separately from each contested nomination race, are reported in table 2.6.

8. For an elaboration on this point, see William G. Mayer, "Election Forecasting as a Parlor Game, or Do Forecasting Models Really Tell Us Anything Worth Knowing about Electoral Politics?" (forthcoming).

9. See, for example, Paul Taylor, *See How They Run: Electing the President in an Age of Mediaocracy* (New York: Knopf, 1990), chap. 5; Mickey Kaus, "Cranking Up the Mario Scenario," *Newsweek*, 11 April 1988, 33; Rhodes Cook, "The Muddled Democratic Field Stirs Brokered Nomination Talk," *Congressional Quarterly Weekly Report*, 12 March 1988, 647–49; George J. Church, "Will Someone Else Leap In?" *Time*, 24 February 1992, 22–23; and Howard Fineman, "Now It's 'Don Quixote' Cuomo," *Newsweek*, 24 February 1992, 27.

10. On these points, see Michael J. Robinson and Margaret A. Sheehan, *Over the Wire and on TV* (New York: Russell Sage, 1983), especially chaps. 4 and 7; Larry M. Bartels, *Presidential Primaries and the Dynamics of Public Choice* (Princeton: Princeton University Press, 1988); William G. Mayer, "The New Hampshire Primary: A Historical Overview," and Henry E. Brady and Richard Johnston, "What's the Primary Message: Horse Race or Issue Journalism?" both in *Media and Momentum: The New Hampshire Primary and Nomination Politics*, ed. Gary R. Orren and Nelson W. Polsby (Chatham, N.J.: Chatham House, 1987).

11. For the argument that a small amount of recent campaign information can dominate a large amount of past political data, see Samuel L. Popkin, *The Reasoning Voter: Communication and Persuasion in Presidential Campaigns* (Chicago: University of Chicago Press, 1991), chap. 4.

12. Perhaps the best-known academic treatment of the nomination process is Bartels, *Presidential Primaries*. Bartels mentions the subject of campaign finance on exactly three pages, and then only in passing. Other works that ignore the role of money in generating momentum include Brady and Johnston, "What's the Primary Message?" and John G. Geer, *Nominating Presidents: An Evaluation of Voters and Primaries* (Westport, Conn.: Greenwood, 1989). One of the few works that does appreciate the critical role of money in the dynamics of the presidential nomination process is John H. Aldrich, *Before the Convention: Strategies and Choices in Presidential Nomination Campaigns* (Chicago: University of Chicago Press, 1980). Another partial exception is Thomas R. Marshall, *Presidential Nominations in a Reform Age* (New York: Praeger, 1981). Marshall clearly recognizes that changes in the campaign finance laws have had a major effect on the selection process (see pp. 50–55). But the model of momentum he presents later in the book (see pp. 142–51) is built entirely around the effects of media coverage.

13. See, among others, Aldrich, *Before the Convention;* and William G. Mayer, "Changing the Rules Really Does Change the Game: The Impact of Rules Reform on the Presidential Nomination Process," paper presented at the annual meeting of the Northeastern Political Science Association, November 1993.

14. Aldrich, *Before the Convention,* 71.

15. On the self-correcting forces inherent in the momentum process that tend to limit its long-term effects, see Bartels, *Presidential Primaries,* 228–36, 287–92; and Brady and Johnston, "What's the Primary Message?" 170–75.

16. Lest this last observation seem speculative, it should be pointed out that this was *exactly* what occurred in 1984. The early field for the Democratic nomination that year included two well-regarded southern politicians: Senator Ernest Hollings of South Carolina and former governor Reubin Askew of Florida. Yet both candidates withdrew from the race within two days after the New Hampshire

primary, before a single southern caucus or primary had taken place.

17. Polls of New Hampshire Republican voters show that Reagan had pulled ahead of Bush before the two debated in Nashua. See Jack W. Germond and Jules Witcover, *Blue Smoke and Mirrors* (New York: Viking, 1981), 124–25, 130.

18. On all these points, see Byron E. Shafer, *Quiet Revolution: The Struggle for the Democratic Party and the Shaping of Post-Reform Politics* (New York: Russell Sage, 1983); Nelson W. Polsby, *Consequences of Party Reform* (New York: Oxford University Press, 1983); and James W. Ceaser, *Presidential Selection: Theory and Development* (Princeton: Princeton University Press, 1979).

19. See, for example, Marshall, *Presidential Nominations,* esp. chaps. 1 and 2; and most of the authors classified as "the 1972 school" in Howard L. Reiter, *Selecting the President: The Nominating Process in Transition* (Philadelphia: University of Pennsylvania Press, 1985), 2–6.

20. On the role of large contributions in the McGovern and Humphrey campaigns, see Herbert E. Alexander, *Financing the 1972 Elections* (Lexington, Mass.: Lexington Books, 1976), 121–24, 126–27, 151–56.

21. For data on this point, see Mayer, "Changing the Rules Really Does Change the Game," tables 2.3 and 2.4.

22. See, in particular, Orren and Polsby, *Media and Momentum;* Hugh Winebrenner, *The Iowa Precinct Caucuses: The Making of a Media Event* (Ames: Iowa State University Press, 1987); and Peverill Squire, *The Iowa Caucuses and the Presidential Nominating Process* (Boulder, Colo.: Westview Press, 1989).

23. Neither Humphrey nor Wallace was even listed on the ballot, though Sam Yorty and Vance Hartke were.

24. A few candidates—most notably, Al Gore in 1988—have *claimed* that they were skipping Iowa and New Hampshire and focusing their efforts on later primaries, especially in the South. But in each case, a closer look at the campaign indicates that the candidate initially made a serious effort in Iowa and New Hampshire, found that his campaign was not catching on, and thus, making a virtue of necessity, proclaimed that he was bypassing the early battlegrounds in order to help dampen media expectations. See Emmett H. Buell, Jr., and James W. Davis, "Win Early and Often: Candidates and the Strategic Environment of 1988," in *Nominating the President,* ed. Emmett H. Buell, Jr., and Lee Sigelman (Knoxville: University of Tennessee Press, 1991), 21, 28; and Jack W. Germond and Jules Witcover, *Whose Broad Stripes and Bright Stars? The Trivial Pursuit of the Presidency 1988* (New York: Warner Books, 1989), 272.

25. Quoted in Rhodes Cook, "In '88 Contest, It's What's Up Front That Counts," *Congressional Quarterly Weekly Report,* 23 August 1986, 1997.

26. On all these points, see Jules Witcover, *Marathon: The Pursuit of the Presidency, 1972–1976* (New York: Viking, 1977), 194–214.

27. Data are based on interviews with the New Hampshire campaign coordinators and are reported in William Mayer, "Take Nothing for Granite," *Boston Magazine,* February 1984, 62.

28. For data on Hart's standing in the New Hampshire polls, see David Moore, "The Death of Politics in New Hampshire," *Public Opinion,* February/March 1984, 56–57.

29. For an elaboration on this argument, see Mayer, "Changing the Rules Really Does Change the Game."

30. As William H. Lucy has shown, in the contested conventions held be-

tween 1936 and 1968, the preprimary poll leader went on to win the nomination in nine of eleven cases, a success rate not very different from the one shown in table 2.2. See Lucy, "Polls, Primaries, and Presidential Nominations," *Journal of Politics* 35 (November 1973): 830–48. See also James R. Beniger, "Winning the Presidential Nomination: National Polls and State Primary Elections, 1936–1972," *Public Opinion Quarterly* 40 (Spring 1976): 22–38.

 31. See Ceaser, *Presidential Selection,* esp. "Introduction" and "Conclusion."

3

Presidential Nomination Activists and Political Representation: A View from the Active Minority Studies

JAMES A. MCCANN

In the late 1960s and 1970s, amid Vietnam war protests, civil rights demonstrations, political scandals, and calls to give "power to the people," leaders from both major parties enacted a series of reforms to increase citizen participation in presidential nomination politics. Party meetings and local caucuses were declared open to the general public; the number of state primaries held each election year was approximately doubled; general affirmative action guidelines were put into place at nominating conventions; and most important, the number of delegates sent to these conventions to support a candidate was tied directly to that candidate's showing in local caucuses and primary elections. Gone were the days when aspiring presidential candidates such as Hubert Humphrey and Adlai Stevenson could win the nomination merely by courting the upper tiers of their party. In this postreform era, all presidential contenders must prove themselves by attracting a bloc of followers early in an election year.[1]

In retrospect, it is clear that the party reformers achieved their most immediate goal. In each presidential election since the reforms, literally tens of millions of individuals have voted in primaries, attended local caucuses, or participated in often short-lived nomination campaigns. Compared to other advanced industrial democracies, the United States has by far the most open system of candidate selection.[2] Citizens interested in becoming active have also generally had a wide array of choices available to them. To take 1988 as an example, a handbook published by Congressional Quarterly Press in the weeks leading up to the primary and caucus season that year listed fifteen prospects (nine Democrats and six Republicans).[3]

By decreasing the power of party elites and allowing candidates of every stripe to compete publicly for support, the reformers hoped ultimately to make the process of candidate selection fairer and more representative. Were they successful in this larger endeavor? Is the system currently in use in fact representative? In the pages that follow I address this concern. At the outset, it is useful to distinguish among three perspectives on political representation.

First, representation can mean "to stand for." The political theorist Hanna Pitkin calls this *descriptive* representation.[4] Under this view, a representative body is a kind of mirror that reflects the characteristics of some constituency. As John Stuart Mill wrote in the last century, representative institutions are forums in which each sentiment within a nation "can produce itself in full light."[5] Today this view of representation comes across most clearly in the context of public opinion polling. If a sample of survey respondents contained a disproportionate number of, say, older Americans, labor union members, or ideologically extreme people, we would conclude that the poll is unrepresentative, that is, biased and untrustworthy. Turning to postreform nomination politics, we may ask whether the citizens turning out to select presidential candidates constitute a representative subset of potential party supporters within the general electorate.

Alternatively, political representation can be thought of in *behavioral* terms.[6] Any individual who acts in place of a group of people, even if he or she is of a different class, race, or religion, can in theory be a good representative (in a behavioral sense) if the group's preferences are furthered. The actions of state legislators and members of the U.S. Congress are often explained in these terms. By communicating with their constituents and submitting to frequent elections, lawmakers are said collectively to represent the American public. Nomination participants may not be in close touch with less active citizens; nor are they themselves held directly accountable for their actions. But in practice, when faced with a choice among many possible contestants, do these individuals seek to act on behalf of the electorate at large? Or do they chiefly pursue their own personal preferences regardless of what the general public may want?

Finally, when examining nomination politics and political representation, it is important to assess how the newer activists might affect the organizational strength of the major parties. After all, the two-party system has long been recognized as essential for coordinated and effective representation in the United States.[7] Parties tie many discrete interest groups together under a shared rubric. They provide policymakers with much needed common ground in an otherwise disconnected political system. By design, the citizens who vote in primary elections, attend local caucus meetings, and travel to nominating conventions are not professional political organizers. Few chair local or state committees, and virtually none are on a party's payroll. Does the presence of so many outsiders help or hurt the parties? Even if nomination participants can adequately "stand for" or "act for" members of the American mass public, we might still conclude that the reformers failed in their effort to make the candidate selection process more representative if the two dominant parties have been severely weakened as a result.

Assessing the Potential for Political Representation among Nomination Activists

The three dimensions of political representation outlined above are explored here using a set of surveys known as the Active Minority study series. In every presidential election since 1980, large samples of party activists in several caucus-convention states have been sent questionnaires asking about their participation in specific campaigns, their attitudes toward the parties, their perceptions of the leading presidential candidates, their positions on a host of important public policy issues, and their involvement in party organizations or interest groups. In 1980, delegates to nominating conventions in eleven states were included in the sampling frame. For the 1984 and 1988 elections, only blocs of delegates in Iowa, Michigan, and Virginia were surveyed. In each state, these activists play a pivotal political role. Decisions made in state-level conventions bear directly on the support given to particular candidates when the parties convene nationally in July or August of an election year.

To get a thorough picture of rank-and-file nomination activists operating at the local level, the Active Minority series also includes several waves of surveys administered to individuals who took part in precinct-level caucuses in Iowa, Michigan, and Virginia during the spring of 1984, 1988, and 1992. The names and addresses of these participants were obtained through local Democratic and Republican organizations. Within each state, sampling was conducted through a multistage procedure; precincts were chosen proportional to a state's population, and within each precinct, caucus attenders were randomly selected in numbers proportional to turnout. Like the delegate groups, these samples were large, ranging from several hundred to several thousand per election year.[8] Although many of the delegates and all the caucus attenders in the Active Minority study come from just three states, it is worth stressing that Iowa, Michigan, and Virginia are quite diverse; the conclusions drawn from these studies are therefore likely to hold in other parts of the United States. Furthermore, each state is vitally important politically. Thus, when assessing the decision making and longitudinal dynamics of nomination politics, these surveys are ideal and unequaled.

How Typical Are Nomination Activists?

Although all American citizens over the age of eighteen are formally free to vote in primary elections or attend local nominating caucuses, help out in a candidate's mobilization efforts, and compete for a position as a delegate to a nominating convention, only a fraction of the electorate will heed the call to become involved. In the American National Election Study from 1988, for example, 36 percent of the respondents reported attending a local caucus or participating in a primary; a comparable survey conducted in 1992 found that 31 percent were active in either setting.[9] Many fewer would have become active in any of the nomination campaigns that year, and only a tiny portion of the electorate (less than one-tenth of one percent) attended a state or national nominating convention.

In their review article on political participation, Norman Nie and Sidney Verba write that "in no society is the activist portion of the population a representative sample of the population as a whole."[10] With respect to nomination politics, a number of scholars commenting on the reforms claim that the people selecting nominees are especially atypical. Chief among these critics is Jeane Kirkpatrick, whose monumental work *The New Presidential Elite,* based on delegates to the 1972 national conventions, shaped much of the current debate on the open nominating system.[11] As the title of her study indicates, Kirkpatrick found that the delegates were disproportionately drawn from the highest socioeconomic strata. Over a quarter of the Democratic delegates and nearly half of the Republicans reported family incomes of over $30,000, a substantial amount in the early 1970s.[12] Furthermore, all but 17 percent of the Democrats and 13 percent of the Republicans had completed at least some college education, and delegates of both parties generally came from high-status occupations.

More recent inquiries confirm the pronounced elitist bent of convention participants.[13] Research on the lower echelons of nomination involvement (principally primary voters) also finds, as Norman Nie and Sidney Verba would expect, higher levels of participation among those with greater socioeconomic resources.[14]

In addition to these biases, Jeane Kirkpatrick and other critics of the reforms find that nomination participants typically express ideological and policy positions that are far from the American mainstream. At the 1972 convention, for instance, nearly eight out of ten Democratic delegates saw themselves as "radical" or "liberal." In striking contrast, 57 percent of the Republicans claimed to be "somewhat" or "very" conservative. Such polarization is unmatched in the mass public.[15] While ideological position taking is somewhat more muted among primary voters and members of local nominating caucuses, a number of studies show participants at this level holding to one degree or another unrepresentative opinions on a host of public policy issues.[16] As one critic remarked on the eve of the 1992 nomination season, "The zealots rule—they're hardy, but hardly representative. Among Republicans, this includes Bible-quoting anti-abortionists, Commie-haters, and those who tolerate public spending only for military hardware. Democrats entertain radical nuns, union bosses, advocates of alternative lifestyles, and beneficiaries of public spending."[17]

Turning to the caucus attenders and delegates in the Active Minority surveys, are the biases among participants indeed this severe? Tables 3.1 and 3.2 describe the socioeconomic status and group affiliations among these groups. For comparative purposes, the first columns in these tables contain mass-level samples—specifically, sets of party identifiers in the American National Election Study.[18] Those citizens who identify with one of the political parties constitute an important foothold for that party. As such, they are a sensible baseline from which to judge the representativeness of the open

TABLE 3.1

ASSESSING SOCIOECONOMIC BIASES AMONG NOMINATION
PARTICIPANTS IN 1988: DEMOCRATS (IN PERCENTAGES)

	Democratic identifiers	Caucus attenders	State-level delegates
Family income			
Less than $20,000	47	26	16
$20,000–$50,000	42	45	45
More than $50,000	11	30	39
Education			
High school or less	62	35	19
Some college	21	37	42
College graduate	18	28	39
Age			
18–29	20	8	12
30–49	41	28	49
50 +	39	64	39
Sex			
Male	39	48	52
Female	61	52	48
Race			
White	72	91	85
Black	22	7	12
Religion			
Catholic	26	30	24
Protestant	63	52	57
Jewish	2	3	2
Born-again	35	23	26

NOTE: The set of Democratic identifiers includes respondents who "lean" toward the Democratic Party. The lowest $N = 872$ (identifiers), 1,040 (caucus attenders), and 1,409 (delegates).

TABLE 3.2

ASSESSING SOCIOECONOMIC BIASES AMONG NOMINATION
PARTICIPANTS IN 1988: REPUBLICANS (IN PERCENTAGES)

	Republican identifiers	Caucus attenders	State-level delegates
Family income			
Less than $20,000	34	14	12
$20,000–$50,000	44	43	47
More than $50,000	22	44	41
Education			
High school or less	48	20	13
Some college	27	52	55
College graduate	25	28	33
Age			
18–29	23	12	12
30–49	40	35	45
50+	37	53	43
Sex			
Male	47	56	58
Female	53	44	42
Race			
White	94	98	97
Black	4	1	1
Religion			
Catholic	22	13	10
Protestant	68	75	79
Jewish	1	1	1
Born-again	37	43	55

NOTE: The set of Republican identifiers includes respondents who "lean" toward the Republican Party. The lowest $N = 766$ (identifiers), 852 (caucus attenders), and $1,360$ (delegates).

nomination system.[19] To simplify matters, I present only survey results from 1988. It is worth noting, however, that if we examine the delegates from 1980 or 1984 and the caucus participants from 1984 or 1992, very similar findings surface.[20]

On the Democratic side (table 3.1), the nomination activists clearly conform to the expectations laid out by Kirkpatrick and the other critics. Although nearly half of the Democratic identifiers in the mass public reported family incomes in 1988 that were less than $20,000, only about a quarter of the caucus attenders and just 16 percent of the delegates were placed in this group. At the high end of the income scale, the percentage of respondents claiming to have incomes in excess of $50,000 was roughly three times as large in the activist samples as in the mass public. The same relationship holds for education levels. Approximately two-thirds of the Democratic identifiers had no college experience, while only 35 percent of the caucus attenders and 19 percent of the delegates reported similarly low levels of schooling.

We also see a number of biases with respect to age, sex, race, and religion, though these are not as profound as for income and education. Younger people are not as inclined to become active in the presidential selection process. Nor are women represented within the activist groups proportional to their numbers within the mass public. In 1988, 61 percent of the Democratic identifiers were female, but women constitute only about half of the caucus and delegate blocs. In a similar vein, although whites made up about three-quarters of the Democratic sample at the mass level, 91 percent of the caucus attenders and 85 percent of the delegates were white. In the case of religion, we find proportionally fewer Protestants and born-again Democrats becoming involved in nomination politics.

For Republicans (table 3.2), nomination activists are likewise better educated and more affluent, though these biases are not as great as among Democrats. Nearly a quarter of the Republican identifiers reported family incomes above $50,000, while roughly four out of ten nomination participants, both caucus attenders and delegates, were this well off. The set of Republican activists is not biased much with respect to gender or race. Approximately half of all samples were female, while virtually no black Americans affiliated at any level with the party. As with the Democratic sample, however, younger people were less represented in the activist groups. With regard to religion, we see the growing influence of evangelical Protestantism within the Republican ranks. While 37 percent of the Republican identifiers in 1988 said they were born-again, over half (55 percent) of the delegates adopted this label.

To what extent do nomination activists take political stands that are unrepresentative of the mass supporters of their party? Tables 3.3 and 3.4 present a number of breakdowns based on the strength of partisan affiliation, ideological self-identification, and four public policy issues. So that readers get a thorough sense of how these stands differ across the various strata of participation, I have divided the caucus attender samples into two groups, those who worked on behalf of a nomination candidate (either by contributing money to his cause, convincing friends to support him, attending a meeting or rally, fund raising, or canvassing one's neighborhood) versus those who did nothing except attend a local caucus. Moreover, survey results from both 1988 and 1992 are presented so that one may gauge the extent to which attitude distributions fluctuate. In 1988, the list of possible candidates put to the caucus attenders included Michael Dukakis, Jesse Jackson, Paul Simon, Richard Gephardt, Al Gore, George Bush, Robert Dole, Pat Robertson, and Jack Kemp. The caucus sample in 1992 was asked to note any involvement on behalf of Jerry Brown, Bill Clinton, Bob Kerrey, Tom Harkin, Paul Tsongas, Pat Buchanan, or George Bush. In total, 75 to 85 percent of

TABLE 3.3
ATTITUDINAL BIASES AMONG NOMINATION PARTICIPANTS:
DEMOCRATS (IN PERCENTAGES)

	Mass identifiers	*Caucus attenders, no campaign activism*	*Caucus attenders, campaign activism*	*State-level delegates*
1988				
Party identification				
Strong	37	32	51	82
Weak/leaning	63	56	42	17
Ideology				
Liberal	38	50	62	68
Moderate	35	31	19	19
Conservative	27	20	19	13
Issues				
Affirmative action (−)	36	30	20	16
Pro-life amendment (+)	44	34	37	24
Defense spending (+)	24	27	21	17
1992				
Party identification				
Strong	36	42	67	
Weak/leaning	64	47	29	
Ideology				
Liberal	44	60	70	
Moderate	32	21	18	
Conservative	24	19	13	
Issues				
Affirmative action (−)	40	30	19	
Pro-life legislation (+)	34	18	14	
Capital punishment (+)	67	50	45	

NOTE: The lowest N = 638 (mass identifiers in 1988), 227 (inactive caucus attenders in 1988), 692 (active caucus attenders in 1988), 1,359 (delegates), 872 (mass public in 1992), 129 (inactive caucus attenders in 1992), and 616 (active caucus attenders in 1992).

the caucus attenders in each year participated in some way for a nomination contender. Many of these respondents were involved in a number of ways, but most did just one or two activities.

For the Democratic groups (table 3.3), we find that involvement in nomination politics is strongly correlated with the strength of partisanship. In both years, nearly four out of ten of the Democratic identifiers stated that their identification was strong, while 51 percent of the caucus participants who were active in a campaign in 1988, and 67 percent in 1992, expressed strong psychological identification. Among the delegates (surveyed only in 1988), fully 82 percent strongly identified with the Democratic Party.

TABLE 3.4
ATTITUDINAL BIASES AMONG NOMINATION PARTICIPANTS:
REPUBLICANS (IN PERCENTAGES)

	Mass identifiers	Caucus attenders, no campaign activism	Caucus attenders, campaign activism	State-level delegates
1988				
Party identification				
Strong	34	37	63	83
Weak/leaning	66	54	35	16
Ideology				
Liberal	10	8	4	3
Moderate	25	12	9	6
Conservative	65	80	87	91
Issues				
Affirmative action (−)	54	59	52	54
Pro-life amendment (+)	46	45	58	63
Defense spending (+)	44	51	65	73
1992				
Party identification				
Strong	30	39	70	
Weak/leaning	70	43	29	
Ideology				
Liberal	10	9	4	
Moderate	27	12	9	
Conservative	64	79	88	
Issues				
Affirmative action (−)	63	66	59	
Pro-life legislation (+)	46	53	58	
Capital punishment (+)	84	81	79	

NOTE: The lowest N = 649 (mass identifiers in 1988), 117 (inactive caucus attenders in 1988), 649 (active caucus attenders in 1988), 1,340 (delegates), 760 (mass public in 1992), 77 (inactive caucus attenders in 1992), and 299 (active caucus attenders in 1992).

Also quite evident in table 3.3 is the higher level of ideological position taking among nomination activists in both years. At the mass level, Democrats leaned only slightly to the left, with 38 percent in 1988 and 44 percent in 1992 calling themselves liberals. Across the participatory strata, the percentage of self-identified liberals rises sharply. Consider, for example, the ideological distribution among the delegates in 1988. Over two-thirds called themselves liberal, but only a very small proportion (13 percent) identified as conservatives.

Turning to the issue positions among Democrats, the extremism noted by reform critics is very much in evidence. For the mass-level surveys, these policy items were worded as follows:

1. Some people feel that the government in Washington should make every effort to improve the social and economic position of blacks. Others feel that the government should not make any special effort to help blacks because they should help themselves. How about you? Where would you place yourself on this (seven-point preference) scale?
2. There has been some discussion about abortion during recent years. Which one of these opinions best agrees with your view? (A) By law, abortion should never by permitted. (B) The law should permit abortion only in the case of rape, incest, or when the woman's life is in danger. (C) The law should permit abortion for reasons other than rape, incest, or danger to the woman's life, but only after the need for the abortion has been clearly established. (D) By law, a woman should always be able to obtain an abortion as a matter of personal choice.
3. Some people believe that we should spend much less money for defense. Others feel that defense spending should be greatly increased. Where would you place yourself on this (seven-point preference) scale? [available only in 1988]
4. Do you favor or oppose the death penalty for persons convicted of murder?

The issue preference questions in the two activist groups were put to respondents in slightly different terms, with each item based on a Likert-type seven-point scale ranging from "strongly favor" to "strongly oppose." The four issues they were asked to evaluate were:

1. Affirmative action programs to increase minority representation in jobs and higher education
2. A constitutional amendment to prohibit abortions except when the mother's life is endangered
3. Keeping defense spending at least at current levels even if it requires cutting domestic programs
4. Elimination of the death penalty [available only in 1992]

Because the four policy attitudes were not measured consistently in the two samples, direct comparisons across strata are not possible. Nevertheless, the tendency for Democratic activists to take more liberal positions is unmistakable for three out of four issues.[21] Significant numbers of Democratic identifiers in both years were opposed to affirmative action programs (36 percent in 1988 and 40 percent in 1992). Among the delegates and caucus attenders who were active in a campaign, opposition to affirmative action did not rise above 20 percent. Democratic activists were also much less supportive of pro-life legislation. And, in 1992, they appeared ambivalent about the death penalty, while two-thirds of the Democratic identifiers supported it.

As with the Democrats, we find in table 3.4 that Republican nomination activists are much more likely to express a firm attachment to their party. They are also more committed ideologues. In 1988, for example, 65 percent of the Republicans at the mass level identified themselves as conservative, a proportion that is much higher than the Democratic identifiers calling themselves liberal. Nearly all the Republican activists (roughly eight out of ten or more) adopted the conservative label. This outlook carries over into Republican policy preferences, with the nomination participants being especially inclined to take conservative positions on abortion rights and defense spending.

After reviewing the various distributions in the preceding four tables, it seems clear that the postreform nominating system, though allowing all in theory to participate, is largely dominated by social elites harboring extreme and unrepresentative political views. A final table in this section, table 3.5, shows that the nomination participants are likewise closely tied to particular interest groups. In the surveys conducted in 1988, both the delegate and caucus samples were asked to describe their level of participation in a host of political, social, and economic organizations. For each type of group, they stated whether they had never been a member, whether they had been just a member, or whether they had been an active member or leader. The breakdown of involvement within six of the more partisan-oriented organizations is presented in table 3.5, where for simplicity's sake I have combined group members and leaders.

Four of the interest groups in this table—women's rights groups, civil rights groups, environmentalists, and labor unions—have close connections to the Democratic Party. We see here that among the active caucus attenders and nomination delegates, these groups were well represented. On the Republican side, evangelical Christian and business organizations were equally prevalent. Few of the Republicans were committed to environmental and labor groups, and almost none participated in the civil rights or women's rights movements.

Reform critics frequently charge that the "special interests" now govern the process of presidential candidate selection. Although this is an overstatement, individuals who become involved in nomination campaigns do have significant ties to organized factions. Given that most American citizens are not equally connected to labor unions, evangelical Christian groups, and the rest of the organizations described in table 3.5, we find further evidence that the newer nomination participants are unrepresentative.

TABLE 3.5
SELECTED GROUP AFFILIATIONS AMONG 1988
NOMINATION ACTIVISTS (IN PERCENTAGES)

	Caucus attenders, no campaign activism	Caucus attenders, campaign activism	State-level delegates
Democrats			
Women's groups	5	10	24
Civil rights	4	13	27
Environmentalist	16	19	30
Labor	19	30	34
Evangelical Christian	1	2	3
Business organizations	10	19	27
Active in any of the above	39	62	81
Republicans			
Women's groups	5	3	5
Civil rights	2	3	4
Environmentalist	12	10	17
Labor	11	14	13
Evangelical Christian	7	17	31
Business organizations	21	31	37
Active in any of the above	41	57	75

NOTE: The lowest $N = 222$ (inactive Democratic caucus attenders); 680 (active Democratic caucus attenders); 1,359 (Democratic delegates); 123 (inactive Republican caucus attenders); 668 (active Republican caucus attenders); and 1,340 (Republican delegates).

How Do Nomination Participants Choose Candidates?

The above analysis portrays those involved in selecting the president as highly atypical. If these participants choose candidates based on their personal ideological, group, or class interest, the end result may potentially be presidential contenders who are far removed from most Americans. Much of the early scholarly literature on the nomination reforms emphasized this danger.

Writing in 1962, a few years before the parties opened up the presidential selection process, James Q. Wilson described the members of three Democratic clubs in Chicago, New York, and Los Angeles as "amateurs." To Wilson, the amateur

> sees the political world more in terms of ideas and principles than in terms of persons. Politics is the determination of public policy, and public policy ought to be set deliberately rather than as the accidental by-product of a struggle for

personal and party advantage. Issues ought to be settled on their merits; compromises by which one issue is settled other than on its merits are sometimes necessary, but they are never desirable.[22]

Wilson was not specifically focused on how amateur activists choose presidential contenders, but many later researchers borrowed his label when describing the decision making of postreform convention delegates.[23]

In a similar spirit, Aaron Wildavsky characterized the 1964 Republicans that selected Barry Goldwater as ideological "purists."[24] Many readers may recall that Goldwater, a senator from Arizona, was known for his outspokenness on a number of conservative issues. At the nominating convention that year, he proclaimed that "extremism in the defense of liberty is no vice ... [and] moderation in the pursuit of justice is no virtue!" According to Wildavsky, such statements fit perfectly with the ideological mindset of the Republican activists who attended local caucuses and conventions. Unfortunately for the Republican Party, Senator Goldwater proved to be a very weak candidate in the fall. Running against the incumbent president Lyndon B. Johnson, the senator managed to gain only 39 percent of the popular vote and 52 electoral votes.

Has the contemporary nominating process been turned over to amateurs and purists? Much of the conventional wisdom about the reforms holds that it has. Thomas Edsall nicely sums up this view: "The political market place in which the delegates were selected shifted ... to an elite group of voters who turn out in disproportionately large numbers and who have no direct interest in seeking representation for political and economic goals that diverge from their own."[25] Similarly, the nomination activists interviewed by Jeane Kirkpatrick in 1972 and Warren Miller and Kent Jennings in 1980 and 1984 frequently stated that their own personal interests and values were more important than those of their party.[26] Respondents taking part in the Active Minority study also voiced solid purist and amateur sentiments. Table 3.6 showcases the extent of these feelings.[27]

In 1980, delegates to state nominating conventions were asked whether they agreed or disagreed with a set of statements about party platforms and decision-making strategies. The caucus attenders in Iowa, Michigan, and Virginia in 1984 were also questioned on these matters. Four statements common to both surveys were:

1. A political party should be more concerned with issues than with winning elections.
2. A candidate should express his convictions even if it means losing the election.
3. The party platform should avoid issues that are too controversial or unpopular.
4. Broad electoral appeal is more important than a consistent ideology.

TABLE 3.6
INDICATORS OF IDEOLOGICAL "PURISM" AND
"AMATEURISM" (IN PERCENTAGES)

	Caucus attenders (1984)		State delegates (1980)	
	Democrats	Republicans	Democrats	Republicans
A political party should be more concerned with issues than with winning elections. (*Agree*)	77	67	76	70
A candidate should express his convictions even if it means losing the election. (*Agree*)	75	67	86	86
The party platform should avoid issues that are too controversial or un-popular. (*Disagree*)	75	71	80	80
Broad electoral appeal is more important than a consistent ideology. (*Disagree*)	72	67	63	70

NOTE: The lowest N = 2,155 (Democratic caucuses), 3,276 (Republican caucuses), 7,958 (Democratic delegates), 8,223 (Republican delegates).

Individuals affirming the first two statements but disagreeing with the third and fourth could be classified as purists or amateurs. Jeane Kirkpatrick, Nelson W. Polsby, and other critics argue that the drive to express themselves regardless of the electoral costs separates postreform activists from the more pragmatic party elites of an earlier generation.[28] A brief look at table 3.6 shows clear evidence of purist/amateur postures. When asked to consider the views and preferences of the wider mass public, the vast majority within nominating caucuses and state conventions appear willing only to further their own immediate political goals. The breakdown for the second item among the delegates is especially telling. Fully 86 percent in each party agreed that "a candidate should express his convictions even if it means losing an election."

Do extreme political preferences in fact lead nomination activists to choose candidates who are ideologically unrepresentative of their party or the electorate in general? Or are participants willing and able to "act for" larger national constituencies? To address this critically important topic, it is necessary to go beyond the statements of activists, which are unabashedly purist and amateur, and build an empirical model of vote choice.

In general, three conditions must hold if, contrary to Edsall's portrayal, the distorting effects of a purist/amateur orientation are to be avoided. First, nomination participants must have some incentive to deviate from their personal ideological or group interests and "act for" others. Second, these activists must be aware that their political preferences differ from those of less involved citizens; that is, they must be at least somewhat aware of the sorts of distributions presented in tables 3.3 and 3.4. And, last, nomination choice must reflect the interests of constituencies beyond what the partisans' ideological concerns would normally encompass.

The incentive that nomination participants have to acknowledge the wider concerns of the electorate is not obvious. But the sequence and logic of presidential elections do suggest a rationale for such behavior. To be successful, nomination participants must not only get their preferred candidates on the presidential ballot but they must also win the general election. Backing a contestant who is close to one's ideological or group interests, but is unlikely to garner much support come November, gains the activist little. In selecting nominees to run on their party's ticket, nomination participants must therefore ponder how their preferred candidate might fare vis-à-vis the opposition's standard-bearer.

As tables 3.3 and 3.4 illustrate, the individuals involved in local caucuses, campaigns, and conventions are more partisan than less active citizens. Consequently, when participants evaluate prospective nominees, it becomes quickly apparent that virtually any contestant within one's own party, even a contender who is not a first choice, is likely to be preferred over an opposition candidate.[29] When facing a set of two or more prospective nominees, where one candidate is more representative of their own policy leanings but another is more moderate or electable, nomination participants may quickly appreciate the age-old political maxim that "half a loaf is better than none at all." The long-term payoff in nomination politics is such that activists have good reason to keep the wider political environment in mind as they vote for a nominee.

Strategic thinking of this sort can introduce a measure of informal political accountability into the candidate selection process. Given the above reasoning, a conservative Republican activist in 1992 who wished to further the agenda of Pat Buchanan, the insurgent challenger to President Bush, would have to judge whether Buchanan or Bush had a better chance to prevail against a Democratic nominee. If Bush were seen as more electable, the activist might well decide to compromise on his or her ideological goals by backing the less conservative, but potentially more popular, Bush. In so doing, participants would be broadly answerable to others within the mass public, despite their unrepresentativeness (in a descriptive sense).

When considering whether candidate choice follows this logic, it is necessary to explore the activists' perceptions of ideological positions across the

American political landscape. Are participants aware of the stands taken by the parties, the major candidates, and typical voters? Are they able to differentiate one nomination contender from another with respect to electability? Figures 3.1, 3.2, and 3.3 show that those involved in nomination politics indeed have a realistic picture of the electoral environment. In 1988, state-level delegates were given a seven-point scale ranging from "extremely liberal" to "extremely conservative" and then asked where along this continuum they would locate themselves, both major parties, President Reagan, an "average American voter," and a number of prominent candidates that year, including Jesse Jackson, Michael Dukakis, Al Gore, Robert Dole, George Bush, and Pat Robertson.[30]

FIGURE 3.1
MEAN IDEOLOGICAL PERCEPTIONS OF 1988
NOMINATION DELEGATES

	Democrats	*Republicans*
Extremely liberal (1)		Jackson
	Jackson	
		Dukakis
Liberal		Democratic Party
		Gore
	Democratic Party	
Slightly liberal	Self-identification	
	Dukakis	
Middle-of-the-road (4)	Gore	
	American Voter	
		American Voter
Slightly conservative		Bush
		Dole
		Republican Party
	Dole	
		Self-identification
Conservative	Republican Party	
	Bush	Reagan
	Reagan	Robertson
	Robertson	
Extremely conservative (7)		

NOTE: The lowest *N* = 1,119 (Democrats) and 1,112 (Republicans).

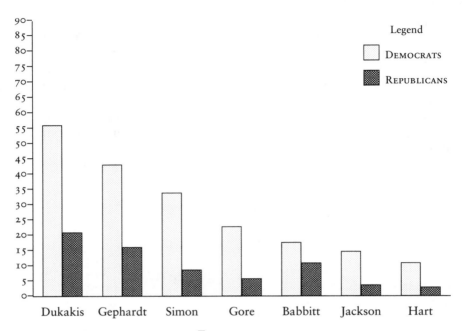

FIGURE 3.2
PERCENT SEEING A CANDIDATE AS LIKELY TO WIN
THE 1988 ELECTION: DEMOCRATS

NOTE: The lowest N = 1,249 (Democrats) and 835 (Republicans).

Delegates in both parties saw the "average American voter" as being very close to the center, just slightly to the right. This perception corresponds quite closely to the citizens' average ideological self-placements in surveys of the mass public.[31] The party activists also see themselves as far from this mainstream. Democrats place themselves on average more than a point away from the American voter, while Republicans position themselves squarely in the conservative camp. Comparable perceptions have been obtained as well for the caucus attenders.[32]

When placing the candidates on this spectrum, however, the delegate blocs diverge markedly. Republicans position members of the Democratic Party much farther to the left than Democrats. Albert Gore, for instance, was seen on average as a centrist by Democrats, but Republicans perceived him as somewhere between "slightly liberal" and "liberal." The same holds for Republican leaders. Democrats were much more liable to position Robert Dole and George Bush to the right, while Republicans saw each as rather

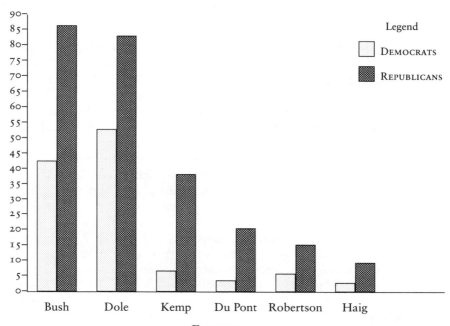

FIGURE 3.3
PERCENT SEEING A CANDIDATE AS LIKELY TO WIN
THE 1988 ELECTION: REPUBLICANS

NOTE: The lowest N = 1,281 (Democrats) and 843 (Republicans).

moderate. This distinction undoubtedly stems from heightened partisan attitudes; it is much easier for activists of one party to perceive candidates from the other party as ideologically extreme. Nevertheless, in relative terms the nomination activists saw the same gradations of ideological positions within each partisan bloc. Consider again Gore's position. On average, the senator was placed about one unit to the right of the Democratic Party by both delegate blocs. Overall, the correlation between Democratic and Republican mean ideological perceptions is a striking .96.

Perceptions of the relative electability of the nomination contestants also vary systematically across the two parties. Figures 3.2 and 3.3 show a number of findings collected from samples of caucus attenders from 1984 who were resurveyed at the start of the nomination season in 1988 (January/February).[33] For each candidate, respondents were asked to rate his chances of victory in November using the following categories: certain to win; probably will win; more likely to win than lose; a toss-up; more likely to lose than win; probably will lose; and certain to lose. In these figures, the percentage that perceived a candidate's chances as "more likely to win than lose" or better is displayed.

We see here that Republicans and Democrats disagree markedly in their estimates, with activists tending to give more pessimistic assessments when evaluating the opposition. Yet the caucus attenders early in 1988 were also quite able to judge the likely popularity of one candidate versus another within the same party. On the Democratic side (figure 3.2), the largest proportion of activists felt that Michael Dukakis was more likely to win, with Paul Simon and Richard Gephardt being thought of almost as positively. Very few of the activists saw Gary Hart, Jesse Jackson, Bruce Babbitt, and Al Gore as likely to win if nominated. For the Republican contestants (figure 3.3), George Bush and Robert Dole were held up as potentially the most successful within each partisan group, with Democrats on the whole rating Dole as slightly stronger. Only small percentages had much faith in the Haig, du Pont, Kemp, and Robertson campaigns that year.

The findings in these figures demonstrate that nomination activists are not blind to the ideological differences among themselves, "average" voters, and the many candidates competing for support. They are also keenly aware of the relative nature of electability.[34] Given that nomination participants have a reasonable stake in getting a member of their party elected president, are they willing to compromise by picking a contestant that is further away from them ideologically if it means running a more electable nominee? In their analysis of delegates to eleven state nominating conventions, Walter Stone and Alan Abramowitz find this to be the case.[35] Table 3.7, which is based on their work, shows that among Democrats who were closer to Senator Kennedy (a committed liberal) but believed President Carter was more electable, 78 percent backed the president's renomination bid. But liberal activists who happened to perceive Kennedy as more electable if nominated were substantially behind the senator; nearly all (98 percent) supported him.

Within the Republican sample, the relationship between electability ratings and candidate choice appears equally strong. More than eight delegates out of ten who were ideologically closer to the more moderate candidate George Bush, but saw Ronald Reagan as more electable, voted for Reagan. In a similar move, those who saw Bush as likelier to succeed, but were ideologically closer to Reagan, overwhelmingly supported Bush. If activists "have no direct interest in seeking representation for political and economic goals that diverge from their own," as Thomas Edsall stressed, we would observe conservatives consistently siding with Reagan and moderates choosing Bush irrespective of electability.

In a more recent work, Stone and his colleagues extend a model of candidate choice to the samples of caucus attenders and present a more systematic account of decision making.[36] In this article, the authors outline three

TABLE 3.7
CANDIDATE PREFERENCE BY PERCEIVED ELECTABILITY
AND IDEOLOGICAL PROXIMITY:
STATE DELEGATES IN 1980

DEMOCRACTS

	Carter more electable	Both equally electable	Kennedy more electable
Closer to Carter	98	57	7
Equal distance	94	57	4
Closer to Kennedy	78	18	2

REPUBLICANS

	Reagan more electable	Both equally electable	Bush more electable
Closer to Reagan	99	75	24
Equal distance	91	60	8
Closer to Bush	83	29	2

NOTE: Entries are percentages of support for Carter (Democrats) and Reagan (Republicans). N = 5,386 (Democrats) and 5,040 (Republicans).

general styles of voting behavior: a strategy based on simple comparisons, where activists pick the contender who is closest to them ideologically, takes policy stands that are most commensurate with their own, or seems to have the most leadership skills and traits; a model predicated solely on perceptions of each candidate's electability (again using a seven-point scale); and an "expected utility" strategy, where ideological, issue, and leadership comparisons are weighted based on differences in candidate electability.[37] This latter model is specified through a series of multiplicative interaction terms.[38] Making nomination choice dependent on the candidates' personal characteristics *times* their relative chances of success implies mathematically that activists withhold their support from an otherwise acceptable contestant if he is deemed unlikely to attract a large national following in the fall. Or, vice versa, a nomination candidate who might be less attractive to nomination participants is upgraded if he appears to be potentially more popular.

Table 3.8 describes some of the results which appear in Stone et al.'s recent article.[39] To simplify matters, the authors limit themselves to candidate selection in the politically charged Iowa caucuses of 1984.[40] Furthermore, the authors concentrate chiefly on the choice between Gary Hart and Walter Mondale. Among the caucus goers, 41 percent expressed a preference for Mondale, while 32 percent supported Hart. Table 3.8 shows how the decision between Hart and Mondale was conditioned by the three strategies cited above. The first column lists the number of respondents whose choice was correctly predicted by a particular theoretical specification. The second

TABLE 3.8

PREDICTORS OF CANDIDATE CHOICE (MONDALE VERSUS
HART) AMONG IOWA DEMOCRATIC CAUCUS
ATTENDERS IN 1984 (IN PERCENTAGES)

	Correct	Error	No prediction
Candidate preferences			
Ideology	38	18	44
Issues	50	21	29
Traits	74	11	15
Candidate chances			
Electability	55	9	36
Expected utility			
Electability × ideology	68	16	15
Electability × issues	74	15	11
Electability × traits	78	13	8

NOTE: The lowest *N* upon which these percentages are based is 656.

column shows how many choices were incorrectly predicted. The percentages in the final column refer to those individuals for whom no prediction was possible because they did not perceive a difference between Hart and Mondale on a given dimension.

At the top of table 3.8 the prediction statistics for the simple "candidate preferences" model are reported. Since respondents tended to see Hart and Mondale as ideologically similar, the breakdown based on ideological proximity yields comparatively few correct predictions (38 percent). The fit improves slightly if we tabulate support based on the distance between survey respondents and candidate positions on four public policy issues, though the number of correct predictions in this case remains fairly low (50 percent).[41] As shown in the third line of table 3.8, when the respondent's perceptions of Hart's and Mondale's leadership traits—their ability to lead, understanding of complex issues, experience, impressiveness on television, and compassion—are taken into account, predictive accuracy rises sharply to 74 percent.[42]

The second set of predictions based on beliefs about relative electability prove to be of little use in differentiating Mondale and Hart supporters. In the bottom section of table 3.8, however, we see that adding perceptions of a candidate's chances improves the fit between nomination choice and the items on ideological proximity, issue preferences, and trait ratings. For ideological proximity and issue preferences, the improvement is quite substantial. Ideological positions, conditioned by the relative electability of Hart versus Mondale, correctly classify 68 percent of the respondents; for the "electability-issue" interaction term, 74 percent of the sample are accurately predicted. Even in the case of trait ratings, which on their own are strongly related to voter preferences, we see an improvement of four points when a candidate's electoral chances are factored in.

Since nomination participants are more ideologically minded than typical American citizens, and many are tied into "special interest" groups, a number of critics charge that the process of presidential candidate selection has become radically distorted and undermined. It is easy to get this impression, since aspiring presidential nominees often run as insurgents and ideologues. Yet surveys administered to activists involved in caucuses and conventions show that to gain a significant following, a candidate must seem electable. Being ideologically close to nomination participants or espousing strong stands on key public policy issues is not enough to ensure support. Even though the individuals who select presidential candidates are unrepresentative in many significant ways, they appear to make choices that reflect the broad preferences of the American electorate.

Have Nomination Activists Weakened the Major Parties?

A frequent criticism of the current nomination system is that it encourages "candidate-centered" politics. To be successful, contestants must fashion a *personal* following. They must recruit staffs for their own local organizations, create their own television commercials, and attract their own funding. Often this means running against traditional party interests; at the least, the present rules seem to reward candidates who seek the support of only particular subsections of their party's constituency base (e.g., labor union members, evangelical Christians, or civil rights activists). As Nelson W. Polsby wrote in his highly influential *Consequences of Party Reform,* "rather than build coalitions, [nomination candidates] must mobilize factions."[43]

One damaging by-product of this strategy is a heightened potential for conflict within each party's ranks. More than two hundred years ago, James Madison, writing as "Publius" in *The Federalist* No. 10, recognized that political factions, if left unchecked, attack one another and can ultimately bring down representative institutions. In the postreform era of nomination politics, critics point to many signs of this tendency. Pat Buchanan's protests in 1992 against the Bush presidency, Robert Dole's blistering attack on George Bush early in the 1988 nomination season, Jesse Jackson's tirades against mainstream presidential candidates in 1984 and 1988, Edward Kennedy's challenge to Jimmy Carter, the incumbent Democratic president in 1980— all are indications of increasing intraparty divisiveness.

Open conflict before the summer nominating conventions may hurt the parties in a number of ways. Often it is the case that the slogans or arguments one contender raises against a fellow partisan competitor resurface in the fall, adopted by the opposition party's candidate. During the 1992 campaign, Pat Buchanan's assault on President Bush for violating his "No new taxes" pledge undoubtedly primed many voters to accept the subsequent Democratic campaign commercials that portrayed Bush as two-faced and unworthy of the voter's trust. A potentially long, costly, and contentious nomination period may also cause many otherwise capable leaders within Congress or in state government to think twice before entering presidential politics. But perhaps the most damaging consequence, and the one that has received most attention from scholars, is the impact of nomination-stage divisiveness on a party's ability to mobilize voters and activists during the fall campaign. Does open conflict within the ranks hobble a party's organizational base?

Many argue that it does. James Lengle, Patrick Kenney, Tom Rice, and a number of other scholars find significant negative relationships between conflict within primary elections and support for a party's presidential ticket in November.[44] Such studies are quite suggestive, though many are based on aggregate data (e.g., federal voting statistics). This being the case, it is difficult to pinpoint the individual-level dynamics of party defection. After all, it may be that the emergence of intraparty conflict during primary elections is not the real culprit behind a party's poor showing in a general election. An incumbent president who is weak or unpopular may invite challengers and intraparty squabbles early in the campaign. Conflict over presidential nominations may therefore be a symptom, rather than a cause, of electoral failure in the fall.[45]

Additional research conducted through surveys has shown that conflict over a nomination may indeed cause losing blocs to defect. Walter Stone and Priscilla Southwell, for example, find a tendency among unsuccessful caucus attenders and primary voters to be less supportive of the party come fall.[46] In one recent work this change of heart has been labeled a *negative carry-over effect*:

> The "negative" view asserts that contemporary presidential nominations are divisive and that the initial factionalism that they excite is difficult or impossible to overcome in the general election stage. Nomination campaigns appear to demobilize those for whom the party should be most appealing. Nomination participants are much more committed to the party than voters generally, and they are part of the natural ideological and issue constituency of their party. Yet, by virtue of their attachment to a losing cause in the nomination campaign, their natural propensity to support the party in the general election campaign against the opposition is subverted.[47]

The implication of this statement for our discussion of political representation is immediately apparent. Although nomination participants keep in mind a candidate's likely popularity as they choose sides (tables 3.7 and 3.8), the parties on the whole suffer if these same activists lose interest when they do not get their way. The eventual result for the major parties could be electoral failure, institutional weakness, and decay.

But before arriving at this dire conclusion, a conclusion that might justify rolling back the democratizing reforms of the 1960s and 1970s, an additional body of research is worth noting.[48] The "negative carryover" literature relies on simple indicators of candidate preferences to isolate supporters of losing versus winning candidates. When nomination factions are compared on these preference measures, it is certainly true that activists who support nomination-round losers work less in the fall campaign than those who backed the eventual nominee. But if one uses the *amount* of participation for nomination candidates instead of preference measures, involvement on behalf of a contestant, whether he succeeds or fails in becoming the party nominee, leads to greater participation for the presidential ticket. In other words, a *positive* carryover effect emerges for campaign involvement.

This reinterpretation of nomination participation is consistent with E.E. Schattschneider's trenchant statement that the purpose of political parties is to expand the "scope of conflict" by alerting citizens to the stakes of political issues and sweeping them into the electoral process.[49] Because nomination politics is now open to the public, candidates have the opportunity to follow a strategy of expansion. Self-styled outsiders like Jesse Jackson or Pat Robertson, for example, may attempt to mobilize previously underrepresented factions; once involved at the nomination stage of an election, these activists become available for recruitment into party politics following the summer conventions. As Emmett Buell recently wrote: "The 'bad news' is that divisive primaries divide parties and render many activists backing losing candidates unwilling to help their party's eventual nominee. The 'good news' is that even a divisive primary attracts some new activists to the process."[50]

Table 3.9 shows that Buell's "good news/bad news" verdict is especially apt for the caucus attenders in 1988. That year, the partisans who participated in the first (preconvention) wave of the survey were sent a follow-up questionnaire after the general election. In this second wave, respondents were asked about their political involvement following the nominating conventions (using the inventory of possible campaign activities discussed earlier). This design allows one to judge the extent to which losing factions defected from the fall presidential campaign.

The first column of table 3.9 documents the potential for activity early in an election year to stimulate postconvention electoral mobilization.[51] In the Democratic sample, roughly 42 percent reported being active in some

TABLE 3.9
THE "CARRYOVER" AND "SPILLOVER" EFFECTS OF 1988
NOMINATION CAMPAIGN INVOLVEMENT
(IN PERCENTAGES)

	Percentage active for their party's 1988 presidential ticket	Percentage active for their party's 1988 House candidate	Percentage active in local committees in 1992
Democrats			
Dukakis activist	81	29	8
Losing activist	65	33	9
Inactive	34	14	0
Republicans			
Bush activist	85	38	31
Losing activist	68	36	24
Inactive	43	15	3

NOTE: $N = 1,047$ (Democrats in 1988); 556 (Democrats in 1992); 857 (Republicans in 1988); 387 (Republicans in 1992).

way in Michael Dukakis's successful nomination campaign, while 36 percent were involved in one of the losing campaigns. Of those who supported Dukakis, 81 percent were active in some way in the Dukakis-Bentsen campaign that fall. This high level of continuity is not surprising. Those factors that drove individuals into the Dukakis campaign early in 1988 also led them to participate later that year. What may be somewhat surprising, given the recent emphasis on candidate-centered campaigning, is the level of participation for Dukakis and Bentsen among losing nomination activists. Nearly two-thirds of this subsample reported involvement. This figure is clearly much lower than the 81 percent found for Dukakis activists. Yet in comparison with respondents who were inactive during the nomination season, nearly twice as many losing partisans become involved after the convention.

A very similar pattern emerges within the Republican bloc. In this case, 85 percent of the early Bush activists (who constitute approximately a quarter of the sample) went on to participate in the Bush-Quayle campaign of 1988. An impressive 68 percent of the losing Republican activists also reported activity for the party ticket. Those who were not drawn into nomination politics, however, were much less likely to participate in the fall.

Research conducted on party activists in 1984 and 1992 confirms the relationships presented here. Furthermore, the positive effect of mobilization on behalf of nomination winners and losers, with the impact being slightly dampened for activists who were unsuccessful at the nomination stage, withstands a number of control variables. When involvement in the presidential campaign of 1984, a personal evaluation of the nominees in 1988, and a number of demographic attributes traditionally linked to political involvement (e.g., being highly educated) are factored in, the influence of preconvention activism remains strong and statistically significant.[52] Once experienced in nomination campaign work, large proportions stay involved during the general election. On balance, then, conflict over candidate selection appears to generate rather than stifle subsequent mobilization.

If nomination campaign work leads to heightened presidential-level activity in the fall, does it increase involvement in other arenas? The second and third columns in table 3.9 explore two such domains: work on behalf of congressional candidates in 1988, and involvement four years later in local party committees. The term "spillover" may be used to describe the positive effect of nomination activism on nonpresidential political involvement. We find in table 3.9 that, as was the case with the carryover effect, a great amount of spillover occurred among the caucus attenders. For Democrats, roughly a third of the nomination participants reported working in some way for their local House candidate, regardless of whether they had initially backed Dukakis or a losing contender. On the other hand, only 14 percent of those who were inactive became involved at this level during the fall. Among Republicans, positive spillover effects seem slightly stronger, with nomination winners and losers alike showing significantly higher rates of congressional-level involvement than nonparticipants.

In 1992, immediately after the general election, the caucus attenders from 1988 were resurveyed. One of the items on the questionnaire sent to them asked whether they were currently a member of their local party committee. As is evident in the third column of table 3.9, nomination involvement in 1988 is also strongly associated with participation at this level. Nearly one out of ten Democrats who had been active in the nomination races of 1988 were committee members in 1992; by contrast, virtually none of the inactive Democrats from 1988 were found to belong to a committee. Within the Republican ranks, the distinction between nomination activists and the inactive surfaces more profoundly. Thirty-one percent of those who had participated for Bush and 24 percent of those who backed a losing contestant reported committee ties in 1992. Those not drawn into nomination politics were quite unlikely to be active at the committee level. As was the case for positive carryover effects, one recent analysis shows that the beneficial impact of nomination-stage involvement on nonpresidential activism holds up well when controls for earlier participation and general predispositions to become involved are introduced in a fuller causal model.[53]

That nomination politics today encourages intraparty divisiveness and can result in heated—perhaps even mean-spirited—debate among a party's leading figures is beyond question. The prospect of winning (or losing) any

zero-sum conflict can be expected to create hostility; when the prize is as important as a major-party presidential nomination, divisions among party activists are probably deeply felt. Thus critics of the open nominating system
are correct in their assertion that the rules for selection emphasize candidate-
centered politics. From this observation, however, it does not necessarily follow that the party system suffers. To the contrary, activity within nominating campaigns, even those that are ideologically extreme or insurgent in
style, can bolster the participants' sense of identification with and attachment to their party.[54] If partisans were denied the opportunity to act on their
preferences at the nomination stage, table 3.9 suggests that they might be
less willing to work in the fall campaigns and partake in less visible (but
quite important) committee activities.

Conclusion

Establishing rules for the selection of presidential candidates has proven to
be one of the most vexing issues facing party leaders and government officials. The U.S. Constitution regulates much of the electoral process; it stipulates the timing of elections, the workings of the Electoral College, and the
breadth of the franchise. It is silent, however, on how candidates should be
chosen. As a result, each political generation has been forced to craft a nomination system that is commensurate with its values and ideals.

The current rules, which are largely a product of the social movements
of the 1960s and 1970s, allow for an unprecedented degree of public input.
This chapter has explored the extent to which greater democracy has made
the process of candidate selection more representative. I began by noting
three distinct dimensions of political representation. In one sense, the people
selecting candidates may be deemed representative if they are similar to
nonparticipants. Alternatively, if those involved in selecting presidential candidates take into account the potential preferences of others beyond their
immediate cohort, they could be characterized as representative. Yet another
facet of representation is related to postconvention participation. If nomination activists seem prepared to work for the presidential ticket and become
"team players," their party's ability to represent large-scale national interests
could be greatly enhanced; in contrast, the wholesale defection of losing factions following the summer conventions undoubtedly would hamper a
party's efforts to connect voters to the policymaking process.

The findings from the Active Minority studies, a set of surveys drawn
on state-level convention delegates and individuals involved in local caucus
meetings over a twelve-year period, allow us to come to some fairly solid
conclusions about political representation. Those who select presidential
candidates are clearly unlike members of the mass public. They tend to be
more affluent, more educated, more connected to specialized lobbying orga-

nizations, and more prone to think in ideological terms. But participants do not necessarily act on these tendencies. Instead, such activists generally understand that they are not like "average voters," and they appear willing to vote against their own immediate concerns in the interest of choosing a contestant who will fare well in the general election. In other words, the *behavior* of the newer participants implies representation even though *descriptively* the caucus attenders and delegates are unrepresentative. Furthermore, investigations based on the panel components of the Active Minority surveys show that involvement in campaigns can encourage fuller participation at a variety of levels within party organizations.

These conclusions stand in stark contrast to the large scholarly literature criticizing the democratic reforms. A claim heard frequently is that the open nomination system weakens the major parties and increases the likelihood that candidates who are ideologically extreme, insurgent, or worse will be chosen as their party's standard-bearers. As the 1996 election nears, political observers seem especially prone to making this charge. While the presence today of many interest groups—evangelical Christians, labor unionists, and members of the civil rights movement, to name just a few—is indeed unmistakable, this chapter suggests that the supposed deleterious effects of activist participation need to be reconsidered.

Acknowledgments

I would like to thank Walt Stone, Stephen Medvic, Lee Wilson, Ron Rapoport, and Bill Mayer for helpful comments.

Notes

1. A commission set up by the Democratic Party after the 1968 election and chaired by Senator George McGovern and Representative Donald Fraser became the principal engine of reform. Under the McGovern-Fraser guidelines, put into effect for the 1972 nominating convention, a quota system put aside delegate convention slots specifically for women and minority-group members. The commission also overturned the "winner take all" rule for choosing slates of convention delegates in favor of "proportional representation" so that candidates receiving as little as 15 percent of the statewide vote could send supporters to the convention. These measures proved to be quite controversial, and they were not replicated on the Republican side. In 1969, however, the Republicans did set up a Delegates and Organization Committee to reassess their nomination rules. This body recommended that state organizations strive to send equal numbers of men and women to the convention and that people under age twenty-five be included in proportion to their voting strength within each state. For good overviews of the reform process, see Barbara Norrander, *Super Tuesday: Regional Politics and Presidential Primaries* (Lexington: University Press of Kentucky, 1992), esp. chap. 1; Thomas R. Marshall, *Presidential Nominations in a Reform Age* (New York: Praeger, 1981);

John G. Geer, *Nominating Presidents* (Westport, Conn: Greenwood Press, 1989); and William Crotty and John S. Jackson, III, *Presidential Primaries and Nominations* (Washington, D.C.: CQ Press, 1985).

2. See Michael Gallagher and Michael Marsh, eds., *Candidate Selection in Comparative Perspective* (London: Sage, 1988), for an interesting overview of nomination politics in other democracies.

3. Congressional Quarterly, *Candidates '88* (Washington, D.C.: CQ Press, 1988).

4. Hanna Pitkin, *The Concept of Representation* (Berkeley: University of California Press, 1967).

5. Ibid., 63.

6. Ibid., chap. 6.

7. See, e.g., the treatment given to parties by two scholarly classics in the field of American politics: E.E. Schattschneider, *Party Government* (New York: Farrar and Rinehart, 1942); and V.O. Key, *Southern Politics in State and Nation* (New York: Knopf, 1950).

8. See Alan I. Abramowitz and Walter J. Stone, *Nomination Politics* (New York: Praeger, 1984); and Ronald B. Rapoport, Alan I. Abramowitz, and John McGlennon, eds., *The Life of the Parties: Activists in Presidential Politics* (Lexington: University Press of Kentucky, 1986), for information about the sampling procedures used to survey the delegates. Technical details concerning the caucus samples may be found in Walter J. Stone, Ronald B. Rapoport, and Alan I. Abramowitz, "Candidate Support in Presidential Nomination Campaigns: The Case of Iowa in 1984," *Journal of Politics* 54, no.4 (1992): 1074–97; James A. McCann, "Nomination Politics and Ideological Polarization: Assessing the Attitudinal Effects of Campaign Involvement," *Journal of Politics* 57, no. 1 (1995): 101–20; Ronald B. Rapoport, Walter J. Stone, and Alan I. Abramowitz, "Sex and the Caucus Participant: The Gender Gap and Presidential Nominations," *American Journal of Political Science* 34, no. 3 (1990): 725–40; Ronald B. Rapoport, Walter J. Stone, Randall W. Partin, and James A. McCann, "Spillover and Carryover: Nomination Involvement and General Election Success," presented at the 1992 meeting of the American Political Science Association, Chicago; and James A. McCann, Randall W. Partin, Ronald B. Rapoport, and Walter J. Stone, "Presidential Nomination Campaign Participation: An Assessment of 'Spillover' Effects," typescript, Purdue University.

9. Warren E. Miller and the National Election Studies, *American National Election Study, 1988: Pre- and Post-Election Study Codebook* (Ann Arbor, Mich.: Interuniversity Consortium for Political and Social Research, 1989); Warren E. Miller, Donald R. Kinder, Steven J. Rosenstone, and the National Election Studies, *American National Election Study, 1992: Pre- and Post-Election Codebook* (Ann Arbor, Mich.: Interuniversity Consortium for Political and Social Research, 1992).

10. Norman H. Nie and Sidney Verba, "Political Participation," *Handbook of Political Science,* 4:1–74, Fred I. Greenstein and Nelson W. Polsby, eds. (Reading, Mass.: Addison-Wesley, 1975), 38.

11. Jeane J. Kirkpatrick, *The New Presidential Elite* (New York: Russell Sage, 1976).

12. Ibid., 64.

13. See, for example, Denise L. Baer and David A. Bositis, *Elite Cadres and Party Coalitions* (Westport, Conn.: Greenwood Press, 1988); Warren E. Miller and

M. Kent Jennings, *Parties in Transition* (New York: Russell Sage, 1986).

14. Note the findings presented in, for example, Crotty and Jackson, *Presidential Primaries;* James I. Lengle, *Representation and Presidential Primaries* (Westport, Conn.: Greenwood Press, 1981); Herbert Kritzer, "The Representativeness of the 1972 Presidential Primaries," *Polity* 10 (1977): 121–29; Everett Carll Ladd, *Where Have All the Voters Gone?* (New York: Norton, 1978); Scott Keeter and Cliff Zukin, *Uninformed Choice* (New York: Praeger, 1983); and Austin Ranney, "Representativeness of Primary Electorates," *Midwest Journal of Political Science* 12 (1972): 224–38. Geer, *Nominating Presidents,* chap. 2, however, provides a contrary view based on the 1976, 1980, and 1984 elections. When primary voters are compared with nonparticipants who usually support the party in general elections, they do not appear to be especially affluent or highly educated. All agree, however, that primary voters are not representative of the mass public in general.

15. On this point, see Robert S. Erikson, Norman R. Luttbeg, and Kent L. Tedin, *American Public Opinion* (New York: Macmillan, 1988), chap. 4.

16. For instance, see Crotty and Jackson, *Presidential Primaries;* Jack Walker, "The Primary Game," *Wilson Quarterly* 12 (1988): 64–77; and Ranney, "Representativeness of Primary Electorates." As with socioeconomic comparisons, the degree of bias changes if primary voters are compared to all nonparticipants, to party identifiers who fail to turn out in primaries, or to citizens who vote in general elections but not in primaries. See, e.g., Geer, *Nominating Presidents;* and Barbara Norrander, "Ideological Representativeness of Presidential Primary Voters," *American Journal of Political Science* 33, no. 3 (1989): 570–87.

17. Steven E. Schier, "A Constituency of Zealots," *Chicago Tribune,* 3 July 1991, 14.

18. These data are publicly available through the Interuniversity Consortium for Political and Social Research at the University of Michigan, Ann Arbor. Of course, the principal investigators for these surveys and the ICPSR bear no responsibility for the analysis and interpretations presented in this essay.

19. On this point, see Lengle, *Representation and Presidential Primaries.*

20. See Walter J. Stone and James A. McCann, "Delegates to State Nominating Conventions," in *Political Parties and Elections in the United States,* ed. L. Sandy Maisel (New York: Garland, 1991), 239–48; Walter J. Stone, Alan I. Abramowitz, and Ronald B. Rapoport, "How Representative Are the Iowa Caucuses?" in *The Iowa Caucuses and the Presidential Nominating Process,* ed. Peverill Squire (Boulder, Colo.: Westview, 1989); and McCann, "Nomination Politics and Ideological Polarization."

21. I do not take into account the intensity of the respondents' issue preferences because such measures might be especially influenced by changes in question wording.

22. James Q. Wilson, *The Amateur Democrat* (Chicago: University of Chicago Press, 1962), 3.

23. See, e.g., John W. Soule and Wilma E. McGrath, "A Comparative Study of Presidential Nomination Conventions: The Democrats of 1968 and 1972," *American Journal of Political Science* 19 (1975): 501–19; John W. Soule and James W. Clarke, "Amateurs and Professionals: A Study of Delegates to the 1968 Democratic National Convention," *American Political Science Review* 64 (1970): 888–98; Thomas H. Roback, "Amateurs and Professionals: Delegates to the 1972

Republican National Convention," *Journal of Politics* 37 (1975): 436–68; and Kirkpatrick, *The New Presidential Elite*.

24. Aaron Wildavsky, "The Goldwater Phenomenon: Purists, Politicians, and the Two-Party System," *Review of Politics* 17 (1965): 386–413.

25. Thomas B. Edsall, *The New Politics of Inequality* (New York: Norton, 1984), 55.

26. Kirkpatrick, *The New Presidential Elite*; Miller and Jennings, *Parties in Transition*.

27. Data on the convention delegates in table 3.4 are taken from Walter J. Stone and Alan I. Abramowitz, "Winning May Not Be Everything, but It's More Than We Thought," *American Political Science Review* 77 (1983): 945–56.

28. Jeane Kirkpatrick, *The New Presidential Elite*; Nelson W. Polsby, *Consequences of Party Reform* (New York: Oxford University Press, 1983).

29. An item from the caucus attender survey conducted in the spring of 1984 dramatically underscores this point. When asked to rank their presidential preferences using a list that included Alan Cranston, John Glenn, Gary Hart, Jesse Jackson, George McGovern, Walter Mondale, and Ronald Reagan, fewer than 7 percent of the Democrats placed Reagan first or second. On the other hand, over three-quarters of the Democratic sample ranked him last or did not even include him in their preference orderings.

30. This information is taken from Stone and McCann, "Delegates to State Nominating Conventions."

31. See, for example, the ideological distributions presented in the classic work *The American Voter* by Angus Campbell, Philip E. Converse, Warren E. Miller, and Donald E. Stokes (New York: Wiley, 1960).

32. McCann, "Nomination Politics and Ideological Polarization."

33. In total, 1,486 Democrats and 945 Republicans from 1984 are included in this wave. See Walter J. Stone, Lonna Rae Atkeson, and Ronald B. Rapoport, "Turning On or Turning Off? Mobilization and Demobilization Effects of Participation in Presidential Nomination Campaigns," *American Journal of Political Science* 36, no. 3 (1992): 665–91, for details regarding response rates and sampling procedures. It is important to distinguish this group of respondents from the 1988 caucus attenders described in tables 3.1 through 3.3. In these earlier analyses, the partisans were independently sampled after the caucus meetings that year in Iowa, Michigan, and Virginia.

34. Figures 3.1 and 3.2 also show that ideological centrism does not automatically make a candidate seem more electable. For example, Al Gore was perceived as the most moderate Democratic contestant, but both partisan groups believed several of his competitors were more likely to be successful.

35. Walter J. Stone and Alan I. Abramowitz, "Winning May Not Be Everything."

36. Stone et al., "Prenomination Candidate Choice."

37. See Peter H. Aranson and Peter C. Ordeshook, "Spatial Strategies for Sequential Elections," in *Probability Models of Collective Decision-Making*, ed. Richard G. Niemi and Herbert F. Weisberg (Columbus, Ohio: Merrill, 1972), for a formalized mathematical treatment of "expected utility" models in political science.

38. Readers unfamiliar with statistical "interactions" may wish to consult James Jaccard, Robert Turrisi, and Choi K. Wan, *Interaction Effects in Multiple*

Regression (Newbury Park, Calif.: Sage, 1990).

39. Stone et al., "Prenomination Candidate Choice."

40. They also replicate their analysis on a set of Democratic delegates to the Iowa convention, but they do not consider Republican activists because Ronald Reagan ran unopposed that year.

41. The four policy issues, all measured using seven-point Likert scales, are a unilateral freeze on deployment of nuclear weapons by the United States; a continued increase in defense spending even if it requires cutting domestic programs; holding down inflation even if it means increases in unemployment; and a constitutional amendment to prohibit abortions except when a mother's life is threatened.

42. A number of studies using mass-level survey data have found equally high correlations between perceptions of a candidate's personal traits and vote choice. See, e.g., Erikson et al., *American Public Opinion*, and Campbell et al., *The American Voter*.

43. Polsby, *Consequences of Party Reform*. On this point, see also Byron Shafer, *Quiet Revolution* (New York: Russell Sage, 1983); Gary R. Orren and Nelson W. Polsby, eds., *Media and Momentum: The New Hampshire Primary and Nomination Politics* (Chatham, N.J.: Chatham House, 1987); James Ceaser, *Reforming the Reforms* (Cambridge, Mass.: Ballinger, 1982); and Martin P. Wattenberg, *The Decline of American Political Parties, 1952–1988* (Cambridge: Harvard University Press, 1990).

44. James I. Lengle, "Divisive Presidential Primaries and Party Electoral Prospects," *American Politics Quarterly* 8 (1980): 261–77; Patrick J. Kenney and Tom W. Rice, "The Relationship between Divisive Primaries and General Election Outcomes," *American Journal of Political Science* 31 (1987): 31–44.

45. On this point, see Alan Ware, "Divisive Primaries: The Important Questions," *British Journal of Political Science* 9 (1979): 381–84.

46. Walter J. Stone, "The Carryover Effect in Presidential Elections," *American Political Science Review* 80 (1986): 271–79, and "Prenomination Candidate Choice and General Election Behavior," *American Journal of Political Science* 28 (1984): 372–89; Priscilla L. Southwell, "The Politics of Disgruntlement: Nonvoting and Defection among Supporters of Nomination Losers, 1968–1984," *Political Behavior* 8 (1986): 81–95.

47. Stone et al., "Turning On or Turning Off?" 668.

48. See, e.g., ibid., as well as McCann et al., "Presidential Nomination Campaign Participation," and Rapoport et al., "Spillover and Carryover."

49. E.E. Schattschneider, *The Semisovereign People* (Hinsdale, Ill.: Dryden, 1975).

50. Emmett H. Buell, Jr., "Divisive Primaries and Participation in Fall Presidential Campaigns: A Study of 1984 New Hampshire Primary Activists," *American Politics Quarterly* 14 (1986): 376–90.

51. These data are taken from McCann et al., "Presidential Nomination Campaign Participation."

52. See, e.g., ibid. In this study, the authors find that for Democratic caucus attenders in 1988, the regression slopes linking nomination activism to postconvention campaign involvement are .401 for those who had backed Dukakis and .125 for losing activists. In the Republican sample, the path linking activism for George Bush to work on behalf of the Bush-Quayle campaign is .528, but for los-

ing partisans it is .155. Standard errors for these paths fall between .03 and .05.

53. Ibid.

54. On this point, see McCann, "Nomination Politics and Ideological Polarization." In 1988, participants in the Jackson, Simon, Dukakis, Bush, and Dole campaigns identified significantly more strongly with their party by virtue of their political activity.

4

Caucuses: How They Work, What Difference They Make

WILLIAM G. MAYER

Plairsville, Maine, is a small town—population about 20,000—located along the southern coast of the Pine Tree State. One of its residents describes it as "about 99 percent Democratic, so it's got a small, very tight Republican Party." And on a cold, sunny afternoon in late February 1988 about fifty of the Republican faithful are crowded into the modest front room of Flo's Deli, a restaurant owned by one of the party's local leaders, for the Plairsville presidential caucuses.[1]

Most of the regular Republicans are sporting Bush buttons, but they have been joined, unexpectedly, by a number of newcomers, most of whom support the presidential candidacy of Pat Robertson. The principal purpose of the caucus is to choose twelve delegates to the Republican state convention (which will be held in mid-April), where the Maine delegation to the Republican National Convention will be selected. As soon as the meeting is brought to order, one of the Robertson backers reads off a list of six names whom he nominates as delegates to the state convention. This slate is quickly voted down, and another caucuser gains the floor to propose a slate composed entirely of Bush supporters. A Robertson partisan then moves that the Plairsville delegation be divided on a proportional basis between Bush and Robertson supporters, but the caucus chairman, who is clearly a Bush supporter, rules this motion out of order. Instead, he takes a yes-or-no vote on the entire pro-Bush slate, which is approved by a wide margin.

At this point, the chairman tries to proceed to a few remaining items of business—the selection of alternate delegates, the election of members to the town and county Republican committees—but the Robertson people are not so easily disposed of. Led by a coordinator from a nearby town with a distinctively loud and squeaky voice, the Robertson forces continue to demand a vote on their motion for proportional representation. The chair says again that the motion is out of order, and when the Robertson coordinator objects, threatens to have him removed from the premises on the grounds that he doesn't live in Plairsville. But everything else the chair tries to say for the next ten minutes is interrupted by cries of "Railroad!" and "Foul play!" Finally, it occurs to the chairman that if he had enough votes to approve the Bush slate, he also has enough votes to reject the motion for proportional representation. So the motion is finally recognized and duly voted down. After that, the chairman is allowed to finish his agenda.

The caucus is adjourned forty-five minutes after it started. As the chairman tries to walk out of the restaurant, a woman who supported Robertson approaches him to complain about the way the meeting was handled. "Lady," he says, "I don't want to hear any more of it."

One day later, it is the Democrats' turn. Most towns in Maine have one voting precinct, which permits all the local Democrats to attend a single caucus. But in Portland, Maine's largest city, there are twenty-six separate precinct caucuses, all of which are being held at Deering High School.

The caucusing is supposed to start at 1:00 P.M., but being Democrats, they of course start late. The formal program begins at 1:30 in the high school gymnasium, where about 1,200 caucus participants are jammed into the bleacher seats. After an opening prayer and the pledge of allegiance, the caucusers hear short speeches by Senate Majority Leader George Mitchell, Congressman Joseph Brennan, and several other party potentates. Representatives from each of the Democratic presidential campaigns are then given one last chance to extol the merits of their candidates and solicit a few last votes among those who have not made up their minds yet.

The gymnasium gathering finally breaks up at around 2:40 P.M., with each of the twenty-six precincts sent to a different classroom in the school. The caucus I decide to observe appears to be one of the larger ones in the city, with about seventy people crammed into a room that only has chairs for forty. The local precinct captain is unanimously elected to chair the caucus, and then all the participants are asked to fill out a card on which they must list their names and addresses and affirm that they are registered voters and enrolled Democrats. For the next half hour, these cards are checked and verified while the room gets hot and the caucusers get restless and one married couple tries to calm down a young and cranky child.

Not until 3:30 do they get around to the task of electing delegates to the Democratic state convention. After a preliminary show of hands, the caucus chairman asks all those who support Michael Dukakis to gather in one corner of the room, points to another corner for the Jesse Jackson supporters, and assigns various other locations for those who favor one of the other candidates or who are still uncommitted. After an interval of counting and recounting, the tally reads Dukakis 35, Jackson 21, Simon 6, Gore 1, and uncommitted 7. Since this particular precinct is allowed to send twelve delegates to the Democratic state convention, and the delegates must be apportioned among the candidates on a proportional basis, that translates into six delegates for Dukakis, four for Jackson, and one each for Simon and uncommitted. (The lone Gore supporter gets nothing for his troubles.)

Now each candidate group caucuses within itself in order to select the people who will actually serve as delegates. In the Dukakis bloc, eight people are vying for six slots, so they decide to take a vote. Before the vote can be taken, however, one woman says she would like each of the eight aspirants to talk briefly about why they would like to be a state convention delegate. The first person asked to speak looks flustered, stammers for a few seconds, and finally blurts out, "To represent the people!" This response is greeted with such laughter and appreciation that the next three delegate candidates say almost exactly the same thing. (Shortly thereafter, two of the eight candidates decide to drop out of the race, making the vote unnecessary.) The Jackson supporters, meanwhile, opt for a simpler method of choosing their four delegates: they draw straws.

In the end, the twelve delegates are finally chosen, and at several minutes after 4:00 P.M., people gradually start to leave the high school.

These are presidential caucuses. And while no one, presumably, will mistake them for a gathering of philosopher kings, they are a very important component of the presidential nomination process. Over the past twenty years, the vast majority of popular and scholarly writing on the American presidential selection system has been focused on the institution of presidential primaries—and with good reason, for in every recent nomination race, a majority of the national convention delegates were selected through primaries. Yet, even in this era of widespread and highly publicized primaries, about a third of all states use a caucus system for selecting their delegates. Equally important, even if caucuses were used less often than they are, they remain one of the principal alternatives to presidential primaries. And as dissatisfaction with the current nomination process has increased, one of the most frequently discussed "reforms" has been the suggestion that the political parties should reduce the number of primaries they hold and move toward a greater reliance on caucuses.[2] This option, moreover, is not just a theoretical one. Of the thirty-nine states that used a presidential primary for delegate selection for at least one election between 1972 and 1988, fourteen of them have, at one time or another, abandoned the primary and adopted a caucus system (though in some cases, they later reinstituted a primary).

In contrast to the huge profusion of writings about presidential prima-ries, there are considerably fewer studies of caucuses. The purpose of this chapter is to help begin to redress that imbalance, by presenting a broad overview of this "invisible component" of the presidential nomination pro-cess.[3] Since most readers of this book have probably never participated in or observed a caucus, I begin with a detailed description of how caucuses work and the national and state party rules that govern their operations. The re-mainder of the chapter is focused primarily on two questions: What differ-ences, if any, are there between caucuses and primaries? And what impact do those differences have on the nomination process as a whole?

How Caucuses Work: The Democrats

As the two narratives that began this chapter have suggested, caucuses are meetings of local Republican or Democratic adherents. Depending on the size and population density of a state, a separate caucus may be held in each voting precinct in the state (this is the pattern, for example, in Iowa, Minne-sota, North Dakota, and Washington) or in each county or state legislative district (as in Arizona, Delaware, and Wyoming). They are usually convened in public places such as town halls or public schools, occasionally in private homes or commercial buildings.[4]

Caucuses, it is important to emphasize, are just the first of several steps in the selection of a state's delegation to the Republican or Democratic na-tional convention. Indeed, in no state do the caucuses directly select any national convention delegates. Instead, each caucus selects a small number of what might be called "intermediate delegates," who will then participate in another round or two of meetings, until finally, at congressional district and state conventions, the national convention delegates are chosen. The number of intermediate delegates that each caucus is allowed to send on to the next level of meetings is determined in advance by the state party and is based on an apportionment formula that takes into account the precinct or county's total population, its vote for past Democratic or Republican candi-dates, or both.

In the delegate selection system used by the Vermont Democratic Party in 1992, for example, each city and town in the state held a Democratic caucus on 31 March. The 1,350 delegates selected at these caucuses then met at the Democratic state convention on 16 May to choose the Vermont delegation to the Democratic National Convention. Iowa has a similar pro-cedure, though with a larger number of intermediate steps (or "tiers," as they are sometimes called). The delegates selected at the Iowa precinct cau-cuses (held on 10 February 1992) attended a series of county conventions (on 28 March), which in turn selected delegates who participated in congres-sional district conventions (on 2 May) and in the state convention (on 20

June). Only at these last two levels were the national convention delegates chosen.

As this discussion should indicate, presidential caucuses, much like presidential primaries, vary from state to state on such matters as the number of stages in the process, the apportionment formula used, and who is allowed to participate in them. In table 4.1 I have tried to summarize the most significant features of the state Democratic caucus rules used in 1992.[5] Such variations notwithstanding, there is a significant measure of uniformity in Democratic caucusing procedures because, unlike the case in the Republican Party, all state Democratic caucuses are closely regulated by the national party's delegate selection rules.

Democratic caucuses are usually convened by a local party official who has been designated to serve as the temporary chairman of the caucus, and the first order of business is frequently that this same person gets elected permanent chairman. A substantial amount of time is then devoted to speeches: welcoming addresses from local or state party officials, pep talks on the merits of the party and the need for unity in the fall campaign, pleas for support from candidates for state or local office. Most caucuses also allow representatives from the various presidential campaigns, or their local supporters, to give short speeches about the candidates, their merits and policies, and why they deserve the support of the caucus participants.

Either before or during the speechmaking, a number of preliminary matters are disposed of, the most important of which is certifying that all the people who have shown up at the caucus are eligible to participate in it. Since 1972, the national Democratic Party has required state parties to make participation in their delegate selection processes open to "all voters who wish to participate as Democrats."[6] This stipulation has two practical implications: it means that all state caucuses and primaries must be open to any *Democrat* who wants to participate in them; but it also puts some burden on state parties to *discourage* participation by independents, the unaffiliated, and those whose principal allegiance is to another party. In states that hold presidential primaries, this latter requirement is frequently slighted or disregarded, since primaries are established and regulated by state law, that is, by governors and state legislatures, who may not be especially worried about the parties' national rules or long-term welfare. Caucuses, by contrast, are usually seen as internal party procedures, which each state party can run as it sees fit (subject to national party rules).

As one reflection of this difference, caucuses generally make a much greater effort to limit their participants to those who have a clear and demonstrable commitment to the party and to exclude independents and members of other parties. In states that have party registration, for example, the state parties almost always mandate that only registered Democrats may take part in the Democratic caucuses. Other states require all participants to

TABLE 4.1

State	Tiers	Date	National convention delegates selected
Alaska	Precinct caucuses	2 April	—
	State house district conventions	2–3 May	—
	State convention[a]	31 May	14
Arizona	Legislative district and county caucuses	7 March	—
	Regional caucuses[b]	25 April	27
	State convention[b]	2 May	15
Delaware	State legislative district caucuses	10 March	—
	State convention[a]	25 April	15
Hawaii	Precinct caucuses	10 March	—
	State convention[c]	31 May	13
	State committee[c]	31 May	8
Idaho	County conventions	3 March	—
	State convention[a]	19 June	19
Iowa	Precinct caucuses	10 February	—
	County conventions	28 March	—
	District conventions	2 May	32
	State convention	20 June	18
Maine	Municipal caucuses	23 February	—
	State convention[a]	16–17 May	24
Minnesota	Precinct caucuses	3 March	—
	County conventions	21 March–5 April	—
	Congressional district conventions	1–10 May	51
	State convention	6 June	29

SOURCE: Based on a detailed examination of Democratic state party rules and delegate selection plan supplemented by interviews with state party officials.

a. State conventions in these states first caucused by congressional district to select district-level delegates, then met as a whole to select at-large delegates.

b. Both the regional caucuses and the state convention in Arizona were bound by the results of the legislative district caucuses.

c. All of the delegates selected at the Hawaii state convention and seven of the eight delegates selected by the state committee were allocated among the presidential candidates according to the division of preferences expressed at the precinct caucuses.

Principal Features of the Democratic Caucus Procedures in 1992

Basis for apportionment	Proportional representation threshold for first-round caucuses[d]	Who may participate in the caucuses
Democratic vote for Congress in 1990	15%	Any registered Democrat (but independents and unregistered voters may register as Democrats at the caucuses)
Democratic vote for president in 1988 and governor in 1990	15%	Any registered Democrat
Democratic vote for president and governor in 1988	15%	Any registered Democrat
Democratic vote in most recent gubernatorial election	Not applicable[e]	Any registered voter who enrolls as a member of the Democratic Party of Hawaii at least 45 days prior to the caucuses
Democratic vote for president in 1988 and governor in 1990	15%	Any registered voter who signs a statement saying that he or she is a "member of the Democratic Party"
Democratic vote for president in 1988 and governor in 1990	15%	Any registered Democrat who signs "a pledge of support for the purposes of the Iowa Democratic Party"
Democratic vote for governor in 1990	No preset minimum[f]	Any registered Democrat (but any independent voter may enroll as a Democrat on the day of the caucus)
Average Democratic vote for five highest-ranking offices in the two most recent elections	No preset minimum[f]	Any person 18 years old or older who is willing to say that he or she agrees with Democratic principles and voted for a majority of Democratic candidates in 1990 or plans to vote for a majority of Democratic candidates in 1992

d. According to the national rules of the Democratic Party, all states must use a 15% threshold at congressional district and state conventions.

e. Since the Hawaii state convention was bound by the presidential preferences expressed by the first-round caucus participants, delegates to the state convention were not required to reveal their presidential preferences at the caucuses or to be elected on a proportional basis.

f. Meaning that no minimum threshold was specified in the state party rules. As a matter of practical necessity, all precinct caucuses must establish a threshold equal to the number of delegates allocated to that precinct divided by the number of caucus participants.

Continued . . .

TABLE 4.1 — CONTINUED

State	Tiers	Date	National convention delegates selected
Missouri	Ward, township, or county mass meetings	10 March	—
	County conventions	24 March	—
	Congressional district conventions	14 April	50
	State committee[g]	24 April	12
	State convention	2 May	17
Nevada	Precinct or assembly district caucuses	8 March	—
	County conventions	10–11 April	—
	State convention[a]	2 May	18
North Dakota	Precinct caucuses	5–19 March	—
	Legislative district conventions	5–19 March	—
	State convention	2 April	15
Texas	Precinct conventions	10 March	—
	County conventions	28 March	—
	State convention[h]	5–6 June	72
Vermont	Town/city caucuses	31 March	—
	State convention[a]	16 May	15
Virginia	City or county caucuses[i]	11 or 13 April	—
	Congressional district conventions	8–23 May	51
	State convention	5–6 June	29
Washington	Precinct caucuses	3 March	—
	County or legislative district conventions	18 or 25 April	—
	Congressional district caucuses	30 May	46
	Election committee[j]	7 June	26
Wyoming	County conventions	7 March	—
	State convention	2 May	14

g. Ten of the twelve delegates selected by the Missouri state committee were determined by the preference results of the congressional district conventions.

h. The Texas state convention also selected 127 district-level delegates, but the allocation of these delegates among the presidential candidates was determined by the results of the 10 March primary.

PRINCIPAL FEATURES OF THE DEMOCRATIC
CAUCUS PROCEDURES IN 1992

Basis for apportionment	Proportional representation threshold for first-round caucuses[d]	Who may participate in the caucuses
Population and combined Democratic vote for president in 1984 and 1988	15%	All registered voters who "declare themselves to be Democrats" and are not members of another party
Democratic vote for president in 1988 and governor in 1990	15%	Any registered Democrat
Democratic vote for governor in 1990	No preset minimum[f]	Any person 18 years old or older who "is willing to be identified with the Democratic-Nonpartisan League"
Democratic vote for governor in the last election	No preset minimum[f]	Anyone who voted in the Democratic primary held earlier on the same day
Population and Democratic vote for president in 1988 and governor in 1990	No preset minimum[f]	Any registered voter who asks to be admitted and has not participated in the nomination process of any other party
Democratic vote for president in 1988 and governor in 1989	15%	Any registered voter who signs a form declaring that "he or she is a Democrat and does not intend to support any candidate opposed to a Democratic nominee in the next election"
Democratic vote for president and governor in 1988	15%	All registered voters who "consider themselves Democrats and are willing to so state publicly"
Population and average vote for Democratic state and national candidates	No preset minimum[f]	Any registered Democrat

i. Cities and counties in Virginia had the option of holding precinct and ward caucuses first, in order to elect delegates to the city or county conventions.
j. The Washington election committee consisted of all national convention delegates elected at the congressional district caucuses.

sign a statement declaring that they are Democrats and/or that they intend to vote for Democratic candidates in the upcoming election. (For a list of the specific rules enforced by the Democratic caucuses in 1992, see table 4.1.) Most states also require that caucus participants be registered voters (though some provide facilities for on-site registration).

When all these preliminaries have been completed, the caucus can finally get down to performing its presidential selection functions. And here we encounter a particularly important influence of the national Democratic rules. Over the past twenty years, the national Democratic Party has required that state delegate selection procedures "provide fair representation of minority views on presidential candidates."[7] That is, a candidate who receives 60 percent of the votes in a given caucus is not allowed to use this majority to claim 100 percent of the delegates that caucus selects. There must, instead, be some attempt at a *proportional representation* of presidential preferences so that a candidate who attracts 60 percent of the caucus participants gets about 60 percent of the delegates, and a candidate preferred by 20 percent of the caucusers is entitled to 20 percent of the delegates.[8]

Accordingly, the first step in selecting the delegates from any Democratic caucus is to *determine the candidate preferences of the caucus attenders*. While a preliminary count is sometimes made with written ballots, in every Democratic caucus I observed, tallying up the candidate preferences was ultimately an exercise in physical democracy. Supporters of the various candidates were asked to gather in different parts of the room: one corner, say, for the Clinton supporters, another corner for the Brown supporters, this table for the Harkin backers, and so on. (The Official Call of the Democratic-Farmer-Labor Party in Minnesota actually refers to this system as a "Walking Subcaucus.") A first count is then made, and on this basis, the caucus chairman announces a preliminary allocation of delegates.

In one caucus I witnessed, for example, a precinct in South Portland, Maine, obtained the following preliminary count of candidate preferences:

Brown	25
Tsongas	17
Clinton	8
Agran	5
Harkin	3
Uncommitted	8

Since sixty-six people were attending this caucus, and the precinct was allowed to select seventeen delegates to the Democratic state convention, this meant, under proportional representation rules, that each candidate group got approximately one delegate for every four supporters present ($66/17 = 3.88$). Put another way, for this particular caucus, there was a *threshold* of four members. Any group that had at least four members would get at least one delegate to the next round of caucusing. Any group with less than four members would be declared "not viable";

it would have to disband and its members would then have the option of joining another candidate grouping. (As indicated in table 4.1, about two-thirds of the Democratic caucuses in 1992 set the threshold at 15 percent, meaning that, no matter how many delegate slots a precinct had been allotted, a candidate group had to attract at least 15 percent of the caucus participants in order to win any delegates to the next round of meetings.[9])

The chairman of this South Portland caucus thus informed the Harkin supporters that they were below the threshold and then allowed a five-minute recess for them to decide what they wanted to do next. As it turned out, one of them joined the uncommitted group and the other two went with Larry Agran.[10] So the final preference tally—and the resulting delegate allocation—looked as follows:

At this point, each candidate group caucuses within itself to decide which of its members will actually be sent as delegates to the state convention. In a different kind of presidential selection system, where state and national conventions had a larger number

	Number of supporters (final count)	Number of delegates
Brown	25	7
Tsongas	17	4
Clinton	8	2
Agran	7	2
Uncommitted	9	2

of uncommitted members and a greater amount of discretion, the selection of individual delegates might be a very significant decision. Under the current system, however, most of the caucus participants seemed to regard this stage of the caucus as distinctly secondary and anticlimactic. What appeared to matter, in other words, was that *Brown* got seven delegates to the state convention—and not which particular people actually served as these delegates.

As a result, this part of the caucus was usually performed in a rapid, even haphazard way. In most instances, the chair of the candidate group simply asked for volunteers, and after a bit of discussion, the number of volunteers expanded or contracted to fit the number of slots available. Votes are occasionally taken, but without any real opportunity for the people within the caucus to learn much about the prospective delegates or their political convictions. The only factor that gives any real structure to this process is, once again, the rules of the national Democratic Party, which require each set of delegates, insofar as possible, to include equal numbers of men and women.

And so the caucus comes to an end. As I have stressed, however, this is only the first step in the full selection process for national convention delegates. While a detailed discussion of county, district, and state conventions is beyond the scope of this chapter, it is worth pointing out that these later stages of the process are usually held weeks or months after the caucuses and that, except in Arizona and Hawaii, delegates to the district and state conventions are *not* bound by the preference votes recorded at earlier levels of the caucus-convention system. Of course, anyone who made the effort to show up at a caucus, join the Brown group, and then get selected as a Brown delegate to the state convention is presumably well disposed toward that candidate and will probably stick with him when the state convention finally meets. But a far different situation occurs when, as is frequently the case, a candidate who did well in a particular state's caucuses drops out of the race at some point between the caucuses and the state convention. The delegates pledged to such a candidate then become, in effect, "free agents," whose behavior at subsequent levels of the process is more difficult to predict. The few studies available of state convention voting suggest that these delegates respond to many of the same factors that influence primary voters, especially ideology and electability.[11]

Republican Caucuses

In many respects, Republican presidential caucuses are similar to those held by the Democrats. They are, quite recognizably, the same basic animal: meetings of the local party faithful that select delegates to district and state conventions, which in turn select delegates to the Republican national convention. But the national rules of the Republican Party, in line with that party's prevailing ideas about federalism, allow somewhat more discretion to state parties; and as a result, Republican caucuses differ from Democratic caucuses in two major ways.

First, Republican national rules allow state parties to be somewhat more restrictive in deciding who can participate in their caucuses. The Democratic Party, as we have seen, requires that participation in the delegate selection process be open to "all voters who wish to participate as Democrats." The sorts of rules described in table 4.1 are designed to keep out the unaffiliated and members of other parties, but any rank-and-file Democrat is allowed and encouraged to participate in a caucus. Republican rules, by contrast, not only limit their caucuses to "legal and qualified voters who are deemed to be Republicans" by state law or party rules, but also allow "the governing Republican committee of each state ... to prescribe additional qualifications not inconsistent with state law."[12] What this means in practice is that a number of Republican state parties, especially in the West, limit their caucuses to people who are party officials or functionaries of some kind. In Arizona and Montana, for example, only precinct committeemen and committeewomen elected in the Republican primary held two years earlier are allowed to participate in the initial round of caucuses. In Wyoming, all registered Republicans are eligible to participate in the precinct caucuses, which elect delegates to the county conventions. But all Republican precinct committeemen and committeewomen become automatic delegates to the county conventions.

Second and more important, there is no provision in the Republican Party's national rules—or, consequently, in any state party rules—requiring proportional representation of the candidate preferences among caucus participants. Indeed, most Republican state bylaws and delegate selection procedure manuals say very little at all about how the caucuses are to select the delegates they send on to the next round of meetings. As the story that opened this chapter indicates, it is thus perfectly permissible in Republican caucuses for a majority to shut out the minority. If one candidate's supporters make up a majority of the caucus attenders, they can, if they wish, select only their own members to serve as delegates to the next stage of meetings or conventions.

There is a sizable literature in political science that discusses the difference between proportional representation and "winner-take-all" delegate allocation formulas, and the implications that such rules have for the nature of the presidential nomination process. According to one major school of thought (which I disagree with), the Democrats' greater reliance on proportional representation rules has worked to the long-term detriment of the party, increasing the power of minority factions and ideological extremists, prolonging the nomination race, and making party unity more difficult to achieve in the November election.[13] Whatever the truth of these claims, the proportional representation requirement in Democratic caucuses—and its absence in the GOP—does have an important effect on the way caucuses are covered by the news media, as well as on political scientists' ability to study them. Simply put, it is vastly more difficult to "keep score" on Republican caucuses.

Every Democratic caucus, as we have seen, produces two clear measures of how well each candidate did: the percentage of caucus attenders who supported each candidate; and the percentage of delegates elected to the next round of meetings who are pledged to that candidate. (With allowance for a bit of rounding error, the two measures are usually equivalent.) So when a Democratic caucus takes place, it is almost always possible for the media to say, shortly after it has ended, who "won" and who "lost" it. But in Republican caucuses, there is no necessity for determining candidate preferences in any kind of formal or systematic way, and thus, frequently, no mathematical box score is available at the end of the day.

In one Republican caucus I attended, for example, the caucus chair asked anyone in the room who wanted to be a state convention delegate to raise his or her hand, wrote all the names on a blackboard, and then passed out slips of paper on which caucus attenders could vote for their favorites. At no time during the entire caucus, however, were any of the delegate candidates asked to reveal anything about whom they supported for president.

Even at the Plairsville caucus described earlier, while it was clear to everyone I spoke with that the town's delegation to the state convention was a pro-Bush slate, it was never formally identified as such during the caucus; and the vote to ratify this slate, taken by a show of hands, was sufficiently one-sided that the caucus chair never bothered to count it.

To give just one example of the effect this can have: During the 1972 and 1976 election cycles, the Iowa Democratic caucuses, which were held in mid-January and thus were the first delegate selection event on the Democratic calendar, emerged as a major media spectacle, attracting a huge flood of television and newspaper coverage. Not surprisingly, the Iowa Republican Party, whose 1972 caucuses were not held until April, soon decided to grab a share of all the publicity, candidate attention, and campaign spending by scheduling their caucuses on the same early date. As a media extravaganza in the making, however, the Iowa Republican caucuses suffered from one major shortcoming. Without a systematic, mathematical measure of how well each candidate did, the Republican caucuses simply did not fit into the way the American media cover contemporary nomination races. Where the Democratic caucusing procedures were tailor-made for the media's horse-race handicappers and those who sought a dramatic story line, the Republican caucuses threatened to be a plot without a climax. To remedy this defect, the Iowa Republicans contrived to hold a nonbinding "straw poll" among their caucus participants. This poll had no formal relationship with the selection of delegates to the Republican county conventions, but it did meet the needs of the news media. These poll results, for example, allowed the media to declare George Bush the upset winner of the 1980 Iowa caucuses, a verdict that obviously had a major impact on Bush's subsequent political career.[14]

The Evolution of Delegate Selection Procedures

Whenever I have tried to explain the convolutions of the caucus process to undergraduates, many students invariably wonder how any state ever decided to use such a complex procedure for selecting its national convention delegates. Where, they wonder, did caucuses come from? Viewed against the broad sweep of American political history, however, a more appropriate question is: where did primaries come from? For the first sixty years or so after American mass parties were created in the 1830s and 1840s, all national convention delegates—indeed, all party-endorsed candidates for any elective office—were selected through party-run caucuses or conventions. Presidential primaries, by comparison, are a relative newcomer to American politics; not until 1901 did Florida pass the first state law allowing for an optional presidential primary.[15]

From this modest beginning, the number of states holding presidential

TABLE 4.2
STATE DELEGATE SELECTION PROCEDURES, 1952–68

	Republicans		Democrats	
	Number of states	*Percentage of delegates*	*Number of states*	*Percentage of delegates*
1952				
Primary	11	29	15	31
Convention	35	52	31	50
Mixed system	3	19	3	19
1956				
Primary	16	34	17	33
Convention	30	49	29	49
Mixed system	3	17	3	18
1960				
Primary	13	29	15	31
Convention	35	54	33	52
Mixed system	3	17	3	18
1964				
Primary	14	32	15	33
Convention	34	51	33	49
Mixed system	3	16	3	18
1968				
Primary	13	29	14	32
Convention	35	55	34	51
Mixed system	3	16	3	17

NOTE: All figures in this table include the District of Columbia but exclude territories such as Puerto Rico and Guam, as well as Alaska and Hawaii in 1952 and 1956.

primaries swelled to twenty-six by 1916, but then declined slightly over the next twenty years. By the mid-1930s, state delegate selection procedures in both parties had taken on a form that persisted, with remarkably little change, up through the nomination races of 1968. As we see very shortly, the presidential nomination process, especially in the Democratic Party, was changed quite radically between 1968 and 1972, with important implications for the nature and functioning of presidential caucuses. In order to appreciate those changes, it is worth taking a quick look back at the final years of the "old system." Table 4.2 summarizes the state of delegate selection procedures during the last five "prereform" nomination contests: the national conventions held between 1952 and 1968. In general, national convention delegates in this period were selected in three principal ways:[16]

Delegate selection primaries. — About a third of all states used primaries to select their delegates to the Republican and Democratic national conventions. From our present-day perspective, many of these states had primary laws that probably seem strange, undemocratic, and scarcely calculated to make these elections a referendum on national issues or candidates. In several states, candidates for national convention delegates were actually prohibited from indicating on the ballot which presidential candidate they supported. In other states, potential delegates *could* list a candidate preference on the ballot, but were not required to do so. Such details notwithstanding, the states in this category did use primary elections as their exclusive means for selecting delegates to the national convention.[17]

Nonprimary selection systems. — About 60 percent of all states abjured primaries entirely in choosing their national convention delegates. The exact procedures they *did* use varied enormously from state to state—even more than current caucusing systems do—but in general, the states in this category selected their delegates through mechanisms that were closely controlled by state party organizations and officials. In almost all cases, the task of choosing the delegates ultimately rested with a state convention or a state committee.[18]

Quite clearly, these selection systems are the direct forerunners of the contemporary caucus-convention systems, but they were considerably less "public" than their modern-day equivalents. In many instances, the state conventions could be attended only by local party functionaries who had been elected two years earlier; where open caucuses were held at the local level, they were usually poorly publicized or lacked formal, written rules or were dominated by local party officials who came to the meetings with large numbers of proxy votes.[19] Much more than the present-day caucus systems, they embodied the belief that a political party was in some sense a "private agency" and that the selection of national convention delegates was therefore an internal matter for party leaders and organization members to handle, not something to be left to ordinary voters or party identifiers.

Mixed systems. — Finally, three states—Illinois, New York, and Pennsylvania—selected some of their delegates through primaries and some of them through conventions. In each instance, a primary was first held to select a certain number of delegates within each congressional district. Then, later in the year, a state convention was held to choose at-large delegates. In 1968, for example, two-fifths of the Illinois delegates to the Democratic National Convention, two-thirds of the New York delegation, and three-fourths of the Pennsylvania delegates were chosen by primary, the balance by convention.

The 1968 Democratic nomination race was an unusually divisive one, however, and on the last day of an especially bitter and chaotic national convention, the Democratic delegates approved a minority report from the Rules Committee that *may* have authorized—it was not at all obvious at first reading—a Special Commission created by another resolution to rewrite the rules by which the party selected its convention delegates and nominated its presidential candidates. Its uncertain mandate notwithstanding, this commission—usually called the McGovern-Fraser Commission after the two men who served as its chairmen—set in motion what is probably the most sweeping revision of nomination rules and procedures since national party conventions were first created in the 1830s.[20] And as the data in table 4.3 make clear, the commission's work had a particularly dramatic impact on delegate selection practices. In the nomination races held since 1972, national convention delegates have been selected in four major ways:

Delegate selection primaries.—The most talked-about change in the new era was the sharp increase in the number of states that selected their national convention delegates through presidential primaries. After staying essentially constant between 1952 and 1968, the number of delegate selection primaries in the Democratic Party jumped from seventeen in 1968 to twenty-three in 1972, and then to twenty-nine in 1976 and thirty in 1980. The number of primaries dipped briefly to twenty-four in 1984, but then shot up to thirty-two in 1988 and thirty-five in 1992.

As table 4.3 also shows, even though the impetus for these changes came initially from the national Democratic Party, its effects were just as pronounced on the Republican side of the aisle. Presidential primaries, as I noted earlier, are creatures of state law; and in the vast majority of cases, the governors and state legislatures who decided to establish Democratic primaries applied the same provisions to the Republican Party. As a result, the number of Republican presidential primaries has grown just as rapidly as the number held by Democrats: from sixteen in 1968 to thirty-eight in 1992.

Advisory primaries.—Though a significant increase in primaries undoubtedly has occurred, that increase has been exaggerated in some tabulations of these data by failing to take note of the fact that some states were holding primaries that were only advisory while using caucuses for the actual task of selecting delegates. Such nonbinding primaries were especially common in the Democratic Party, which held three of them in 1988, four in 1992.

Caucuses.—For states not inclined to hold a primary, the only alternative permitted under the new Democratic rules was a caucus-convention system.[21] As I suggested earlier, however, such caucuses were quite different from those held under the old, prereform rules. In order to comply with the McGovern-Fraser guidelines—that is, in order to have their delegates certi-

fied as valid participants in the Democratic National Convention—all state
Democratic parties had to take their old, organization-dominated convention systems and completely rewrite their rules in order to comply with a

TABLE 4.3
STATE DELEGATE SELECTION PROCEDURES, 1972–92

	Republicans		Democrats	
	Number of states	Percentage of delegates	Number of states	Percentage of delegates
1972				
Primary	22	59	23	67
Caucus	29	41	28	33
1976				
Primary	28	70	29	77
Caucus with advisory primary	2	2	1	0.4
Caucus	21	28	21	23
1980				
Primary	33	76	30	71
Caucus with advisory primary	2	2	4	10
Caucus	16	22	17	19
1984				
Primary	28	67	24	54
Caucus with advisory primary	2	2	5	4
Caucus	21	31	22	28
Superdelegates	—	—	—	14
1988				
Primary	34	77	32	64
Caucus with advisory primary	3	4	3	1
Caucus	14	19	15	15
Mixed system[a]	—	—	1	4
Superdelegates	—	—	—	16
1992				
Primary	38	84	35	66
Caucus with advisory primary	1	1	4	4
Caucus	12	15	11	9
Mixed system[a]	—	—	1	5
Superdelegates	—	—	—	16

NOTE: All figures in this table include the District of Columbia but exclude territories such as
Puerto Rico and Guam.
a. In 1988 and 1992, the Texas Democratic Party selected about two-thirds of its base delegation by primary, the remainder by caucus.

lengthy new list of procedural requirements. In particular, after 1968, all Democratic caucuses had to

- Have "explicit, written rules"
- Make all meetings "open to all members of the Democratic Party regardless of race, color, creed, or national origin"
- "Forbid proxy voting"
- "Forbid the use of the unit rule"
- Ensure that party meetings were held "on uniform dates, at uniform times, and in public places of easy access"
- "Ensure adequate public notice" of all meetings
- "Adopt procedures which will provide for fair representation of minority viewpoints"
- "Conduct the entire process of delegate selection . . . within the calendar year of the Convention"[22]

And here, too, the Republican nomination process was significantly influenced by the Democratic initiatives. Though the national Republican Party has not seen fit to regulate its caucuses in quite the same detail as the Democrats, its national rules have, with little fanfare or attention from the media, changed substantially since 1968, incorporating many of the same procedural guarantees first promulgated by the Democrats.[23] The rules adopted at the 1992 Republican convention, for example,

- Ban automatic or ex-officio delegates
- Require advance public notice of all caucuses, meetings, and conventions
- Ban proxy voting at district and state conventions
- Ban discrimination for reasons of "sex, race, religion, color, age, or national origin"
- Require each Republican state committee to adopt explicit "rules, procedures, and policies" governing the selection of delegates[24]

The result in both parties, as we later see, was to transform what had once been a relatively closed, party-run delegate selection process into a considerably more public and plebiscitary system.

Superdelegates. — Another clear result of the new rules was to make it considerably more difficult for Democratic Party leaders—governors, senators, representatives, and national committee members—to become delegates.[25] According to many critics, this was an especially critical defect because it removed from the nomination process precisely those people who knew the candidates best and might therefore have been most capable of assessing their strengths and weaknesses. Hence, beginning in 1984, the Democratic Party created a new category of delegates, usually referred to as "superdelegates."

About one-sixth of the votes at the national convention were automatically set aside for Democratic governors, members of Congress, and members of the Democratic National Committee. Such delegates are selected completely outside the normal primary and caucus systems and are in no way bound by their results. (Nothing remotely similar exists in the Republican Party.)

The result of all this rewriting can be seen in table 4.3. Obviously, there has been a significant reduction in the use of caucus-convention methods for selecting national convention delegates. Especially since 1976, the nomination process in both parties clearly has been dominated by the institution of presidential primaries. Nevertheless, about a third of all states continued to rely on a caucus-convention system.

Participation and Democracy

As the preceding discussion should suggest, from the perspective of the typical Democratic or Republican voter, caucuses differ from primaries in at least three significant ways:

1. Caucuses are a more complicated procedure than presidential primaries, with a less direct link between a person's expression of a presidential preference and the final selection of national convention delegates.
2. Caucuses require a considerably more significant investment of time from those who participate in them. The seven caucuses I attended lasted, on average, about an hour and forty-five minutes. The shortest took forty-five minutes; the longest ran about three hours. (Indeed, the Democratic Party rules in several states actually *require* that caucuses last at least one hour.) Unfortunately, I know of no study that has measured how long it typically takes a person to vote; but based on observations at a small sample of Massachusetts precincts in 1992, I calculated that the average voter was able to leave the polling place about seven minutes after arriving there.
3. Caucuses require a more public revelation of a person's political beliefs than voting does. The basic act of voting is performed, of course, in the privacy of a polling booth; the only public aspect of it is that, in most states, one must request a ballot for either the Democratic or Republican primary, an act usually witnessed only by a couple of election judges and perhaps one or two poll watchers.

(Even this is not necessary in states that have open primaries.) A caucus, by contrast, requires one to show up at a meeting attended by fifty or a hundred of one's neighbors, an act that clearly marks one out as a supporter of one party or the other. And at most caucuses, people are further required to make some kind of public declaration as to which presidential candidate they support, either by raising their hands or moving to a particular part of the room. For political activists, none of these activities is likely to be especially disconcerting; most of them have had considerable past experience in affirming and advocating their convictions in public. But many Americans clearly regard their political beliefs, especially their choice of candidates, as a very private and personal matter and will therefore be more reticent about participating in a caucus.[26]

For one or all of these reasons, one clear difference between caucuses and primaries is that substantially fewer people participate in caucuses. Table 4.4 presents turnout data for the Democratic presidential caucuses and primaries held in 1988 and 1992. For reasons noted earlier, it is considerably more difficult to obtain reliable data about the numbers participating in Republican caucuses; but figures were available for about two-thirds of the 1988 GOP caucuses. These data, along with the Republican primary participation rates from that year, are shown in table 4.5.

The turnout rates presented here are calculated according to a method developed by Barbara Norrander, which uses a "normal vote" based estimate of the Democratic and Republican voting-age population in each state.[27] But the basic pattern is so clear and robust that it emerges in any reasonable treatment of the data.[28] Simply put, the level of participation in presidential caucuses is far, far lower than it is in presidential primaries. In the 1988 Democratic nomination race, for example, the average presidential primary attracted about 30 percent of a state's voting-age Democrats, but an average caucus had a turnout rate of about 3 percent. In general, in about 85 percent of the caucuses for which turnout data are available, the participation rate was 4 percent or less. In a few cases, it rises to 6 percent. Only in the exceptional circumstances of Iowa did more than 10 percent of the potential party electorate take part in a state's caucuses.

A particularly compelling demonstration of the gap between primary and caucus participation rates can be seen in the seven instances in table 4.4 where a state held both a caucus and an advisory primary. In all these cases, the primary had no formal relationship to the selection of national convention delegates; that task was performed entirely through the caucus process. Yet, in every single instance, *the nonbinding primary had a higher turnout than the binding caucuses,* often by a margin of eight or nine to one.

Turnout rates of the kind shown in tables 4.4 and 4.5 are not, however,

TABLE 4.4
PARTICIPATION RATES IN DEMOCRATIC PRIMARIES AND
CAUCUSES, 1988 AND 1992 (IN PERCENTAGES)

	1988		1992	
	Primary	*Caucus*	*Primary*	*Caucus*
Alabama	21		25	
Alaska		2		1
Arizona		4		3
Arkansas	43		44	
California	30		27	
Colorado		3	20	
Connecticut	19		14	
Delaware		2		1
District of Columbia	21		17	
Florida	24		21	
Georgia	19		14	
Hawaii		1		1
Idaho	(21)[a]	2	(20)[a]	1
Illinois	36		35	
Indiana	38		25	
Iowa		12		3
Kansas		1	20	
Kentucky	20		23	
Maine		2		3
Maryland	22		23	
Massachusetts	24		28	
Michigan		6	16	
Minnesota		6	(11)[a]	3
Mississippi	30		17	
Missouri	26			1
Montana	42		39	
Nevada		1		1
New Hampshire	42		58	

the only or necessarily the best standard for evaluating participation. If caucuses involve fewer people than primaries, it might be argued that caucuses also make possible a higher *quality* of participation: one that involves considerably more political and civic education; some interchange of views and opinions with one's fellow citizens; and, perhaps, some opportunity for bargaining, compromise, and persuasion.

My own observation of caucuses provided mixed support for this view. On the one hand, as I have already indicated, six of the seven caucuses I sat in on were preceded by speeches—sometimes by party leaders and local

TABLE 4.4 — CONTINUED

	1988		1992	
	Primary	*Caucus*	*Primary*	*Caucus*
New Jersey	25		15	
New Mexico	35		30	
New York	21		13	
North Carolina	23		25	
North Dakota	(2)[a]	1	(16)[a]	2
Ohio	33		24	
Oklahoma	32		33	
Oregon	40		34	
Pennsylvania	34		27	
Rhode Island	11		11	
South Carolina		3	8	
South Dakota	42		32	
Tennessee	31		16	
Texas	28	2	23	N.A.
Utah		3	—	
Vermont	(27)[a]	3		3
Virginia	15			N.A.
Washington		6	(7)[a]	3
West Virginia	40		37	
Wisconsin	57		42	
Wyoming		2		1
Average turnout[b]	30	3	25	2

NOTE: The numerator for each entry is the total number participating in that state's primary or caucus. The denominator is a normal vote-based estimate of the Democratic voting-age population. For further details, see note 27, p. 154. 1992 figures exclude Utah, whose delegate selection system was based on a party-run primary that is not comparable with primaries held in other states.

a. Figures in parentheses indicate that the primary was only advisory; delegates were actually selected via caucus.

b. Average primary turnout figure excludes advisory primaries.

elected officials, more often by representatives and supporters of the presidential candidates. In the 1992 South Portland Democratic caucuses, for example, participants heard five- to ten-minute speeches by U.S. Senate Majority Leader George Mitchell, Paul Tsongas's wife, Bob Kerrey's sister, Congressman Stephen Solarz (who was supporting Bill Clinton), and local supporters of Jerry Brown, Tom Harkin, Jesse Jackson, and Larry Agran. In a small town north of Portland that held its caucuses later that day, the proceedings began with about forty-five minutes of short speeches by the caucus participants themselves, who explained, often in very thoughtful and eloquent terms, why they were there and whom they supported.

TABLE 4.5
PARTICIPATION RATES IN REPUBLICAN PRIMARIES
AND CAUCUSES, 1988 (IN PERCENTAGES)

	Primary	Caucus		Primary	Caucus
Alabama	21		Nevada		1
Alaska		2	New Hampshire	31	
Arkansas	12		New Jersey	8	
California	22		New Mexico	18	
Colorado		1	North Carolina	14	
Connecticut	9		North Dakota	15	
District of Columbia	8		Ohio	22	
Florida	21		Oklahoma	21	
Georgia	30		Oregon	27	
Hawaii		2	Pennsylvania	19	
Idaho	16		Rhode Island	6	
Illinois	21		South Carolina	21	
Indiana	19		South Dakota	29	
Iowa		11	Tennessee	15	
Kansas		3	Texas	19	
Kentucky	11		Vermont	$(23)^a$	
Maryland	19		Virginia	$(11)^a$	
Massachusetts	15		Washington		1
Minnesota		4	West Virginia	28	
Mississippi	26		Wisconsin	21	
Missouri	23		Wyoming		0.4
Montana	$(32)^a$		Average turnout[b]	19	3

NOTE: The numerator for each entry is the total number participating in that state's primary or caucus. The denominator is a normal vote-based estimate of the Republican voting-age population. For further details, see note 27, p. 154.
a. Figures in parentheses indicate that the primary was only advisory; delegates were actually selected via caucus.
b. Average primary turnout figure excludes advisory primaries.

On the whole, however, it was my strong impression that most of the people who attended these caucuses showed up with a fairly clear idea of which candidate they intended to support (or that they were going to be counted as uncommitted) and that whatever education and discussion went on had little impact on their ultimate decisions. Probably the best single speech I observed at any caucus was given by a supporter of Gary Hart at a small 1988 caucus in central Maine. Speaking from carefully prepared notes, she presented a remarkably thorough and concise analysis of Hart's policy views and general approach to governing. But when the caucus participants broke down into candidate preference groups several minutes later, it became clear that she was the only Hart supporter in the room. At the 1988 Portland Democratic caucuses, each major candidate sent a representative to address the assembled participants. But the speeches were almost all general

in tone, clearly designed to rally the faithful more than to convert the unde-
cided. The audience, not surprisingly, reacted to them in the same spirit.
Various parts of the auditorium were clearly marked out, by signs and buttons, as places where the Jackson supporters or the Dukakis supporters were
sitting. Each such group gave polite applause to all speakers, but reserved
the loudest and most enthusiastic cheering for the representative of their
own candidate.

And once it was time for the caucus participants to register their candidate preferences and select delegates to the state conventions, the whole process seemed to be a fairly mechanical one of counting up votes and figuring
out delegate allocations. I saw conspicuously little evidence of any bargaining or coalition building of the kind that is sometimes said to be an important characteristic of a convention system.[29] At Democratic caucuses, as
soon as the speeches were finished, the precinct chair would ask people to go
to different parts of the room, depending on which candidate they supported. And if the number of supporters for one candidate (or the uncommitted) fell below the threshold, the chair would then advise them to join
another group. But I never observed such a group trying to bargain with one
of the larger candidate factions; the only attempt to "persuade" those who
had to make a second choice was that someone would occasionally say, in a
loud voice, "Come on and join us," or, "You're welcome over here." The
Republican caucuses I observed featured, if anything, even less of this activity. In one instance, the voting for delegates was done by secret ballot. In another case, a pro-Bush slate of delegates was proposed and then endorsed by
a simple show of hands.

Caucuses, in short, are a more engaging form of participation than voting, but they fall well short of the standard of deliberative or "strong" democracy envisioned by many modern political theorists.[30] Caucuses are less
an opportunity for citizens to "come and reason together" than an occasion
in which candidate enthusiasts come together to be counted.

Representation

The fact that fewer people participate in caucuses than in primaries will
hardly come as shocking news to anyone familiar with the basic mechanics
of the current nomination system. The more significant and controversial issue concerns the consequences of this difference. Are certain kinds of people
more likely to participate in caucuses than in primaries? And do these differences, in turn, mean that some candidates do better in one kind of delegate
selection procedure than in the other?

Over the past twenty years or so, two quite different answers have been
provided to such questions. On the one hand, caucuses have sometimes been
recommended as an antidote to primaries on the grounds that caucuses are

more likely to be controlled by state party leaders and thus give more weight to the views of party regulars and professionals. As Michael Malbin summarized this position a number of years ago:

> Most people active in presidential politics agree that the emphasis on primaries helps those candidates who are relying on a devoted following, frequently a minority, to run against a party organization or an incumbent. [George] McGovern in February 1972 said that Sen. Edmund S. Muskie of Maine would have the Democratic nomination sewn up if the choice was up to the party leaders. Similarly, the supporters of former Gov. Ronald Reagan and [George] Wallace feel that the proliferation of primaries is what gives their campaigns life.... "I have never met a Wallace supporter who ever has been to a party function," let alone a caucus, Wallace aide [Mickey] Griffin said. "They're literally afraid, they don't know what to expect, and they don't know parliamentary procedure."[31]

Much like the state committee and convention systems of the old, prereform nomination process, this view asserts, caucuses are a mechanism through which established party organizations can maintain at least some measure of influence over the selection of the presidential ticket.

But according to many observers, the Democratic nomination race of 1972, the first conducted under the new caucus rules, produced exactly the opposite result. The chief beneficiary of the caucuses in 1972, it has often been argued, was actually George McGovern, whose support among a small but zealous group of antiwar activists allowed him to gain considerably more delegates in many caucus states than he might have won in contested primaries. Witness this account from *Congressional Quarterly:*

> In 1972, well-organized cadres of McGovern supporters blitzed lightly attended caucuses across the country. They won large chunks of delegates in such unlikely places as Mississippi, Oklahoma and Virginia, states where the liberal South Dakota senator had little popular appeal.[32]

Far from helping party regulars, this second view asserts, caucuses are dominated by ideological zealots, who are likely to support extremist candidates who are out of sync with the mainstream electorate.

My effort to resolve this controversy begins with an assessment of the demographic characteristics of caucus participants, as set forth in tables 4.6 and 4.7. These tables have been compiled to permit comparison of four distinct groups within each major party: those who participated in the Iowa, Michigan, and Virginia caucuses in 1988; those who voted in a 1988 presidential primary; each party's voters in the 1988 general election; and all party identifiers.[33]

TABLE 4.6
SELECTED DEMOGRAPHIC TRAITS OF CAUCUS ATTENDERS,
PRIMARY AND GENERAL ELECTION VOTERS, AND
PARTY IDENTIFIERS: REPUBLICANS, 1988
(IN PERCENTAGES)

	Caucuses			Primary voters	General election voters[a]	All party identifiers[b]
	Iowa	Michigan	Virginia			
Education						
No high school degree	4	2	3	13	12	16
High school graduate	28	13	15	30	30	32
Some college	25	25	22	26	28	26
College graduate	25	29	33	23	23	19
Graduate school degree	18	31	27	8	7	6
Income						
Under $9,999	5	2	1	10	9	14
$10,000–$19,999	15	8	6	17	18	20
$20,000–$29,999	23	13	10	18	17	18
$30,000–$39,999	18	21	19	15	16	15
$40,000–$59,999	24	27	29	22	22	18
$60,000 or more	15	29	36	18	18	15
Gender						
Male	57	58	60	43	48	47
Female	43	42	40	57	52	53
Age						
17–29	2	7	6	8	15	23
30–39	10	14	6	20	24	24
40–49	15	21	14	19	18	16
50–64	40	41	45	26	23	19
65 and over	32	17	29	27	20	18
Smallest *N*	(379)	(343)	(311)	(214)	(586)	(766)

SOURCE: Data on caucus attenders come from a survey in the "Activists in the United States Presidential Nomination Process" studies and were graciously provided by Walter J. Stone of the University of Colorado. Data on primary voters, general election voters, and party identifiers are taken from the 1988 American National Election Study.
a. Includes only those who voted for George Bush in the 1988 general election.
b. Includes those who say they lean toward the Republican Party.

One might sum up the patterns in tables 4.6 and 4.7 in terms of three general propositions. First, as a number of recent studies have argued, the voters in presidential primaries are not very different from those who support that party's candidate in the general election.[34] Second, both primary and general election voters are, in a number of respects, not very representative of party identifiers as a whole. In particular, voters tend to be older, better educated, and wealthier than party identifiers.

TABLE 4.7
SELECTED DEMOGRAPHIC TRAITS OF CAUCUS ATTENDERS,
PRIMARY AND GENERAL ELECTION VOTERS, AND
PARTY IDENTIFIERS: DEMOCRATS, 1988
(IN PERCENTAGES)

	Caucuses		Primary voters	General election voters[a]	All party identifiers[b]
	Iowa	Michigan			
Education					
No high school degree	10	15	17	19	25
High school graduate	31	27	32	33	37
Some college	21	22	22	23	21
College graduate	18	16	17	15	11
Graduate school degree	20	21	11	10	7
Income					
Under $9,999	10	9	15	15	23
$10,000–$19,999	18	24	21	23	24
$20,000–$29,999	21	19	16	21	19
$30,000–$39,999	20	15	19	17	15
$40,000–$59,999	22	21	17	15	14
$60,000 or more	8	12	12	8	6
Gender					
Male	47	54	42	41	39
Female	53	46	58	59	61
Age					
17–29	4	7	14	15	20
30–39	16	13	24	24	24
40–49	17	16	22	20	17
50–64	33	33	20	21	20
65 and over	30	31	20	20	19
Smallest N	(580)	(387)	(344)	(514)	(872)

SOURCE: See table 4.6. Figures for Virginia Democrats are excluded because the party selected its delegates via primary in 1988.
a. Includes only those who voted for Michael Dukakis in the 1988 general election.
b. Includes those who say they lean toward the Democratic Party.

Third, and most important for our purposes, the data in tables 4.6 and 4.7 clearly establish the distinctly unrepresentative character of caucus participants—no matter which other group one uses as a standard of comparison. Education provides a particularly good example of the differences. Among all Republican identifiers in 1988, 25 percent either graduated from college or had a graduate school degree. The comparable figure for primary and general election voters was about 30 percent. Among Republican caucus attenders, however, between 40 and 60 percent were college graduates (the figure varies a bit between the three caucuses). For Democrats, those with at least a college degree made up about 18 percent of identifiers, 26 percent of voters, and about 38 percent of the caucus participants. In a similar way, those with a family income of less than $20,000 accounted for 47 percent of Democratic identifiers, about 37 percent of voters, and about 30 percent of those attending the Iowa and Michigan caucuses. Among Republicans, only about 15 percent of caucus attenders were between the ages of seventeen and thirty-nine—as compared to 28 percent of primary voters, 39 percent of general election voters, and 46 percent of party identifiers.[35]

Depending on one's perspective, these data may be either very disturbing or business as usual. Caucus participants are demographically different from the general public, but so is any small group of political activists and elites. (Caucus attenders are considerably more representative of the American adult population in this regard than members of Congress or presidential appointees are.) A few chronic malcontents such as Rousseau notwithstanding, most political and social philosophers have not seen this kind of discrepancy as a conclusive argument against representative democracy. The more important question is whether these activists or elites are capable of representing the interests and opinions of more ordinary citizens. In particular, those who defend caucuses as a way of increasing the role and power of the regular party organization almost certainly do not expect that caucuses will be demographically representative. Instead, their hope is that caucus participants, regardless of their demographic characteristics, will be more likely to take into account the long-run needs and interests of the party and, for this reason, ultimately do a better job of reflecting rank-and-file opinions and preferences than the more numerous but more casually interested primary voters.[36]

Beyond their demographic characteristics, then, what do the surveys tell us about the people who participate in presidential caucuses? Are they ideological activists or party regulars? According to the data in tables 4.8 and 4.9, the answer may well be: both. On the one hand, caucus participants in both parties do have a pronounced ideological tilt to them, far more so than primary voters or party identifiers. Liberals and even moderates were an extremely scarce commodity at the 1988 Republican caucuses: in all three instances, at least 83 percent of the caucusers described themselves as some variety of conservative (though only about 10 percent chose the label "extremely conservative"). Republican voters and identifiers are scarcely very liberal groups, but "only" about 65 to 70 percent of them say they are conservatives. Democratic caucuses are more ideologically diverse than those held by the Republicans, but their center of gravity is clearly on the liberal side. Overall, about 65 percent of the Democratic caucus attenders said they were liberals, as compared to about 40 percent of Democratic voters and party identifiers.

But caucus attenders are not simply ideological zealots who come out of

TABLE 4.8
IDEOLOGICAL AND PARTISAN COMMITMENTS OF CAUCUS
ATTENDERS, VOTERS, AND PARTY IDENTIFIERS:
REPUBLICANS, 1988 (IN PERCENTAGES)

	Caucuses			Primary voters	General election voters[a]	All party identi-fiers[b]
	Iowa	Michigan	Virginia			
Ideology						
Extremely liberal	0	0	0	0	0	1
Liberal	1	0	0	2	2	2
Slightly liberal	3	2	1	5	5	7
Moderate	13	11	6	22	26	25
Slightly conservative	24	30	15	26	28	28
Conservative	52	50	66	35	33	31
Extremely conservative	7	8	11	10	6	6
Party identification						
Strong Republican	67	77	73	48	35	
Weak Republican	27	13	15	25	24	
Independent Republican	4	10	8	18	20	
Pure Independent	1	0	1	4	8	
Independent Democrat	0	0	1	3	2	
Weak Democrat	0	0	1	1	9	
Strong Democrat	0	0	1	1	2	

	Caucuses:	Iowa	Michigan	Virginia
How long active in state party politics				
0–5 years		9	7	11
5–10 years		25	29	29
10–20 years		27	30	31
More than 20 years		39	34	30
Positions held, previously or currently				
Member of local party committee		61	73	77
Chairman of local party committee		24	24	18
Elected local government office		11	29	6
Elected state or national office		2	3	2
Appointed government office		8	20	17
Paid campaign staff		2	11	6
Delegate to state convention		41	87	66
Any of the above		76	93	86
Work for the party				
Year after year, regardless of the candidate or issues		58	69	61
Only when there is a particularly worthwhile candidate or issue		42	31	39

NOTE: Smallest N = Iowa (378), Michigan (359), Virginia (320), primary voters (194), general election voters (519), all party identifiers (649).
a. Includes only those who voted for George Bush in the 1988 general election.
b. Includes those who say they lean toward the Republican Party.

TABLE 4.9
IDEOLOGICAL AND PARTISAN COMMITMENTS OF CAUCUS
ATTENDERS, VOTERS, AND PARTY IDENTIFIERS:
DEMOCRATS, 1988 (IN PERCENTAGES)

	Caucuses		Primary voters	General election voters[a]	All party identifiers[b]
	Iowa	*Michigan*			
Ideology					
Extremely liberal	6	8	4	4	4
Liberal	35	42	12	15	14
Slightly liberal	22	19	19	21	20
Moderate	22	18	33	34	34
Slightly conservative	8	8	18	17	15
Conservative	6	5	12	7	10
Extremely conservative	1	1	2	2	2
Party identification					
Strong Democrat	56	54	41	40	
Weak Democrat	26	16	29	25	
Independent Democrat	13	23	16	21	
Pure Independent	2	4	4	5	
Independent Republican	2	2	4	4	
Weak Republican	0	1	4	5	
Strong Republican	0	0	1	1	

	Caucuses:	*Iowa*	*Michigan*
How long active in state party politics			
0–5 years		22	29
5–10 years		22	16
10–20 years		25	15
More than 20 years		32	40
Positions held, previously or currently			
Member of local party committee		32	20
Chairman of local party committee		10	4
Elected local government office		4	6
Elected state or national office		0	1
Appointed government office		2	6
Paid campaign staff		2	2
Delegate to state convention		18	10
Any of the above		42	27
Work for the party			
Year after year, regardless of the candidate or issues		42	42
Only when there is a particularly worthwhile candidate or issue		58	58

NOTE: Smallest N = Iowa (534), Michigan (339), primary voters (272), general election voters (416), all party identifiers (638).
a. Includes only those who voted for Michael Dukakis in the 1988 general election.
b. Includes those who say they lean toward the Democratic Party.

the woodwork to support a particular candidate or cause and then drop out of sight. As tables 4.8 and 4.9 indicate, large numbers of them have a clearly demonstrated, long-term commitment to their party. Most obviously, caucus participants do think of themselves as party members: only 2 to 3 percent of the people at the 1988 Democratic caucuses told pollsters that they were actually Republicans; independents accounted for, at most, another 4 percent of the caucus goers. But the caucusers' sense of attachment to their party goes well beyond this minimal level. Among Democrats, for example, about 55 percent of the caucus participants said they had been active in their state party for at least ten years; another 15 to 20 percent claimed to have been active for five to ten years. (Many of the newcomers, of course, are young people and those who have recently moved to the state.) In the Republican caucuses, about 90 percent had worked in the state party for at least five years.

Indeed, the Republican caucuses, at least in 1988, were dominated by members of the party organization. About 70 percent of the participants in all three caucuses said they were members of a local party committee; about 20 percent had chaired such a committee. Except in Iowa, two-thirds had been delegates to a previous state convention. On all these measures, it might be noted, Democratic caucus participants clearly stand out as being less firmly attached to their party than their Republican counterparts. If the ideological activist versus party regular split is still relevant to party nomination processes in the late twentieth century, the data in tables 4.8 and 4.9 suggest that it is a distinctly Democratic phenomenon. Yet even among Democrats, 30 to 40 percent of the caucusers had served in some kind of party or government position, and 42 percent said that they worked "for the party year after year, win or lose, whether or not [they] like the candidate or issues."

Delegate Selection Procedures and Convention Voting

To summarize the analysis in the last section, there is strong reason to believe that caucuses and primaries differ in the kinds of people who participate in them. But the more important issue, for both candidates and would-be party reformers, concerns the influence of these differences on the actual convention balloting. Is there a relationship between the kind of delegate selection procedure a state adopts and the sort of candidate it is likely to support at the Democratic or Republican national convention?

To see what such a relationship might look like, let us start by taking a look at the effects of delegate selection procedures in the years before 1972. In table 4.10, I have taken the first-ballot convention roll-call votes for seven contested nomination races held between 1952 and 1968, and calculated the

TABLE 4.10
MEAN VOTE PERCENTAGE FOR CANDIDATES
IN CONTESTED NOMINATION RACES
BY DELEGATE SELECTION METHOD,
1952–68

Candidate or position	Convention states	Primary states	Difference (convention – primary)	Difference, controlling for region and other factors
1952 Democratic				
Kefauver[a]	14	53	–39	–46**
Russell[a]	30	13	17	5
Stevenson[a]	25	9	16	31**
Harriman[a]	6	7	–1	4
Favorite son and other[a]	24	18	6	
1952 Republican				
Yes on seating of Louisiana delegation[b]	60	43	17	3
No on seating of Louisiana delegation[b]	40	57	–17	–3
Eisenhower	47	40	7	17
Taft	50	42	8	1
Favorite son and other	2	18	–16	
1956 Democratic				
Stevenson	65	87	–22	–15
Harriman	10	8	2	4
Favorite son and other	25	5	20	
1960 Democratic				
Kennedy	44	66	–22	–7
Johnson	39	8	31	21*
Stevenson	5	4	1	–2
Symington	6	5	1	–3
Favorite son and other	6	14	–8	

Continued ...

mean vote percentage that each major candidate received from primary and nonprimary states. The difference between these two figures, shown in the third column of table 4.10, indicates whether a particular candidate fared better in conventions or in primaries.

Before one spends too much time scrutinizing these results, I should immediately point out that such comparisons are, in some cases, misleading. During the 1950s and 1960s, the vast majority of presidential primaries were held in the Northeast and the Midwest; states in the South and the West were much more likely to use convention systems to select their

TABLE 4.10 — CONTINUED

Candidate or position	Convention states	Primary states	Difference (convention – primary)	Difference, controlling for region and other factors
1964 Republican				
Goldwater	75	63	12	−9
Scranton	12	27	−15	−2
Rockefeller	1	9	−8	−9
Favorite son and other	12	1	11	
1968 Democratic				
Humphrey	79	43	36	31**
McCarthy	13	36	−23	−24**
McGovern	4	11	−7	−1
Favorite son and other	3	9	−6	
1968 Republican				
Nixon	60	68	−8	−25*
Rockefeller	16	12	4	17*
Reagan	11	8	3	7
Favorite son and other	14	12	2	

* p < .05.
** p < .01.

NOTE: "Convention" and "primary" categories exclude those states that used "mixed" systems. For the number of states in each category, see table 4.2. For details on how the figures in column 4 were computed, see the appendix to this chapter.
a. Figures are for the first-ballot voting; Stevenson was ultimately nominated on the third ballot.
b. A "yes" vote supported the pro-Taft position on a credentials dispute; a "no" vote endorsed the pro-Eisenhower position.

national convention delegates. Hence, any candidate with a distinctively regional appeal—a candidate, for example, who was especially popular in the South—might appear to run unusually well (or poorly) in convention states for reasons that actually had nothing to do with the selection procedure being used. Accordingly, in the final column of table 4.10, I present a set of estimates that show how much better or worse each candidate did in convention states, after controlling for such variables as region, ideology, demographic composition, and the home states of the major candidates. (For details on how these estimates were computed, see the appendix to this chapter.)

Controlling for these other factors clearly does change the conclusions we might draw about a number of specific races, but it does not affect the overall pattern. For the clear lesson that emerges from this table is that, at least from 1952 to 1968, delegate selection procedures mattered—*they mat-*

tered a lot. Even though the presidential primaries of this era were sometimes designed to disguise as much as to reveal popular preferences, the
states within each category often threw their support behind different presidential candidates.

The divergence is particularly striking in a number of the Democratic
nomination races and corresponds closely to the standard historical accounts of those elections. In the 1952 Democratic contest, for example, Estes Kefauver demonstrated considerable support among primary voters (who
knew about him partly through a series of televised hearings he had conducted on organized crime) but had very little rapport with party leaders.
The result was that on the first convention ballot, Kefauver won 53 percent
of the votes from an average primary-state delegation, but averaged only 14
percent in convention states. After controlling for region and a number of
demographic variables, I estimate that Kefauver received 46 percent less support in convention states than in states that held primaries. Adlai Stevenson,
by contrast, became a reluctant aspirant for the 1952 Democratic nomination only after the convention itself was under way. His support, especially
after allowances are made for its regional character, came overwhelmingly
from convention states. A similar pattern clearly characterized the Democratic nomination race of 1968. Hubert Humphrey, who did not contest a
single presidential primary that year, not surprisingly drew disproportionate
support from convention states. Eugene McCarthy, in contrast, garnered
about one-third of the delegates selected in primary states, but only about
one-eighth of the delegates selected through conventions.

Both of these races involved a fairly clear contest between one candidate who was favored by the "regular" party organization and another who
tried to bypass the organization by entering the primaries. But the primary-
convention distinction could surface in other situations as well. In 1968,
Richard Nixon did have strong support among the Republican Party leadership, especially in the South. But his victory in that year's GOP convention
also owed much to the fact that he was the only Republican candidate who
made a serious effort in the presidential primaries. Overall, my estimate is
that Nixon ran about 25 percent better in primary states than in those that
held conventions. His principal opponents—Ronald Reagan and, especially,
Nelson Rockefeller—attracted much stronger backing from convention
states.[37]

Not every nomination race from this period can be characterized as a
showdown between primary states and states that held conventions. In the
1952 Republican nomination race, for example, *both* Robert Taft and
Dwight Eisenhower registered a number of impressive victories in the presidential primaries (Taft won six of them, Eisenhower five) and both had considerable support among party leaders (though from different regions of the
country). Since Taft was particularly popular among southern Republicans,

whose delegations were selected via state convention, Taft appeared to draw disproportionate support from convention states. After controlling for region, however, there was essentially no difference between primary and convention states in the way they voted on an early credentials dispute, which is probably the best single test of strength between the Taft and Eisenhower forces.[38] Still, the basic pattern is clear: In the "old" nomination process, delegate selection procedures frequently *did* matter. In four of the seven races shown here, at least one major candidate ran 20 percentage points better in one kind of selection system than in the other.

And what about the years after the McGovern-Fraser Commission? Table 4.11 presents the results of the contested nomination roll-call votes held between 1972 and 1992, once again broken down by delegate selection method. And again, in the fourth column of this table, I present a series of estimates showing the net advantage or disadvantage each candidate received in the caucus states, after controlling for region, ideology, the candidates' home states, and a number of demographic variables.

The nomination races of the "postreform" era present one additional complication. Where the nomination battles of 1952–68 were usually fought all the way down to the actual convention balloting, contemporary races frequently have a much shorter effective life span. While the primaries and caucuses themselves may feature a spirited, even bitter contest between a large number of presidential aspirants, most of the candidates soon drop out of the race, and one candidate finally accumulates enough pledged delegates so that he is declared the winner and certain nominee by all the major media organizations, weeks or even months before the convention opens. The result may be a misleading display of consensus and unity in the first-ballot voting, one that can obscure patterns and relationships that were quite important during the earlier stages of the race.

To overcome this problem, I have turned to two other sources of evidence. In some cases, such as the 1972 and 1980 Democratic conventions, it is possible to identify an earlier convention roll-call vote, usually on a procedural issue, that was widely seen as the decisive showdown between supporters and opponents of the leading candidate. For the Republican nomination contest of 1980 and the Democratic races of 1984 and 1988, I have used the state-by-state tabulations of delegate strength maintained by various media organizations, as they appeared on or shortly after the day when the eventual nominee finally reached the "magic number" needed to assure a first-ballot victory.[39]

No matter which set of figures one looks at in table 4.11, however, the interesting result is that in the postreform nomination races, the caucus versus primary distinction generally did *not* matter. There are a number of exceptions to this pattern, all of which are discussed shortly. But the exceptions should not be allowed to obscure the general finding. In the Demo-

TABLE 4.11
MEAN VOTE PERCENTAGE FOR CANDIDATES
IN CONTESTED NOMINATION RACES
BY DELEGATE SELECTION METHOD,
1972–92

Candidate or position	Caucus states	Primary states	Difference (caucus – primary)	Difference, controlling for region and other factors
1972 Democratic				
Yes on California resolution[a]	48	63	–15	–16*
No on California resolution[a]	52	37	15	16*
McGovern	47	60	–13	–12
H. Jackson	27	10	17	16*
Wallace	3	21	–18	–25**
1976 Democratic				
Carter	73	78	–5	–4
Udall	14	9	5	4
Brown	7	8	–1	0
1976 Republican				
Ford	46	56	–10	1
Reagan	54	44	10	–1
1980 Democratic				
Yes on binding delegates[b]	41	41	0	–1
No on binding delegates[b]	59	59	0	1
Carter	68	65	3	2
Kennedy	27	34	–7	–5
1980 Republican				
Reagan as of 26 May 1980	68	72	–4	–7
Bush as of 26 May 1980	14	20	–6	–4
Uncommitted as of 26 May 1980	16	3	13	13*
1984 Democratic				
Mondale as of 27 June 1984	49	49	0	8
Hart as of 27 June 1984	34	34	0	–10*

Continued ...

cratic nomination contests of 1976, 1980, and 1992, and the Republican races of 1976 and 1980, no major candidates did very much better in one delegate selection procedure than in another.

As I noted earlier, contemporary caucuses have been lionized and criticized for the advantages they supposedly confer on two quite different categories of nomination participants: the regular party organization and ideological activists. Of these two alleged biases, the claim that caucuses favor party regulars fares particularly poorly when evaluated against the results in

TABLE 4.11 — CONTINUED

Candidate or position	Caucus states	Primary states	Difference (caucus − primary)	Difference, controlling for region and other factors
J. Jackson as of 27 June 1984	7	11	−4	2
Uncommitted as of 27 June 1984	9	5	4	1
Mondale (actual balloting)	54	53	1	7
Hart (actual balloting)	34	33	1	−10*
J. Jackson (actual balloting)	9	13	−4	2
1988 Democratic				
Dukakis as of 8 June 1988	51	54	−3	−18**
J. Jackson as of 8 June 1988	28	25	3	12**
Gore as of 8 June 1988	5	10	−5	1
Uncommitted as of 8 June 1988	14	9	5	6
Dukakis (actual balloting)	65	72	−7	−16**
J. Jackson (actual balloting)	31	27	4	14**
1992 Democratic				
Clinton	79	84	−5	0
Brown	12	11	1	−2
Tsongas	5	3	2	0

* $p < .05$.
** $p < .01$.

NOTE: Primary includes only those states in table 4.3 that used primaries for delegate selection purposes. Caucus includes all states in the "caucus"and "caucus with advisory primary" categories. For details on how the figures in column 4 were computed, see the appendix to this chapter.
a. A "yes" vote was the position endorsed by George McGovern; a "no" vote supported the position of McGovern's principal opponents.
b. A "yes" vote was the position endorsed by Edward Kennedy; a "no" vote supported the position of Jimmy Carter.

table 4.11. If there is any candidate who ought to receive preferential treatment from the regular organization, it is an incumbent president. Yet, of the two recent incumbents who have faced serious opposition in their quests for renomination, neither Ford in 1976 nor Carter in 1980 ran significantly better in caucuses than in primaries.

Indeed, of all the candidates between 1976 and 1992 who might plausibly be dubbed "the candidate of the party regulars," only Walter Mondale in 1984 seems to have derived any perceptible advantage from the caucuses. Even here, the result is not very impressive. To begin with, Mondale's relative success in the 1984 caucuses may have had more to do with the assistance he received from a number of powerful interest groups, especially labor unions, women's groups, and teachers' organizations, than with his strong support among Democratic Party leaders and elected officials. Yet, even with the AFL-CIO, NOW, and the regular organization all solidly in his corner, Mondale's advantage in the caucus states was a remarkably narrow one (especially when compared with the experiences of Adlai Stevenson in 1952 and Hubert Humphrey in 1968). With region, ideology, and a number of other factors held constant, I estimate that Mondale ran about 7 percent better in caucus states than in those that held primaries, while Gary Hart gained an edge of about 10 percent in the primaries (only the latter figure is statistically significant).

The claim that caucuses favor ideological extremists fares somewhat better. In the 1988 Democratic nomination race, Jesse Jackson clearly did run much better—and Michael Dukakis much worse—in the presidential caucuses. The relationship is partially obscured by the fact that most caucuses that year were held in small, mostly white states that were not generally sympathetic to Jackson's candidacy. After controlling for such influences, my estimate is that Jackson derived an advantage of about 14 percent from the caucus procedure.

Another race in which the caucus versus primary distinction seems to have mattered was the Republican nomination contest of 1988, where television evangelist Pat Robertson's "invisible army" showed impressive strength in many caucuses but remained largely invisible in the GOP primaries. Unfortunately, the Republican race that year ended so soon after it had begun that it is impossible to obtain a state-by-state delegate tabulation that would permit a meaningful estimate of the major candidates' relative success rate in the caucuses and primaries.[40]

Instead, table 4.12 provides an analysis of a somewhat different performance measure: the percentage of primary votes or first-round caucus preferences that each candidate received during the *contested phase* of the 1988 Republican nomination race.[41] Since Republican rules do not require proportional representation of candidate preferences, there is no easy way to estimate how the percentages in table 4.12 would have translated into actual convention votes. But at least in terms of the preferences expressed by ordinary party voters and activists, the caucuses really were a significant boon to the Robertson campaign. With ideology and the religious composition of the states held constant, Robertson could generally count on getting 24 percent more support among caucus attenders than among primary voters. George Bush and Robert Dole, whose positions presumably gave them much closer ties to the regular party leadership, both ran substantially better in the primaries.

So there *is* evidence that presidential candidates with a special appeal to ideological activists and extremists can fare better in caucuses than in primaries. Yet, even here, the difference seems to have surfaced only in two exceptional cases, where the advantaged candidate managed to receive ample me-

TABLE 4.12
CANDIDATE SUPPORT AMONG PRIMARY VOTERS
AND FIRST-ROUND CAUCUS ATTENDERS
DURING THE CONTESTED PHASE OF THE 1988
REPUBLICAN NOMINATION RACE

Candidate	Average support in first-round caucuses	Average vote in primaries	Difference (caucus − primary)	Difference, controlling for ideology and demographic composition
Bush	23	53	−30	−19*
Dole	33	27	6	−13*
Robertson	30	12	18	24*
Uncommitted	4	1	3	4

NOTE: Results include all Republican primaries and all Republican caucuses for which first-round preference tallies are available, up through 29 March, the day Robert Dole formally withdrew from the nomination race. For details on how the figures in column 4 were computed, see the appendix to this chapter.

* p < .01.

dia attention even though he was well outside the party mainstream and generally did not possess the qualifications that parties and voters conventionally demand of their presidential candidates. All the other candidates in table 4.11 who might be characterized as having a special appeal to ideological activists—Morris Udall in 1976, Ronald Reagan in both 1976 and 1980, Jerry Brown in 1992, even Jesse Jackson in 1984—showed about the same level of success in the caucuses as in the primaries.

One final result in table 4.11 deserves a brief mention, if only to dispel one more myth about recent party reforms. Caucus systems, as we have seen, first became controversial during the Democratic nomination battle of 1972 for the advantages they supposedly conferred on the legions of antiwar activists who supported George McGovern. As the figures in table 4.11 make clear, however, McGovern actually won a larger share of the delegates in primary states than in those that held caucuses. McGovern did, it is true, fare better in *southern* caucuses than in southern primaries. But in the Northeast, the Midwest, and the West, just the opposite pattern occurred: McGovern's showing in primary states exceeded his success rate in the caucuses by at least 20 percentage points. All told, on the first (and only) ballot at the 1972 Democratic convention, McGovern averaged 60 percent of the votes in primary states versus 47 percent in caucus states. Almost the same pattern occurred in the vote, held two days earlier, on whether McGovern's victory in the California primary entitled him to all of that state's delegates.

How can we account for this exception? A closer look at the 1972 race suggests two general points. The first is that McGovern happened to do very well in a number of states that had winner-take-all or loophole primaries (most of which would later be banned or discouraged by national party rules) and thus won nearly all of their delegations. McGovern received more than 87 percent of the delegate votes in Massachusetts, Nebraska, Oregon, Rhode Island, California, and New York, even though he never won more than 53 percent of the presidential preference vote in any of these states.[42] Second, the McGovern campaign, perhaps because its candidate had chaired the Democratic reform commission, seems to have had a significantly greater understanding of the new primary rules and thus, in a number of states, won substantially more delegates than it might have against better-prepared opponents. In Pennsylvania, for example, McGovern came in third in the preference tally, getting 20 percent of the vote to George Wallace's 21 percent and Hubert Humphrey's 35 percent. But because McGovern fielded an entire slate of delegate candidates, while Wallace had only 4 such candidates pledged to him, McGovern won 37 of Pennsylvania's national convention delegates, while Wallace received exactly 2 delegates for his showing.[43]

Conclusion

The preceding discussion does not exhaust the list of dimensions on which one might profitably compare caucuses and primaries. Caucuses have also been defended on the grounds that they help strengthen state and local party organizations; that they are cheaper to campaign in; and that they permit a more intensive dialogue between candidates and ordinary party members. Some proponents also claim that caucuses are less influenced by the mass media; on the other side, there is evidence that governors and state legislatures are attracted to primaries precisely because they *do* bring more publicity and attention to a state.[44]

But the analysis in this chapter does cover the issues and distinctions usually regarded as most significant by both party reformers and academic students of the presidential selection process. To summarize the principal findings:

1. It is well established that considerably fewer people participate in caucuses than in primaries.
2. In return for the reduction in numbers, caucuses are probably a more involving and educational form of participation than primary voting, though they fall well short of the strong democratic ideals propounded by many political theorists.
3. Judged by their demographic traits, caucus attenders are substantially less representative than primary voters, whether one uses general election voters or party identifiers as the comparison group. Much as

one might predict from their low turnout rates and our more general knowledge about the structure of political participation in the United States, caucus attenders in both parties are considerably older, wealthier, and better educated than rank-and-file party members.

4. Those who participate in presidential caucuses also differ from ordinary party voters and identifiers in their ideological profile, with Republican caucusers being significantly more conservative and Democratic caucusers substantially more liberal. Yet most caucus attenders, especially in the Republican Party, also appear to have a strong, long-term commitment to their party and considerable previous experience in party affairs.

5. In most recent nomination races, the caucus versus primary distinction does not seem to have had a very significant influence on the final convention voting. Most presidential candidates have succeeded or failed at about the same rate in both kinds of selection systems.

6. In particular, there is little indication that caucuses confer a special advantage on party regulars or candidates with strong ties to the established party leadership.

7. There *is* evidence, however, that caucuses can be fertile territory for presidential candidates who are supported by a highly committed ideological or demographic faction, but lack a similar appeal to the average party voter. The two best recent examples of this phenomenon are Jesse Jackson and Pat Robertson, both of whom seem to have run significantly stronger in caucuses than in primaries.

Depending on one's preconceptions before reading this chapter, these findings may raise one (or both) of two further questions. On the one hand, some may wonder why caucuses have provided so little apparent benefit to party regulars and the established party leadership. Others, looking at the data in tables 4.8 and 4.9, may be surprised that candidates with a strongly ideological message have not derived a *greater* advantage from the caucuses.

As to the first question, there are two major reasons why party regulars have had such an undistinguished record in recent caucuses. First and most obvious, it reflects the significant changes in the nomination process worked by the party reforms of the early 1970s. As almost every introductory text in American government points out, one important consequence of the Democrats' decision to rewrite their delegate selection rules was a huge increase in the number of presidential primaries. Less often recognized is that the new Democratic rules—and the less substantial changes in the Republican by-laws—also transformed the nature of nonprimary selection procedures.

In the nomination system that existed up through 1968, the two principal methods for selecting national convention delegates also embodied distinct philosophies of party governance. Presidential primaries, even in the rather murky form they often assumed, represented a triumph of the Progressive ideology, which held that political parties were in some sense a public institution, whose choice of leaders and policies should be open to anyone who wanted to participate, whose internal operations could and should be regulated by government. Convention states, by contrast, operated as if parties were private associations, in which leaders and other members of long standing deserved a privileged place in their deliberations, which accepted the dictum of E.E. Schattschneider that "democracy is not to be found *in* the parties but *between* the parties."[45] And precisely because these two selection methods did express such different philosophies, they often, as we have seen, produced very different results. It was possible, under the old system, for a candidate to do quite well in the primaries yet acquire relatively few votes at the state conventions, or to rack up large delegate totals from convention states even though he had never entered a single primary.

If the disjunction between these two methods was simply one reflection of a perennial tension in American politics, as Austin Ranney has argued,[46] the McGovern-Fraser Commission was apparently plagued by no such ambivalence. For the Democratic Party reform movement of the late 1960s and early 1970s came down clearly, explicitly, and unequivocally on the side of public, open, and participatory parties. It is one of the major, unifying threads that runs through all of the commission's guidelines and recommendations. No longer did local caucuses and state conventions accord a privileged place to party insiders and the established party leadership. Instead, the regular organization became just one more group that could, if it wanted, try to mobilize its members to do battle against other interest and candidate groups for a proportionate share of the delegate slots.

Given their low turnout rates and complex rules, presidential caucuses are still the sort of arena in which a strong, disciplined party organization could do very well.[47] But, and this is the second major reason that caucuses have failed to help party regulars, such parties have become almost totally extinct in the United States. The traditional urban machines and rural county courthouse cliques have been declining steadily since at least the mid-1940s; and whatever was left of them was dealt a death blow by a series of Supreme Court decisions that essentially declared political patronage unconstitutional. The result, as chapter 3 shows particularly well, is that contemporary party activists are motivated overwhelmingly by considerations of policy and ideology. (Indeed, given the always uncertain character of solidary incentives and the almost complete absence of patronage, what else *besides* issues could motivate people to work for a political party?) To be sure, these new party/issue activists are more pragmatic and politically astute than the old amateurs and purists were generally portrayed to be. They recognize that their own views are not shared by all Americans and that nominating their ideal candidate is of little use if that person cannot win in the general election. Still, they scarcely seem like the sort of group that will ever march in lockstep behind some party leader, to be reliably delivered to whichever candidate that leader chooses to endorse.

If caucuses are unlikely to be a propitious venue for candidates with strong ties to the party leadership, there is good reason, as we have seen, to think that caucuses might provide an advantage to candidates supported by a small but intense ideological or demographic faction. Put another way, the decision about whether to use a caucus or a primary for selecting national convention delegates probably matters most when one candidate is especially good at mobilizing activists to attend the caucuses but lacks equivalent support among more ordinary, rank-and-file voters. According to the evidence presented in this chapter, however, not many candidates fit this description. Most candidates with a strongly ideological appeal will be capable of attracting support among *both* caucus attenders and primary voters (Ronald Reagan and Edward Kennedy are two good examples), or they will fail with both (witness Fred Harris in 1976, Philip Crane in 1980, Alan Cranston in 1984, and Patrick Buchanan in 1992).

More generally, when caucuses and primaries no longer embody distinct philosophies of party governance, when both selection systems are open to essentially anyone who wants to participate in them, the caucus versus primary distinction typically will *not* matter very much. That is, once you have already made a momentous and far-reaching decision as to what a party is and who its members are, the question of whether to use a caucus or a primary as a device for recording preferences is of distinctly secondary importance. Above all, it seems most unlikely that any attempt to cut back on the number of primaries and increase the use of the caucus system will help undo or moderate the "reforms" of the last several decades. To do that would require a considerably more radical restructuring of the basic ground rules under which state and local parties now operate. And while a few cranky academics might think this a good idea, there is very little support for it in the rest of the country.

APPENDIX

As noted in the main text, the states that decide to hold primaries or caucuses are not, in most years, randomly distributed around the country. During the 1950s and 1960s, the vast majority of presidential primaries were held in the Northeast and Midwest. In the years since 1972, caucuses have more often been held in the West and in states with smaller, less urban populations. Hence, to get a proper estimate of how each candidate was helped or hurt by a particular delegate selection procedure, it is necessary to control for other factors that might be correlated with both the candidate's vote and the selection system employed.

The general procedure used to produce the estimates in tables 4.10 and 4.11 was to calculate a regression equation in which the dependent variable was the percentage of each state's convention vote received by a particular candidate or position. (In table 4.12, as noted above, the dependent variable is the percentage of the primary vote won by each candidate in states that held primaries, the percentage of first-round caucus preferences for each candidate in caucus states.) The independent variables were somewhat different from equation to equation, but generally broke down into six categories: selection system used, region, ideology, the candidate's home state, the home states of other leading candidates, and other demographic variables.

Selection system. — For the nomination races from 1952 to 1968, two dummy variables were used, one for convention states (1 if yes, 0 if no) and one for the three states that used mixed selection systems (New York, Pennsylvania, and Illinois). The coefficient for the convention state variable thus represents the average difference between a candidate's vote in the convention states and his vote in the "pure" primary states, with all other influences held constant. It is the value of this coefficient that is reported in the fourth column of table 4.10, along with an indication of its statistical significance.

For most of the races of 1972–92, I used a single dummy variable, which assumed a value of 1 for all states that used caucuses to select their national convention delegates, 0 for primary states. An additional dummy variable was used to control for the mixed system in Texas in the Democratic nomination races of 1988 and 1992.

Region. — Separate dummy variables were used for the South, the West, and the Northeast. The South consisted of the eleven former Confederate states plus Kentucky. The West included Alaska, Arizona, California, Colorado, Hawaii, Idaho, Montana, Nevada, New Mexico, Oregon, Utah, Washington, and Wyoming. The Northeast was made up of Connecticut, Delaware, the District of Columbia, Maine, Maryland, Massachusetts, New

Hampshire, New Jersey, New York, Pennsylvania, Rhode Island, Vermont, and West Virginia.

Unfortunately, the abbreviated character of the 1988 Republican race made it impossible to control for region. By the time that race was effectively over (i.e., on the day Dole withdrew), only primaries had been held in the South and Northeast, and only caucuses in the West. To add in the region variables under these circumstances would both create a serious multicollinearity problem[48] and mean that any estimate of the caucus-primary difference would, in effect, simply be an estimate of what had occurred in the Midwest. Accordingly, the region variables were dropped from these equations and, as detailed below, a somewhat larger number of demographic variables were added in.

Ideology. — For the nomination races of 1960, 1964, and 1968, the ideological measure used was Rosenstone's New Deal Social Welfare Liberalism index. For the races of 1972–92, I have used the survey-based measure developed by Wright, Erikson, and McIver.[49] I was unable to locate a reliable ideological measure for 1952 and 1956, so no such variable was included for the candidate equations for these years. Instead, a larger number of demographic variables were added to the equations, in the hopes of controlling for the most significant variations in state economic and social structure. The results do not change appreciably, however, if one adds the Rosenstone values to the equations for these years.

Candidate's home state, — in the form of a dummy variable that had a value of 1 for the candidate's home state and 0 for all other states. As a result of preliminary analysis and the work of Barbara Norrander,[50] I included such variables only for candidates clearly identified with their home state who had run for statewide office at some time in the recent past. Candidates who did not meet these criteria were Dwight Eisenhower in 1952, Adlai Stevenson in 1960, Richard Nixon in 1968, Jesse Jackson in 1984 and 1988, and George Bush and Pat Robertson in 1988.

Home states of the other leading candidates, — with one dummy variable designating all such states. For the 1972 Democratic nomination race, the list included Terry Sanford of North Carolina.

Other demographic variables, — which were felt, on the basis of contemporary accounts and/or other published work, to have played a significant role in a particular candidacy or nomination race. These include:

- 1952 Democratic race, 1952 Republican race, 1956 Democratic race: percentage living in urban areas, percentage working in manufactur-

ing occupations, percentage foreign stock
- 1960 Democratic race: percentage Catholic
- 1972 Democratic race: percentage college educated
- 1976 and 1980 Democratic races: percentage Catholic, percentage Southern Baptist
- 1980 Republican race: percentage Episcopalian (as a measure of old-stock Yankee ethnicity and culture)
- 1984 Democratic race: percentage union members, percentage black
- 1988 Democratic race (actual vote): percentage black
- 1988 Democratic race (as of 8 June): percentage black, percentage Southern Baptist
- 1988 Republican race: percentage living on farms, percentage Catholic, percentage Southern Baptist

Acknowledgments

I would like to thank Amy Logan, Richard Boylan, Hemal Vaidya, James McCann, Walter Stone, Ronald Rapoport, Evans Witt, Barbara Norrander, Duane Oldfield, and Valerie Therrien for their generous help with this chapter.

Notes

1. The account of this caucus and all other caucus anecdotes presented in this chapter are based on my own observations of seven caucuses held in Maine and Vermont during the 1988 and 1992 presidential nomination races. In order to preserve the anonymity of the Democrats and Republicans who allowed me to observe their caucuses, I have not identified the specific precincts in which they were held and have, in this instance, changed the name of the town and restaurant.

2. See, among others, Wilson Carey McWilliams, "Parties as Civic Associations," in *Party Renewal in America: Theory and Practice,* ed. Gerald M. Pomper (New York: Praeger, 1980), 51–68; James MacGregor Burns, "Party Renewal: The Need for Intellectual Leadership," in ibid., 194–99; Michael Walzer, "Democracy vs. Elections," *New Republic,* 3 and 10 January 1981, 17–19; Thomas R. Marshall, "Delegate Selection in Nonprimary States: The Question of Representation," *National Civic Review* 65 (September 1976): 390–93; David E. Price, *Bringing Back the Parties* (Washington, D.C.: CQ Press, 1984), 205–13; Pope McCorkle and Joel L. Fleishman, "Political Parties and Presidential Nominations: The Intellectual Ironies of Reform and Change in the Mass Media Age," in *The Future of American Political Parties,* ed. Joel L. Fleishman (Englewood Cliffs, N.J.: Prentice Hall, 1982), 140–68; *Report of the Commission on Presidential Nomination* [the Hunt Commission] (Washington, D.C.: Democratic National Committee, 1982); and the comments of David Broder in John Charles Daly et al., *Choosing Presidential Candidates: How Good Is the New Way?* (Washington, D.C.: American Enterprise Institute, 1980), 14.

3. The phrase is quoted from Marshall, "Delegate Selection in Nonprimary States," 390.

4. My description of caucusing rules and procedures is based on four principal sources: (1) My own observations of seven caucuses, which were held in Maine and Vermont in 1988 and 1992. Five of the seven were Democratic caucuses; two were held by Republicans. (2) The delegate selection plans adopted by the sixteen states holding Democratic caucuses in 1992, all of which are on file with the Rules and Bylaws Committee of the Democratic National Committee. (3) Republican state party rules and caucus plans, which were provided by the Republican state committees in Alaska, Arizona, Delaware, Iowa, Missouri, Montana, Nevada, Utah, Virginia, and Wyoming. (4) The national party bylaws and delegate selection rules.

5. Table 4.1 includes every state that held a Democratic caucus in 1992 for delegate selection purposes. It excludes Utah, which was often classified as a caucus state in 1992 but actually had a process that more closely resembled a presidential primary. The Utah system began with what its own rules describe as a "firehouse primary" (a primary run entirely by the party organization). Precinct caucuses were then held a month and a half later, but all delegates selected at these caucuses (and at the later county and state conventions) were allocated according to the presidential preferences expressed earlier at the primary. For further details, see "The Utah Delegate Selection Plan for the 1992 Democratic National Convention."

6. This particular quotation is taken from the "Delegate Selection Rules for the 1992 Democratic National Convention," sec. 2A; but similar statements may be found in the rules and guidelines used in other years.

7. This was the phrasing used in the Commission on Party Structure and Delegate Selection, *Mandate for Reform* (Washington, D.C.: Democratic National Committee, 1970), Guideline B-6, p. 44. The same principle is enunciated in "Delegate Selection Rules for 1992," sec. 12.

8. Where the proportional representation rules for Democratic primaries have changed a lot over the years, and have often allowed states to elect delegates on a winner-take-all basis within congressional districts, party rules since 1974 have consistently required proportional representation for all caucuses.

9. In 1992, the Democratic national rules required a 15 percent threshold at congressional district and state conventions, but left state parties free to use a different threshold at other levels of the process. See "Delegate Selection Rules for 1992," sec. 12A.

10. Agran was a former mayor of Irvine, California, who ran a very long-shot campaign for the Democratic nomination in 1992.

11. See, in particular, Alan I. Abramowitz and Walter J. Stone, *Nomination Politics: Party Activists and Presidential Choice* (New York: Praeger, 1984); and Ronald B. Rapoport, Alan I. Abramowitz, and John McGlennon, eds., *The Life of the Parties: Activists in Presidential Politics* (Lexington: University Press of Kentucky, 1986).

12. See "The 1992 Rules of the Republican Party," Rule 32(c)4.

13. See, among others, James I. Lengle and Byron Shafer, "Primary Rules, Political Power, and Social Change," *American Political Science Review* 70 (March 1976): 25–40; Elaine Ciulla Kamarck, "Structure as Strategy: Presidential Nominating Politics in the Post-Reform Era," in *The Parties Respond*, ed. L. Sandy

Maisel (Boulder, Colo.: Westview Press, 1990), 160–86; and Martin P. Wattenberg, *The Rise of Candidate-Centered Politics: Presidential Elections of the 1980s* (Cambridge: Harvard University Press, 1991), chap. 3.

14. For further details about the rise of the Iowa caucuses and the Republican straw poll, see Hugh Winebrenner, *The Iowa Precinct Caucuses: The Making of a Media Event* (Ames: Iowa State University Press, 1987); and William G. Mayer, "The New Hampshire Primary: A Historical Overview," in *Media and Momentum: The New Hampshire Primary and Nomination Politics,* ed. Gary R. Orren and Nelson W. Polsby (Chatham, N.J.: Chatham House, 1987), 9–41.

15. This history of the presidential primary draws on James W. Davis, *Springboard to the White House* (New York: Crowell, 1967), 24–37.

16. Information about delegate selection procedures for 1952 and 1956 is drawn from Paul T. David, Ralph M. Goldman, and Richard C. Bain, *The Politics of National Party Conventions* (Washington, D.C.: Brookings Institution, 1960); Paul T. David, Malcolm Moos, and Ralph M. Goldman, *Presidential Nominating Politics in 1952,* 5 vols. (Baltimore: Johns Hopkins University Press, 1954); and Richard M. Scammon, "The Road to 1960," *American Government Annual, 1959–60* (1959), 23–43. Selection procedures for 1960 to 1968 are based on the coverage in *Congressional Quarterly Weekly Report,* especially the issues of 12 February 1960; 4 March 1960; 17 January 1964; 13 March 1964; 8 May 1964; 12 June 1964; 29 September 1967; 8 March 1968; and 22 March 1968. Additional information on the 1968 Democratic procedures can be found in Commission on Party Structure and Delegate Selection, *Mandate for Reform,* 56–63.

17. Also included in this category are three states—Maryland, Indiana, and Montana—that actually selected their delegates at state conventions; but these conventions were legally bound by the results of presidential preference primaries held earlier in the year.

18. For further details, see David, Goldman, and Bain, *Politics of National Party Conventions,* chap. 11. Also included in this category is the Texas Republican delegation of 1964. The Texas Republicans did hold a primary that year, but it had no legal impact and seems to have been designed principally to aid the state Republican ticket in the fall. The Texas delegates to the Republican National Convention were chosen at a state convention.

19. For a vivid description of some of the prereform practices in nonprimary states, see Kenneth A. Bode and Carol F. Casey, "Party Reform: Revisionism Revisited," in *Political Parties in the Eighties,* ed. Robert A. Goldwin (Washington, D.C.: American Enterprise Institute, 1980), 6–11.

20. Two especially good studies of the Democratic Party rules revisions are Byron E. Shafer, *Quiet Revolution: The Struggle for the Democratic Party and the Shaping of Post-Reform Politics* (New York: Russell Sage, 1983); and Nelson W. Polsby, *Consequences of Party Reform* (New York: Oxford University Press, 1983).

21. The McGovern-Fraser guidelines actually sanctioned three different methods for choosing delegates: primaries, caucuses (the commission actually calls them "conventions"), and committees created by the state parties. But having first said that it had "no authority to eliminate committee systems in their entirety," the commission then made it clear that such procedures were "undesirable" because they offered "fewer guarantees for a full and meaningful opportunity to participate," and required that no state choose more than 10 percent of its delegates by

committee. See *Mandate for Reform,* 47–48.

22. All phrases are quoted from the commission's final report, *Mandate for Reform.* But similar or identical provisions may be found in any edition of the Democratic delegate selection rules issued over the last twenty years.

23. Recent writings about the transformation of the presidential nomination process have almost always focused on changes initiated within the Democratic Party. Among the few studies that give sustained attention to the evolution of Republican national rules are Price, *Bringing Back the Parties,* 156–59; and John F. Bibby, "Party Renewal in the National Republican Party," in *Party Renewal in America: Theory and Practice,* ed. Gerald M. Pomper (New York: Praeger, 1980), 102–15.

24. See "The Rules of the Republican Party, 1992," especially rules 32–34.

25. For data on this point, see Howard L. Reiter, *Selecting the President: The Nomination Process in Transition* (Philadelphia: University of Pennsylvania Press, 1985), 65–71.

26. One of the more striking findings in Jane J. Mansbridge's excellent study of a Vermont town meeting is about the difficulties that many citizens have in dealing with political matters in a public setting. See Mansbridge, *Beyond Adversary Democracy* (New York: Basic Books, 1980), chap. 6.

27. The method is described and defended in Barbara Norrander, "Measuring Primary Turnout in Aggregate Analysis," *Political Behavior* 8 (1986): 356–73; and Barbara Norrander and Gregg W. Smith, "Type of Contest, Candidate Strategy, and Turnout in Presidential Primaries," *American Politics Quarterly* 13 (January 1985): 28–50. A variation on the same method is employed in Lawrence S. Rothenberg and Richard A. Brody, "Participation in Presidential Primaries," *Western Political Quarterly* 41 (June 1988): 253–71.

I have modified Norrander's procedure slightly by using a somewhat different set of election results for computing the normal partisan vote in each state. My results are based on an average of each party's percentage of the total vote in the last three presidential elections held prior to the primaries and caucuses; each party's percentage of the total vote in the last three gubernatorial elections; and each party's share of the seats in the lower house of the last three state legislatures. For the District of Columbia, I have substituted the party vote for mayor and delegate-at-large for the gubernatorial and state legislative figures, respectively. Both tables exclude Nebraska, which elects its state legislature on a nonpartisan basis, and Louisiana, which uses a runoff system for selecting its governor.

28. See Austin Ranney, *Participation in American Presidential Nominations, 1976* (Washington, D.C.: American Enterprise Institute, 1977).

29. On the distinction between bargaining and voting as the operative principles of conventions and primaries, respectively, see Henry E. Brady, "Conventions or Primaries?" Occasional Paper No. 85-9, Center for American Political Studies, Harvard University, 1985.

30. See, especially, Benjamin R. Barber, *Strong Democracy: Participatory Politics for a New Age* (Berkeley: University of California Press, 1984); and James S. Fishkin, *Democracy and Deliberation: New Directions for Democratic Reform* (New Haven: Yale University Press, 1991).

31. Michael J. Malbin, "Democratic Delegate Rules Influence Candidates' Strategies," *National Journal,* 6 December 1975, 1670. Others subscribing to this view include William Crotty and John S. Jackson III, *Presidential Primaries and*

Nominations (Washington, D.C.: CQ Press, 1985), 95–97; and Terry Sanford, *A Danger of Democracy: The Presidential Nomination Process* (Boulder, Colo.: Westview Press, 1981), 125.

32. *Congressional Quarterly Weekly Report,* 6 August 1983, 1613. Other sources who see caucuses as more likely to favor ideological activists include James W. Ceaser, *Presidential Selection: Theory and Development* (Princeton: Princeton University Press, 1979), chap. 6; Robert E. DiClerico and Eric M. Uslaner, *Few Are Chosen: Problems in Presidential Selection* (New York: McGraw-Hill, 1984), 27; and McCorkle and Fleishman, "Political Parties and Presidential Nominations."

33. These tables are not, I would concede, absolutely ideal for answering the set of questions I have posed. In particular, some may wonder about how representative the caucuses held in these three states were; and about how meaningful it is to compare caucus participants from three states with a primary electorate drawn from twenty or so other states or with a nationwide sample of party identifiers. My defense is simply that this is the best I could do given the data available.

In particular, outside the caucus surveys from the "Activists in the United States Presidential Nomination Process" studies, usable survey data on caucus attenders are essentially nonexistent. Given how low caucus turnouts usually are, and how few states hold them, a conventional national survey will usually include no more than about twenty or thirty respondents who claim to have attended a caucus. And while various news organizations often conduct exit polls of primary voters, they have never shown a similar interest in sampling the characteristics and opinions of caucus participants. Insofar as I can tell, the only caucus that has ever been the subject of a media exit poll is that in Iowa, which, as the data in tables 4.4 through 4.7 indicate, is probably not representative of the caucuses held in the rest of the country.

34. See, especially, Michael G. Hagen, "Voter Turnout in Primary Elections," in *The Iowa Caucuses and the Presidential Nominating Process,* ed. Peverill Squire (Boulder, Colo.: Westview Press, 1989), 51–87; John G. Geer, *Nominating Presidents: An Evaluation of Voters and Primaries* (Westport, Conn.: Greenwood Press, 1989), chap. 2; and Barbara Norrander, "Selective Participation: Presidential Primary Voters as a Subset of General Election Voters," *American Politics Quarterly* 14 (January 1986): 35–53.

35. Though they do not provide comparative data on primary voters, a similar portrait of caucus attenders in 1984 is provided in Walter J. Stone, Alan I. Abramowitz, and Ronald B. Rapoport, "How Representative are the Iowa Caucuses?" in *The Iowa Caucuses and the Presidential Nominating Process,* 19–49.

36. For a good statement of this position, see Penn Kemble and Josh Muravchik, "The New Politics and the Democrats," *Commentary,* December 1972, 78–84.

37. This should not be taken to mean that Rockefeller was a favorite of the regular Republicans. The point is that, aside from a few northeastern states, Rockefeller won essentially no primary delegates at all. By contrast, he did pick up at least small pockets of support from a number of convention states in the West and Midwest.

38. As a result of that vote and another held the next day, a substantial number of southern delegates, all of whom were selected at state conventions, were transferred from Taft to Eisenhower, which helps explain Eisenhower's advantage

in convention states on the presidential roll-call vote.

39. The tally for the 1980 Republican nomination race is taken from *Congressional Quarterly Weekly Report,* 31 May 1980, 1471; the 1984 Democratic count appears in *Congressional Quarterly Weekly Report,* 30 June 1984, 1570. For the 1988 Democratic contest, I have used the Associated Press tabulation, previously unpublished, which was graciously made available by Evans Witt of the AP's Washington bureau.

40. According to the *New York Times,* Bush clinched a first-ballot nomination victory on 26 April, about two and a half months after the Iowa caucuses (see *New York Times,* 27 April 1988, 1). But Jack Kemp had formally withdrawn from the race on 10 March, Dole on 29 March. Robertson announced that he was "no longer an active candidate" on 6 April but apparently did not shut down his campaign organization and did not formally withdraw from the race until 16 May (*New York Times,* 7 April 1988, D23; 12 May 1988, A32; and 17 May 1988, A23). From the perspective of this chapter, the problem is that since caucus systems are a multistage process, very few caucus delegates were actually selected until May. The on-going media delegate tabulations from March and April thus tend to understate Robertson's potential delegate take.

41. For reasons discussed in the preceding note, I have defined the "contested phase" of the 1988 race to include every Republican primary and caucus held up through 29 March, the day of Dole's withdrawal. Caucus and primary results are taken from *Congressional Quarterly Weekly Report,* 13 August 1988, 2254–55.

42. The New York primary did not have a presidential preference vote in 1972. McGovern's average primary vote in the other five states was 46 percent.

43. The same point is made in the Ripon Society and Clifford W. Brown, Jr., *The Jaws of Victory* (Boston: Little, Brown, 1973), 121–31. For an argument that McGovern's advantage in the 1972 primaries may have derived from a somewhat more sinister manipulation of the party rules, see Kemble and Muravchik, "The New Politics," 81–82. If either version of this theory is accurate, it would explain why this kind of caucus-primary difference appears only in 1972. Since this was the first nomination race held under the new rules, McGovern probably derived a significant advantage by being farther along the "learning curve" than his rivals. By 1976, with one election behind them, the candidates were more nearly equal in this respect.

44. On all these points, see the discussion in Roundtable 2 in John Foley, Dennis A. Britton, and Eugene B. Everett, Jr., eds., *Nominating a President: The Process and the Press* (New York: Praeger, 1980), 31–53.

45. E.E. Schattschneider, *Party Government* (New York: Farrar and Rinehart, 1942), 60 (emphasis in the original).

46. Austin Ranney, *Curing the Mischiefs of Faction: Party Reform in America* (Berkeley: University of California Press, 1975), esp. chaps. 3 and 5.

47. For anecdotal evidence on this point, see Joe Mathewson's account of what happened in 1972 when a group of Chicago liberals led by Jesse Jackson and Bill Singer tried to hold a series of open caucuses to choose a slate of delegates that would challenge the slate fielded by the Daley organization. In almost every instance, the regular organization heard about these caucuses in advance and showed up with so many members that the anti-Daley forces had to adjourn or abandon the meetings and choose their delegate slates in private, closed-door meetings—in total violation of the McGovern-Fraser guidelines. See Mathewson,

Up Against Daley (LaSalle, Ill.: Open Court, 1974), chap. 10.

48. The three region variables alone account for 67 percent of the variation in the selection system variable. In other years, the region variables typically account for only about 15 to 20 percent of the variation in type of selection system.

49. Average state values on the Rosenstone index for the 1960–80 time period are reported in Thomas M. Holbrook-Provow and Steven C. Poe, "Measuring State Political Ideology," *American Politics Quarterly* 15 (July 1987): 406. Both the methodology and the values for the survey-based measure are presented in Gerald C. Wright, Robert S. Erikson, and John P. McIver, "Measuring State Partisanship and Ideology with Survey Data," *Journal of Politics* 47 (May 1985): 469–89.

50. Barbara Norrander, "Nomination Choices: Caucus and Primary Outcomes, 1976–88," *American Journal of Political Science* 37 (May 1993): 343–64.

5

The Southern Super Tuesday: Southern Democrats Seeking Relief from Rising Republicanism

Charles D. Hadley and Harold W. Stanley

On 8 March 1988 and 10 March 1992 most southern Democrats converged on the polls for a one-day presidential primary in hopes of (1) increasing the influence of the South in the Democratic presidential nomination and shifting attention and influence from earlier events in Iowa and New Hampshire; (2) increasing voter turnout in the Democratic primaries and caucuses and bringing moderate voters back to the Democratic Party; and (3) increasing the likelihood of nominating a more centrist candidate than the likes of Walter Mondale, George McGovern, or Hubert Humphrey. The ideal was to find an electable Democrat, but if not that, at least a candidate southern Democrats could politically afford to be seen with in public.[1]

Did they succeed? This chapter, after describing the establishment of Super Tuesday, considers the ways in which Super Tuesday did and did not fulfill its founders' expectations. The founders' goals frame the analysis, but the discussion also incorporates the expectations and reactions of the critics and political opponents. It ends with a look toward Super Tuesday 1996.

The Establishment of a Southern Regional Primary

In 1976 Jimmy Carter's election to the presidency showed that a centrist could be nominated by the Democratic Party without the benefit of a southern primary. Carter's quest for renomination in 1980, however, carried the regional primary idea closer to realization. The Democratic National Committee's Commission on Presidential Nomination and Party Structure—the Winograd Commission—considered rule reforms for the 1980 nomination process. The Winograd Commission report criticized national and regional presidential primary proposals, arguing that a national primary would favor well-known and well-financed candidates. The commission also warned that "the most important objection to a national primary is that it would drastically change and possibly disrupt the institutional roles in the arena of national politics. . . . [A national primary] would probably spell the end of the national party system as we know it." The Winograd Commission rejected the notion that holding national or regional primaries would save presidential candidates time, energy, and money or increase voter turnout.[2] The Winograd Commission concluded that "even if the length, expense, and wear on candidates is seen to be a problem, there is no guarantee that national or regional primary proposals would yield better results."[3] The then-current nomination system enjoyed a relative advantage: "While some think that the current hodgepodge system turns off and confuses the voters, others point out that an advantage of the present primary system is that it allows many voters to look at the candidates over time and in many different contexts. The exposure to a 'constant barrage of information, speculation and evaluation' . . . is seen by many as a positive feature of the present system in that it educates the public."[4]

With a possible challenge to President Carter's renomination from Senator Edward M. Kennedy (D-Mass.), aides and supporters of the two candidates worked within the Winograd Commission to have the rules serve each candidate's interests.[5] The delegate selection period, the "window," was shortened from six to three months, and various rules were modified by the commission. The shortened window did not prevent any state from changing a primary or caucus date as long as the date remained within the three-month period.

Carter supporters, seeking a sizable southern setting to allow Carter to win immediately after an expected Kennedy victory in New Hampshire, persuaded several southern party leaders to establish uniform delegate selection dates for their states. Thus, a southeastern regional primary first took place on 11 March 1980, when Alabama, Georgia, and Florida held primaries at the opening of the window.[6] While this small-scale regional primary ultimately aided President Carter's renomination, an additional justification was that it drew attention to the region. Carter later claimed that a southern regional primary, especially a larger one like the 1988 version, "will not hurt the South; it will focus a great deal of attention on the region." He went on to note that a southern primary would improve campaign efficiency because television markets cross state borders. More attention to the South might also pay off politically for the Democrats because the arithmetic of the Electoral College makes it very difficult for a Democratic presidential candidate to win in November without southern electoral votes.[7]

For 1984, the second Tuesday in March through the second Tuesday in June was left open as a window by the Democratic National Committee's Commission on Presidential Nomination—the Hunt Commission—though concern was expressed about "front-loading," namely, the movement to select delegates toward the opening of the window. The Hunt Commission thought that front-loading threatened "the pacing and responsiveness of the process." Undue influence went to primaries or caucuses in such early states as Iowa and New Hampshire, which, by special dispensation, preceded the opening of the window. Moreover, well-known candidates could prematurely "lock up" the nomination. The Hunt Commission reacted to this problem and the recently reduced convention presence of Democratic elected officials by creating a large bloc of delegates—dubbed Superdelegates—composed of party and elected officials formally uncommitted to any candidate (Rule 8). The commission urged the "national and state party leadership to keep the front-loading problem uppermost in their minds as they schedule primaries and caucuses for 1984 and to do all within their power to maintain an even spread of events through the entire delegate season."[8] This caution aside, for 1984 five nonsouthern states joined Alabama, Florida, and Georgia at the opening of the window in what the news media dubbed "Super Tuesday." Other groups of state primaries clustered around 8 May and 5 June, but not around distinct regional divisions.[9]

Southern Super Tuesday Realized

The Southern Governors' Association had an interest in a southern regional primary, but the successful push in 1988 to establish the primary came from the Southern Legislative Conference, especially its chair, Texas State Senator John Traeger.[10] In September 1982 the organization had adopted a resolution urging member states to establish a southern regional primary for 1984. Given state legislative timetables, however, there was insufficient time to bring the proposal to fruition. The Southern Legislative Conference renewed the effort to establish a regional primary at its September 1985 Executive Committee meeting when it created a Regional Primary/Caucus Task Force, with each member state represented by one member each from of its senate and house. On 31 October 1985, the task force adopted a recommendation that member states hold presidential primaries on the second Tuesday of March or presidential caucuses on the following Saturday. At the meeting, Jay E. Hakes, an aide to Bob Graham, noted that "Governor Graham of Florida [chair of the Southern Governors' Association] had discussed the regional primary with each of the southern governors . . . 'and none are publicly opposed.' " It also was reported that the region's secretaries of state "could be counted on to assist in the implementation of a common primary or caucus date in their states." Subsequently, the Executive Committee of the Southern Legislative Conference received and endorsed the task force recommendation on 4 December 1985.[11]

The driving force behind the southern regional primary was the 1984 rout of the Democratic Mondale-Ferraro ticket in the region and in the nation at the hands of Ronald Reagan. One anonymous southerner dubbed it "the Fritz Mondale Memorial Southern Regional Super Tuesday."[12] The liberal Democratic nominees in 1984 were perceived to be out of step with the South's more moderate political proclivities.[13] Speaking of the national Democratic Party and the need for a southern regional primary, Traeger noted: "We think our voice is not being heard."[14] Dick Lodge, the Democratic state chair in Tennessee, resorted to metaphor: "When your dog bites you four or five times, it's time to get a new dog. We've been bitten and it's time for the South to get a new dog."[15] The reformers' rhetoric frequently recalled secession. Senator Traeger: "We're getting more cooperation on this regional primary than in any movement since the Confederacy. More even, because we've picked up some border states."[16] "If we'd got this much action in the Civil War, we'd have won it."[17] State Senator Bill Harpole of Mississippi said: "You can go back home and gather up your Confederate money, 'cause the South is going to rise again!"[18] Mississippi State Representative Charlie Capps declared: "We're excited that we can have more impact on presidential and vice-presidential nominations than any time since the War of Northern Aggression. Our Confederate money is about to become worth a whole lot more."[19]

With about one-third of the total Democratic National Convention delegates at stake in the South and border states in 1988, reformers expected the southern regional primary to diminish the kingmaker role of Iowa and New Hampshire. Rather than hang back in the nomination process—waiting to choose among the surviving candidates after more favorable ones had fallen by the wayside—advocates sought an early date to allow selection from a broader field. As then governor of Texas Mark White complained, "Many candidates who would have done well in Texas were already out. We are tired of getting leftovers."[20] The early date had added appeal because early results influence later ones. But early did not mean earliest. Dislodging New Hampshire or Iowa from the start of the nomination process was deemed impossible, although desirable in the eyes of some. As Robert Slagle, the Texas Democratic Party chair, put it, "Texas is damn tired of Iowa and New Hampshire exercising a disproportionate impact on the outcome."[21] Southerners had agreed on a resolution calling on the Democratic National Committee to make the Iowa caucus and New Hampshire primary go within the "window" rather than before it.[22] Simultaneous scheduling of a southern regional primary with New Hampshire and Iowa would have altered the nomination calendar dramatically, as well as the implications of the southern primary.

Southern regional primary advocates sought to maximize southern clout in the Democratic presidential nomination, not for its own sake, but to facilitate the selection of a Democratic presidential nominee palatable to moderate and conservative southern voters—at best a nominee capable of retaking the White House for the Democrats, at least a nominee comfortable for southern Democrats to be associated with in the general election campaign. The nominee need not be a southerner but, in the eyes of the regional primary reformers, if a southern primary were to favor a suitable southerner, so much the better.[23] By coordinating the dates for the region's caucuses and primaries, the reformers hoped to make candidates campaign longer in the South, making them address regional concerns such as textiles, farming, and energy to a greater extent than they would have otherwise. Moreover, the campaign coverage for weeks before the primary date was expected to produce extensive free publicity for the region (presumably a blessing).

The southern regional primary idea, as David Broder put it, "spread like kudzu."[24] Given the institutional barriers that stopped previous attempts to set up regional primaries, achieving the unity and coordination required to enact the southern regional primary was a major accomplishment. With the national Democratic Party closely monitoring the progress of the southern primary, the Southern Legislative Conference systematically shepherded the 8 March 1988 primary date and 12 March 1988 caucus date through the legislatures of member states. Task force members prefiled the necessary legislation and guided it through both houses to their governors for signature. In each instance, the Southern Legislative Conference issued press releases with appropriate quotations from state legislators, heralded the primary's enactment by yet another member state, and summed up the progress to date. In short, the southern regional primary was kept in the public eye so as to maintain momentum. On 26 March 1987, Virginia became the fifteenth of the Southern Legislative Conference's sixteen members to fix its primary date for 8 March.[25]

Although southern state Democrats built Super Tuesday, many southern Republican leaders, including Haley Barbour, then chair of the Southern Republican Exchange, saw Super Tuesday as a golden opportunity for the GOP in 1988. Their expectations ran high that Democrats had given southern Republicans a superb opening for party growth. Republicans were confident that the Democrats had erred in establishing Super Tuesday and planned to make the event a referendum on conservative versus liberal values. The Republicans portrayed Democratic presidential candidates as liberals, painted their candidates as conservatives, and encouraged comparative partisan shopping. In the words of President Reagan in 1988:

"Super Tuesday" presents our party with a tremendous opportunity—to convince those who share our values to vote for the Republican candidate of their choice in the Republican primary. Now, in my humble opinion, it shouldn't be too hard.... Any one of our Republican candidates stands head and shoulders above those running in the other party. And Republican candidates all agree with the people of the South.... Yes, the values of Southern voters are best represented by our Republican candidates for President.[26]

Republicans had other goals, such as increasing turnout in Republican presidential primaries. Greater Republican turnout, it was hoped, would draw centrist whites away from the Democrats, leaving the Democratic primary voters (and thus the favored candidates) all the more left-of-center.[27]

Critics of Super Tuesday flourished. They contended that a southern regional primary was politically naive. Why? First, it would serve as an echo chamber for Iowa and New Hampshire rather than a launching pad for a mainstream candidate. Second, Republicans, not Democrats, might benefit more from the South focusing on presidential politics. And third, moderates attracted to the Republican primaries would leave the Democratic primaries even more under the sway of left-of-center influences.[28]

Critics proved more right than wrong about 1988, as evidenced by several southern states subsequently jumping off the Super Tuesday bandwagon. In 1992 Super Tuesday was scaled back—only seven southern and border states participated: Florida, Louisiana, Mississippi, Oklahoma, South Carolina, Tennessee, and Texas. Some commentators contended that in 1992 Super Tuesday did what its Democratic creators had intended—aid the nomination of a moderate Democrat (Bill Clinton) who could win back the White House. Such a conclusion outstrips the facts, as this discussion shows.

Super Tuesday was a Democratic device designed in part to counter the drift of the South toward the Republican Party. Yet the 1994 midterm election results emphasize just how far the South has drifted toward the Republicans, both in Congress and in the statehouses. Republicans gained a majority of House seats (64 Republican to 61 Democratic) and Senate seats (12 to 10) in the region. By contrast, after the 1964 election, Republicans had held only 2 of the 22 southern Senate seats and 16 of the 106 southern House seats. Republicans also won 4 governorships, giving them a 7–4 advantage in the states of the former Confederacy. Republicans picked up 28 state senate seats and 70 state house seats in the seven southern states holding elections in 1994, enabling them to gain control of three legislative chambers (the Florida Senate, North Carolina House, and South Carolina House).[29] Continued Republican advances raise strong doubts about the political efficacy of Super Tuesday in halting movement in the South toward the Republicans.[30] Direct consideration of Super Tuesday results raises even stronger doubts.

Super Tuesday Results

Reforms often bring unanticipated consequences.[31] When southern state Democrats enacted Super Tuesday, hoping it would settle the presidential nomination, they did not intend to help the Republicans rally around George Bush. Yet, Republicans did rally to Bush in both 1988 and 1992. In 1988 the Democrats were left divided: Michael Dukakis, Al Gore, and Jesse Jackson gained almost equal shares of delegates and votes. The Democratic muddle contrasted vividly with the Republican clarity.

In 1988 the Bush sweep—sixteen out of seventeen Republican contests went his way on 8 March[32]—and winner-take-all rules gave Bush enough delegates to make the Republican nomination all but inevitable. Prior to Super Tuesday, Bush and Dole had secured the support of equal shares of national convention delegates (table 5.1). After Super Tuesday, Bush had the backing of 74 percent of the delegates selected, while Dole had only 17 percent. Not only was the nomination nearly settled, but Pat Robertson's candidacy, potentially divisive for the Republican Party, essentially was laid to rest. The poor Robertson showing on 5 March in South Carolina, a state he had targeted for a showdown with Bush, was followed by weak showings throughout the South.[33]

On the Democratic side in 1988, three candidates could claim victory. Gore's southern strategy paid off in that he carried five states. Jackson combined solid support among blacks with enough white votes to place first in five states. Dukakis finished first in Florida and Texas, the two largest southern states, and he carried Massachusetts, Maryland, and Rhode Island to yield five primary wins. Prior to Super Tuesday, Dukakis had led Richard Gephardt 14 to 10 in percentage of delegates secured (table 5.1). After Super Tuesday, Dukakis led with a larger percentage (28), but Jackson had surged (24 percent), as had Gore (21 percent).[34]

Winnowing also took place. Gephardt carried his home state of Missouri, but doing this and nothing more doomed him. Super Tuesday occurred before some candidates dropped out, but it would be an overstatement to say that Super Tuesday eliminated them. Gary Hart was finished after New Hampshire (if not before), but remained in the race and quit on 11 March. Jack Kemp was doomed after his poor showing in South Carolina before Super Tuesday, but postponed withdrawing until 10 March.

In 1992 the candidate field and expectations differed. The election calendar for the 1992 nomination process appeared to favor Democrats Tom Harkin from Iowa, Paul Tsongas from Massachusetts (across the border from New Hampshire), and southerner Bill Clinton. Harkin's home-state advantage devalued the Democratic caucuses in Iowa. No other candidate except Jerry Brown even visited the state, necessitating treks to New Hampshire by the *Des Moines Register*'s famed David Yepsen in search of presidential campaign news to report. Ultimately, Harkin received 76.5 percent

TABLE 5.1
DELEGATE SUPPORT BEFORE AND AFTER
SUPER TUESDAY, 1988 AND 1992

	1988			1992	
Candidate	1 March	9 March	Candidate	4 March	11 March
Dukakis	14.2%	27.8%	Clinton	29.6%	49.6%
Gephardt	10.4	8.7	Tsongas	16.4	24.3
Gore	3.8	21.2	Brown	5.3	5.7
Jackson	6.2	24.2	Harkin	11.9	—*a*
Others and un-			Others and un-		
committed	65.4	18.1	committed	36.7	20.3
(Delegates			(Delegates		
selected)*b*	(451)	(1,638)	selected)*b*	(668.5)	(1,424.75)
Bush	35.1	73.5	Bush	85.5	91.5
Dole	34.5	17.0	Buchanan	11.6	7.5
Kemp	20.1	4.1	Others and un-		
Others and un-			committed	2.9	1.0
committed	10.4	5.4			
(Delegates			(Delegates		
selected)*b*	(174)	(959)	selected)*b*	(173)	(403)

SOURCES: Calculated from Associated Press tallies as reported in *National Journal,* 5 March 1988, 616, and 12 March 1988, 692; *Congressional Quarterly Weekly Report,* 7 March 1992, 562, and 14 March 1992, 632.

NOTE: Candidate delegate support percentages are based on delegates selected through the date indicated.

a. Withdrew from the race 5 March.

b. Includes "superdelegates" and projected caucus results, as well as delegates allocated by primary election voting.

of the "delegate equivalents," but few Iowans bothered to participate—an estimated 30,000 in contrast to 125,000 in 1988. (Perhaps because the Iowa Republican establishment was so solidly behind President Bush, Buchanan and Duke also chose not to participate.)[35]

In economically depressed New Hampshire, the Democratic front-runner Clinton survived the marital infidelity and draft evasion explosions that surfaced two and a half weeks before the Iowa caucuses. This gave some credibility to Clinton's claim to be the "Comeback Kid," as he garnered 25 percent of the vote in a record voter turnout and a second-place finish to New Hampshire neighbor Tsongas (33 percent). Tsongas had invested substantial campaign time, rather than dollars, to duplicate former Massachusetts governor Michael S. Dukakis's 1988 victory. By one count, Tsongas spent nearly twice as many campaign days there as did Clinton (70 versus 43). Interestingly, House of Representatives Speaker Tom Foley publicly dismissed the Tsongas victory and declared Clinton the winner.[36] On the Republican side, Pat Buchanan, endorsed by the conservative *Manchester Union Leader,* seriously wounded President George Bush. Bush received 53 percent of the vote to Buchanan's 37 percent, in large measure due to an ailing economy and Bush having broken his "Read my lips. No new taxes" pledge.

With primaries coming up in Georgia, Maryland, and Colorado (3 March), South Carolina (7 March), and Super Tuesday (10 March), the election calendar now favored regional native son and political centrist Clinton. In Georgia and Maryland voters were free to participate in the primaries of their choice, while Colorado voters were restricted to their party of registration with independents free to choose between them. On 3 March the three primary contests produced three winners. Colorado was a near three-way tie among Brown (29 percent), Clinton (27 percent), and Tsongas (26 percent). Maryland proved to be a two-way contest between Tsongas with 41 percent and Clinton with 34 percent, the other candidates each gaining only single-digit support. Georgia, on the other hand, was a Clinton rout of Tsongas by 57 to 24 percent, the next closest competitor being Brown with but 8 percent. The clear loser was Bob Kerrey, who folded his tent two days later, withdrawing from the race on 5 March.[37] Clinton widened his victory margin in South Carolina on 7 March, garnering 63 percent to 19 percent for Tsongas. Harkin had not fared well. His endorsement by fifteen labor unions with 7.7 million members had not translated to his benefit given their predominant location in the "rust belt" states holding later primaries. Harkin ended his campaign on 9 March.[38]

Only Tsongas and Brown remained to challenge Clinton for the nomination. On Super Tuesday, Clinton registered impressive victories in the southern states, victories ranging from 52 percent in Florida, where Tsongas was banking on a win but took only 34 percent of the vote, to 65 percent in Texas (versus Tsongas's 19 percent), to a high of 73 percent in Mississippi with the remaining challengers in single digits. Expectedly, Massachusetts and Rhode Island belonged to Tsongas, who trounced Clinton and Brown by 67 percent to 11 and 21 percent in Massachusetts and by 53 percent to 21 and 19 percent in Rhode Island. With the Super Tuesday votes aggregated, Clinton was the clear winner with 54 percent, followed by Tsongas (28 percent), and distantly by Brown (11 percent).[39] The designers of Super Tuesday had hoped to rally the southern states behind a moderate Democrat who could win the presidency in 1988. What they failed to accomplish in 1988 did not elude them in 1992.

Bush solidified his hold on the Republican nomination with Super Tuesday. Having voluntarily yielded to Buchanan the role of major challenger to Bush and having been kept off the Republican ballot by many determined state Republican parties, David Duke was about as invisible as his former

Invisible Empire. Unable to raise campaign funds to qualify for public funding, let alone sustain even a regionwide campaign organization, Duke mostly remained in single digits on Super Tuesday, even in his home state of Louisiana (9 percent). Only in Mississippi did Duke amass 11 percent. Pat Buchanan had assumed the role of legitimate conservative opposition or "thorn," consistently pulling about 25 to 30 percent of the vote away from President Bush. The president, on the other hand, continued to gain disproportionate shares of delegates in "winner-take-all" contests. In stark contrast to Super Tuesday 1988, after which Bush had the Republican nomination virtually sewn up with 73 percent of the delegates needed for nomination, he had only a third of the delegates needed for 1992, a result due more to a changed election calendar than to southern disunity.[40]

Super Tuesday and Southern Influence in the Democratic Presidential Nomination Process

There are several reasons to doubt that Super Tuesday has magnified the influence of the South in the presidential nomination process. Political influence turns in part on numbers. Scheduling southern delegate selections for the same day called attention to the substantial southern share of convention delegates. But influence through numbers depends on the degree of unity. Southern Democrats divided their votes among three candidates in 1988, results that attest to their political diversity. Expectations of political unity were met more in 1992, but Clinton's commanding lead turned partially on Jackson's noncandidacy. Had Jackson run and captured the black vote in 1992, as he did in 1988, southern unity behind Clinton would have lessened considerably. Southern clout was most evident in the 1988 Republican contest when Super Tuesday did for the Republicans what some had hoped it would do for the Democrats, namely, winnow the field and solidify the party behind one candidate.

For Democrats, even the larger 1988 Super Tuesday did not deliver what its creators had hoped. The size of Super Tuesday 1988 fuzzed its focus. Democratic candidates did not compete seriously in all the Super Tuesday states. Sensibly, candidates husbanded their resources and targeted presumably responsive states. "They were forced to pitch their campaigns to geographical, racial, cultural, and ideological slices of the electorate rather than appeal to the whole—exactly the opposite of what the southern leaders had planned."[41] Moreover, since Super Tuesday did not decide the Democratic nomination, the South essentially sat out the rest of the contest. Other than superdelegates, after Super Tuesday there were few additional southern delegates to be secured by the candidates. The "sorting out" of Dukakis,

Jackson, and Gore took place in nonsouthern states. In 1992, in contrast, Clinton emerged as the clear front-runner after Super Tuesday, but still had to nail down the nomination in nonsouthern states.

In one sense, the early organizational success of Super Tuesday 1988 helped doom its impact. As was clearly evident, bunching all southern and border state primaries on a single day robbed a candidate with southern appeal of similar state primaries in which to follow up with wins. After Super Tuesday, Gore's forays into midwestern and northern primaries found less receptive voters. Jackson's campaign was disadvantaged outside the South in that blacks made up smaller shares of the Democratic primary voters and in that his white support was not sufficient to overcome the vote totals of Dukakis, especially after Gore suspended his campaign. Unlike Gore and Jackson, Dukakis's candidacy was relatively advantaged by the location of primaries after Super Tuesday 1988.[42]

Voters in later contests did not seem to take their cues from Super Tuesday voters in 1988. No bounce from Super Tuesday was visible in Illinois, the next primary. Senator Paul Simon skipped Super Tuesday, but had little trouble in his home state fending off two Super Tuesday "winners"—Gore and Dukakis. Jackson, however, proved more formidable because of the sizable black vote in Illinois.

Was Super Tuesday an echo chamber for Iowa and New Hampshire? For 1988 the answer is no and yes; for 1992, more no than yes. Super Tuesday 1988 reversed the results of Iowa. The first-place finishers there, Gephardt and Dole, came to grief on Super Tuesday. Both later dropped out. Robertson's fortunes were raised by Iowa, but turned down in New Hampshire and in the South. The eventual nominees for both parties, Dukakis and Bush, placed no higher than third in Iowa. Super Tuesday essentially echoed the New Hampshire results in that Dukakis did well, Bush very well.[43] In 1992 Harkin's home-state advantage rendered Iowa meaningless. On the other hand, the 1992 New Hampshire results were ones that Super Tuesday revised. Clinton, the "Comeback Kid," rebounded to amass impressive delegate totals and turn back Tsongas. Bush's stumble in New Hampshire was righted by Buchanan's not-so-impressive showings on Super Tuesday.

Reformers had hoped that the pile of delegates at stake on Super Tuesday—nearly one-third of the total—would encourage candidates to downplay, perhaps even skip, Iowa and New Hampshire, to come down south and start the serious campaigning there. Gore *claimed* to do that in 1988, others did not. Gephardt took the opposite tack, deciding in December to shut down his southern operations and reassign his southern staffs to Iowa.[44] Gephardt won Iowa, thereby getting into the ranks of the front-runners. Gephardt's stumble on Super Tuesday may have had more to do with money management than with his early emphasis on Iowa at the expense of the South. Dukakis and Gore outspent Gephardt in the southern and border

Super Tuesday states by two to one. The money shortage restrained Gephardt from responding to critical ads run by Dukakis and Gore immediately before Super Tuesday.[45] Although polls showed that Gephardt remained competitive in the days leading up to Super Tuesday, the four-way split became a three-way split as late-deciding voters spurned Gephardt in favor of Gore or Dukakis.[46]

Super Tuesday creators desired to downplay the importance of Iowa and New Hampshire. The strategy backfired because the delegates at stake on Super Tuesday increased the importance candidates attached to doing well in the early contests in order to gain momentum for Super Tuesday. No major candidate in 1992 repeated Gore's gamble of "jump starting" his campaign on Super Tuesday.

Where candidates spent their time is one measure of the relative importance of Iowa, New Hampshire, and the Super Tuesday states.[47] Simply counting the number of appearances candidates made on separate days leads to a striking conclusion. While not available for 1992, the 1988 data speak eloquently to the lingering importance of New Hampshire and Iowa. Only Gore and Jackson spent more days down south than they did in Iowa and New Hampshire (table 5.2, p. 170). Every other candidate spent at least as much time in the two early states as in the fifteen southern Super Tuesday states combined—as many as two (Dukakis) or three (Gephardt) to four (Simon) days in Iowa or New Hampshire for every day in the South.

How candidates campaigned in the South also led to some discontent. The size of Super Tuesday voting meant wholesale politicking replaced the retail politics of Iowa and New Hampshire.[48] As one journalist described 1988: "The three-week run-up to Super Tuesday had the feel of a mass airplane hijacking, as planeloads of desperate candidates and their journalistic hostages flew from tarmac to tarmac, stopping only to refuel and blink into television lights."[49] In the words of one campaign strategist, "Super Tuesday's a black hole. It eats up your money and energy. You break it into three components—Tarmac, Debates, Ads—and try to survive."[50]

Candidates did more than airport hops, but campaigning understandably took on the appearance of scrambling to be seen favorably in as many of the more than 150 Super Tuesday media markets as possible. Free media through news coverage was important, but not under the control of a candidate or his staff. Paid media required hefty finances.[51] Jackson's campaign reported that buying adequate advertising time on a single Dallas television station for a week would easily run to $300,000. They did not do it. Jackson spent only $447,644 on Super Tuesday, although initially claiming $100,000. Dukakis and Gore spent $3 million and Gephardt spent $1.5 million (table 5.3, pp. 172–73), principally on television advertising.[52] An editorial in *The New York Times* suggested that the day should have been spelled $uper Tuesday.[53]

TABLE 5.2
CAMPAIGN DAYS IN IOWA, NEW HAMPSHIRE, AND
THE SOUTHERN SUPER TUESDAY STATES, 1988

| | Iowa | N.H. | Iowa & N.H. | South and Border South | | | Iowa & N.H. to South ratio |
				a	b	c	
Democrats							
Babbitt	118	60	178	18	—	—	—
Dukakis	84	36	120	34	42	60	2.0
Gephardt	144	51	195	26	32	58	3.4
Gore	32	51	83	54	86	129	0.6
Hart*	18	22	40	—	2	—	—
Jackson	62	19	81	40	75	85	0.9
Simon	88	49	137	15	26	32	4.3
Republicans							
Bush	38	25	63	21	28	51	1.2
Dole	48	56	104	40	53	70	1.5
Du Pont	91	87	178	8	10	—	—
Haig	24	80	104	30	37	—	—
Kemp	69	83	152	20	24	—	—
Robertson	30	36	66	21	28	56	1.2

SOURCES: Iowa: *USA Today*, 9 February 1988, 4a. New Hampshire: *USA Today*, 9 February 1988, 5A, and the campaign schedules in subsequent issues through 16 February. South and Border South: 14 southern and border south states (excluding South Carolina). Days of campaign appearances in the region since 1 July 1987 are as reported in press releases of the Southern Legislative Conference:
a. Release of 20 November 1987, covering days through 15 November 1987.
b. Release of 2 February 1988, covering days through 15 January 1988.
c. Release of 10 March 1988, covering days through 29 February 1988, updated through campaign staff contacts.
* Since 15 December 1987.
"—" indicates data not available. Candidates withdrew as follows: Babbitt, 18 February; Dole, 29 March; du Pont, 18 February; Gephardt, 28 March; Haig, 16 February; Hart, 11 March; and Kemp, 10 March. Campaigns were suspended by Simon on 7 April and Gore on 21 April.

Where candidates spent their money corroborates the lingering importance of Iowa and New Hampshire relative to the southern Super Tuesday states (table 5.3, p. 172). Among Democrats, even Gore spent more money in New Hampshire than in any single Super Tuesday state with the exception of Texas. Dukakis (again, excepting Texas), Gephardt, Jackson, and Simon spent more in Iowa than in any Super Tuesday state. Among Republicans, Bush spent more in Florida and Robertson in Texas than in any other state. Expressing expenditures as a percentage of Federal Election Commission state spending limits shows a similar emphasis on Iowa and New Hampshire. For 1992, campaign spending emphasized the greater importance of New Hampshire relative to southern Super Tuesday states: no Democratic candidate spent more in a southern Super Tuesday state than in New Hampshire. Among Republicans, only Bush spent more in Florida and Texas than in New Hampshire, a phenomenon related more to Federal Election Commission state spending limits. Bush actually spent over twice the amount per Republican vote cast in New Hampshire ($2.43) than in Florida ($1.11) and one and a half times that spent in Texas ($1.56).[54]

Candidates spent more time and money in Iowa and New Hampshire than they did down south; and the media covered the two early events more extensively (table 5.4, p. 174).[55] The southern states varied in 1988 news coverage received: South Carolina stands out for the Republicans (thanks chiefly to its pre–Super Tuesday primary scheduling) as do Florida and Texas for the Democrats. From early 1987 until the end of the 1988 primaries and caucuses, nomination contests in the southern states voting on Super Tuesday received 106 mentions on the evening news of the three major networks. The Iowa contest received 285, the New Hampshire contest 210. Including all states voting on Super Tuesday and non-state-specific mentions of Super Tuesday raises the total to 228—slightly ahead of New Hampshire but behind Iowa. Yet considering that more than 2,000 Republican and Democratic delegates were at stake on Super Tuesday but only 130 in Iowa and New Hampshire, the emphasis on the early events is clear.[56]

Southern Super Tuesday states, in fact, did not receive appreciably more media attention in 1988 as a fifteen-state mega-event than they did in 1984 as a mere three-state event encompassing Alabama, Florida, and Georgia. By one measure, in 1984 those three states received 8 percent of all presidential nomination news coverage; in 1988 the fifteen southern Super Tuesday states received 10 percent (table 5.4, p. 174). The level of attention did climb to 14 percent in 1992, even though only seven states took part.

Enhancing southern influence on the Democratic presidential nomination was one objective behind Super Tuesday. The media treated Super Tuesday as a major event, but media coverage, candidate schedules, and campaign spending for 1988 and 1992 do not indicate that Super Tuesday eclipsed Iowa and New Hampshire.[57]

Super Tuesday and Centrist Voters

Expectations ran high for increased voter turnout when Super Tuesday was put together in 1988, especially that of more centrist voters. Consider, first, the question of overall participation rates. Did Super Tuesday increase voter turnout? Republican turnout set records in most states in 1988, while Democratic turnout was neither the disaster the Republicans desired nor the delight the designers intended (table 5.5, pp. 176–77). Overall, 1988 voter turnout increased dramatically in the eight states that switched from cau-

TABLE 5.3

1988	State limit	Democrats					
		Dukakis		Gephardt		Gore	
		Amount	%	Amount	%	Amount	%
Iowa	$775,217	$755,366	100.0	$729,677	94.1	$261,350	33.7
New Hampshire	461,000	438,437	95.1	344,045	74.6	434,401	94.2
Super Tuesday states total	$23,207,474	$2,988,788	12.9	$1,545,719	6.6	$2,892,043	12.5

1992	State limit	Democrats					
		Clinton		Tsongas		Brown	
		Amount	%	Amount	%	Amount	%
Iowa	$775,217	$11,623	1.5	$18,894	2.4	$21,869	2.8
New Hampshire	461,000	485,628	105.3	369,395	80.1	279,544	60.6
Super Tuesday							
Florida	3,436,847	268,992	7.8	225,040	6.5	6,247	0.2
Louisiana	1,159,876	23,070	2.0	20	—	0	—
Mississippi	676,010	14,093	2.1	0	—	825	0.1
Oklahoma	877,375	11,242	1.3	2,500	0.3	80	—
South Carolina	916,099	78,647	8.6	312	—	2,500	0.3
Tennessee	1,329,155	34,897	2.6	4,596	0.3	1,445	0.1
Texas	4,353,684	270,713	6.2	4,783	0.1	34,307	0.8
Total	$12,749,046	$701,654	5.5	$237,251	1.9	$45,404	0.4

SOURCE: 1988: calculated from "Presidential Primary Spending at $200 Million Mark," Federal Election Commission Press Release, 18 August 1988, 5–6; 1992: Federal Election Commission, unpublished data, 31 December 1992.

cuses to primaries. But this compares apples and oranges, as caucuses traditionally have very low voter turnout. Turnout in presidential primaries, while lagging behind that for state and local election primary contests, far outstrips the voter turnout for caucuses.[58]

For 1992, the most striking turnout result came in Georgia, where Republicans virtually matched Democrats in absolute numbers of voters. This Republican rise was echoed only in South Carolina, where the absolute number of Republican voters actually exceeded that of Democratic voters. As a percentage of voting-age population, turnout in southern Super Tuesday states had climbed from 18 percent in 1984 to 22 percent in 1988 but fell back to 18 percent in 1992. (In 1980 turnout had been an even higher 19 percent of the voting-age population.)

Although Republican presidential primary turnouts set records in many states, Republican voters were still outnumbered two to one by Democratic voters on Super Tuesday in 1988, by three to two in 1992. The Republican

CANDIDATE CAMPAIGN SPENDING IN IOWA, NEW HAMPSHIRE,
AND THE SOUTHERN SUPER TUESDAY STATES, 1988 AND 1992

		Republicans					
		Bush		Dole		Robertson	
Jackson							
Amount	*%*	*Amount*	*%*	*Amount*	*%*	*Amount*	*%*
$195,032	25.2	$774,698	99.9	$775,564	100.0	$763,391	98.5
72,892	15.8	481,449	104.4	469,288	101.8	430,902	93.5
$447,644	1.9	$3,980,108		$3,785,271	16.3	$3,768,701	16.2

| Republicans | | | |
| Bush | | Buchanan | |
Amount	*%*	*Amount*	*%*
$13,997	1.8	0	0
422,678	91.7	$456,866	99.1
994,886	28.9	4,745	.1
33,710	2.9	0	—
344,048	50.9	109,826	16.2
156,245	17.8	13,041	1.5
250,007	27.3	173,005	18.9
174,474	13.1	9,000	0.7
1,247,668	28.7	5,000	0.1
$3,201,038	25.1	$314,617	2.5

NOTES: In Iowa and New Hampshire, Democrat Babbitt spent 83% and 48% of the state limits. Republicans du Pont spent 79% and 96% of the limits and Haig 5% and 36%. South Carolina is included, although in 1988 the Republican primary occurred on 5 March and the Democratic caucus on 12 March. In 1992 both parties held primaries on Saturday, 7 March. "—" Less than 0.1%.

share of the vote rose from 28 percent in 1980 to 34 percent in 1988 to 39 percent in 1992. Despite gains in voter turnout in 1988, Republicans still had a long way to go in the South. Super Tuesday in 1988 or 1992 did not provide the vehicle for Republicans to pull even with the Democrats by achieving substantial, enduring political gains from a single event.

Did Republicans or Democrats secure the support of the targeted ideological middle? Consider crossover voting. Network exit polls in 1988 indicate that crossover voting in the open primary states did not materialize in any significant sense. Only 5 percent of the voters in the Republican primaries considered themselves Democrats, while only 6 percent of voters in Democratic primaries considered themselves Republicans.[59] Gore's candidacy, endorsed by about 800 Democratic officeholders and party officials

TABLE 5.4
NEWS COVERAGE OF IOWA, NEW HAMPSHIRE, AND
THE SOUTHERN SUPER TUESDAY STATES,
1984–92 (IN PERCENTAGES)

	1984	*1988*	*1992*
Iowa	13	23	2
New Hampshire	19	17	23
Super Tuesday*	8	10	14
Alabama	3*	0*	0
Arkansas	0	0*	0
Florida	1*	2*	4*
Georgia	4*	1*	7
Kentucky	0	1*	0
Louisiana	1	0*	2*
Maryland	1	0*	4
Mississippi	0	0*	1*
Missouri	1	0*	0
North Carolina	1	1*	0
Oklahoma	0	0*	1*
South Carolina	0	3*	3*
Tennessee	1	0*	1*
Texas	4	2*	2*
Virginia	1	0*	1
All others	60	50	61

SOURCES: 1984 news coverage: William C. Adams, personal communication, content analysis of *New York Times* and of ABC, CBS, and NBC evening news as summarized in *Television News Index and Abstracts* (Nashville, Tenn.: Vanderbilt Television News Archive, Vanderbilt University); 1988 news coverage: Center for Media and Public Affairs content analysis of the ABC, CBS, and NBC evening news from 8 February 1987 through 7 June 1988; 1992 news coverage: Center for Media and Public Affairs content analysis of the ABC, CBS, and NBC evening news from 1 January 1991 through 2 June 1992. The data are presented in Harold W. Stanley and Richard G. Niemi, *Vital Statistics on American Politics,* 4th ed. (Washington, D.C.: CQ Press, 1994), 60–61.
NOTE: Media coverage in a given state is the percentage of seconds of TV coverage or of column inches of print coverage of primary, caucus, or general election contests that mention the state.
* Super Tuesday 1988 included all the southern and border states listed, while Super Tuesday 1984 and 1992 included only the state figures marked by an asterisk. Together the group of southern states participating in Super Tuesday in 1988 had received 18 percent of the news coverage in 1984 and 26 percent in 1992.

(whose constituents were the most likely to desert the Democrats), undoubtedly helped hold down Democratic crossovers.[60] Although large numbers of Democrats did not spurn the party to take part in the Republican primary, those Democrats who did turn out were less conservative in 1988 than in 1984 (table 5.6, p. 178).[61] The goal of bringing centrists back into the Democratic party was not realized.

Neither party registered turnout gains to the desired extent. Moreover, Republicans failed to secure Democratic crossover voters and Democrats fell short of attracting more moderate voters into their primaries.

Super Tuesday and Moderate Candidates

Many southern Democrats supported Super Tuesday in order to advantage moderate candidates who would move the national party toward a more centrist, more competitive position. Yet, moderate candidates, such as former governor Charles Robb and U.S. Senator Sam Nunn, never entered the fray in 1988, despite the existence of Super Tuesday.[62]

One Super Tuesday 1988 reformer initially claimed that after Iowa and New Hampshire, there would be one conservative candidate and one liberal candidate (Jackson may not have registered on the mental map of this partisan), and voting in the South would advantage the conservative candidate. Iowa and New Hampshire did not cooperate, of course, as the joint results there helped send Paul Simon back to Illinois and elevated Gephardt. As former Democratic National Committee political director Ann Lewis described the dynamics before Super Tuesday: "This is not a sudden death playoff, but a game of musical chairs. There will probably be one more chair gone after Super Tuesday."[63] Gephardt lost his chair. Although close to the center, Gephardt was mortally wounded on Super Tuesday and later folded his campaign.

Gore, a self-styled "raging moderate,"[64] did come alive on Super Tuesday, but his chief competition was Gephardt, another Democratic candidate capable of claiming moderation. If the Gore and Gephardt votes are combined, this combination would place first in Alabama, Louisiana, and Texas, in addition to the six states Gore or Gephardt carried as individuals. A Super Tuesday result in which the moderate candidate carried nine primary states, Dukakis four, and Jackson three, might have produced far more momentum for the moderate than did the actual results, in which Gephardt carried one state and Dukakis, Gore, and Jackson each carried five.

Gore's actual success on Super Tuesday did not provide a lasting lift. He had run as a centrist and "jump started" his campaign on Super Tuesday but he ran out of gas in subsequent contests, finally suspending his campaign six weeks after Super Tuesday. Dukakis and Jackson, despite their evident strength and appeal, were not the centrists the architects of Super Tuesday had in mind. In 1992, in contrast, Clinton's comeback bid for the nomination was strengthened considerably by his showings over Tsongas in Georgia and across the South on Super Tuesday.

Table 5.5

Presidential Primary Voter Turnout and Political Party Vote Share, Southern Super Tuesday States, 1984–92

| | 1984 | | | | | 1988 | | | | | 1992 | | | | |
| | Democrat | | Republican | | Turn- | Democrat | | Republican | | Turn- | Democrat | | Republican | | Turn- |
	N^a	%	N^a	%	out^b	N^a	%	N^a	%	out^b	N^a	%	N^a	%	out^b
Alabama	428	—	c	—	15%	406	66	214	34	21%	451	73	165	27	20%
Arkansas	c	—	c	—	—	498	88	68	12	32	507	90	55	10	32
Florida[d]	1,182	78	344	22	18	1,273	59	900	41	23	1,124	56	893	44	20
Georgia	685	93	51	7	17	623	61	401	39	22	455	50	454	50	19
Kentucky[d]	c	—	c	—	—	319	72	121	28	16	371	79	101	21	17
Louisiana[d]	319	95	17	5	11	624	81	145	19	24	384	74	135	26	17
Maryland[d]	507	87	74	13	18	531	73	201	27	22	567	70	240	30	22
Mississippi	c	—	c	—	—	353	69	157	31	27	191	55	155	45	19
Missouri	c	—	c	—	—	534	57	400	43	24	c	—	c	—	—
N. Carolina[d]	961	—	c	—	21	680	71	274	29	19	692	71	284	29	19
Oklahoma[d]	c	—	c	—	—	393	65	209	35	25	416	66	218	34	27

S. Carolina	c	—	c	—	—	45[c]	19	195	81	—	116	44	149	56	10
Tennessee	322	80	83	20	12	576	69	254	31	24	318	56	246	44	15
Texas	c	—	320	—	—	1,767	64	1,015	36	23	1,483	65	797	35	18
Virginia	c	—	c	—	—	367	61	235	39	13	c	—	c	—	—
Super Tuesday states	1,867	83	395	17	18	8,904	66	4,594	34	22	4,032	61	2,593	39	18
Region[e]	4,404	89	569	11	16	8,904	66	4,594	34	22	7,075	65	3,892	19	35

SOURCES: 1984: compiled from Richard M. Scammon and Alice V. McGillivray, eds., *America Votes 16* (Washington, D.C.: CQ Press, 1984), 37, 41, 59–60, 66–67; U.S. Bureau of the Census, "Projections of the Population of Voting Age, for States: November 1988," *Current Population Reports*, Series P-25, No. 1019 (Washington, D.C.: Government Printing Office, January 1988). 1988: reports of the secretaries of state or state boards of elections, 1988. Alabama turnouts in 1988 are from the state parties. 1992: compiled from "Official Primary Election Results for United States President," *Federal Elections 92* (Washington, D.C.: Federal Election Commission, June 1993): 101–18; voting-age population figures are from Federal Election Commission Press Release 12 February 1992, "FEC Announces 1992 Presidential Spending Limits," 2.

a. Number voting in thousands (e.g., 428,000 Democrats in Alabama for 1984).

b. Primary turnout is based on voting-age population.

c. A caucus rather than a primary election was held.

d. States with party registration enabling the holding of closed primaries.

e. Voter turnout for the region is based on the total votes cast in states where both major political parties held primary elections. Consequently, in 1984 Alabama, North Carolina, and Texas turnout is not included in the regional figure.

TABLE 5.6
IDEOLOGY OF DEMOCRATIC PRIMARY VOTERS,
1984 AND 1988 (IN PERCENTAGES)

Question: "Regardless of the party you may favor, do you lean more toward the liberal side or the conservative side politically?"

Date	Liberal	In-between	Conservative
Alabama			
13 March 1984	22	37	41
8 March 1988	32	39	29
Change	+10	+2	−12
Florida			
13 March 1984	30	37	33
8 March 1988	30	41	29
Change	0	+4	−4
Georgia			
13 March 1984	23	40	37
8 March 1888	32	41	27
Change	+9	+1	−10

SOURCE: ABC exit polls.

Conclusion

Super Tuesday was hyped so high that it was bound to disappoint. Some supporters declared that it would nominate the next president.[65] It did in 1988, but Republican George Bush was not the candidate the designers had in mind. Actually, the "Super Tuesday experiment . . . produced results that were considerably less spectacular than the ballyhoo that preceded it. . . . After all the dust settled . . . there was little in the way of earth-shaking change."[66] Super Tuesday did contribute mightily toward settling the nomination in the Republican Party. Yet, the Republican reaction to Super Tuesday, which proclaimed it the "political boo-boo" of the century[67] or a "political tar-baby,"[68] was more hype and hope than reality, although certain results were what the Democrats wanted to avoid rather than accept. Nor was Super Tuesday the disruptive force predicted by the Winograd Commission. Iowa and New Hampshire remained dominant in 1988, but Iowa's days as a trend-setter appear numbered, especially since it was sidelined in 1992. Although voter turnout increased somewhat for 1988, it fell back in 1992. Super Tuesday neither settled the Democratic nomination nor gave meaningful momentum to the more moderate candidates in 1988, although it went a long way toward these goals with Clinton in 1992.

Does the South have greater prominence in Democratic presidential politics because of Super Tuesday? Just as southern Democrats could not lay an exclusive claim to the Super Tuesday dates in 1988, the place and prominence of southern delegate selection turns on how the southern and non-southern states arrange their primaries and caucuses. For example, even though Super Tuesday was reduced from fifteen to seven states in 1992, circumstances—the popularity of President George Bush narrowing the field of prominent Democrats, including Gore and Jackson, before the contest began, widespread organization, fund-raising success, name recognition, and endorsements—were such that the event helped seal the nomination of regional native son Clinton.[69] Hence, one can argue that Super Tuesday gave the South greater prominence in 1992 Democratic presidential politics.

Did Super Tuesday work? Super Tuesday, in several senses, was less than super in 1988 since it produced a three-way contest for the nomination. In 1992 the results matched more closely the founders' hopes, but Clinton's failure to rejuvenate the Democratic Party in the South during his first two years in office with his "New Democrat" credentials set the party back. In 1994 Republican gains in the South reached beyond the presidential level, handing Democrats defeats at the congressional and state levels as well. The bunching of southern presidential primaries into a Super Tuesday failed to stop—indeed, may not have even slowed—Republican advances in the region.[70]

Looking toward 1996

With forty-two of the fifty state presidential candidate selection contests set at this writing in early 1995 (table 5.7, p. 180), three important changes in the election calendar have the potential to impact Super Tuesday 1996: (1) competition with New Hampshire by the establishment of same-day primary elections for Maine (20 February); (2) the movement of New York to the week before Super Tuesday (7 March); and (3) the movement of California two weeks behind Super Tuesday (26 March).[71] The continued movement to front-load the presidential nomination process with, for instance, the election of 57 percent of the available Republican National Convention delegates by the end of March, is slightly tempered by the movement of North Dakota, Washington, and Wyoming (and potentially others) to later dates.[72]

Take the case of California. In reaction to Super Tuesday 1988, an attempt was made to move California from the first Tuesday in June to the first Tuesday in March 1992, a date in advance of Super Tuesday, with the blessing of the Democratic National Committee, which expanded the election calendar window to accommodate the move. The political realities of cost ($42 million to hold separate presidential and state primary elections), completion of the required redrawing of congressional district boundaries prior to the new date, and the fear of ballot initiatives mobilizing a more lib-

TABLE 5.7
TENTATIVE PRESIDENTIAL PRIMARY AND CAUCUS SCHEDULE
AND ALLOCATION OF NATIONAL CONVENTION
DELEGATES, 1996

			Republicans	Democrats
20 February	Arizona	primary	39	36
	Maine	primary	15	23
	New Hampshire	primary	16	20
24 February	Delaware	primary	12	14
27 February	South Dakota	primary	17	15
5 March	Colorado	primary	26	49
	Georgia	primary	42	76
	Maryland	primary	32	68
	Vermont	primary	12	24
7 March	New York	primary	102	244
12 March	Florida	primary	98	152
	Louisiana	primary	27	59
	Massachusetts	primary	37	93
	Mississippi	primary	32	38
	Oklahoma	primary	38	44
	Rhode Island	primary	14	22
	Tennessee	primary	37	68
	Texas	caucus	123	194
19 March	Illinois	primary	69	164
	Michigan	primary	57	128
	Ohio	primary	67	147
26 March	California	primary	163	363
	Connecticut	primary	27	53
2 April	Kansas	primary	31	36
	Minnesota	caucus	33	76

eral primary electorate in the absence of any opposition to President Bush combined to kill the move.[73] Instead, South Dakota (25 February), Colorado, Georgia, Idaho (Republicans), Maryland, and Washington (Republicans) (3 March), and South Carolina (7 March) moved before Super Tuesday; California remained at the end of the window (2 June), as it had in the past.

With redistricting settled, with an open field of Republican candidates, and with a continuing sensitivity to being last, California moved its presidential and state and local primaries from the first Tuesday in June to the fourth Tuesday in March 1996, as a one-time experiment. In the words of Democratic State Assemblyman Jim Costa, who had tried to change the primary date since the late 1970s to give the state more clout in the selection

TABLE 5.7 — CONTINUED

			Republicans	Democrats
	Wisconsin	primary	36	79
23 April	Pennsylvania	primary	73	167
4 May	Wyoming	caucus	20	13
7 May	D.C.	primary	14	17
	Indiana	primary	52	74
	North Carolina	primary	58	84
14 May	Nebraska	primary	24	25
	West Virginia	primary	18	30
21 May	Arkansas	primary	20	36
	Oregon	primary	23	47
28 May	Idaho	caucus	23	18
	Kentucky	primary	26	51
	Washington	primary	36	74
4 June	Alabama	primary	39	54
	Montana	primary	14	76
	New Jersey	primary	48	104
	New Mexico	primary	18	25
11 June	North Dakota	primary	18	14

SOURCES: "Tentative 1996 Presidential Primary/Caucus Dates; 1996 Republican National Convention Preliminary Delegate Allocation," Chief Counsel's Office, Republican National Committee, December 1994. The primary/caucus dates were not set for Iowa, South Carolina, Virginia, and five other states at the time of the RNC survey of the chief election officer in the states. Some delegate allocations (e.g., Louisiana) may change based on elections held in 1995. The allocation of pledged Democratic delegates is from Office of Party Affairs, Democratic National Committee, "1996 Democratic National Convention Delegate/Alternate Allocation," 18 January 1995, 41–44.

process, California had "become the automatic teller machine for presidential politics. Candidates come to California the year before the primaries and raise substantial amounts of dollars that they take to the likes of New Hampshire, Iowa, Illinois, New York, and Pennsylvania. But we played virtually no role in the selection process." California was expected to play an important role in 1996. Republican strategist Steven A. Merksamer likened the change to a big earthquake: "It's got tremendous implications for both parties. If someone loses New Hampshire, loses Iowa, and comes in second or third on Super Tuesday but wins California, they're right back as the front-runner."[74] In the presidential election itself, Electoral College-rich California, with 54 members (or 20 percent of the number necessary to win), "is like hitting a $15 million lottery. None of the rest [of the states] is worth more than $2 or $3 million."[75]

While positioned to seal the renomination of President Clinton, California also is positioned to make it a nasty contest should former governor

Jerry Brown decide to take advantage of his California organization and challenge Clinton, as he did in 1992. On the Republican side, the most advantaged potential candidate is California Governor Pete Wilson, who hosts the 1996 Republican National Convention in San Diego.[76]

When California leap-frogged its primary a week ahead of New York by moving it to the fourth Tuesday in March, Mario Cuomo, then governor of New York, reacted by having his state legislature move New York's to the first Tuesday in March (the first Thursday in March only for 1996, due to religious holidays), a week before Super Tuesday. Cuomo was blunt: "By moving our primary to the first Tuesday in March, New York will continue to be an important state in the primary process, which may encourage Washington, D.C., to pay closer attention to our needs as a state." With this move, a political consultant with close ties to Senator Alphonse M. D'Amato (R-N.Y.), stressed the necessity of a large campaign war chest, political organization, and visibility to compete in the presidential candidate selection process: "You will need to have enough money to sustain a primary campaign in multiple states by 1 January 1996.... It's going to be much more difficult for a Jimmy Carter or a Gary Hart to emerge by doing well in the first two primaries and then trying to contest the rest."[77]

What is the potential impact of these changes on the presidential candidate selection process? On Super Tuesday?[78] To a large extent the impact of the election calendar depends on the mix of Republican and Democratic candidates. For the Democrats, Super Tuesday aided the renomination of Jimmy Carter in 1980, saved the nomination of Walter Mondale in 1984, produced a three-way contest among eventual nominee Michael Dukakis, Al Gore, and Jesse Jackson in 1988, and sealed the 1992 nomination of regional native Bill Clinton, the perceived centrist it was designed to produce. The respective repositioning of New York and California immediately before and two weeks after Super Tuesday is likely to work for the nomination of a liberal Democrat in 1996.

On the other hand, Super Tuesday, with 20 percent of the available delegates at stake—90 percent of whom are southern—remains positioned to help nominate a conservative Republican candidate, as it did Vice-President George Bush in 1988. Depending on the nature of the "first in the nation contests," the First Tuesday contests in Colorado, Georgia, Maryland, and Vermont (with New York two days later) have the potential of sustaining, even accelerating, any generated momentum going into Super Tuesday to improve the position of a conservative southern candidate such as U.S. Senator Phil Gramm (Texas).

Democrats initially designed the southern Super Tuesday but, as in the past, Republicans may now reap the rewards. Given the rising Republican tide in the South in recent years, Super Tuesday has yet to prove super for southern Democrats.

Notes

1. For an analysis of these goals and whether Super Tuesday seemed an appropriate means of realizing them, see Harold W. Stanley and Charles D. Hadley, "The Southern Presidential Primary: Regional Intentions with National Implications," *Publius: The Journal of Federalism* 17 (Summer 1987): 83–100; Stanley and Hadley, "Expect a Super Tuesday Muddle," *New York Times,* 4 March 1988, 27; and David S. Castle, "A Southern Regional Presidential Primary in 1988: Will It Work as Planned?" *Election Politics* 4 (Summer 1987): 6–10. For a detailed analysis of the 1988 Super Tuesday, see Charles D. Hadley and Harold W. Stanley, "Super Tuesday 1988: Regional Results, National Implications," *Publius: The Journal of Federalism* 19 (Summer 1989): 19–37. Our analyses are tracked and expanded on by Barbara Norrander in *Super Tuesday: Regional Politics and Presidential Primaries* (Lexington: University Press of Kentucky, 1992).

2. Morley A. Winograd, chair, Commission on Presidential Nomination and Party Structure, "Openness, Participation and Party Building: Reforms for a Stronger Democratic Party," Democratic National Committee, 9 June 1978, pt. 1., pp. 31–35.

3. Ibid., 36.

4. Winograd quoted in Rhodes Cook, "Democrats to Adopt Final Rules for 1980," *Congressional Quarterly Weekly Report,* 3 June 1978, 1396.

5. Patrick Caddell, U.S. Congress, House, Subcommittee on Elections of the Committee on House Administration, *Hearings on the Presidential Nominating Process,* 99th Cong., 2d sess., 1986, 107–8; Cook, "Democrats to Adopt Final Rules for 1980," 1392–94; and Rhodes Cook, "Helpful to Carter: Democrats Adopt New Rules for Picking Nominee in 1980," *Congressional Quarterly Weekly Report,* 17 June 1978, 1571–72.

6. Rhodes Cook, "Delegate Selection: Democratic Commission Approves Leadoff Spots for Iowa, New Hampshire," *Congressional Quarterly Weekly Report,* 1 September 1979, 1898; James R. Dickenson, "Spare Us Primary Reform: Tinkering with the System Is a Prescription for More Mischief," *Washington Post,* 12 May 1985, B5; Dave Doubrava and Bill King, "Southern Democrats Pushing for 'Super-Grits' Primary," *Washington Times,* 14 January 1986.

7. Remarks, Jimmy Carter, annual meeting of the Southern Political Science Association, Atlanta, Georgia, 7 November 1986. Carter noted his effort to establish a southern regional primary in 1980 by bringing party leaders and executives together from Alabama, Georgia, Florida, North Carolina, and Tennessee for that purpose.

8. James B. Hunt, chair, Report of the Commission on Presidential Nomination, Democratic National Committee, 26 March 1982, 11–12, 19–20.

9. Rhodes Cook, "Strong in the Frost Belt: Mondale's Primary Weakness Bodes Ill for November Hopes," *Congressional Quarterly Weekly Report,* 16 June 1984, 1141–43.

10. The Southern Legislative Conference of the Council of State Governments includes sixteen southern and border states as well as Puerto Rico.

11. "Policy Position: Southern Presidential Preference Primary/Caucus," Southern Legislative Conference, release SO-85-PR45, n.d.; "Key Southern Legislators Voice Overwhelming Support of Early Regional Primary/Caucus Day in 1988," Southern Legislative Conference, press release, 31 October 1985.

12. James R. Dickenson, "South Moving to '88 'Super Tuesday': 12-State Regional Primary Could Transform Presidential Race," *Washington Post,* 24 December 1985, A1.

13. For example, Dan Balz, "Democrats Sift '84 Rubble, Assess Rebuilding in South," *Washington Post,* 20 January 1985, A31; Dickenson, "South Moving," A1; Eugene Carlson, "Southern States Have a Plan for Choosing Next President," *Wall Street Journal,* 17 December 1985, 35.

14. Quoted in Dickenson, "South Moving."

15. Quoted in Phil Gailey, "Southern Democrats Press Plan for a Regional Primary," *New York Times,* 8 March 1986, 9. Lodge had tried and failed to get the Democratic National Committee to approve regional primaries for 1988. See Mary Deibel, "Vote Plan May Gain Foothold," *Memphis Commercial Appeal,* 8 February 1986, 4:E7. (Page references such as 13:F4 are to Newsbank, Political Development, fiche.)

16. Bob Dart, "Southern States Seem to Be Lining Up for 'Mega-Super' Primary," *Atlanta Journal,* 8 February 1986, 4:E5.

17. Richard Cohen, "A Southern Illusion," *Washington Post,* 2 September 1986, A19.

18. David Treadwell, "Eight Dixie States Plan Same-Day Primary," *Los Angeles Times,* 19 April 1986, pt. 1, p. 4.

19. Quoted in Dickenson, "South Moving."

20. Quoted in Maralee Schwartz, "Simultaneous Primaries Being Urged for South: Governor Graham Leads Democratic Effort," *Washington Post,* 11 September 1985, A6.

21. Quoted in Paul Taylor, "Regional Primary a Political Wild Card: Prospective Change Is Beyond the DNC's Control," *Washington Post,* 6 March 1986, A13.

22. Phil Gailey, "Democratic Leaders in South Favor Regional Primary Idea," *New York Times,* 12 May 1985, 22.

23. Dart, "Southern States," 4:E5.

24. David S. Broder, "The Southern Primary: Another Mistake," *Washington Post,* 12 March 1988, A23. Kudzu, imported from the Orient to help halt soil erosion in the South, has proven to be a pesky plant. Its phenomenally rapid rate of growth meant this "solution" caused problems of its own.

25. West Virginia was the only Southern Legislative Conference member to consider and reject the southern regional primary because some West Virginia legislators objected to the high cost of an early presidential primary date. Other legislators contended West Virginia was not a southern state (*Washington Post,* 27 February 1986). For the adoption dates, see Stanley and Hadley, "Southern Regional Primary," 89, table 1. Southern Democrats did not go it alone on Super Tuesday 1988. Five nonsouthern states and American Samoa combined to create, short of the conventions themselves, the largest single-day event ever in the presidential nomination process. Republican as well as Democratic contests were involved. In 1992, sixteen rather than twenty states took part.

26. Videotaped remarks by the president, Southern Republican Leadership Conference, New Orleans, 11 February 1988.

27. Haley Barbour, 9 January 1988, memorandum to the Southern Republican Exchange on the Southern Republican Primary Project.

28. Dick Lodge, chair of the Tennessee Democratic Party and one of the ar-

chitects of Super Tuesday, responded to such criticisms in this way: "Nothing is without risk and our friends in the Washington political community are happy to tell us why it's a bad idea. . . . But it can't be any worse than now, and if this doesn't work, we'll change it again." Quoted in Phil Gailey, "Southern Democrats Press Plan for a Regional Primary," *New York Times,* 8 March 1986, 9. For broad-ranging critical assessments, see R.W. Apple, Jr., "Super Tuesday: An Experiment Whose Time May Be Past," *New York Times,* 8 March 1988, 11; and David S. Broder, "No More Super Tuesdays," *Washington Post,* 2 March 1988, A17.

29. In this section the South is defined as the eleven states of the former Confederacy, a definition that entails revision of Congressional Quarterly figures based on a thirteen-state South in Rhodes Cook, "Dixie Voters Look Away: South Shifts to the GOP," *Congressional Quarterly Weekly Report,* 12 November 1994, 3231; and Dave Kaplan, "Southern Democrats: A Dying Breed," *Congressional Quarterly Weekly Report,* 19 November 1994, 3356. For Republican officeholding between 1948 and 1974, see Jack Bass and Walter DeVries, *The Transformation of Southern Politics: Social Change and Political Consequence Since 1945* (New York: Basic Books, 1977), 36–37. Data for 1994 taken from National Conference of State Legislatures, "Preliminary Partisan Composition of the State Legislatures," 15 November 1994.

30. For a similar assessment prior to the 1994 midterm elections, see Charles D. Hadley, "Southern Politics After the Election of President Clinton: Continued Transformation toward the Republican Party?" *American Review of Politics* 14 (Summer 1993): 197–212.

31. On the reforms, see William Crotty and John S. Jackson III, *Presidential Primaries and Nominations* (Washington, D.C.: CQ Press, 1985), 27–54. On the dynamics of the reformed nomination process, see Larry M. Bartels, "Expectations and Preferences in Presidential Nominating Campaigns," *American Political Science Review* 79 (September 1985): 812–14, and *Presidential Primaries and the Dynamics of Public Choice* (Princeton: Princeton University Press, 1988); and John H. Aldrich, *Before the Convention: Strategies and Choices in Presidential Nomination Campaigns* (Chicago: University of Chicago Press, 1980).

32. Bush had won the Republican primary in South Carolina on Saturday, 5 March. He won all sixteen primaries on Super Tuesday, losing only the Republican caucuses in Washington State to Robertson.

33. The dismal results doomed Robertson's 1988 candidacy, but the divisive potential his candidacy posed still lingers. Robertson supporters have had greater success transforming southern Republican organizations by taking control at the grassroots. On this point, see John C. Green and James L. Guth, "The Christian Right in the Republican Party: The Case of Pat Robertson's Supporters," *Journal of Politics* 50 (February 1988): 150–65, esp. 162.

34. Dukakis nosed out Jackson for the most delegates gained in all states voting on Super Tuesday (31.8 to 31.5 percent, Gore was third with 28). In southern and border states, the ranking was reversed: Gore 29, Jackson 27, and Dukakis 22.

35. Rhodes Cook, "Iowa Caucuses Lose Limelight as Nominating Season Opens," *Congressional Quarterly Weekly Report,* 1 February 1992; Rhodes Cook, "Tsongas Passes Clinton in N.H.; Harkin Wins in Iowa Caucuses," *Congressional Quarterly Weekly Report,* 15 February 1992, 372.

36. Rhodes Cook, "New Hampshire May Hold Recipe for Moveable Feast,"

Congressional Quarterly Weekly Report, 22 February 1992, 423–27; and Ronald D. Elving and Beth Donovan, "Candidates Spread Their Bets in Presidential Gamble," *Congressional Quarterly Weekly Report,* 22 February 1992, 419–22. Even if Cuomo's write-in bid had been successful, filing deadlines remained open in only nine states and Washington, D.C., with a mere 751 delegates (19 percent of the convention total). See also Charles D. Hadley and Harold W. Stanley, "Surviving the 1992 Presidential Nomination Process," *America's Choice: The Election of 1992,* ed. William Crotty (Guilford, Conn.: Dushkin, 1993), 33–37.

37. Rhodes Cook, "Clinton, Brown Taste First Wins; Bush-Buchanan Duel Rolls On," *Congressional Quarterly Weekly Report,* 7 March 1992, 554–62.

38. Rhodes Cook, "'Super' Kick Propels Front-Runners onto Fast Track to Nomination," *Congressional Quarterly Weekly Report,* 14 March 1992, 634; and Beth Donovan, "Harkin Signs Out of Race," *Congressional Quarterly Weekly Report,* 14 March 1992, 633.

39. Cook, "Super Kick," 631–32, 634; Jeffrey L. Katz, "Clinton Sweep Shows Strength, Justifies Regional Primary," *Congressional Quarterly Weekly Report,* 14 March 1992, 641–42; Dave Kaplan, "Bush, Clinton Win Overwhelmingly in Central South States," *Congressional Quarterly Weekly Report,* 14 March 1992, 643–44; and Ines Pinto Alicea, "Low-Turnout Victories Go to North's Favored Sons," *Congressional Quarterly Weekly Report,* 14 March 1992, 645–46.

40. Hadley and Stanley, "Super Tuesday 1988," 22; Cook, "Super Kick," 631–32, 635, 638–40. Duke finally abandoned his futile challenge to President Bush on 22 April; see Rhodes Cook, "Duke Out of Race: 'My Role Is Over,'" *Congressional Quarterly Weekly Report,* 25 April 1992, 1086.

41. Apple, "Super Tuesday," 11.

42. Bartels, *Presidential Primaries,* 181–83, has a suggestive ranking of states by liberalism scores.

43. For an examination of the previous influence of the New Hampshire primary, see William G. Mayer, "The New Hampshire Primary: A Historical Overview," in *Media and Momentum: The New Hampshire Primary and Nomination Politics,* ed. Gary R. Orren and Nelson W. Polsby (Chatham, N.J.: Chatham House, 1987), 9–41.

44. Only the Florida Gephardt campaign remained operative, primarily for fund-raising reasons. See Kenneth S. Allen, "Gephardt Curtailing Campaign in South, Except Florida," *St. Petersburg Times,* 23 December 1987, 4A.

45. Unlike Gore, Gephardt spent a disproportionate amount in his home state (conveniently located next to Iowa): 18 percent of his total Super Tuesday campaign spending was in Missouri versus less than 1 percent by Gore in Tennessee.

46. Exit polls conducted by the *New York Times* and CBS News in fourteen southern and border states interviewed 9,176 Democratic voters. Of the 31 percent who claimed to have decided how to vote on Super Tuesday or "since Saturday," Dukakis and Gore were backed by about 30 percent each and Gephardt and Jackson by 16 percent each. *New York Times/*CBS News Poll, "Southern Democratic Primary Exit Poll, 8 March 1988," 1.

47. For comparable Iowa figures in earlier years, see Hugh Winebrenner, *The Iowa Precinct Caucuses: The Making of a Media Event* (Ames: Iowa State University Press, 1987), esp. 141 (data for 1984), and Norrander, *Super Tuesday,* 102 (data for 1976).

48. The size meant that those in some states felt slighted. For example, Mary-

land Governor William Donald Schaefer stated that Maryland was "lost in the shuffle" and should move its presidential primary back to May. Quoted in *USA Today,* 9 March 1988, 7A.

49. Hendrik Hertzberg, "Campaign '88: The Wind Tunnel," *New Republic,* 2 May 1988, 10.

50. As quoted by Sandy Grady, "Super Tuesday Means Video Politics in 30-Second Bites," *Nashville Banner,* 5 March 1988, A8.

51. Richard L. Berke, "Dukakis Funds Mount as His Rivals Face Bills," *New York Times,* 10 March 1988, 11.

52. Despite the seemingly large sums spent overall, individual states and stations felt slighted. For example, one report from Kentucky compared state spending to hold the special Super Tuesday presidential primaries ($4.22 million) with what candidates spent in Kentucky ($.50 million). See "Super Tuesday to Cost State Eight and One-Half Times More Than It Raised," *Louisville Courier-Journal,* 27 April 1988, B1. "Most of the major television stations in Louisville and Lexington budgeted three to four times more in campaign ad revenues than actually came in," *Louisville Courier-Journal,* 8 March 1988, 1. For an overview of such Super Tuesday letdowns, see "Political TV Ad Race Off to Sluggish Start," *Broadcasting,* 14 March 1988, 27–29.

53. "The Shock of Super Tuesday," editorial, *New York Times,* 10 March 1988, 26.

54. "Presidential Primary Spending at $200 Million Mark," Federal Election Commission Press Release, 18 August 1988, 5–6; and Federal Election Commission, unpublished data dated 31 December 1992. The FEC cautions that data for different campaigns may not be comparable since each campaign employs its own method for determining the distribution of state-by-state expenses. Some expenditures may not be allocated to any state if they more closely relate to the campaign's "national" effort.

55. If we consider news coverage of primaries and caucuses in the *New York Times* and *Washington Post* in 1984 and 1988, we note that, ironically, coverage of the Democratic nomination process in the southern and border states surpassed the coverage given to Iowa and New Hampshire combined in 1984, but not in 1988. Calculated from data presented in David S. Castle, "Media Coverage of Presidential Primaries," *American Politics Quarterly* 19, no. 1 (1991): 33–42.

56. S. Robert Lichter, Daniel Amundson, and Richard Noyes, *The Video Campaign: Network Coverage of the 1988 Primaries* (Washington, D.C.: American Enterprise Institute, 1988), 13.

57. See also Paul Henri-Gurian, "Less Than Expected—an Analysis of Media Coverage of Super Tuesday 1988," *Social Science Quarterly* 72, no. 4 (1991): 761–73.

58. Crotty and Jackson, *Presidential Primaries,* 11–25; and David E. Price, *Bringing Back the Parties* (Washington, D.C.: CQ Press, 1984), 205–13.

59. *New York Times/* CBS News Poll, 2.

60. Dick Kirschten, "The New South Vote," *National Journal,* 9 April 1988, 936. These endorsements resulted from recognition that Gore could attract voters who might otherwise be crossovers. As Dolph Briscoe, former governor of Texas, said when endorsing Gore: "It is my opinion that Senator Gore ... will bring back into the Democratic Party those who have been lost in elections in the past." Quoted in Terrence Stutz, "63 in Texas Endorse Gore," *Dallas Morning News,* 13

January 1988, 6A.

61. The comparisons that can be made are restricted to Alabama, Florida, and Georgia, but among these states the trend is evident. Admittedly, comparing 1988 with 1984 is comparing a year (1988) when both parties had presidential contests with a year when only Democrats had one (1984) and focusing on these three states does not deliver a regionwide perspective. Moreover, these three states constituted the southern Super Tuesday in 1980 and 1984. Directly comparable data are not available for 1992.

62. Gore's quest for the presidency had more to do with strong support among fund raisers than the existence of Super Tuesday. (He had initially declared he would not be a candidate.) Gore settled on a Super Tuesday strategy in the fall of 1987, several months after entering the race: Gore "adopted his Super Tuesday strategy in early October after finding his campaign in Iowa and New Hampshire going nowhere." See Donna Blanton, "Gore Sees Logic in Betting All on Super Tuesday," *Orlando Sentinel*, 1 February 1988.

63. Quoted in Cook, "8 March Offers Clues," 574.

64. Gore's shifts before Super Tuesday were not all in a more moderate direction. Gore had moved in a more conservative direction on military spending in the fall of 1987. As Super Tuesday approached, this military nationalism was less emphasized in favor of a more populist stance, an economic nationalism that was at the core of Gephardt's appeal in Iowa. Whether this shift helped account for late shifts in support to Gore for Super Tuesday, or Gore's late media blitz with a basically acceptable message mattered more, must await further analysis of survey data.

65. One of the founders of Super Tuesday, Georgia House Speaker Tom Murphy, said, "I truly believe when Super Tuesday is over you're going to know who the next president will be." Southern Legislative Conference press release, 20 November 1987.

66. Kirschten, "The New South Vote."

67. Lee Atwater, as quoted in Michael Oreskes, "GOP Gains Seen in South's Turnout," *New York Times*, 10 March 1988, 12.

68. Steve French, Alabama Republican political director, as quoted in *Montgomery Advertiser and Alabama Journal*, 13 March 1988, B1.

69. Hadley and Stanley, "Surviving the 1992 Presidential Nomination Process," 31–39.

70. On this point, see Hadley, "Southern Politics After the Election of President Clinton;" Earl Black and Merle Black, *The Vital South* (Cambridge: Harvard University Press, 1992).

71. Chief Counsel's Office, Republican National Committee, "Tentative 1996 Presidential Primary/Caucus Dates; 1996 Republican National Convention Preliminary Delegate Allocation" (revised December 1994); and Richard L. Berke, "Arizona Moves Up Its Primary to Catch Political Limelight," *New York Times*, 30 January 1995, A10. Alaska, Hawaii, Iowa, Missouri, Nevada, South Carolina, Utah, and Virginia have yet to set election dates.

72. Republicans and Democrats respectively selected 54 and 49 percent of their delegates by 31 March 1992. Calculated from "Nominating Season at a Glance," *Congressional Quarterly Weekly Report*, 1 February 1992, 259.

73. Norrander, *Super Tuesday*, 195–97.

74. Costa and Merksamer are quoted in Richard L. Berke, "California Guar-

antees Warm Primary Season," *New York Times,* 23 September 1993, A16. See also Jerry Gillam, "Assembly OKs March Primary," *Los Angeles Times,* 9 September 1993, B1.

75. Republican strategist Stuart Spencer, quoted in R.W. Apple, Jr., "California Race May Be the Key to White House," *New York Times,* 21 March 1994, A1.

76. Apple, "California Race," A1, B6; Berke, "California Guarantees," A16.

77. Kevin Sack, "Albany Poised to Advance 1996 Primary," *New York Times,* 6 March 1994, 33A, 36A. Cuomo and Republican political consultant Kieran V. Mahoney are quoted in this article. See also Kevin Sack, "Presidential Primary to Be Held in Early March," *New York Times,* 1 July 1994, B4.

78. At the time of this writing, the election calendar is still in flux. Eight states, including Iowa, have yet to set their dates. Furthermore, the statutes establishing the dates for Iowa and New Hampshire require them to hold the first caucuses and primary election, regardless of whether other states (such as Maine for 1996) have statutes that establish dates tied to New Hampshire. This date problem is one for resolution either by the parties, the courts, or both.

6

Press Treatment
of Front-Runners

MICHAEL G. HAGEN

Most of what Americans can learn about the candidates for a party's presidential nomination comes to them through the news media. Few people —excepting residents of Iowa and New Hampshire, perhaps—meet the candidates face to face. Many see political advertising, but no billboard, button, bumper sticker, or thirty-second commercial, carefully crafted though it may be, can offer as much information as a newspaper or a newscast. For all practical purposes, most people acquaint themselves with presidential candidates only through the news.

If the public relies on the news media for the wherewithal to make a well-informed choice at the polls, the quality of the news about nominating campaigns is of critical importance. The charge to journalists is a formidable one. The quadrennial concern is that they furnish voters with the right kind of information, in the appropriate quantities, gathered and disseminated impartially, so that the best possible presidential candidates are chosen.

Measured against this ideal, news coverage of nominating campaigns every four years comes up short. The reason, in general, is not that journalists inject their partisan or ideological orientations into the news they produce; there is precious little credible evidence that news coverage of politics reliably tilts toward Democrats or Republicans, liberals or conservatives. Much more than political bias, the news displays what has been called "structural bias," imperfections that reflect the process through which news is made.[1] News is the product of interactions between and among newsmakers and journalists. To manage the daunting task of gathering and processing the information that newsmakers and events present, journalists make use of fairly standardized routines and principles, which in turn reflect the professional, economic, and technical incentives and constraints under which they work.[2] The routines and principles that journalists employ shape the news they produce, leading to coverage that highlights some aspects of the political world and obscures others.

During a presidential nominating campaign, the most prominent illustration of structural bias is the preoccupation of journalists with the competitive aspects of the campaign. Journalists accept and share an outlook that includes a particular definition of "news," a set of presumptions about politicians, an enthusiasm for indisputable facts and figures, and a firm belief about what appeals to readers and viewers; all these elements foster a focus on the successes and failures of the candidates, rather than on, for instance, the merits and defects of alternative policy proposals. This orientation pervades the news about presidential nominating campaigns. Its most obvious manifestation, confirmed by practically every analyst of preconvention news coverage, is in the copious coverage the news media give to the questions of who's ahead and who's behind in the race for the nomination.[3] News accounts of nominating campaigns play up the competition, reporting the campaign as if it were a game or a sporting event. The metaphor of choice is a horse race. The news focuses on favorites, dark horses, and also-rans, on candidates neck and neck, gaining ground, or running far behind. At every turn, each candidate's strategy is scrutinized, each candidate's chances of winning reckoned. Journalists' primary preoccupation is with identifying the candidate who has, at any given moment, the inside track.

For the glut of news coverage devoted to the horse race, journalists have been roundly castigated. Some critics argue that by overplaying the dynamic, ephemeral properties of the campaign, journalists underplay the enduring, meaningful properties of candidates for the presidency. The news about nominating campaigns is said to be superficial, shallow, frivolous, useless. In particular, critics charge, too little nomination coverage communicates the views and qualities of the candidates. The media devote insufficient attention to the candidates' backgrounds and pertinent personal qualities, even less to their policy positions. When the media do cover substantive concerns, they tend to dwell less on issues of government policy than on incidents and controversies that develop during the campaign—usually misstatements and missteps made by the candidates. What coverage there has been of policy issues has been skewed toward issues on which the candidates disagree relatively vociferously, on which they take stands that can be distinguished easily and described in simple terms. In short, these critics fault the news media for failing to supply the public with enough detailed, substantive information during a presidential nominating campaign.[4]

Journalists' attention to who's ahead and who's behind shows up in other well-established patterns of the coverage nominating campaigns elicit. The amount of coverage devoted to a given candidate, for example, hinges on that candidate's standing in the race: front-running candidates accumulate volumes of coverage, long-shots hardly any.[5] And a candidate's prospects of winning the nomination influence not only how much the candidate is covered but also the way the candidate is covered. Only a small fraction of the news about a dark-horse candidate, for instance, typically is given over to discussing the candidate's organization, strategy, and resources, while such matters dominate the news about a front-runner.[6] It seems clear that the candidates' positions in the race influence the decisions journalists make about how to cover them.

In at least one other critical respect, however, the influence of a candidate's position in the race is not so clear. Many observers of nominating campaigns argue that a candidate's standing in the competition influences not just the quantity of coverage the candidate receives but also its *message,* the degree to which the coverage is positive or negative.[7] Variations in the message about a single candidate over time and differences in the message across candidates both have been attributed to changes in the state of the contest. But there is no consensus about the direction of the impact of a candidate's position in the race on the message of the candidate's coverage. Some argue that candidates running ahead receive more negative coverage.[8] Others argue that candidates who are doing better receive more positive coverage.[9] And still others argue that the relationship between a candidate's position and the message in the news about the candidate was positive in the 1970s but has been negative since.[10]

As a means of exploring some general questions about the way in which the news media cover presidential nominating campaigns, this chapter investigates further the particular question of how a candidate's position influences the message conveyed by the news about the candidate. The question merits close inspection, for several reasons. The most straightforward, of course, is to resolve the confusion about the nature of the influence. But there are more general considerations at issue as well. If it is well established that a candidate's ranking in the race for a presidential nomination influences many features of the news coverage that candidate receives, the limits of the influence are not. Just how pervasive is the preoccupation of journalists with who's ahead and who's behind? What else might affect the message in the news about a candidate? Who is responsible for the content of the news about presidential nominating campaigns?

The data for this investigation come from a content analysis of United Press International's coverage of the 1984 Democratic nomination campaign.[11] The content analysis, which yielded quantitative information about some 1,800 stories carried by UPI between 1 January and 31 July 1984, provides an extraordinarily rich portrait of how one news organization covered the 1984 campaign. Nonetheless, the data have two important limitations. The first is the possibility that conclusions based on data from one campaign may not apply with equal force to other campaigns. In its most salient features, the campaign for the right to face Ronald Reagan in the 1984 presidential election was an archetypical nominating campaign, with just the sorts of twists and turns that have been characteristic of preconvention campaigns over the past twenty-five years. But while there seems to be no reason to believe that the argument to follow reflects something peculiar to one campaign, the possibility ought to be acknowledged from the outset.

The second limitation is similar to the first: UPI is but one news organization, and generalizing from one organization to all the news media must be done only with some caution. In most respects, however, the news reported by UPI is probably much like the news reported by the other major outlets. What little has been done to compare the election coverage produced by UPI and by the other major wire service, the Associated Press, has turned up little in the way of differences.[12] The wire services are an important source of the news that most Americans read in the papers.[13] Even a wire-service story that is not picked up and printed probably guides many editors and reporters in choosing what to cover and how to cover it, because papers that use wire-service stories only sparingly show the same patterns of news coverage as those that use them liberally.[14] The stories written by UPI reporters may differ in some ways from those written by reporters for such prestigious newspapers as the *New York Times* and *Washington Post*. But because most working journalists have undergone similar professional socialization and because most news organizations in business for profit face similar economic constraints, the news reported in prestige papers is probably much the same as the news carried on the wires.[15] For many of the same reasons, although it is common to allege a great watershed in campaign news coverage between the print media and television news, the differences in content actually documented are not nearly as impressive as the similarities.[16] In sum, there are good reasons to believe that the news produced by other print outlets was very similar to that produced by UPI and that the television news also was not much different. It seems likely that the stories crossing the UPI wire constitute a fairly accurate and exhaustive record of all the stories written about the Democratic presidential campaign in 1984.

One additional restriction must be noted. As an African American, Jesse Jackson broke new ground running for the 1984 Democratic nomination. As a result, Jackson received exceptional treatment from the press.[17] Reporters and editors at UPI appear to have discarded the usual decision rules when it came to covering Jackson. Over the course of the campaign, for example, the amount of coverage devoted to seven of the eight Democratic candidates was positively associated with coverage of the others: when the space allocated to one candidate rose, the space allocated to each of the others tended to rise as well. The lone exception was Jackson. The space allotted to Jackson's campaign followed the opposite pattern, rising when coverage of the others fell. UPI coverage of Jackson also was qualitatively different from coverage of the other candidates: while the horse race dominated coverage of each of the other candidates following the first primaries and caucuses in 1984, only a small fraction of Jackson's coverage discussed his chances of winning the nomination. Moreover, journalists seem to have judged Jackson's performance in the primaries and caucuses according to qualitatively different standards than they did the performance of other candidates.[18] On the grounds, then, that both Jackson's campaign and his treatment by the press were in many respects atypical, coverage of Jackson has been excluded from the analysis that follows.

Identifying the Front-Runner

To investigate the treatment that front-running candidates receive at the hands of the press requires a means of identifying who, at any point during the campaign, is running in front. One tack might be to calculate, insofar as possible, the proper expectations—to compute, for each day of the campaign, each candidate's chances of winning the nomination.[19] But it is not just anyone's expectations that are of interest in accounting for news coverage; it is the expectations of journalists that matter. Journalists, after all, produce the stories that are at issue. Whether journalists' expectations might be accurate or at times might be systematically erroneous is an interesting question, but it is not the question at hand. Evaluating press treatment of front-runners requires a measure of journalists' own expectations—of journalists' own estimates, accurate or not, of a candidate's chances of winning the nomination.

Elaborate techniques are hardly necessary to characterize journalists' expectations at the start of 1984. As the election year began, nearly every observer regarded Walter Mondale as the candidate most likely to win the Democratic presidential nomination. Judging from the news they produced, reporters and editors at United Press International shared that view. Virtually every story that mentioned Mondale early in the year labeled him the front-runner or "the odds-on favorite." To the extent that distinctions were made among the other seven candidates, John Glenn's campaign was regarded as the most viable challenge to Mondale's. Even as Glenn's chances were compared favorably with those of the other six, however, they usually were contrasted unfavorably with Mondale's. In January, for example, UPI stories said that Glenn was "the man they say has the best chance of catching Mondale" and "generally regarded as Mondale's most dangerous rival." Among the remaining candidates (with the exception of Jackson) distinctions rarely were made: the candidacies of Reubin Askew, Alan Cranston, Gary Hart, Ernest Hollings, and George McGovern, when their presidential prospects were mentioned at all in UPI stories in January, were described in no uncertain terms as the longest of long-shots.

Capturing in rigorous detail journalists' assessments of the chances of each candidate over the course of the campaign requires more than just looking for common phrases in the news. Perhaps the ideal measure would be constructed from responses to direct questions put to reporters and editors each day of the campaign, asking about each candidate's chances; but such data are, of course, unavailable. What are available are the stories that UPI journalists wrote, stories that offer obvious clues to what their authors thought about each candidate's chances for nomination. Some parts of some stories are more useful than others in this regard, for a news report typically contains not only the reporter's assessments, of course, but also the pronouncements of his or her sources. Most notable among those sources are the candidates themselves, whose self-interested public predictions might not coincide with the judgments of journalists at all. Coverage attributed to other sources—the infamous spin doctors, for instance—also might be shaped by the axes those sources have to grind. It is coverage not attributed to other sources that would seem to reflect best the journalist's own sense of the situation. News coverage not attributed to other sources obviously does not reliably reveal a reporter's innermost thoughts, nor does it contain only judgments at which the reporter has arrived independently. But unattributed coverage is in some sense more directly under the control of the journalist than coverage attributed to other sources, at minimum in the sense of being written in his or her own words. The portions of news stories that discuss the various candidates' chances without reference to other sources would seem to provide the best available evidence of what journalists themselves thought about the candidates' chances.

The correspondence between a measure of journalists' expectations based on unattributed coverage and the anecdotal evidence reported earlier attests to the validity of the quantitative measure. Figure 6.1 displays the average message conveyed each week, from January through mid-June, by unattributed UPI statements about the chances of the three most prominent Democratic candidates in 1984.[20] As the year began, by this measure as by every other, Mondale was considered the heavy favorite: UPI journalists during January put the probability of Mondale winning the nomination between .36 and .51. By contrast, UPI journalists rated the chances of Mondale's nearest competitor in January, John Glenn, at about .1. Gary Hart's chances were put at .05, and no other candidate was given better than 1 chance in 20 of becoming the Democratic nominee.

Journalists' judgments of all three candidates' chances underwent dramatic changes once the primaries and caucuses began. In the first major delegate selection event of the year, the 20 February Iowa caucuses, Glenn finished a distant fifth, with just 4 percent of the vote. As a result, Glenn's

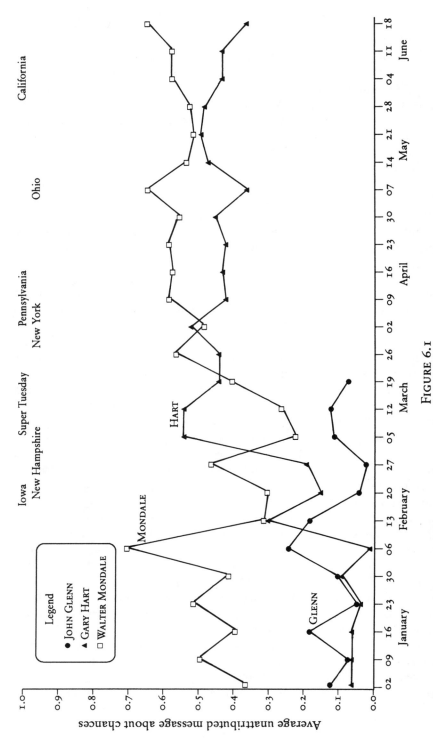

FIGURE 6.1

UNATTRIBUTED UPI MESSAGES ABOUT CHANCES OF GLENN, HART, AND MONDALE, BY WEEK

chances fell to barely 1 in 25 during the week after Iowa, according to UPI. His prospects brightened a bit the following week, in the wake of the New Hampshire primary, where he came in third. But the eleven primaries and caucuses held on Super Tuesday (13 March in 1984) finished off Glenn's campaign. Failing to win a single event on Super Tuesday, Glenn withdrew three days later.

Hart, meanwhile, emerged as the leading challenger to Mondale. Hart's chances began to climb just before the Iowa caucuses, in the estimation of UPI journalists. After the caucuses, in which Hart placed second to Mondale, Hart's chances of winning the nomination were put at almost 1 in 5.[21] Between Iowa and New Hampshire, UPI still rated Mondale's chances about twice as good as Hart's. But Hart's victory in the New Hampshire primary made him the front-runner, in the opinion of UPI journalists. Between New Hampshire and Super Tuesday, during which time Hart won caucuses in Maine and Wyoming and a nonbinding "beauty contest" primary in Vermont, unattributed UPI coverage put Hart's probability of winning at better than .5. Mondale's chances plummeted at the same time: between New Hampshire and Super Tuesday UPI coverage put Mondale's probability of winning at only about .25.[22] Super Tuesday, however, got Mondale back on track, in the view of UPI journalists, with his victories in the Alabama and Georgia primaries. Four days later Mondale also won the Arkansas, Michigan, and Mississippi caucuses. The week made Mondale the front-runner once again, in the eyes of those at UPI.

One week later, Hart and Mondale had changed places again, following Hart's victory in the Connecticut primary and Wisconsin's nonbinding primary. When Mondale later won the Wisconsin caucuses and the Pennsylvania primary, however, he was back in the lead for good, according to UPI. The gap between the two did not stay constant, however; it widened after Mondale won the Texas caucuses, and it narrowed when Hart won the Oregon primary and began to look good in California. Only after the last primaries and caucuses had been held—and Mondale had won in New Jersey and West Virginia—did the journalists at UPI once again come to regard Mondale's nomination as inevitable.

The News about the Front-Runner

Overall, the news in January 1984 about Walter Mondale, the consensus front-runner as the election year got under way, was decidedly mixed. While his campaign was discussed in only the most glowing terms, Mondale himself came in for substantial criticism. The two most common charges were that he was overly cautious and that he was the pawn of special interests. The following passage, part of a UPI story describing a 15 January New

Hampshire debate among the eight contenders, illustrates the critical coverage typical of this period:

> The exchange began after Mondale, former vice president and acknowledged
> front-runner for the Democratic nomination, outlined his program to cut fed-
> eral deficits.
>
> Glenn, the Ohio senator and Mondale's closest rival, said with disgust:
> "That's the same vague gobbledygook we've been hearing for years."
>
> "Is this going to be a Democratic Party that promises everything to every-
> body and runs up a $170 billion bill?" Glenn asked, using the figure he says
> Mondale's campaign promises would cost.
>
> "I'm disgusted and tired of all the vague promises," Glenn said, adding
> that Mondale would add to the deficits he has pledged to cut.

Scoring every line produced about Mondale by UPI during the month of
January on a scale ranging from +2 for "very favorable" to −2 for "very unfavorable," the average is a mildly positive .15.

The rather balanced message conveyed by the coverage UPI gave the
early front-runner overall conceals a more telling systematic pattern, however, a pattern that only emerges after one takes into account the subject to
which each piece of news is devoted. Coverage of the horse race—of the
candidate's chances of winning the nomination, his tactics and strategy, his
sources of support and opposition, his campaign organization, and his fund-
raising efforts—delivered a decisively positive impression about Mondale
during January, averaging .46. In contrast, coverage of substance—of the
policy views and the personal qualities of the candidate—carried a distinctly
negative message about Mondale as the year began, averaging −.24 during
January. Only coverage of the hoopla—of the events of the campaign, the
activities of the candidate, and the other personalities involved—was nearly
neutral with regard to Mondale during the first month of the campaign, averaging .07. If Mondale's status as front-runner influenced the message of
the news coverage he received early in 1984, the direction of that influence
depended on the subject of the coverage.

The conditional nature of the relationship between journalists' assessments of a candidate's chances and the news coverage the candidate receives
is evident throughout the 1984 campaign. Coverage of Hart's standing in the
horse race, for example, for the most part paralleled journalists' judgments
about his chances of winning the nomination (figure 6.2). Horse race coverage of Hart was most favorable in early to mid-March, just when those at
UPI apparently rated his chances most highly. It was at just about the same
time, too, that coverage of Hart on substantive matters reached its most negative level. The dominant criticism was that Hart's candidacy lacked real

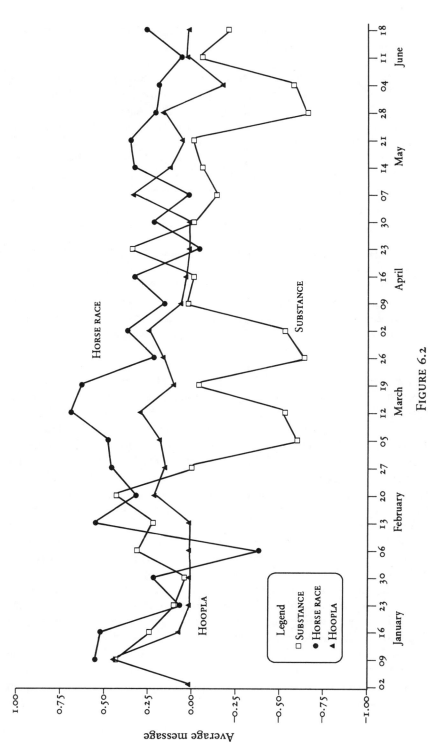

FIGURE 6.2

UPI MESSAGES ABOUT HART, BY SUBJECT AND WEEK

substance, as exemplified by the following passage from a story appearing on the eve of Super Tuesday.

> Mondale kept up the attack as he landed in Tampa Sunday night after the debate, calling Hart naive and inconsistent, particularly on foreign affairs.
>
> "The differences are now becoming clearer," Mondale said.
>
> He said that Hart once had said that Cuba was not a totalitarian dictatorship while "the fact is that Castro is a communist dictator."
>
> He also said Hart had said that if Persian Gulf oil was blocked at the Straits of Hormuz, U.S. allies are on their own. "That's naive," he said.
>
> Mondale charged that Hart had taken seven separate inconsistent positions on arms control.
>
> "We're not electing momentum," he said. "We're not electing a can of hair spray."
>
> Mondale said he was pleased by the outcome of the debate. "I made the points I wanted to," he said.
>
> Most of the points Mondale raised were aimed at poking holes in Hart's campaign theme of "new ideas."
>
> "When I hear your new ideas, I keep being reminded of that ad—'Where's the beef?'" Mondale taunted Hart after he had explained his program for economic recovery.

Not until early April, when Mondale overtook Hart in the race, according to UPI, did the harsh coverage of Hart on substance subside, even turning decidedly positive for one week later that month. The only other burst of negative press Hart received on substantive concerns appeared in late May, when his chances had rebounded a bit in the eyes of those at UPI. Coverage of Hart on the other aspects of the campaign, on the hoopla, remained relatively neutral throughout. Coverage of the horse race and of the substance of the campaign, however, both were affected strongly—in opposite directions —by journalists' perceptions of where Hart stood in the competition.

Across candidates and over time, in short, journalists' assessments of a candidate's chances of winning the Democratic presidential nomination in 1984 strongly influenced the message in the coverage that candidate received. Table 6.1 shows the effects of assessments by UPI journalists of each candidate's chances, as manifested in unattributed coverage, on the average message of the coverage devoted to the candidate in the three subject areas each week he was in the race. The impact of journalists' assessments on coverage of the horse race was positive and powerful: an increase of .25 in journalists' perceptions of a candidate's chances produced coverage of the candidate's standing in the horse race that was nearly one-half point more favorable on the five-point scale. The impact of assessments of chances on substantive coverage was strong and negative: a difference of .25 in the

TABLE 6.1
EFFECTS OF JOURNALISTS' ASSESSMENT OF A CANDIDATE'S
CHANCES ON AVERAGE WEEKLY MESSAGE ABOUT
THE CANDIDATE, BY SUBJECT

	Message about the horse race	Message about substance	Message about the hoopla
Standardized effect	.66	−.41	.11
Unstandardized effect	1.84	−.77	.11
(Standard error)	(.22)	(.18)	(.10)
Constant	−.44	.13	.08
(Standard error)	(.07)	(.06)	(.03)
R^2	.43	.17	.01
N	96	90	96

judgments of UPI journalists about the probable outcome of the race—either across candidates or over time—produced a difference of almost one-fifth of a point on the five-point scale representing the message about a candidate on substantive subjects. Assessments of chances made little difference in the coverage of the hoopla surrounding a candidate. But a candidate who was doing better in the eyes of journalists simultaneously received much more positive coverage when the subject was the horse race and more negative coverage when the subject was a matter of substance.

The Agendas of Journalists

To find a close positive association between unattributed coverage of a candidate's chances of winning the presidential nomination and the overall coverage the candidate receives on the subject of the horse race is not surprising. Unattributed coverage of candidates' chances makes up a substantial portion—35 percent in 1984—of all coverage of the horse race. Then, too, the various aspects of the horse race—devising an effective strategy; building a sturdy organization; securing the support of important groups; raising funds; showing well in polls, primaries, and caucuses—all tend to run together. Moreover, the sources of most news coverage—whether partisans, nonpartisans, or journalists themselves—all are watching the same campaign. All have access to much the same information about how well each candidate is doing. Sources with rooting interests in the outcome no doubt can be counted on to exaggerate the chances of some candidates and disparage the chances of others. But they also are constrained by facts that are available for all to see: one candidate's poor finish in the recent primary, another's strong showing in a new poll, another's dwindling bank balance. Nearly all the sources to which a reporter might turn when writing a story about the horse race, therefore, are likely to say something roughly congruent with the reporter's own view of each candidate's chances.

Evidence favoring this reasoning can be found in the effect of journalists' expectations on UPI horse race coverage in 1984, controlling for the source of the news (table 6.2). Unattributed coverage of the horse race is closely related to journalists' assessments of the candidates' chances, of course, because much of the unattributed coverage of the horse race is unattributed coverage of chances. But so too is horse race coverage attributed to nonpartisan and to partisan sources—supporters and opponents of the candidate alike—strongly associated with journalists' judgments of the candidate's chances: the more positive the reporter's evaluation of a candidate's chances, the more positive the evaluations of other sources of horse race news about the candidate. To be sure, supporters and opponents do not offer the same evaluation of a candidate's chances; the news from his opponents tends to play down a candidate's chances, while the news from his supporters plays them up.[23] Given this divergence, it also should be noted, it seems unlikely that the views of reporters and the views attributed to partisan sources are associated simply because the reporters chose from among the statements of their sources those that agreed with their own views. Instead, on this evidence the more appropriate conclusion is that the journalists employed by UPI in 1984 for the most part faithfully reported the views of their sources on the horse race, and the views of their sources tended to coincide with those of the journalists themselves. It is for this reason that the message conveyed by coverage of the horse race overall is strongly and positively associated with journalists' expectations.

The negative association between journalists' expectations and the overall coverage a candidate receives on substantive matters is not so easily explained. The difficulty is not a shortage of explanations but a surplus. Deciding which among them is the most accurate would seem to require an intimate familiarity with the instincts, reflexes, and habits of political reporters as a species.

One way to explain harsh press treatment of front-runners begins with the proposition that journalists see themselves as the watchdogs of the political process. Devoted to their duty, these dogs take a dim view of anyone getting too close to the White House. It is the role of the press, from this perspective, to scrutinize carefully any candidate who does get close. Critical coverage does not occasion censure from others in the profession; on the contrary, journalists who report negative news about a candidate win the plaudits of their colleagues. "The political press corps," according to one member of that corps, "prides itself on how quickly it can knock the stuffing out of those who would run for president."[24] Critical treatment of front-running candidates, according to this view, is the product of journalists who are just doing their job as they see it.[25]

TABLE 6.2

EFFECTS OF JOURNALISTS' ASSESSMENT OF A CANDIDATE'S
CHANCES ON AVERAGE WEEKLY MESSAGE ABOUT
THE CANDIDATE, BY SUBJECT AND SOURCE

	Message about the horse race	Message about substance	Message about the hoopla
Unattributed coverage			
Effect of chances	2.51 (.20)	−.60 (.16)	.14 (.08)
Constant	−.72 (.06)	.17 (.06)	.05 (.03)
R^2	.63	.16	.03
Attributed to nonpartisans			
Effect of chances	.95 (.46)	−1.53 (.53)	.10 (.66)
Constant	−.10 (.19)	.44 (.19)	.04 (.32)
R^2	.08	.20	.00
Attributed to partisans			
Effect of chances	.71 (.29)	−.67 (.23)	−.26 (.32)
Constant	.04 (.10)	.09 (.08)	.28 (.13)
R^2	.07	.09	.01
Attributed to supporters			
Effect of chances	1.18 (.28)	.35 (.21)	−.05 (.28)
Constant	.07 (.10)	.17 (.07)	.28 (.12)
R^2	.19	.03	.00
Attributed to opponents			
Effect of chances	.84 (.42)	.07 (.25)	1.27 (.99)
Constant	−.87 (.18)	−1.08 (.11)	−1.27 (.50)
R^2	.08	.00	.19

NOTE: Entries are unstandardized regression coefficients, with standard errors in parentheses.

A second explanation proceeds from the assumption that journalists are more defensive creatures than protective ones. In particular, journalists are sensitive to the charge that they might contribute to a particular candidate's acquisition of the precious commodity known as "momentum," thereby fueling a bandwagon and affecting the outcome of the contest. So, according to this line of reasoning, journalistic norms increasingly prescribe the practice of "compensatory journalism," reporting with a bias against front-runners and in favor of challengers.[26] Journalists may wish to preempt the critics and keep the race even, "dewheeling" the bandwagon by running down the leading candidate and preventing him from getting too far ahead.[27]

A third explanation might be founded on the belief that journalists are not so much defensive or protective as they are selfish. It is in their economic interest for the nomination contest to be close because a close race is more likely to attract and hold the attention of readers and viewers, boosting circulation and advertising rates. The bottom line, from this angle, is that journalists put front-runners down in order to keep the competition tight and interest up.[28]

What is most notable is not what distinguishes these explanations from each other, but what ingredient is common to all three. All three ascribe negative coverage of front-runners to the agendas of journalists. According to all three, the message of the substantive coverage a candidate receives is inversely related to the candidate's standing in the horse race because reporters and editors, following their judgments about who's ahead and who's behind, elect to produce more negative stories about front-runners than about underdogs. According to all three of these explanations, journalists generate more critical news about front-running candidates because, for one reason or another, they intend to do so.

Support for this proposition may be found in UPI coverage of the 1984 nominating campaign. Again, the most fertile ground to search for clues to the intentions of journalists (absent the answers of reporters and editors to direct questions) is the news coverage over which journalists exercise the most control—the portions of stories that are in their own words, rather than in the words of their sources. As in the case of unattributed coverage of candidates' chances, this is not to say that unattributed coverage of substantive subjects somehow provides access to a reporter's innermost thoughts and feelings about a candidate. Unattributed coverage would seem to provide the best opportunity, however, for insight into the messages journalists themselves wish to convey about the substance of the various candidacies.

Consistent with the proposition that journalists intend to produce more critical news of front-running candidates, the message conveyed by unattributed UPI coverage of a candidate on substantive matters was negatively influenced by the judgments of UPI journalists about the candidate's chances (table 6.2). The effect is substantial and statistically significant. To a degree, it seems evident, the harsh press treatment received by front-running candidates may result from a desire on the part of journalists to cover candidates who are doing better less favorably than candidates who are doing worse. When journalists take it upon themselves to comment on the substance of a candidate's campaign in their own words, rather than in the words of others, they apparently are guided to some extent by how well they think the candidate is doing in the race for the nomination.

Nevertheless, only a small fraction of the substantive coverage a candidate receives is reported in the words of journalists; in UPI's coverage of the substance of the 1984 campaign, only one line in seven was not attributed to other sources. Substantive coverage attributed to nonpartisan observers of the campaign also was negatively related to journalists' expectations, but such coverage made up even less of the total devoted to substance, just one line in twenty-five. More than three-quarters of the substantive coverage produced by UPI in 1984 was attributed to partisans in the campaign—44 percent to the candidates themselves or their supporters, 34 percent to their opponents.

What is striking about the partisan coverage is that while the message it conveyed about each candidate overall was negatively associated with journalists' expectations, both the message of coverage attributed to the candidate's supporters and the message of coverage attributed to his opponents were not. Substantive news based on statements made by a candidate's opponents is unfailingly derogatory, as might be expected, and it is altogether unrelated to journalists' assessments of the candidate's chances. Substantive news based on the statements of the candidate or his supporters tends to be mildly favorable, and if it changes at all with an improvement in the candidate's chances, it becomes more favorable, not less. Again, the marked difference between the average messages attributed to supporters and opponents argues against the possibility that journalists merely report statements that square with their own views. Even more telling than the difference in average tendencies is their resilience in the face of changes in journalists' expectations. If it was the intention of those at UPI in 1984 to tilt the news on substantive matters against the front-runner, they nevertheless did not do so with the two largest categories of news, coverage based on what the candidates and their confederates had to say about themselves and on what they had to say about each other.

The Changing Sources of News

The bulk of the news on substantive matters presents a paradox. Journalists' expectations heavily influence the message about the candidate conveyed by substantive news coverage attributed to partisan sources: front-runners receive decidedly more negative coverage than underdogs. Yet journalists' expectations affect neither the message of coverage attributed to a candidate's supporters nor the message of coverage attributed to a candidate's opponents. The explanation for this apparent paradox lies in systematic changes in the sources on which news is based.

Among the most well-established patterns of news coverage during a presidential nominating campaign, noted earlier, is the robust relationship between a candidate's standing in the race and the amount of news coverage the candidate receives: the candidate ahead receives more coverage than the candidate behind. UPI coverage in 1984 followed this typical pattern. A rise of just .1 in a candidate's chances, in the judgment of journalists, was worth more than 200 additional lines of coverage per week from UPI. In terms of substantive coverage alone, the gain from such a rise overall was 64.5 lines. (The estimates on which these calculations are based appear in table 6.3.)

The increase in the volume of coverage resulting from an improvement in a candidate's prospects is not distributed uniformly over the sources of

TABLE 6.3

EFFECTS OF JOURNALISTS' ASSESSMENT OF A CANDIDATE'S
CHANCES ON AMOUNT OF COVERAGE
DEVOTED TO THE CANDIDATE,
BY SUBJECT AND SOURCE

	Coverage of the the horse race	Coverage of substance	Coverage of the hoopla
All coverage			
Effect of chances	1113 (144)	645 (75)	250 (39)
Constant	56 (45)	23 (24)	29 (12)
R^2	.37	.42	.28
Unattributed coverage			
Effect of chances	639 (78)	48 (17)	181 (34)
Constant	23 (25)	19 (6)	24 (11)
R^2	.40	.07	.22
Attributed to nonpartisans			
Effect of chances	79 (13)	25 (8)	17 (4)
Constant	1 (4)	2 (2)	0 (1)
R^2	.25	.09	.15
Attributed to partisans			
Effect of chances	395 (61)	572 (61)	51 (13)
Constant	33 (19)	3 (19)	5 (4)
R^2	.29	.46	.13
Attributed to supporters			
Effect of chances	295 (52)	245 (33)	43 (13)
Constant	34 (17)	20 (10)	5 (4)
R^2	.24	.36	.10
Attributed to opponents			
Effect of chances	100 (14)	328 (41)	7 (2)
Constant	−2 (4)	−17 (13)	0 (1)
R^2	.34	.38	.13

NOTE: Entries are unstandardized regression coefficients, with standard errors in parentheses.

coverage. When the subject is either the horse race or the hoopla, the increase in coverage produced by an increase in a candidate's perceived probability of winning is largely concentrated in coverage not attributed to other sources. The effect on horse race coverage of a .1 rise in a candidate's putative chances was an increase of 64 lines of unattributed coverage per week, compared with an increase of 40 lines of coverage attributed to partisans and just 8 lines attributed to nonpartisan observers of the campaign. The effect on coverage of the hoopla was even more heavily skewed toward unattributed coverage. In sharp contrast, the effect on coverage of the substance of a candidacy when a candidate was judged to be more likely to capture the nomination was much less pronounced on coverage not attributed to other sources, much more pronounced on coverage attributed to partisans. A jump of .1 in journalists' expectations produced an increase in unattributed substantive coverage of less than 5 lines per week; the increase in coverage attributed to nonpartisan sources was only half that. On the other hand, the same jump produced an increase in coverage attributed to partisan sources of 57 lines per week—an increase more than ten times as great as that in unattributed coverage of substance. Thus, doing better in the eyes of journalists chiefly drives up unattributed coverage of the horse race and the hoopla surrounding a candidate's campaign, while it chiefly drives up coverage of the substance of the candidate's campaign that is based on the statements of partisan observers.

More important still, the increase in coverage attributed to partisans is not evenly divided between supporters and opponents of a candidate. Again, the contrast between coverage of substance and of other subjects is instructive. The increment in horse race coverage attributed to a candidate and his supporters is three times as great as the increment in horse race coverage attributed to his opponents, and the difference is similar, and even greater, for coverage of the hoopla of the campaign. But the pattern is reversed for substantive coverage: when a candidate did better in the eyes of UPI journalists in 1984, substantive coverage based on the statements of his competitors and their allies rose one-third more than did coverage of substance based on the candidate's own statements and those of his allies.

The upshot of the differences across sources in the effects of journalists' expectations is that changes in those expectations alter the balance of sources on which a candidate's coverage is based. Because substantive coverage attributed to a candidate's opponents rises faster than coverage based on other sources with an increase in the candidate's putative chances, the percentage of the substantive coverage a candidate receives that is based on what his opponents say increases as his chances improve, while the percentage based on what he and his supporters say and the percentage not attributed to any other source decrease. Before the Iowa caucuses in 1984, for instance, more than one-third of Walter Mondale's coverage was attributed to Mondale's opponents, and almost one-sixth of John Glenn's coverage was attributed to Glenn's opponents, but neither Gary Hart nor any of the other candidates received any coverage at all attributed to their opponents. After the New Hampshire primary, however, the fraction of Hart's coverage attributed to his opponents skyrocketed, to more than two-thirds. The share of Hart's coverage attributed to his opponents remained high the following week—and substantially higher than the share of Mondale's coverage attributed to his opponents. But after Super Tuesday, the percentage of coverage attributed to opponents increased for Mondale, who again was regarded as the front-runner, and fell for Hart, who was again regarded as the underdog.

In general, 50 percent of the substantive coverage devoted to a candidate whose chances were rated at one in ten in 1984 was attributed to the candidate and his supporters, and 27 percent was not attributed to any other source; just 18 percent was attributed to the candidate's opponents (figure 6.3). A candidate whose chances were rated at four in ten, in contrast, received coverage that was much less likely to be unattributed (only 14 percent was not attributed to other sources), and almost as likely to be based on the statements of his opponents (40 percent) as on statements made by himself or his supporters (42 percent). The better a candidate's chances of winning the nomination, in short, the greater the fraction of his substantive coverage that is based on what the candidate's opponents have to say. Much more of the coverage devoted to front-runners than of the coverage devoted to underdogs reflects the pronouncements of their opposition.

It is the effect of journalists' expectations on the percentage of coverage attributed to opponents, and not the effect on changes in the message attributed to any particular source, that is primarily responsible for the overall relationship between journalists' expectations and the message conveyed by coverage of the candidates on substantive subjects. Figure 6.4 displays the evidence for this conclusion, comparing the observed pattern of messages on substantive subjects with the results of two simulations. The first represents the pattern of messages that would have been produced if only the average message of coverage attributed to each type of source had varied over the campaign and the mix of sources had remained fixed after the first half of January. Those circumstances, it is clear, would have yielded a very different pattern of messages on substantive subjects, one only mildly correlated (.57) with the observed pattern. Changes in the message from each type of source alone can account for neither the pro-Hart shifts in substantive coverage during late February and mid-April nor the pro-Mondale shifts during mid-March and late May. The tendency for front-running candidates to receive negative news coverage is not due, it is evident, to changes in the message of coverage attributed to any particular type of source.

The second simulation represents the pattern that would have been produced if the average message attributed to each type of source had remained fixed after the first two weeks of January and only the percentage of coverage attributed to each type of source had varied. Variation in the mix of sources alone would have produced messages closely following the observed pattern. The results of the second simulation are strongly and positively correlated with the observed pattern of messages on substantive subjects (.88).[29] The reason a front-runner, on average, receives more negative news coverage than an underdog is that a larger proportion of the front-runner's coverage is based on what his opponents say.

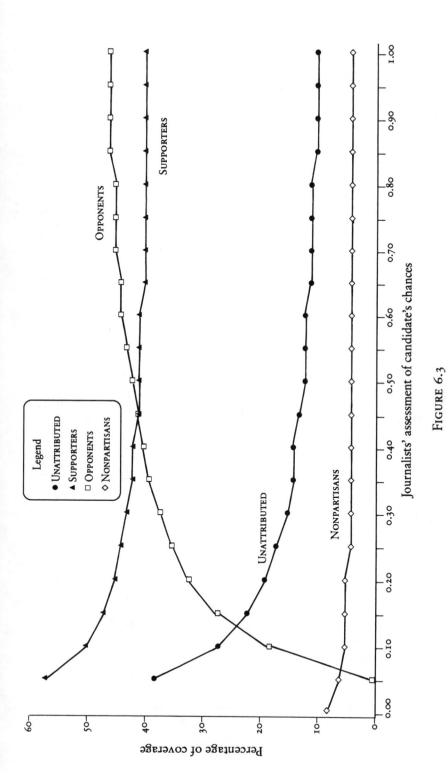

FIGURE 6.3

EFFECTS OF JOURNALISTS' ASSESSMENT OF A CANDIDATE'S CHANCES
ON DISTRIBUTION ACROSS SOURCES OF SUBSTANTIVE COVERAGE

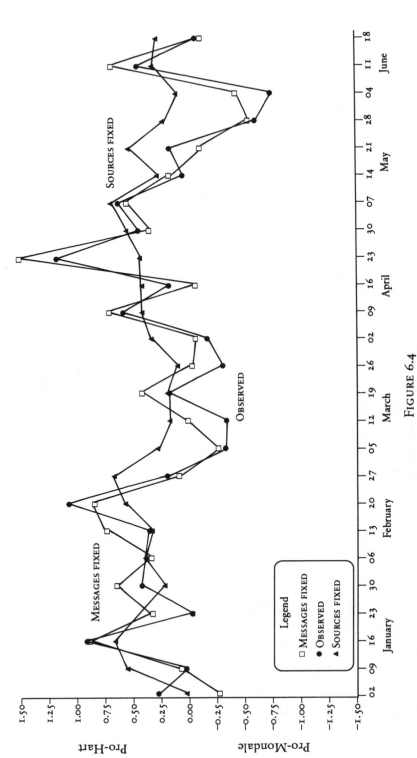

FIGURE 6.4

OBSERVED AND SIMULATED DIFFERENCES BETWEEN AVERAGE MESSAGES
ABOUT HART AND MONDALE, SUBSTANTIVE COVERAGE, BY WEEK

The Agendas of Candidates

Across candidates and over time, the message of the substantive news coverage a candidate receives changes with journalists' expectations because the mix of sources on which journalists base his coverage changes with their estimates of his chances. Why, then, does the mix of sources change? Why is substantive coverage of a front-runner based on different sources than coverage of an underdog?

The explanation may be that portraying the front-runner in a negative light is very high on the agendas of journalists. After all, the choice of sources is under the control of journalists. To produce a more negative overall message about the front-runner, all one need do is include in stories about the front-runner more of the statements made by his opponents and fewer of the statements made by the candidate and his backers. Perhaps journalists are so intent on producing coverage critical of the candidate in the lead that they are not content to criticize in their own words—they also may manipulate the mix of sources on which the leading candidate's media coverage is based.

If the sole explanation for critical coverage of front-runners were the designs of journalists, however, it would seem that the negative relationship between the message conveyed by substantive news and journalists' expectations should hold for all coverage, irrespective of its source. The news about the front-runner should include not only the more negative statements of nonpartisan observers and journalists themselves but also the less positive statements of allies and the more negative statements of the enemy. But this is not the case. Neither the message of coverage attributed to a candidate's supporters nor the message of coverage attributed to a candidate's opponents is related to journalists' assessments of the candidate's chances of winning the nomination. If journalists' agendas alone are what prescribe critical coverage of front-running candidates, journalists nevertheless are unable to achieve that goal when they report the statements of the candidates, their advocates, and their adversaries.

The obvious explanation for the absence of a negative relationship between journalists' expectations and the news from a candidate's supporters and opponents would seem to be that supporters rarely have anything at all unfavorable to say about their candidate and opponents rarely say anything favorable. Journalists, for their part, generally are unwilling to put words into the mouths of their sources; they must work with the raw materials available to them. When writing about the campaign, journalists are to a great extent constrained by what the candidates and their other sources say. And because candidates rarely offer disparaging pronouncements on their own personal qualities and policy views, substantive news that reflects badly on a candidate rarely is attributable to that candidate. It is no doubt the combined effect of candidates and journalists adhering to their respective rules of conduct that produces substantive news attributed to supporters and opponents that is unrelated to where journalists believe the candidate stands in the race.

If the behavior of candidates can affect the message conveyed by news coverage attributed to them, the behavior of candidates also can affect the mix of sources on which news coverage is based, for journalists are constrained not only by what the candidates say but also by whom the candidates discuss. Consider what goes on in the real world of politics during a presidential nominating campaign, leaving aside for a moment the news media's representation of that world. All the candidates routinely say glowing things about themselves and nasty things about each other, of course. But the candidates do not choose the targets of their attacks at random, nor do they distribute their negative remarks uniformly across all their opponents. A candidate who trails in the race for a presidential nomination chooses his target so that, if his attack is effective, it will reduce the difference between his chance of winning and that of the candidate with the best chance. Most underdogs do not need high-priced political consultants to tell them that the target at which they should direct their fire is, therefore, the front-runner. The front-runner's circumstance is different, of course, but the front-runner is not likely to engage in indiscriminate attacks either. With the goal of maximizing the distance between himself and his closest competitor, the front-runner's primary target will be the candidate in second place. In general, then, when a candidate talks about an opponent, the candidate is more likely to talk about an opponent who has a good chance of winning than about one who has a poor chance. A candidate with a good chance of winning, as a result, is more likely than a candidate with a poor chance to be the object of statements made by opponents.[30] And because the norms of the profession compel journalists, at least to some degree, to report what their sources say, the tendency for the front-running candidates to draw most of their opponents' fire is likely to show up in the news.[31]

If candidates and their allies choose whom to attack with an eye to the standings in the race, then it is possible to explain the negative press that front-runners receive in terms of the behavior of candidates, without reference to the intentions of journalists. Demonstrating unequivocally the superiority of a candidate-based explanation over a journalist-based explanation for changes in the sources of news is, however, not easy. A direct empirical test would require systematic data about the statements made by candidates, independent of the data on news coverage—that is, a random sample of everything the candidates said, not just what was reported in the news; collecting such a sample is difficult to imagine. What nevertheless can be shown clearly is that UPI coverage of the 1984 Democratic nomination campaign is perfectly consistent with an explanation that rests on the candidates, not on journalists.

Changes over the course of the campaign in the targets of news coverage attributed to opponents square readily with a candidate-based explanation. From the beginning of the year until the Iowa caucuses in late February, the vast majority of substantive UPI coverage attributed to a candidate's opponents went to Walter Mondale, the consensus front-runner (figure 6.5). Before Iowa, the only other candidate who accumulated coverage based on the comments of his opponents was John Glenn, widely regarded to be second in the standings at the time. Less than 5 percent of the coverage attributed to opponents during that period was devoted to the other five candidates combined. After Iowa, however, Gary Hart entered the picture, as the other candidates, Mondale in particular, shifted their fire. As Hart's standing in the race improved, his share of the comments made by other candidates that were reported in the news increased. By the week preceding Super Tuesday, nearly three-quarters of the comments reported were directed at Hart. With the rejuvenation of the Mondale campaign during late March, and the reduction of the contest to a two-man race (plus Jackson), Mondale's share of substantive coverage attributed to the opposition surged once again, and Hart's dropped; with the nomination seemingly in hand, Mondale sought to minimize intraparty conflict and to project a more positive image by turning his own attention away from Hart and toward Ronald Reagan. Only when Hart seemed to surge back into contention, with victories in a string of primaries early in May, did Mondale resume criticizing Hart regularly.[32] In short, the sources of news coverage followed just the pattern that would be expected from the incentives of the candidates.

To repeat, these data can provide only a mediated account of what the candidates said about each other, which for any number of reasons is unlikely to match exactly an unmediated account. What these data underscore, however, is that even if UPI's coverage of what the candidates said constituted a perfectly random sample of what the candidates actually said, this same pattern would have been the result; and the consequence of this pattern, in turn, would have been an apparent tendency for front-runners to receive more negative press coverage. The tendency for the front-runner to receive harsh treatment in the press does not necessarily imply that journalists are slanting the news against the front-runner. At least as plausible an interpretation is simply that the other candidates are inclined to disparage the front-runner.

Conclusion

Without question, the news media wield enormous influence in American politics. That influence is manifest perhaps in no domain more than in the presidential nomination process. Nominating campaigns are among the principal exhibits to which critics can point when making a case against me-

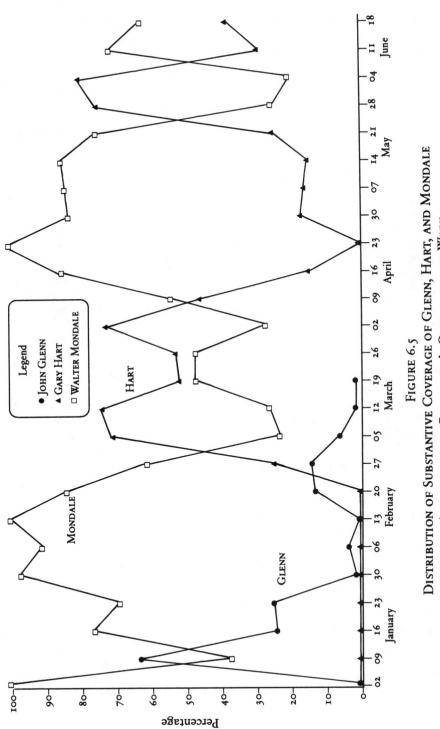

FIGURE 6.5

DISTRIBUTION OF SUBSTANTIVE COVERAGE OF GLENN, HART, AND MONDALE
ATTRIBUTED TO CANDIDATE'S OPPONENTS, BY WEEK

dia power in politics. It sometimes seems that everything the candidates do, they do for the media, and that whatever reporters fail to prompt the candidates to do before the day's news is delivered, their editors take care of in postproduction. Journalists shape the news both by influencing the behavior of the candidates and then by determining whether and how it is covered.

If all this is widely believed, less frequently acknowledged is the fact that the influence of journalists—in the nomination process as on politics in general—is limited. One source of restraint, perhaps the most important one, is the fact that others, too, influence the process. As obvious as the point may seem, too often the motivations and strategies of those other actors are overlooked when news coverage of nominating campaigns is evaluated; when they are cited, the actions of others often are written off as second-order media effects, on the ground that they were contrived with news coverage in mind. But an accurate assessment of the influence of journalists requires a more meticulous account of the influence of others on the news. Alternative explanations for the news we read, see, and hear need to be entertained. To identify the parameters of media power, one must discover not only where journalists are influential, but also where they are not.

The specific case considered here illustrates this general proposition. The negative treatment front-runners receive can easily be explained without falling back on the notion that journalists are both omniscient and omnipotent but not benevolent: most of the criticism directed at the front-running candidate originates not with journalists at all, but with other candidates. And this candidate-based explanation does not depend on media influence in either of the senses noted above, for it can account for the observed distribution of statements made by candidates in the news without assuming that journalists choose among those statements in any systematically biased manner, and it specifies a strategy that candidates probably would adopt even in the absence of the news media. The evidence at hand cannot discriminate perfectly between the candidate-based and journalist-based explanations; it includes no information about the candidates that has not passed through the hands of journalists. But while the data on UPI coverage of the 1984 Democratic campaign cannot be fashioned into an airtight case, they provide quite solid circumstantial evidence of the importance of attending to what candidates do, not just to what journalists do.

All this is not to say that journalists do nothing to contribute to the kind of press a front-runner receives. Journalists certainly do make decisions about, for example, how to allocate the resources necessary to investigate some candidates more thoroughly than others. Moreover, the sample of candidates' attacks that make the news is certainly not a random sample of all candidates' attacks; it is not mere chance, after all, that among the most enduring legacies of the 1984 Democratic campaign is the phrase "Where's the beef?" Packaging is surely important. It also might be true, however, that sometimes the candidates say just what they would say if they were talking to the public directly, not through the media, and sometimes journalists might report just what the candidates say. If this is so, then some of what passes as the impact of journalists' assessments of the candidate's chances is in fact the product of a more complex process, one that involves the perceptions and strategies of candidates as well as those of journalists. And if just where and how journalists influence the presidential nominating process is to be understood with any precision, careful attention must be paid to the distinction between the political decisions journalists make and the political decisions candidates make and journalists report.

Acknowledgments

Earlier versions of this chapter were presented at the 1992 annual meeting of the Midwest Political Science Association, Chicago, 9–11 April, and at "The Mass Media in the Electoral Process," the 1992 Stuart Symposium on Communications and Public Affairs, Woodrow Wilson School of Public and International Affairs, Princeton University, 30 April–1 May. I am grateful for the comments and encouragement of Larry Bartels, Henry Brady, and Raymond Wolfinger.

Notes

1. Austin Ranney, *Channels of Power* (New York: Basic Books, 1983).

2. Bernard C. Cohen, *The Press and Foreign Policy* (Princeton, N.J.: Princeton University Press, 1963); Leon V. Sigal, *Reporters and Officials: The Organization and Politics of Newsmaking* (Lexington, Mass.: D.C. Heath, 1973); Edward Jay Epstein, *News from Nowhere: Television and the News* (New York: Vintage Books, 1974); and Herbert Gans, *Deciding What's News* (New York: Vintage, 1979).

3. For documentation, see Thomas E. Patterson and Robert D. McClure, *The Unseeing Eye: The Myth of Television Power in National Politics* (New York: Putnam, 1976); Thomas E. Patterson, *The Mass Media Election: How Americans Choose Their President* (New York: Praeger, 1980); Michael J. Robinson and Margaret A. Sheehan, *Over the Wire and on TV: CBS and UPI in Campaign '80* (New York: Russell Sage, 1983); Henry E. Brady and Richard Johnston, "What's the Primary Message? Horse Race or Issue Journalism?" in *Media and Momentum: The New Hampshire Primary and Nomination Politics,* ed. Gary R. Orren and Nelson W. Polsby (Chatham, N.J.: Chatham House, 1987), 127–86; and S. Robert Lichter, Daniel Amundson, and Richard Noyes, *The Video Campaign: Network Coverage of the 1988 Primaries* (Washington, D.C.: American Enterprise Institute, 1988).

4. See Patterson and McClure, *The Unseeing Eye;* Patterson, *The Mass Media Election;* Scott Keeter and Cliff Zukin, *Uninformed Choice: The Failure of the New Presidential Nominating System* (New York: Praeger, 1983); and Thomas E.

Patterson, *Out of Order* (New York: Knopf, 1993).

5. William C. Adams, "Media Coverage of Campaign '84: A Preliminary Report," *Public Opinion* 7 (1984): 9–13; William C. Adams, "As New Hampshire Goes ...," in *Media and Momentum: The New Hampshire Primary and Nomination Politics,* ed. Gary R. Orren and Nelson W. Polsby (Chatham, N.J.: Chatham House, 1987), 42–59; Emmett H. Buell, Jr., "'Locals' and 'Cosmopolitans': National, Regional, and State Newspaper Coverage of the New Hampshire Primary," in *Media and Momentum: The New Hampshire Primary and Nomination Politics,* ed. Gary R. Orren and Nelson W. Polsby (Chatham, N.J.: Chatham House, 1987), 60–103; Emmett H. Buell, Jr., "Meeting Expectations? Major Newspaper Coverage of Candidates during the 1988 Exhibition Season," in *Nominating the President,* ed. Emmett H. Buell, Jr., and Lee Sigelman (Knoxville: University of Tennessee Press, 1991), 150–95.

6. Michael G. Hagen, "Sources of Information in Presidential Nominations," Ph.D. dissertation, University of California, Berkeley, 1991.

7. Others who have investigated the degree to which news coverage is positive or negative typically have termed this quality *tone* or *good press/bad press.* This terminology, however, seems to emphasize the voice of the journalist over all others. For reasons that will become clear, the more inclusive term *message* seems preferable here.

8. Donald R. Matthews, "'Winnowing': The News Media and the 1976 Presidential Nominations," in *Race for the Presidency: The Media and the Nominating Process,* ed. James David Barber (Englewood Cliffs, N.J.: Prentice Hall, 1978), 55–78; Richard A. Joslyn, *Mass Media and Elections* (Reading, Mass.: Addison-Wesley, 1984); Lichter, Amundson, and Noyes, *The Video Campaign;* and Buell, "Meeting Expectations?"

9. Patterson, *The Mass Media Election;* Judy Woodruff and Edward Fouhy, "The Message: Advertising, Sound Bites, and Reporting Polls," in *Campaign for President: The Managers Look at '88,* ed. David R. Runkel (Dover, Mass.: Auburn House, 1989), 130–68; Harrison Hickman, "Public Polls and Election Participants," in *Polling and Presidential Election Coverage,* ed. Paul J. Lavrakas and Jack K. Holley (Newbury Park, Calif.: Sage, 1991), 100–33; and Kathleen Hall Jamieson, *Dirty Politics: Deception, Distraction, and Democracy* (New York: Oxford University Press, 1992).

10. Michael J. Robinson, "The Media in 1980: Was the Message the Message?" in *The American Elections of 1980,* ed. Austin Ranney (Washington, D.C.: American Enterprise Institute, 1981), 177–211; Michael J. Robinson, "Where's the Beef? Media and Media Elites in 1984," in *The American Elections of 1984,* ed. Austin Ranney (Washington, D.C.: American Enterprise Institute, 1985), 166–202; Michael J. Robinson, "News Media Myths and Realities: What Network News Did and Didn't Do in the 1984 General Election Campaign," in *Elections in America,* ed. Kay Lehman Schlozman (Boston: Allen & Unwin, 1987), 143–70; Robinson and Sheehan, *Over the Wire and on TV;* and Michael J. Robinson and S. Robert Lichter, "'The More Things Change ...': Network News Coverage of the 1988 Presidential Nomination Races," in *Nominating the President,* ed. Emmett H. Buell, Jr., and Lee Sigelman (Knoxville: University of Tennessee Press, 1991), 196–212.

11. The data were collected as part of a project organized and directed by Henry E. Brady of the Department of Political Science, University of California,

Berkeley. For the funds to acquire and process the data, my thanks go to Henry Brady, Nelson W. Polsby and the Institute of Governmental Studies, Austin Ranney and the Department of Political Science, and Percy Tannenbaum and the Survey Research Center, all of the University of California at Berkeley, and to the Department of Government at Harvard University. For their diligence as coders, thanks to John Bickel, Ramon Bolanos, Brian Bunger, Laurie Freeman, Mike Green, Marissa Martino Golden, Ted Lascher, Karin Martin, Mitch McClure, Liz Norville, Chris Rohmberg, and Chris Young. For further details on sampling and coding procedures, see Hagen, "Sources of Information."

12. Robinson and Sheehan, *Over the Wire and on TV.*

13. Ibid., 15.

14. Doris A. Graber, *Mass Media and American Politics,* 3d ed. (Washington, D.C.: CQ Press, 1989), 209.

15. Graber, *Mass Media and American Politics,* 207.

16. Robinson and Sheehan, *Over the Wire and on TV,* 25; Graber, *Mass Media and American Politics,* 214.

17. Jackson also received exceptional treatment in the television news. See C. Anthony Broh, *A Horse of a Different Color: Television's Treatment of Jesse Jackson's 1984 Presidential Campaign* (Washington, D.C.: Joint Center for Political Studies, 1987); and Robinson and Lichter, " 'The More Things Change. . . .' "

18. For further details on these points, see Hagen, "Sources of Information."

19. For attempts to implement this approach, see Larry M. Bartels, *Presidential Primaries and the Dynamics of Public Choice* (Princeton: Princeton University Press, 1988), and Hagen, "Sources of Information."

20. The impression conveyed by each line of each UPI story devoted to discussing a candidate's chances of winning the nomination was scored on a five-point scale running from "very favorable" to "very unfavorable." The raw values have been transformed so that their sum across all the candidates in the race (excluding Jackson) in each week is equal to one; an individual candidate's score, therefore, can be regarded as his probability, in the judgment of UPI journalists, of winning the nomination.

21. That journalists' assessments of Hart's chances should rise so much when Hart was a *distant* second to Mondale is a matter of some interest, but not directly relevant here. Again, the purpose of this chapter is not to explain or to evaluate journalists' expectations, only to describe them. For a fuller treatment of the question of accuracy, see Hagen, "Sources of Information."

22. In part, of course, the relationship between weekly messages about Hart's and Mondale's chances is negative by construction—their sum is constrained to be constant. The raw data, however, show the same changes over time in the rank order of the two candidates.

23. This is apparent in the difference between the constants on table 6.2: .07 for supporters, −.87 for opponents.

24. Margaret Carlson, "Bill Clinton: Front Runner by Default," *Time,* 30 December 1991, 19–21. For corroboration, see the quotations of Jeff Greenfield (p. 107) and Bill Plante (p. 116) in Robinson and Sheehan, *Over the Wire and on TV.*

25. Matthews, " 'Winnowing' "; Robinson and Sheehan, *Over the Wire and on TV;* and Robinson, "Where's the Beef?"

26. Robinson, "News Media Myths and Realities"; Robinson and Lichter, " 'The More Things Change. . . .' "

27. Robinson, "The Media in 1980"; Joslyn, *Mass Media and Elections.*

28. The explanatory power of this account may vary over time, according to the analysis of Senator Phil Gramm and Representative Newt Gingrich. The recession, the two Bush supporters maintained in a press conference early in 1992, made journalists so concerned about their jobs that they were inspired to promote the candidacy of Pat Buchanan.

29. Another measure of the fit between the two simulations and the observed pattern confirms the superiority of the second: the mean squared difference between the second simulation and the observed pattern is just .056, compared with .175 for the first.

30. According to Nelson W. Polsby and Aaron Wildavsky, for example, both Jimmy Carter in 1976 and Richard Gephardt in 1988 faced a concentrated, although formally uncoordinated, barrage of criticism from their opponents once they threatened to move out into the lead in their respective races. Nelson W. Polsby and Aaron Wildavsky, *Presidential Elections: Contemporary Strategies of American Electoral Politics,* 8th ed. (New York: Free Press, 1992), 132.

31. Richard A. Brody argues that a roughly analogous process explains the typically rosy news coverage of presidential actions during international crises, when journalists find themselves reporting an unusually uncritical mix of news about the president's performance because during a crisis few members of the Washington elite openly criticize the president. See Richard A. Brody, *Assessing the President: The Media, Elite Opinion, and Public Support* (Stanford: Stanford University Press, 1991).

32. I am indebted to Bill Mayer for pointing out this feature of the Mondale strategy late in the campaign.

7

The Changing Environment
of Presidential Campaign
Finance

ANTHONY CORRADO

In the early 1970s Congress completely restructured the system for financing presidential prenomination campaigns. Alarmed by rapidly rising campaign costs and the growing importance of wealthy donors as a source of campaign funds, Congress passed a series of laws to control the flow of money in presidential campaigns and reduce the influence of private wealth in national elections. The hallmark of this regulatory effort was the Federal Election Campaign Act of 1974, the most ambitious campaign finance law ever adopted. This legislation established a new regulatory regime for candidates seeking their party's presidential nomination. It imposed strict limits on political contributions, established national and state spending ceilings, and required full public disclosure of contributions and expenditures. It created an innovative system of public funding, which was designed to supplement private donations with public subsidies and thus reduce the emphasis on fund raising in political campaigns. To ensure its effectiveness, the law also established a new agency, the Federal Election Commission, to administer and enforce the new regulations.

These new rules, as well as other changes in the presidential selection process, forced candidates to change their fund-raising approaches and adopt new financial strategies. Some of these strategies were intended by the law; others were not. Some were prompted by efforts to comply with the regulations, others to circumvent them. The result has been a dynamic process of adaptation and response, in which federal regulators seek to control the flow of money in presidential campaigns and uphold the integrity of the law, while candidates seek to accommodate changing circumstances and maximize the amounts of money they can spend.

This chapter traces the major developments that have taken place in the financing of presidential prenomination campaigns under the system established by the Federal Election Campaign Act. In order to assess the degree to which these reforms have achieved their objectives, it specifically examines how presidential candidates have responded to the modern regulatory environment. In doing so, it highlights the inventiveness of candidates in circumventing the law and the problems that continue to confront federal regulators in light of the ever-changing strategic circumstances that shape the financial activity in presidential prenomination campaigns.

The Regulatory Framework

From the mid-1950s to the early 1970s, presidential campaigns became increasingly sophisticated as candidates began to make extensive use of television advertising, telephone banks, and specialized mail programs to spread their message to the electorate. These new communication techniques, especially paid television advertisements, substantially increased the costs of presidential campaigns. For example, in the 1956 election, President Dwight Eisenhower and his Democratic challenger Adlai Stevenson spent a total of $11.6 million. By 1972, the amount spent by the Republican and Democratic presidential nominees had skyrocketed to over $90 million, or more than eight times the sum spent just sixteen years earlier, and almost ten times the rate of inflation during this period. Richard Nixon alone spent a staggering $61.4 million in 1972, more than twice the amount he had spent in winning the presidency in 1968, while George McGovern, his Democratic challenger, spent approximately $30 million, or almost three times the amount spent by Democrat Hubert Humphrey in 1968.[1]

This dramatic rise in campaign spending forced candidates to place a greater emphasis on fund raising, since they had to devote more attention to the burdensome task of soliciting the funds needed to fuel their campaigns. In order to ease this burden yet continue to generate the amount of money needed for television advertising and other expenses, candidates increasingly turned to wealthy donors, or "fat cats," as their primary source of campaign dollars. In 1952, 110 individuals contributed $10,000 or more to a presidential candidate, for a total of $1.9 million. In 1972, 1,254 individuals contributed $10,000 or more, for a total of $51.3 million, or an average gift of more than $40,000 per person. This group of well-heeled donors included W. Clement Stone, chairman of the Combined Insurance Company of America, who gave more than $2 million to President Nixon's reelection campaign; Richard Mellon Scaife, an heir to the Mellon family fortune, who gave more than $1 million to Nixon; and Stewart Mott, an heir to the General Motors fortune, who gave about $400,000 to McGovern. In addition, the number of individuals giving $500 or more rose from 9,500 in 1952 to 51,230 in 1972.[2]

This growing dependence on large contributions raised fundamental concerns about the health of the presidential campaign finance system. Advocates of reform charged that "fat cat" donors were playing too great a role in the financing of campaigns. They noted that wealthy contributors were undermining the integrity of the political process, since their generous contributions permitted gross inequities in the relative influence of individual citizens on electoral outcomes, exacerbated the role of special interests in politics, and encouraged many citizens to regard the electoral system as a process corrupted by money. Critics also argued that the system led to unacceptable disparities in the resources available to candidates, which served to reduce the level of competition and fairness in presidential contests. These issues became a focal point of congressional and public attention after the 1972 election, as the Watergate investigations revealed that the Nixon campaign had accepted a number of extraordinarily large gifts, solicited illegal donations from corporations and foreign interests, and promised ambassadorial appointments and legislative favors in exchange for campaign contributions.[3]

Congress responded to these concerns by adopting the Federal Election Campaign Act (FECA) in 1974. Although technically a set of amendments to the Federal Election Campaign Act of 1971, the 1974 legislation thoroughly revised the rules governing the funding of presidential campaigns in an effort to protect the integrity of the presidential selection process and prevent the types of abuses exposed in the aftermath of the 1972 election.[4] The FECA addressed the problems associated with large gifts by placing a limit on campaign contributions. The law set a ceiling of $1,000 per election on the amount an individual could contribute to a presidential candidate and limited an individual's total annual contributions to all federal candidates and political committees to $25,000. Political action committees (PACs) were allowed to give no more than $5,000 per election with no annual aggregate limit, while other types of political committees were limited to donations of $1,000 per election.

To restrain the growth in expenditures and equalize the potential resources available to candidates, the law imposed a set of stringent spending ceilings on presidential campaigns. Different ceilings were applied to each stage of the selection process: the act established one ceiling for the nomination contest, another for the amount national party organizations could receive in public funding for costs associated with their presidential nominating conventions, and a third for the general election campaign. With respect to the prenomination contest, the act established an aggregate spending limit of $10 million per candidate.[5] Each candidate was also allowed to spend up to 20 percent of this amount, or $2 million at the time the law was adopted, for fund-raising expenses, since it was assumed that the new regulations would force candidates to incur higher fund-raising costs as a result of the need to finance their campaigns through smaller donations. This aggregate ceiling is indexed to account for inflation, so with each new election cycle the amount that candidates may spend has increased. By 1992, the limit had been raised to $27.6 million, with an additional $5.5 million for fund-raising expenses (see table 7.1).

In addition, the act established state-by-state expenditure ceilings so that relatively unknown presidential aspirants would have an opportunity to compete effectively against better-known or better-financed candidates in individual states.[6] These limits are set at the higher amount of either sixteen cents times the voting-age population of the state or $200,000. As with the aggregate ceiling, these state limits are indexed for inflation. By 1992, these limits ranged from $552,400 in the states with the smallest populations, such as New Hampshire, Delaware, and Rhode Island, to $9.8 million in the largest state, California.[7]

TABLE 7.1
PRESIDENTIAL PRENOMINATION CAMPAIGN SPENDING LIMITS,
1976–92[a]

Year	National spending limit[b]	Exempt fund raising[c]	Overall spending limit[d]
1976	10.9	2.2	13.1
1980	14.7	2.9	17.7
1984	20.2	4.0	24.2
1988	23.1	4.6	27.7
1992	27.6	5.5	33.1

SOURCE: Federal Election Commission.
a. Figures represent dollars in millions.
b. Based on a ceiling of $10 million plus cost-of-living adjustments (COLAs) using 1974 as the base year. Candidates eligible for public subsidies may receive no more than one-half the national spending limit in public matching funds.
c. Candidates may spend up to 20 percent of the national spending limit for fund-raising costs.
d. Legal and accounting expenses to ensure compliance with the law are exempt from the spending limit.

While limiting contributions and expenditures, the FECA also recognized the need to ensure that presidential candidates have access to the resources needed to mount a viable national campaign. The law therefore provided candidates with a new source of campaign money by creating a voluntary program of public financing. The purpose of this subsidy is to reduce the fund-raising burdens placed on candidates and at the same time encourage them to seek smaller donations. To become eligible for matching funds, a candidate has to raise at least $5,000 in contributions of $250 or less in at least twenty states, for a total of $100,000. Once eligible, a candidate may receive public matching funds on a dollar-for-dollar basis on the first $250 received from an individual, provided the contribution is received after 1 January of the year before the election year. The aggregate amount a candidate may receive in public matching funds is limited to one-half the aggregate spending limit for a presidential prenomination campaign, or about $13.8 million in 1992. As a result of the Supreme Court's 1976 decision in *Buckley* v. *Valeo*,[8] candidates who accept public funds must not only abide by the aggregate and state spending limits but must also agree to limit personal contributions to their own campaigns to no more than $50,000. Candidates who do not accept public money are exempt from the spending limits and may donate unlimited amounts to their own campaigns.

While the 1974 law clearly delineated how to qualify for matching funds, it did not set forth specific guidelines as to when a candidate's eligibility for these subsidies ended. This raised the concern that the availability of public funds might serve to encourage a presidential candidate with little hope of gaining the nomination to stay in the race simply because enough money was available to do so. To guard against this possibility, Congress modified the regulations in 1976 and established the "ten percent rule." This rule stipulates that a presidential candidate who receives less than 10 percent of the vote in two consecutive primaries in which he or she is qualified for the ballot is ineligible for additional matching fund payments. These payments are restored if that candidate receives 20 percent of the vote in a later primary. The law also requires that candidates who withdraw from the nomination race after receiving matching funds must return any remaining monies to the Treasury.[9]

Revenues for the public financing program are provided by a voluntary tax checkoff on individual federal income tax forms. Under the original terms of this program, an individual could designate $1 and a married couple filing jointly could designate $2 to be used for the public financing program by marking the appropriate box on the income tax form. In 1993, Congress increased the amount of the checkoff to $3 for individuals and $6 for joint filers in order to ensure that the program would have the revenues needed to finance future elections.

Financing Prenomination Campaigns

Prior to the adoption of the FECA, candidates could generate the money needed to launch a viable presidential campaign by relying on the generosity of wealthy supporters. Since there were no effective limits on campaign giving, candidates could raise sizable amounts of money quickly and efficiently by soliciting large gifts or loans from a handful of individuals. Such gifts were especially important in the early stages of the race, when candidates were looking for seed money that could be used to start up a campaign or when they were trying to raise the sums needed to finance their efforts in a crucial primary state. In 1972, for example, George McGovern had five supporters who gave close to $500,000 and loaned over $850,000 to his campaign during the primaries.[10] These funds provided McGovern with the resources he needed early on to sustain his direct mail fund-raising efforts and establish himself as a serious contender for the Democratic nomination. In 1968, Robert Kennedy did not decide to run for the presidency until mid-March, weeks after the crucial New Hampshire primary. But in less than three months, he managed to raise millions of dollars and mount a nationwide campaign.[11]

The contribution limits established by the FECA made it impossible for candidates to raise large sums so quickly and efficiently. Although they did not prevent candidates from raising substantial amounts of money, they did change the way candidates went about this task. Instead of relying on a relatively small group of large donors for a significant portion of their campaign funds, candidates had to solicit donations of $1,000 or less and finance their campaigns through tens of thousands of small gifts. This did not, however, reduce the amount of money involved in presidential campaigns. In 1972, for example, eighteen candidates for the Democratic presidential nomination spent an estimated $32.7 million during the prenomination period. In 1976, thirteen Democrats reported spending $40.7 million.[12] Overall, the major-party presidential candidates raised almost $68 million in 1976 and more than $100 million in each subsequent race. In 1988, the first contest since the FECA was adopted in which there was no incumbent seeking reelection in either party, sixteen candidates raised more than $213 million, an amount equal to the total raised in the 1980 and 1984 elections combined (see table 7.2).

In 1992 the aggregate amount raised by the presidential candidates fell well below the amount generated in 1988; the ten major-party challengers and three minor-party challengers received about $126.2 million, or approximately 60 percent of the amount generated by their 1988 counterparts. The primary reason for this decline was the lack of an "open" race in the Republican Party. President George Bush was seeking reelection, so only one candidate, former Nixon speechwriter and conservative television commentator Patrick Buchanan, decided to contest the Republican nomination. Bush and Buchanan raised a combined $50.2 million, as compared to $135.6 million for the six candidates who sought the Republican Party mantle in 1988.[13]

Another factor accounting for the lower fund-raising totals in 1992 was the relatively late start to the Democratic race. In recent years, candidates for the presidential nomination have begun to raise money well in advance of the election year. But in the 1992 election cycle, President Bush's post

–Gulf War popularity caused most of the putative Democratic candidates to adopt a "wait and see" attitude toward the presidential contest. Ultimately, the most well-known prospective challengers, including Governor Mario Cuomo of New York, Representative Richard Gephardt of Missouri, Senators Bill Bradley of New Jersey and Jay Rockefeller of West Virginia, and the Reverend Jesse Jackson, decided not to run. Consequently, the Democratic field consisted largely of less well-known contenders who decided to enter the race relatively late, with the exception of former Senator Paul Tsongas of Massachusetts, who declared his candidacy in the spring of 1991. As a result, the Democrats generated relatively modest sums by the standards of other recent presidential contests.[14] Only Bill Clinton, the eventual Democratic nominee, solicited more than $10 million, as compared to five Democrats who passed this threshold in 1988.[15] Overall, the eight Democrats who ran in 1992 raised about $70 million, as compared to $115 million for the eight who ran in 1988; the seven who failed to win the nomination in 1992 raised a total of less than $33 million, as compared to over $80 million for the seven who failed to win in 1988.[16] The decline in campaign revenues was thus largely a result of the unique dynamics of the 1992 race.

As noted in table 7.2, most of the money raised by presidential candidates comes from individual donors and the public funds generated by small individual gifts. On average, more than 95 percent of the total funds received by presidential candidates comes from individuals and public funding, with individual gifts constituting about 65 percent of total receipts and matching funds about a third.

While PACs and other political committees often provide up to 40 percent of the money raised by congressional candidates, they account for only 1 or 2 percent on average of the amounts raised by presidential candidates. Even candidates who specifically target PAC money as a source of campaign dollars, such as Democrats Richard Gephardt in 1988 and Thomas Harkin in 1992, rarely receive more than 5 percent of their total funds from these committees. There are a number of reasons for this pattern. PACs and other political committees generally prefer to concentrate their gifts in congressional races, and many have a policy of not participating in presidential nomination campaigns. PAC contributions are not eligible for matching under the public funding program, so candidates have less incentive to solicit such gifts. PACs are such a minor source of funding that a number of recent presidential candidates, including all of the Democrats in 1992 except Harkin and Robert Kerrey, decided to refuse PAC donations. While some who have refused PAC money have done so because of their general opposition to this source of funding (e.g., Democrats Paul Tsongas and Jerry Brown in the 1992 campaign), most have based their decision on strategic considerations, hoping that such a stance would prove more beneficial politically than the marginal amount of money they might receive from such groups.

TABLE 7.2
PRESIDENTIAL PRENOMINATION CAMPAIGN RECEIPTS, 1976–92

	1976		1980		1984		1988		1992[a]	
Number of candidates[b]	15		10		11		16		13	
Total receipts[c]	67.9		108.0		105.0		213.8		126.2	
Individuals	42.5	(62.6)	72.8	(67.4)	62.8	(59.8)	141.1	(66.0)	82.3	(65.2)
Public funds	24.3	(35.8)	30.9	(28.6)	34.9	(33.2)	65.7	(30.7)	42.7	(33.8)
PACs	0.8	(1.2)	1.6	(1.5)	1.3	(1.2)	3.0	(1.4)	0.9	(0.7)

SOURCE: Federal Election Commission.

a. Based on amounts reported as of 30 September 1993.

b. Includes all candidates who received public funds, as well as Republican John Connally in 1980 and Libertarian Andre Marrou in 1992.

c. Figures represent dollars in millions. Figures in parentheses represent the percentage of total receipts. All figures based on adjusted receipts, which exclude transfers between affiliated committees, refunds, and loan payments. The itemized receipts do not equal the total amount received in each election cycle because candidates have other sources of revenue, including interest, transfers from other committees, and loans.

Although all candidates for the presidential nomination rely on individual donations to finance their campaigns, there is a great variety in the approaches used to solicit the tens of thousands of individual gifts needed to finance a viable national campaign. For example, in 1992, President George Bush entered the race with the most solidly established financial base in recent electoral history. He had essentially spent twelve years recruiting financial support, first as a candidate for the 1980 presidential nomination, then as vice-president, and finally as president. Over these years he had developed an extensive, nationwide base of donors, many of whom were capable of making large contributions. In his 1988 bid for the Republican nomination, he adopted a fund-raising approach designed to exploit his ability to attract large gifts. In addition to soliciting those who had contributed to his efforts in the past, Bush recruited a network of supporters who were responsible for soliciting large donations on behalf of the campaign. These solicitors contacted other Bush supporters or relied on their personal contacts to identify individuals who could give $1,000 to the campaign. This "networking" or "pyramiding" approach produced the bulk of the revenues for his campaign. Bush raised more than $27 million, the maximum amount allowed under the spending limit, $16.5 million of which came from $1,000 donors.[17]

In 1992, Bush pursued a similar strategy. He raised about $27.1 million through individual contributions, which accounted for about 70 percent of his total campaign revenues (see table 7.3). Of this amount, more than two-thirds came in the form of $1,000 donations; according to Federal Election Commission records, the campaign received the maximum contribution from over 18,500 individuals, for a total of more than $18.5 million.[18] If contributions of $750 or more are considered, this reliance on large contributions is made even clearer, since donations in these amounts accounted for 82 percent of Bush's total individual receipts. Bush also sought contributions through direct-mail programs designed to raise smaller gifts, but this tactic proved to be less successful than campaign officials had hoped. Bush thus raised less than 10 percent of his campaign monies from contributions of under $500.[19]

Bush's 1992 opponent for the Republican nomination, Patrick Buchanan, entered the race without an extensive donor network and therefore adopted a different fund-raising strategy. His campaign emphasized the solicitation of small contributions through direct mail and the accumulation of public matching funds. Buchanan sent letters seeking donations to his newsletter subscriber list and other mailing lists of conservative donors, including supporters of national defense causes, antidrug campaigns, evangelical groups, and 1988 Bush contributors. Each of these mailings generated thousands of contributions, the vast majority of which were eligible for matching funds, and produced substantial amounts of money for Buchanan's insurgent campaign. Buchanan's approach was so effective that direct-mail expert David Tyson described it as "the most successful direct-mail effort in the history of conservative politics."[20] By the end of February, 50,000 people had contributed an average of $48 to the campaign, with about 80 percent of these early funds a result of direct mail. By May, Buchanan had raised more than $4 million through direct mail, and more than 85 percent of these donations had qualified for matching funds.[21] In total, he raised more than 76 percent of the $7.2 million he received from individuals in contributions of $200 or less, and about 83 percent in contributions of less than $500. He also earned about $5 million in public matching funds, which constituted about 40 percent of his total campaign revenues. Moreover, in stark contrast to Bush, Buchanan received only about 600 donations of $1,000, or approximately one for every 30 received by the president.[22]

Democrat Jerry Brown, Buchanan's polar opposite ideologically, pursued a similar, albeit more radical, fund-raising strategy. Brown based his fund raising solely on small gifts and public subsidies, a position consistent with his central campaign message advocating political reform. He refused to accept any contribution in excess of $100 and established a twenty-four-hour-a-day 800 telephone service as the primary means for soliciting donations. Brown regularly mentioned or advertised the 800 number in his campaign appearances, encouraging voters to telephone the number and make a contribution. This innovative, grassroots approach to fund raising proved to be effective. With the exception of some loans his campaign received in anticipation of matching fund payments, all of his campaign's finances were based on small gifts. Brown raised $5.2 million through small donations, with nearly 85 percent of this amount solicited through the 800 number system. He accepted over 84,500 contributions, at an average of $52 each, that were eligible for matching funds, resulting in $4.2 million in public revenue, which represented about 45 percent of his total campaign funds.[23]

Democrats Bill Clinton and Paul Tsongas used more varied approaches designed to raise both large and small contributions. Both candidates relied on networks of supporters to solicit contributions on their behalf, as well as small donor events and direct mail. Clinton raised about 42 percent of the $25.1 million he received from individuals in contributions of $750 or more, including approximately $7.2 million from $1,000 donors, and 38 percent of these funds from contributors of less than $500. About a third of his total receipts, $12.5 million, came from public monies. Tsongas was less successful in soliciting large donations than Clinton, raising about 26 percent of his $8.1 million in total individual receipts from contributors of $750 or more, including about $1.2 million from $1,000 donors. More than half of the funds he received from individuals were in the form of contributions of less than $500, with roughly 43 percent of his total individual receipts from gifts of $200 or less. As a result, he had a slightly higher percentage of funds from public monies than Clinton did, 36 percent.

TABLE 7.3

PRESIDENTIAL PRENOMINATION CAMPAIGN RECEIPTS AND EXPENDITURES BY CANDIDATE, 1992

Candidate	Total adjusted receipts[a]	Individual contributions	PAC contributions[a]	Public funds	Total adjusted expenditures[b]
Democrats					
Larry Agran	$610,831	$331,631	$0	$269,691	$607,218
Jerry Brown	9,420,374	5,176,336	0	4,239,345	8,994,722
Bill Clinton	37,641,819	25,105,044	5,204	12,518,130	33,900,254
Thomas Harkin	5,681,056	3,069,474	492,069	2,103,351	5,227,520
Robert Kerrey	6,466,079	3,913,332	349,757	2,198,284	6,461,751
Lyndon LaRouche	1,599,861	1,599,840	0	100,000	1,605,386
Paul Tsongas	8,099,564	5,056,620	3,566	3,003,973	7,682,978
Douglas Wilder	799,334	508,519	750	289,026	805,972
Republicans					
Patrick Buchanan	12,205,269	7,157,808	24,750	4,999,983	11,551,379
George Bush	38,013,375	27,088,825	44,250	10,658,513	37,945,656
Minor parties[c]					
John Hagelin	926,304	561,820	449	353,160	875,143
Andre Marrou	578,067	562,770	181	0	575,795
Lenora Fulani	4,137,368	2,201,577	0	1,935,524	4,206,857
Totals	$126,179,301	$82,333,596	$920,976	$42,668,980	$120,440,631

SOURCE: Federal Election Commission, as of 30 September 1993.

a. Includes contributions from party organizations and other political commitees.

b. Totals have been adjusted to account for any transfers between affiliated committees, refunds, or loan payments.

c. John Hagelin was the presidential nominee of the Natural Law Party; Andre Marrou, the Libertarian Party; and Lenora Fulani, the New Alliance Party.

Although the differences in the fund-raising patterns in the 1992 cycle were more pronounced than in previous elections, they were not atypical. An examination of comparable data for candidates in previous nomination contests reveals similar patterns (see table 7.4). In 1988, for example, the Reverend Jesse Jackson, a Democrat, and Pat Robertson, a Republican, adopted fund-raising strategies along the lines of Buchanan's approach, raising close to 90 percent of their individual receipts in contributions of less than $500. Republicans Robert Dole and Jack Kemp, as well as Democrat Michael Dukakis, the eventual Democratic nominee, employed the more varied approach used by Clinton and Tsongas in 1992. Dole and Dukakis were particularly successful at soliciting larger donations through fund-raising networks. The Dole campaign created a team of fund raisers, each of whom pledged to raise $50,000. The Dukakis campaign created a finance committee consisting of individuals who pledged to raise $10,000. By May 1992, 900 individuals had fulfilled this requirement. The campaign also recruited 230 individuals who each raised at least $25,000, and 130 supporters who each raised at least $100,000.[24]

One of the primary objectives of the FECA was to encourage presidential candidates to expand their fund-raising bases and, by providing matching funds for contributions of $250 or less, to place greater reliance on small contributions. The law has certainly had this effect; serious contenders for the presidential nomination now must solicit contributions from tens of thousands of donors in order to raise the money needed for a viable national campaign. The data in table 7.4, however, indicate that in recent elections increasing numbers of candidates have placed greater emphasis on larger donations in their efforts to build campaign war chests. In the 1980 election only Jimmy Carter, an incumbent president seeking reelection, and Republican John Connally, the only major-party candidate to refuse public matching funds, raised a greater proportion of their campaign monies from large donations than from contributions of less than $500. In 1984, only Democrat John Glenn followed this pattern. In the 1988 and 1992 elections, however, almost half the candidates who seriously contested the nomination raised more money from large donors than small donors.

Part of the explanation for this shift in the general fund-raising patterns in presidential prenomination campaigns is the decline in the real value of a contribution. Although a $1,000 contribution may seem high to the average voter, who could not afford such a gift, the erosion of the dollar since this limit was established in 1974 has been substantial. Had the FECA's contribution limit been indexed to inflation, the maximum contribution in 1992 would have been about $2,495. In other words, a $1,000 donation in 1992 was comparable to a donation of roughly $350 to $400 in 1974. Moreover, given the substantial sums needed to mount a presidential campaign, an increasing number of candidates have found it to be more efficient to concen-

TABLE 7.4
INDIVIDUAL CONTRIBUTIONS: DISTRIBUTION BY SIZE
OF DONATION, 1980–92[a]

	Amount of contribution		
Candidate[b]	$1–499	$500–749	$750–1,000
1980			
Brown	55	13	33
Carter	32	18	50
Kennedy	59	11	31
Anderson	87	6	8
Baker	65	14	20
Bush	57	18	25
Connally	43	13	44
Crane	91	4	5
Dole	43	18	39
Reagan	59	11	30
1984			
Askew	59	15	27
Cranston	47	14	39
Glenn	37	18	45
Hart	68	10	23
Hollings	60	13	27
Jackson	86	6	8
Mondale	52	17	31
Reagan	63	9	29
1988			
Babbitt	35	12	54
Dukakis	37	20	42
Gephardt	43	19	38
Gore	44	17	39

trate on soliciting larger gifts. This is especially true of candidates who are well known or who enter the race with a preestablished donor base; they seek to capitalize on such support to gain a financial advantage over their opponents. By focusing on large donations, they can raise money more efficiently, amass sizable amounts of money relatively quickly, and still earn matching funds.

Another conclusion that may be drawn from table 7.4 is that the FECA's small-donor incentives have particularly benefited the more ideological candidates in presidential nomination contests. Liberal candidates such as Jesse Jackson in 1984 and 1988 and Jerry Brown in 1992 have received the vast majority of their campaign funds from smaller donations and thus

TABLE 7.4 — CONTINUED

Candidate[b]	Amount of contribution		
	$1–499	*$500–749*	*$750–1,000*
Hart	44	11	45
Jackson	88	4	7
Simon	61	12	27
Bush	22	12	66
Dole	36	12	51
Du Pont	45	14	40
Haig	22	17	61
Kemp	68	9	22
Robertson	89	3	8
1992			
Brown	100	0	0
Clinton	38	20	42
Harkin	73	8	19
Kerrey	41	16	43
Tsongas	60	13	26
Buchanan	83	6	12
Bush	9	9	82

SOURCE: Federal Election Commission. For elections prior to 1992 see the Commission's quadrennial Reports on Financial Activity: Final Report, Presidential Prenomination Campaigns.
a. Figures represent the percentage of the total amount raised from individuals that was received in contributions of the specified dollar amounts. For example, in 1980, Democrat Jerry Brown raised $938,086 in contributions of less than $500, which equaled 55 percent of the total amount he received from individual contributions.
b. Includes the major Democratic and Republican candidates, with the Democrats listed first in the groupings for each election cycle.

qualified for substantial amounts of public money. The public subsidy helped them muster the resources needed to mount a viable national campaign. Jackson raised a combined $17.4 million from individuals in his two bids for the presidency and earned $10.7 million in public funds; Brown raised $5.2 million from individuals and earned $4.2 million in public funds. Similarly, conservative candidates such as Philip Crane in 1980, Pat Robertson in 1988, and Patrick Buchanan in 1992 have been able to capitalize on the support of a broad base of conservative small donors. Crane received $3.5 million from individuals and $1.8 million in matching funds; Robertson $20.6 million and $9.7 million in matching funds; and Buchanan $7.2 million and $5.0 million in matching funds. This latter group might even be extended to include Ronald Reagan, who even as president in 1984, relied on smaller donations for about 60 percent of the total amount his campaign raised from individuals. As a result, Reagan was the first, and to date the only, presidential candidate to qualify for the maximum amount of matching money allowed under the law.

The matching funds that accompany small contributions have also helped lesser-known aspirants who entered the presidential sweepstakes without access to a broad base of large donors. For these individuals, such as Jimmy Carter in 1976, Gary Hart in 1984, and Bill Clinton and Paul Tsongas in 1992, public subsidies served as a source of sorely needed revenues, providing the money needed at crucial points in the delegate selection contest to help them continue in the race or communicate their ideas to voters.[25] Public funding has thus fulfilled its objective of enhancing competition in presidential contests. It has provided candidates who lack access to financial support from established party donors with a means of raising funds, while providing lesser-known candidates with the resources to wage viable campaigns.

To argue that lesser-known candidates and those from outside the party mainstream have benefited from public funding, however, is not to claim that better-known or established candidates have been unduly disadvantaged. Well-known candidates, especially perceived front-runners, also gain an advantage under the public financing program. Because these candidates usually enter the race with a much broader base of financial support than their less prominent challengers, they can solicit a greater number of small donations or matchable contributions. By doing so, they can significantly increase the resource gap they enjoy over their opponents. So although public funding provides less prominent candidates with sorely needed revenues and increases their relative resources, the program provides the most money in absolute terms to better-known contenders and thus helps them maintain their financial superiority over lesser-known challengers.

The potential advantage public funding offers to more established candidates can be especially important in the earliest stages of a presidential race. Under the provisions of the FECA, the first matching fund payments are not issued by the Treasury Department until 1 January of the election year. By beginning to raise money early, as much as a calendar year before the election, and capitalizing on their ability to solicit funds, well-known candidates can accrue a substantial amount in public matching funds and thus gain a major resource advantage over their competitors when the first matching checks are issued, just weeks before the crucial Iowa caucuses and New Hampshire primary. For example, in 1984 Democrat Walter Mondale followed this strategic approach and gained a sizable financial windfall when the first payment was made. His first matching fund check totaled almost $4.3 million, or about $2 million more than that of his closest rival, John Glenn, who received about $2.3 million.[26] In 1988 George Bush had amassed over $6.1 million in matching funds by the time of the first payment, which was almost $1 million more than the amount raised by his chief rival, Robert Dole, but was close to $3 million more than the amount earned by Jack Kemp and more than $4 million over the amount earned by Pierre "Pete" du Pont.[27] Similarly, in 1992, by the time of the New Hampshire primary, Clinton led all Democrats with $1.4 million in matching funds, compared to $556,000 for Tsongas and $393,000 for Brown, while Bush had banked about $3.6 million in public subsidies, as compared to $100,000 for Buchanan.[28]

Matching funds have therefore been an important source of revenues for all presidential aspirants. Their value is demonstrated by the fact that every candidate except Connally in 1980 has relied on this source of funding for a substantial portion of campaign monies. On average, public subsidies have provided about a third of the total amount raised in each election since 1976. Even those candidates who primarily solicit large donations receive about 25 to 30 percent of their campaign funds from the public treasury. Bush, for example, received about $10.7 million in matching funds in 1992, even though more than 80 percent of the individual gifts he solicited were in large dollar amounts. Candidates who raise the majority of their funds from small donors often receive at least 40 percent of their total campaign monies from public financing.[29]

The provisions of the FECA have thus provided presidential aspirants with a variety of effective fund-raising options. Candidates no longer have to rely on their success in soliciting large contributions from a small cadre of wealthy donors in order to be financially competitive or raise the sums needed to finance a viable campaign. Instead, they can craft fund-raising strategies to conform to their political strengths and maximize the revenue potential of their individual bases of support. Candidates without access to large donors or those with broad bases of support can focus on the solicitation of small, matchable contributions to double the revenue produced by their fund-raising efforts. Those with access to large donors can concentrate on building networks designed to solicit larger gifts and thus raise money more efficiently. Others may choose a more differentiated approach that taps both small and large donors, although it appears that candidates are increasingly choosing one approach or the other. That is, the evidence from recent elections suggests that fund-raising practices are becoming more polarized, with some candidates primarily seeking smaller gifts through mail and telemarketing programs, and others primarily seeking donations in larger amounts through personal solicitations and donor networks.[30]

The Strategic Pressures of the FECA

THE NEED TO RAISE MONEY EARLY

While the provisions of the FECA have provided candidates with alternative means of financing their campaigns, they have also increased the financial pressures aspirants face and thus compelled them to begin fund raising early in the election cycle—in most cases, at least a year before the beginning of the delegate selection process. Developing the broad base of financial support and soliciting the thousands of contributions needed to finance a truly national campaign is a burdensome and time-consuming task, regardless of the fund-raising approach a candidate employs. Developing a network of individuals capable of raising substantial amounts for a presidential campaign is a highly labor-intensive process that often requires the candidate's participation in the recruiting process. Identifying such individuals and securing their support can often take months, even for candidates who begin the process with an established base of financial supporters.

Building an extensive list of small donors through direct-mail or telemarketing programs can be an even lengthier and more expensive process. Candidates initially have to rent or purchase lists of possible donors and then conduct a number of "prospecting" mailings to identify actual donors. These mailings generally result in donations from 2 to 3 percent of the individuals solicited and often lose money. Moreover, any money raised through initial prospecting efforts is usually reinvested in additional mailings, with as many as five separate mailings often needed to develop a list capable of generating substantial profits. The process of creating a profitable direct-mail program capable of producing thousands of small donations can therefore often take three to six months.[31]

In addition to the basic mechanics of fund raising required by the FECA, the law's public funding provisions encourage candidates to begin raising money early because of the timetable it establishes for eligible donations. Any contribution made or received after 1 January of the year before the election is eligible for matching. This provision offers candidates an incentive to begin soliciting matchable gifts as early in the preelection year as possible. As noted earlier, candidates who begin raising funds early, and do so successfully, usually receive a sizable sum when the first matching payments are issued. Lesser-known candidates therefore have a reason to begin raising money early because the matching funds they earn can help them raise the sums needed to be perceived as a credible candidate by the press as well as the voters, and thus to be competitive in the crucial early stages of the delegate selection process. Well-known contenders are also encouraged to make an early start because they can capitalize on their established bases of support and preexisting name recognition to gain a substantial financial advantage over their opponents.

These incentives to begin raising money early intensified throughout the 1980s as a result of the operational effects of the FECA's spending limits. The law adjusts spending limits for inflation, but not contribution limits. Thus, while the amount a candidate may spend has grown from $12 million when the law was established in 1974 to more than $33 million in 1992, the maximum contribution has remained static at $1,000. In each succeeding election, candidates have had to devote more time to fund raising in order to generate the increasingly large number of contributions needed to raise the amount legally permitted by the spending limit. The effect of this imbalance in the regulations has been to encourage candidates to begin raising money earlier and earlier in each new election cycle.

Early campaigning has also been encouraged by the changes that have taken place in the delegate selection process. Throughout the 1980s and early 1990s, the primary calendar has become "front-loaded" as a growing number of states have decided to hold their delegate selection contests during the six-week period extending from mid-February to the end of March. In addition, a number of states have changed from more party-oriented caucuses to more open primary elections. These decisions have dramatically increased the financial demands of the initial weeks of the formal selection process. Candidates must now build organizations and conduct expensive media campaigns in a number of states simultaneously, sometimes beginning as early as mid-January, to attract the wide support needed to win primary contests, especially the crucial first primary in New Hampshire. Candidates must therefore accrue large sums of money before the beginning of February if they are to be assured of having the resources needed to wage an effective campaign.

This need to raise a substantial campaign war chest before the start of the formal delegate selection process has been exacerbated in recent elections by the increasingly tight schedule of primaries and caucuses. The early state elections are grouped so closely together that they take place in relatively rapid succession. Candidates therefore have little time to raise money in between state contests. As a result, it is difficult for any candidate other than the front-runner to build any sort of "financial momentum"; even candidates who win early must often compete in a number of additional primaries or caucuses before they begin to realize the financial gain that can accompany an early victory.

For example, in 1984, only New Hampshire held a primary between 20 February and 10 March, with three other states holding caucuses. Democrat Gary Hart finished second in the Iowa caucuses and won the New Hampshire primary the following week, and in doing so experienced a surge in fund raising that provided him with the revenues needed to campaign in the bloc of contests that were held in the last two weeks of March. Hart reportedly raised as much in the first week of March as he did in the entire month of February, as he saw his individual contributions jump from $342,000 in February to $3 million in March.[32]

By contrast, in 1988 twenty states held primaries between 16 February and 10 March.[33] State delegate selection contests were scheduled so tightly that candidates who won early had little time to raise additional funds in advance of the next major set of contests. Republican Robert Dole and Democrat Richard Gephardt, the winners in Iowa, did not experience a fund-raising surge after their victories because, as Clyde Wilcox has noted, "Super Tuesday occurred before most contributors had much time to react to the outcomes of Iowa and New Hampshire."[34] In 1992 both Tsongas, who won the New Hampshire Democratic primary, and Buchanan, who had a strong showing against the president in the Republican primary, experienced a financial windfall after their showings. But the surge in fund raising that accompanied Tsongas's victory came too late to help him the next week in South Dakota, or in most of the Super Tuesday states, where he was soundly defeated. Buchanan witnessed a dramatic increase in his fund raising, taking in an estimated $1 million in the two weeks between New Hampshire and the 3 March Georgia primary. But he still trailed far behind the president, who began 1992 with $7 million in the bank and therefore had the resources needed to compete in most of the southern states, unlike Buchanan, who could afford only to concentrate on Georgia.[35]

The campaign finance regulations and changes in the nominating process have thus combined to force candidates to begin campaigning early, especially if they are entering the race without a well-developed donor base. Those who fail to start early risk the prospect of lacking the funds needed to mount a serious campaign or of facing challengers who enjoy a significant financial advantage in the initial contests. The need for early fund raising has become a strategic imperative that determines the financial strategies of most presidential candidates.

THE PROBLEM OF SPENDING LIMITS

Pressures to begin campaigning early would not be of great concern to candidates were it not for the FECA's spending limits. Without spending limits, candidates could simply adapt to the strategic and operational demands of the law by beginning their campaigns early enough to accommodate them. But this option is not readily available to all candidates in a system that restricts the amount a campaign may spend. The FECA's ceilings on state-by-state and aggregate expenditures are designed to compel candidates to limit the length of their campaigns and their level of early campaigning. Thus, one of the largely unexpected outcomes of the presidential campaign finance system is that it has presented candidates with a central strategic problem: how to accomplish the early campaigning necessitated by the law without violating the campaign spending limits.

Candidates who begin to organize well in advance of the first contests and spend substantial amounts in the preelection year run the risk of having to curtail their campaigning during the election year in order to comply with the limits, and may have to face an opponent legally capable of outspending them by significant amounts in the latter stages of the selection process. No candidate wants to face these possibilities. Instead, challengers, especially prospective front-runners, want to maximize the amounts they can spend during the primaries and caucuses in hopes that their ability to outspend others will prove to be a strategic key that helps them gain the nomination.

Candidates found that this central strategic problem became more difficult to resolve over the course of the 1980s. As with the pressures generated by the FECA's funding provisions to expand the length of campaigns, the pressures created by the law's expenditure limits to restrain spending intensified during this period because the ceilings increasingly failed to reflect the financial realities of presidential campaigning. Although the limits are adjusted according to the Consumer Price Index, the real costs of such items as air travel, hotels, postage, polling services, and television advertising have increased at rates much faster than that of inflation. As FEC Commissioner Lee Ann Elliott has noted, "In truth, campaign costs don't go up at market-basket inflation; instead of going up about four or five percent every year, they go up *ten, twelve, fifteen* percent every year."[36] Moreover, because state spending limits are based on population, they fail to reflect the enhanced revenue demands of the changing delegate selection process or the relative importance of particular states. For example, in New Hampshire candidates may spend only the minimum amount allowed for any state, even though it is the nation's most important primary.

The ceilings are supposed to force candidates to control the costs of their campaigns and make judgments about how to allocate resources. And they have induced some candidates to restrict their spending. In the first four elections conducted under the FECA, at least five candidates had to cut back significantly on their anticipated spending or were reluctant to spend available funds because of the aggregate limit: Ford and Reagan in 1976, Reagan in 1980 (and perhaps 1984 when he spent the limit, although he essentially ran without opposition), Mondale in 1984, and Bush in 1988.[37] The predominant response to the law, however, has not been to reduce spending. Instead, candidates have either violated the law or sought ways to circumvent the limits.

Circumventing the Limits

The penalties for exceeding spending limits are not extremely severe. Since 1984, the Federal Election Commission has required that a candidate simply pay a fine in the form of a repayment to the Treasury in an amount equal to the percentage of excess spending that represents the use of public funds, which is usually about 33 percent. Most candidates would not find such a penalty onerous, particularly since no fines are assessed until the commission completes its audit of a campaign, which normally occurs more than a year after the primaries have been completed.

Why, then, are candidates concerned about breaking the law? The reason is that they fear the potential political consequences of violating or approaching the limits in the midst of a campaign. If a candidate reaches a state's spending threshold before a primary, or the aggregate limit before the convention, press reports would note that he or she had "violated the law," a story that might raise questions about the candidate's integrity. Opponents might attempt to exploit such stories and make them an issue in the campaign. Even if a campaign does not exceed the limit, heavy early spending could place a candidate in a vulnerable strategic position. In such a case, a candidate risks being outspent by an opponent in the final stages of a race or may have to face press stories speculating whether the candidate is "in trouble" because of the spending constraints his or her campaign will be forced to operate under for the rest of the campaign.

These kinds of considerations initially induced candidates to find ways to minimize the expenditures they had to report under the spending ceilings. This was particularly true in Iowa and New Hampshire, where candidates felt compelled to spend as much as possible given the importance of these states in the presidential selection process. Candidates thus routinely began to evade the limits in these states by employing sophisticated allocation schemes and exploiting some of the technical exemptions contained within the law.

For example, the presidential campaign finance regulations acknowledge some of the practical realities of campaign spending by exempting certain expenditures from the state spending limits. Certain fund-raising costs and expenses associated with efforts to comply with the law do not have to be reported as state expenditures. The costs of television advertising are allocated on the basis of the potential statewide audience; so if a candidate running in New Hampshire airs commercials on Boston television stations, only about 16 percent of the cost of the advertising (in 1992) is charged against the New Hampshire limit, since only 16 percent of the Boston television market consists of New Hampshire viewers. Campaign lawyers and accountants have taken these exemptions and applied them in creative ways, such as defining as many types of expenditures as possible as fund-raising and compliance activities exempt from state limits. They have also applied the allocation principle established for media spending to a wide range of functions, including "regional headquarters," out-of-state telephone banks, and polls that interview voters in more than one state. Such tactics have allowed candidates to spend hundreds of thousands of dollars more than the amounts permitted in Iowa and New Hampshire.

An even more subversive practice that became increasingly common among prospective candidates during the 1980s was the establishment of a precandidacy political action committee (PAC) or some other organizational vehicle that would allow a presidential hopeful to engage in political activities yet remain an undeclared candidate for as long as possible. Because a PAC is a legally separate organization from a candidate's campaign committee, it is not subject to the contribution and spending limits imposed on presidential candidates. Even if a potential presidential candidate heads a PAC, the money raised and spent by the committee is not considered to be a presidential campaign expense, so long as that individual or the PAC avoids a handful of specific activities that the Federal Election Commission regards as signs of presidential candidacy.[38] A PAC can therefore serve as an effective vehicle for circumventing the FECA's restrictions; it can essentially be used to conduct a wide range of activities relevant to a presidential campaign without having any of the expenses charged against the FECA spending limits. It is therefore not surprising that an increasing number of presidential aspirants turned to the PAC alternative as a means of resolving the strategic problems generated by the campaign finance laws.

The first candidate to use this tactic was Ronald Reagan, who formed a PAC, Citizens for the Republic, after his unsuccessful bid for the Republican presidential nomination in 1976. Reagan's committee, which was initially organized to disburse $1.6 million in surplus funds from his 1976 campaign, was established to provide assistance to conservative candidates and causes. But Reagan and his advisers soon discovered that this committee could also be used to conduct an array of campaign-related activities that would keep Reagan in the political spotlight and allow him to expand his donor list and political organization in preparation for a possible run in 1980. This insight became the PAC's operative principle, and over the next three years the committee spent over $6 million. Only about 10 percent of this amount, however, was disbursed in the form of contributions to other candidates for federal office. Most of the money was used to hire a staff, establish fund-raising networks, build direct-mail lists, develop a political operation, recruit volunteers, and subsidize Reagan's travel.[39]

Following Reagan's lead, an increasing number of prospective presidential candidates established PACs of their own throughout the 1980s. Before the 1980 election, three Republican hopefuls formed PACs in an effort to keep pace with Reagan's efforts. In advance of the 1984 contest, five candidates formed committees, as four Democratic challengers joined Reagan in adopting this organizational approach. In the 1988 election cycle, ten of thirteen major-party candidates established PACs before declaring their candidacies.[40] The amounts spent by these committees rose even more dramatically, growing from $7.48 million in the 1980 cycle to more than $25.2 million in 1988. In all, the use of these committees led to more than $40 million in expenditures outside the spending limits.

One of the primary benefits of a precandidacy PAC is that it provides a potential candidate with a solution to the strategic dilemma created by the FECA because it facilitates early fund raising without triggering the spending limits. Through a PAC, a prospective presidential candidate can develop contacts with potential future financial supporters, build a donor network, and launch a direct-mail program. The PAC can finance the costs of these efforts, carry out the initial prospecting mailings, and maintain a list of donors who have responded to fund-raising appeals made by the prospective candidate on behalf of the PAC. When the presidential hopeful officially becomes a candidate, his or her campaign can then purchase or rent the PAC's donor list for a tiny fraction of the cost of constructing it, thus saving the campaign a substantial amount of money in fund-raising costs, as well as providing it with an established base of potential donors, most of whom will be likely to give to the presidential campaign. For example, in 1980 Reagan's PAC developed a list of 300,000 donors, mostly small contributors, all of whom were likely to contribute to a Reagan presidential campaign. In 1984 Democrat Walter Mondale saved an estimated $1 million in fund-raising costs by using a PAC, which provided his presidential campaign with a list of 25,000 proven donors. Similarly, in 1988 Jack Kemp and Robert Dole each saved about $2 million in fund-raising costs by relying on their personal PACs for their initial list of campaign donors.[41]

Yet, despite these tactics and machinations, candidates have still exceeded the spending limits. Three candidates, Mondale in 1984 and Bush and Robertson in 1988, have violated the aggregate spending ceiling. On average, about a third of those who have sought the presidency since 1976 have spent more than the limit in Iowa and New Hampshire. Throughout the 1980s, the number of candidates guilty of violating the Iowa and New Hampshire limits rose, and the extent of overspending increased significantly. In 1976, only two candidates (Reagan and Democrat Morris Udall) exceeded the New Hampshire limit, spending an average of $20,000 more than the law allowed. In 1988, eight candidates surpassed the Iowa limit by an average of $360,000, while six candidates exceeded the New Hampshire limit by an average of $219,000.[42]

Consequently, the relatively level playing field supposed to be created by the adoption of state spending ceilings was never realized in practice. While some candidates may have spent less than they could have because of the limits, for the most part candidates have discovered ways to spend more than allowed in the crucial early primaries, even if this meant exceeding the limits and having to pay a fine after the campaign was over. Yet the experience in these early contests suggests that the inefficacy of these ceilings has not significantly undermined the ability of lesser-known candidates to be competitive in such contests, which was the major concern that led to these regulations. Among others, Jimmy Carter in 1976, George Bush in 1980, Gary Hart in 1984, and Paul Tsongas in 1992 demonstrated that it was possible for a lesser-known candidate to win in Iowa or New Hampshire, even if outspent by a more prominent opponent.

Following the 1988 election, the Federal Election Commission admitted that the state ceilings "have had little impact on campaign spending in a given state" and have "proven a significant accounting burden for campaigns and an equally difficult audit and enforcement task."[43] Accordingly, in 1990 and 1991, the commission revised its rules regarding state spending. The new rules, which were first implemented in the 1992 election, state that a candidate's expenditures apply to a state limit only if they fall within one of five specific categories: media expenses, mass mailings, overhead expenses, special telephone programs, and public opinion polls. Any other expenses only count against the campaign's aggregate spending limit. In addition, the rules allow a candidate to treat up to 50 percent of the expenditures allocable to a state as fund-raising expenses that count against the overall fund-raising limit rather than the state limit.[44]

The revised regulations have essentially turned the state limits into an accounting exercise. They allow such broad leeway in allocating costs that they should have little, if any, effect in terms of restricting a campaign's spending in a particular state. Under these guidelines, a candidate in 1992 could easily spend close to $2 million in New Hampshire, even though the state's ceiling was $552,000.[45] Candidates will still, however, have to be concerned with the overall spending limit. Candidates who take advantage of the opportunities to spend early that exist under the revised rules may find themselves at a disadvantage at a subsequent stage in the process because they have less room remaining under the cap than their opponents. So although the Federal Election Commission's action has reduced some of the pressures on candidates, it has not eliminated all the concerns that have encouraged candidates to seek out ways of avoiding the law.

The 1992 Experience and Beyond

The 1992 prenomination campaign did not follow the general patterns or fund-raising tactics that became manifest in the 1980s. In its earliest stage, it appeared that 1992 would. A number of the potential Democratic challengers to President Bush had PAC operations after the 1988 election and began to engage in the activities associated with the beginnings of a presidential candidacy. The most prominent was the Reverend Jesse Jackson, who formed a PAC called Keep Hope Alive after his unsuccessful 1988 candidacy and, according to Federal Election Commission records, raised more than $700,000 by the end of 1990. Most of this amount was used to support Jackson's political activities, as well as develop a national direct-mail effort and lists of supporters.[46] Richard Gephardt's Effective Government Committee, which was formed in anticipation of the 1988 election and spent about $1.2 million before he declared his 1988 candidacy, raised close to $850,000 by the end of 1990 and contributed $252,000 to seventy-four federal candidates, according to Federal Election Commission reports. Governors Mario Cuomo of New York and L. Douglas Wilder of Virginia also considered the PAC option early in the election cycle.[47]

Despite these initial efforts on the part of some prospective candidates, there was little early campaigning in the 1992 cycle because of the unique political circumstances that characterized the two-year period leading up to the election. President Bush's high popularity throughout most of 1989, the invasion of Kuwait, and the subsequent war in the Persian Gulf discouraged Democratic politicking. As previously noted, the result was a late start to a Democratic nomination contest in which the most prominent prospective challengers decided not to run. Only one candidate, Paul Tsongas, began to campaign early in the preelection year. The other Democrats all waited until late August or thereafter to declare their candidacies. As a result, there was no precampaign activity comparable to that of previous elections.

The late start in 1992, however, is also the exception that proves the rule. Because the Democratic aspirants did not enter the presidential race with well-established fund-raising bases, as did President Bush, and did not begin to campaign early, they had to devote an inordinate amount of time to fund raising after declaring their candidacies. Moreover, they failed to build up their bank accounts before the start of the delegate selection process and therefore lacked the resources needed to run a truly national campaign and develop organizations in the many states holding contests in the first three weeks of the formal selection process. As a result, most candidates were forced to concentrate their resources on New Hampshire and failed to establish campaign organizations in a majority of the states holding early contests.

By November 1991, less than four months before the New Hampshire primary, most of the Democrats were spending at least half of their time raising money.[48] Even so, all of these campaigns were relatively underfinanced in comparison to previous contests. By the end of January 1992, Bill Clinton had raised about $5.4 million, which was almost $2 million more than his nearest challenger. In 1988, Clinton would have been fifth in the fund-raising rankings with this amount, or more than $9 million behind Michael Dukakis. Having failed to build sizable war chests in the preelection year, most Democrats had to secure loans by mid-February to help finance their campaigns. Federal Election Commission records show that Clinton ended February over $600,000 in debt and had to rely on $1.5 million in loans to outspend Tsongas in the early weeks of March. Bob Kerrey dropped out of the race during the first week of March with more than $1 million of debt, while Tom Harkin dropped out a few days later more than $300,000 in debt. At the time, Harkin's campaign manager Tim Raftis noted, "We are stopping because we just ran out of money. . . . It's difficult to get your message through when you don't have any money."[49] Two weeks later Tsongas suspended his campaign, noting a lack of financial support, as his campaign stood $500,000 in debt despite the fact that it was taking in about $93,000 in cash each day.[50]

Patrick Buchanan, who also began to campaign relatively late in his bid to unseat President Bush, shared the Democrats' plight. At the start of the election year, Buchanan was already acknowledging that "we didn't start to raise money early enough."[51] By the end of January, his campaign had received close to $2 million, which was less than every Republican candidate had raised at a comparable point in 1988 and was more than $10 million less than comparable totals reached by Bush, Dole, Kemp, and Robertson.[52] More important, he trailed President Bush in fund raising by more than $12 million.

The earliest stage of the open race for the 1996 Republican presidential nomination signals a return to the patterns of the 1980s. Changes in the scheduling of state delegate selection contests have created "a virtual national primary in March" that will significantly increase the already intensive pressures to begin fund raising early.[53] New York has moved its primary to the week before Super Tuesday. Ohio, Illinois, and Michigan will vote a week after Super Tuesday, and California has moved its winner-take-all Republican contest from June to 26 March. The eight largest states in the nation will therefore cast their votes for a presidential nominee within a three-week period. As a result, once the formal delegate selection process begins, there will be almost no time for traditional fund raising because the lead time will be too short for direct mail and the primary schedule too demanding to provide candidates with many opportunities to raise additional money after New Hampshire.[54]

Because of these changes, most observers believe that those who seek to be serious contenders for the presidential nomination will have to amass large campaign war chests before the start of the election. Charles Black, one of Bush's former campaign advisers, has noted that a candidate will have to have at least $10 million *in the bank* before New Year's Day 1996.[55] Many others have estimated that a candidate will have to raise up to $25 million before the Iowa caucuses in order to be competitive.[56]

In an effort to develop the capacity to raise such large sums, many of those considering a 1996 presidential bid established PACs or nonprofit foundations after the 1992 election. These organizations, like those created before previous prenomination contests, are designed to serve as shadow campaign organizations, responsible for developing donor networks, direct-mail lists, and political contacts that will provide the initial resources for a possible presidential campaign.[57] As listed in table 7.5, at least five potential Republican challengers—Lamar Alexander, former Tennessee governor and secretary of education; Richard Cheney, former defense secretary; Senate Majority Leader Robert Dole; Senator Phil Gramm; and a former represent-

TABLE 7.5
PACs Associated with Potential 1996 Candidates

Potential candidate	PAC	Total receipts[a]
Lamar Alexander	Republican Fund for the 90s	$250,400
Richard Cheney	Alliance for American Leadership	514,000
Robert Dole	Campaign America	6,261,900
Phil Gramm	Leadership for America	147,500
Jack Kemp	Campaign for a New Agenda	180,200

SOURCE: Federal Election Commission.
a. Receipts reported as of 30 June 1994, with the exception of Kemp's Campaign for a New Agenda, which is registered in Illinois. Data for Kemp's committee based on reported receipts as of 13 February 1994.

ative, Jack Kemp—established PAC operations in advance of the 1996 election. Only Dole's committee was active before 1992. In addition, Kemp is affiliated with a tax-exempt foundation, Empower America, which was formed in January 1993 to serve as a conservative think tank/advocacy organization.[58] Dole has also founded a tax-exempt foundation, the Better America Foundation, which will also serve as a think tank and advocacy organization. Dole's foundation, whose president is the executive director of Dole's PAC and a former Dole presidential campaign staffer, was formed, according to at least one report, in part as a reaction to Kemp's foundation.[59]

The value of these organizations to a prospective 1996 presidential campaign was already becoming clear early in 1994. Kemp's Empower America conducted an aggressive direct-mail program in 1993 that had produced a list of more than 100,000 donors by the beginning of 1994.[60] Dole's Campaign America had raised over $6 million by July 1994, developing an extensive nationwide donor base in the process. His Better America Foundation had reportedly raised more than $1 million.[61] The PAC operation had also helped Dole develop potential future political support by contributing about $178,000 to sixty-two federal candidates and more than $100,000 to Republican candidates at the state level.[62] Alexander had relied on his Republican Fund for the 90s, which had spent $230,000 by mid-1994, to pay for his travel throughout the country.[63] Phil Gramm had capitalized on his position as chair of the National Republican Senate Campaign Committee and head of a PAC to build a donor list of 88,000 names, attend political events in at least thirty-four states, and develop a computerized mailing list of people he has met since 1991, which totaled 164,000 names by 1994, including 62,000 Iowans.[64]

Given the anticipated revenue demands of the 1996 election, it is likely that many of the candidates will begin campaigning early. Unless candidates have an extensive preestablished donor base, they will find it very difficult, if not impossible, to start after mid-1995 and still raise the sums needed to finance a viable presidential campaign, even if they plan to wage campaigns and advertise only in selected states. Accordingly, Phil Gramm formed a presidential campaign committee and announced his intention to run in early November 1994, more than fifteen months before the 1996 Iowa caucuses. A few days later, Senator Arlen Specter of Pennsylvania announced the formation of an exploratory committee to investigate whether he should seek the Republican presidential nomination. A number of other candidates, including Dole, followed their lead early in 1995.

Conclusion

The rules governing the presidential selection process never operate in a vacuum; instead, they operate within the context of the process as a whole and the particularities of each election. The interaction between these rules and the broader strategic environment of the selection process, which includes such factors as the delegate selection system, the political context of the race, and the particular candidates involved in an election, largely determines the efficacy of these regulations, because it influences how individual actors will respond to their provisions. This is particularly true in the case of campaign finance regulations, since these rules attempt to regulate one of the most essential and dynamic components of the presidential selection process—money.

Candidates as strategic actors are always looking for ways to maximize the resources available to their campaigns and gain a competitive advantage over their opponents. The central purpose of the FECA's regulatory scheme, however, is to limit the resources available to candidates and reduce the potential financial inequities among candidates. Consequently, the experience with the FECA has been one of adaptation and innovation. Candidates have adapted to the regulations in ways both intended and unintended, in part as a result of the effects of the law and in part because of changes in the broader strategic environment the law was not designed to accommodate. In general, they have responded to the FECA's regulatory structure by developing innovative means of fulfilling their resource needs, many of which were not intended by the reforms. As a result, the FECA has not achieved all its purposes.

The FECA has had a dramatic effect on the financing of presidential prenomination campaigns. It eliminated "fat cat" contributions from the early stages of the presidential selection process, compelled candidates to raise money in smaller amounts from thousands of donors, and created a new source of funds through its public funding program. By doing so, the law provided candidates with a variety of alternative strategies for raising the money needed to wage a campaign. Candidates can therefore shape their fund-raising strategies to conform to their particular strengths or take advantage of the resources available to their campaigns: for example, candidates who enjoy the support of the party establishment can seek larger gifts through individuals capable of giving large sums or of soliciting large sums from others; candidates with strong ideological convictions can try to solicit smaller donations from those who share their convictions; lesser-known candidates can raise funds from their core supporters and use the public monies earned as a result as seed money for developing further support.

The FECA's contribution limits and public funding program have thus helped to increase the representativeness of the selection process and improved the alternatives available to voters. Candidates do not need to rely on the support of the party establishment to contest the presidential nomination. But they do need to develop a financial constituency capable of providing them with the monies needed to spread their message to the electorate. A wide array of candidates, including many from outside the respective mainstreams of the two major parties, has been able to develop such constituencies under the new regulatory regime. Voters have therefore had a wider choice of candidates from which to select their presidential nominees.

In each subsequent election since the FECA was adopted, however, candidates have found it increasingly difficult to meet the rapidly growing financial demands of the selection process, yet remain within the spending parameters established by the law. Because the FECA's spending limits were not designed to account for the dramatic changes that have taken place in the delegate selection process over the past two decades, the effect of the limits has been to induce—even compel—candidates to seek out ways of raising and spending money outside the framework established by the regulations. By the time of the 1988 election, the disparity between the financial demands of the selection process and the financial dictates of the regulations had become so great that many candidates eagerly took advantage of the opportunities available to circumvent the law. This disparity, especially with respect to state-level expenditures, also placed such a strain on the enforcement apparatus that federal regulators responded to the situation by easing the restraints imposed on candidates, essentially trying to adapt the law to the new realities of the campaign finance system. In doing so, they acknowledged that the regulations had failed to achieve their goals.

The experience in presidential prenomination campaigns thus highlights the difficulty of regulating so dynamic a component of the electoral system as political finance. Given the stakes of a presidential contest, candidates will constantly be searching for ways to gain access to the resources they feel are necessary to win the nomination. While campaign finance regulations can help define the parameters of this quest and eliminate the most flagrant abuses, they will be effective only if they also recognize changes in the broader strategic context in which they operate. The current campaign finance system has not kept pace with the broader changes that have taken place in the presidential selection process. Acknowledging this reality is the first step that is needed in considering future campaign finance reforms.

Notes

1. Herbert E. Alexander, *Financing Politics,* 3d ed. (Washington, D.C.: CQ Press, 1984), 7.

2. Herbert E. Alexander, *Financing Politics,* 4th ed. (Washington, D.C.: CQ Press, 1992), 21.

3. See Herbert E. Alexander, *Financing the 1972 Election* (Lexington, Mass.: Lexington Books, 1976), 39–75 and 513–57.

4. The FECA of 1971 (Public Law 92-225) was signed into law by President Nixon on 7 February 1972 and went into effect sixty days later. The FECA of 1974 (Public Law 93-443) was signed into law by President Ford on 15 October 1974. For the text of the legislation, see 86 Stat. 3 and 88 Stat. 1263, respectively. The 1976 amendments to the law (Public Law 94-283) can be found at 90 Stat. 475 and the 1979 amendments (Public Law 96-187) at 93 Stat. 1339. A thorough review of the history of this legislation is provided in Robert E. Mutch, *Campaigns, Congress, and Courts: The Making of Federal Campaign Finance Law* (New York: Praeger, 1988).

5. For convention and general election expenditures, the act established aggregate limits. The public subsidy for convention spending was originally set at $2 million, plus an adjustment for inflation. This base amount was increased to $3 million under the 1979 FECA amendment and increased again in 1984 to $4 million. By 1992, cost-of-living adjustments had raised the limit to $11 million. In the general election, candidates who accept public funding are limited to the amount of the general election grant given to each candidate, which was originally set at $20 million plus adjustments for inflation. By 1992, this limit had increased to $55.2 million. In addition, the national party committee of each presidential nominee is allowed to spend an amount equal to two cents times the voting-age population in coordinated spending to help elect its candidate.

6. Federal Election Commission, *Legislative History of the Federal Election Campaign Act Amendments of 1974* (Washington, D.C.: Government Printing Office, 1977), 107.

7. Federal Election Commission, "FEC Announces 1992 Presidential Spending Limits," press release, 12 February 1992.

8. 424 U.S. 1 (1976).

9. 26 U.S.C. 9033(c)(1)(B).

10. The five supporters were Max Palevsky, Miles Rubin, Henry Kimmelman, Morris Dees, and Stewart Mott. See Alexander, *Financing the 1972 Election,* 122–23.

11. See Herbert E. Alexander, *Financing the 1968 Election* (Lexington, Mass.: Lexington Books, 1971), 54–55.

12. Ibid., 98; and Federal Election Commission, *FEC Disclosure Series Report No. 7: 1976 Presidential Campaign Receipts and Expenditures* (Washington, D.C., May 1977), 7.

13. The candidates in 1988 were George Bush, Robert Dole, Pete du Pont, Alexander Haig, Jack Kemp, and Pat Robertson.

14. Jack W. Germond and Jules Witcover, "Money Is Tight for the Democratic Six," *National Journal,* 7 December 1991, 2984.

15. These five Democrats included Michael Dukakis, the Democratic Party nominee, $28.5 million; Jesse Jackson, $20.0 million; Albert Gore, $12.3 million; Richard Gephardt, $10.3 million; and Paul Simon, $10.1 million. Figures reflect adjusted receipts as reported in Federal Election Commission, "FEC Releases Final Report on 1988 Presidential Primary Campaigns," press release, 25 August 1989.

16. For purposes of comparison, this analysis excludes Joseph Biden, who dropped out of the 1988 presidential race in late 1987, months before the first delegate selection contest. The 1988 candidates included in the analysis are Bruce Babbitt, Michael Dukakis, Richard Gephardt, Albert Gore, Gary Hart, Jesse Jackson, Lyndon LaRouche, and Paul Simon. The 1992 Democratic candidates are listed in table 7.3.

17. Herbert E. Alexander and Monica Bauer, *Financing the 1988 Election* (Boulder, Colo.: Westview Press, 1991), 22–23.

18. Based on an analysis of Federal Election Commission contributor files conducted by the author. See also Carol Matlack, "Money Rolls in for Bush," *National Journal,* 23 May 1992, 1229.

19. Bush campaign officials hoped to collect an average of $2 or $3 for each of the letters mailed, but averaged only about $1. See Herbert E. Alexander and Anthony Corrado, *Financing the 1992 Election* (New York: M.E. Sharpe, 1995), chap. 3.

20. Quoted in Sara Fritz, "Buchanan's Direct Mail Drive Delivers Substantial Dividends," *Los Angeles Times,* 7 March 1992.

21. Alexander and Corrado, *Financing the 1992 Election,* chap. 3.

22. Based on an analysis of Federal Election Commission contributor records conducted by the author.

23. Alexander and Corrado, *Financing the 1992 Election,* chap. 3. Although all of Brown's campaign contributions fell below the $250 limit for matching funds, all of his campaign funds were not matched on a dollar-for-dollar basis. The campaign received a loan of $1.2 million with anticipated matching funds as collateral, and not all of the campaign's contributions were eligible for matching due to the campaign's failure to provide complete information about the contributor or due to some other technical problem with his campaign's submissions. These problems are common among candidate matching fund requests; usually an average of 1 to 4 percent of the contributions submitted for matching are deemed ineligible for various technical reasons.

24. Clyde Wilcox, "Financing the 1988 Prenomination Campaigns," in *Nominating the President,* ed. Emmett H. Buell, Jr., and Lee Sigelman (Knoxville: University of Tennessee Press, 1991), 96.

25. See Herbert E. Alexander, "Yes: Public Financing is a Desirable Policy," in *Controversial Issues in Presidential Selection,* ed. Gary L. Rose (Albany: SUNY Press, 1991), 159–60; and Anthony Corrado, *Paying for Presidents* (New York: Twentieth Century Fund Press, 1993), 43–44.

26. Federal Election Commission, *Reports on Financial Activity, 1983–84, Final Report: Presidential Prenomination Campaigns* (Washington, D.C., April 1986), 44.

27. Federal Election Commission, *Record* 14, no. 2 (February 1988): 1.

28. Figures based on Federal Election Commission data on the adjusted receipts for presidential candidates through 29 February 1992.

29. Corrado, *Paying for Presidents,* 39–41.

30. For a more extensive analysis of presidential fund-raising practices that reaches a similar conclusion, see Clifford Brown, Lynda Powell, and Clyde Wilcox, *Serious Money* (Cambridge: Cambridge University Press, 1996).

31. On the economics of direct mail, see, among others, R. Kenneth Godwin, *One Billion Dollars of Influence* (Chatham, N.J.: Chatham House, 1988), 10–12; Larry J. Sabato, *The Rise of Political Consultants* (New York: Basic Books, 1981), 226–29; and Richard Armstrong, *The Next Hurrah: The Communications Revolution in American Politics* (New York: Morrow, 1988), 70–73. It should be noted that Patrick Buchanan's direct-mail program in 1992 proved to be an exception to these general rules. Buchanan's first mailing had a response rate of 13.8 percent and an average contribution of nearly $62, compared to the typical response rates of less than 3 percent with an average contribution of about $25. Alexander and Corrado, *Financing the 1992 Election,* chap. 3.

32. For a discussion of the fund-raising surge Hart experienced after the initial contests, see Herbert E. Alexander and Brian A. Haggerty, *Financing the 1984 Election* (Lexington, Mass.: Lexington Books, 1987), 223–25; and Wilcox, "Financing the 1988 Prenomination Campaigns," 101.

33. Gerald Pomper et al., *The Election of 1988* (Chatham, N.J.: Chatham House, 1989), table 2.6.

34. Wilcox, "Financing the 1988 Prenomination Campaigns," 101.

35. Alexander and Corrado, *Financing the 1992 Election,* chap. 3.

36. Lee Ann Elliott, "Campaign Finance," *Journal of Law and Politics* 8 (Winter 1992): 302.

37. For a discussion of these cases, see Herbert E. Alexander, *Financing the 1976 Election* (Washington, D.C.: CQ Press, 1979), 308, 314, 322–23, 328; Herbert E. Alexander, *Financing the 1980 Election* (Lexington, Mass.: Lexington Books, 1983), 172–74; Alexander and Haggerty, *Financing the 1984 Election,* 165; and Rita Beamish, "GOP Funds Trip as Bush Nears Spending Cap," Associated Press release, 4 July 1988.

38. These activities include the financing of a media campaign to announce an individual's intention to seek a party's presidential nomination, the use of PAC money to qualify an individual for state ballots, and describing an individual as a future presidential candidate in materials paid for by the PAC.

39. For a detailed account of Reagan's Citizens for the Republic and a discussion of the role of presidential PACs in the modern presidential selection process, see Anthony Corrado, *Creative Campaigning* (Boulder, Colo.: Westview Press, 1992), esp. chaps. 4–6.

40. In the 1980 election cycle, Republicans Ronald Reagan, George Bush, Robert Dole, and John Connally had PACs; in 1984, Ronald Reagan and Democrats Walter Mondale, John Glenn, Alan Cranston, and Ernest Hollings; in 1988, Republicans George Bush, Robert Dole, Pierre du Pont, Alexander Haig, Jack Kemp, and Pat Robertson, and Democrats Bruce Babbitt, Joseph Biden, Richard Gephardt, and Paul Simon.

41. Corrado, *Creative Campaigning,* 152–53.

42. Data based on the Final Audit Reports issued by the Federal Election

Commission for each election cycle.

43. Federal Election Commission, *Annual Report 1992* (Washington, D.C., June 1993), 52.

44. For an outline of the new regulations, see Federal Election Commission, *Record* 17, no. 9 (September 1991): 2–5; and 56 *Federal Register* 91 (29 July 1991), 35896–950.

45. For example, in 1992, Democrats Bob Kerrey and Tom Harkin spent well over $550,000 in New Hampshire on television advertising alone. See L. Patrick Devlin, "Television Advertising in the 1992 New Hampshire Presidential Primary Election," *Political Communication* 11 (January–March 1994): 81–99.

46. Tom Sherwood, "PUSHing and Rainbowing and Keeping Hope Alive," *Washington Post National Weekly Edition,* 6–12 November 1989, 14.

47. Cuomo's federal PAC, the Empire Leadership Fund, was relatively inactive after the 1988 election as Cuomo's supporters concentrated on his 1990 re-election campaign. Wilder filed with the FEC to establish a PAC, the Committee on Fiscal Responsibility, which he reportedly planned to finance in part with left-over inaugural funds (see "Wilder Still Keeps Inaugural Fund Secret," *Campaign Practices Reports,* 24 June 1991, 8). Instead, Wilder decided to establish an exploratory committee to examine the prospects for a 1992 bid.

48. Daniel J. Swillinger, "Reflections on Fifteen Years of Presidential Public Financing," *Journal of Law and Politics* 8 (Winter 1992), 340.

49. Sam Fulwood, III, "Harkin Withdraws from Democratic Presidential Race," *Los Angeles Times,* 10 March 1992.

50. Robin Toner, "Tsongas Abandons Campaign," *New York Times,* 20 March 1992; B. Drummond Ayres, Jr., "Tsongas Declares He Won't Re-enter Democratic Race," *New York Times,* 10 April 1992; and "Tsongas's Money Ceiling," *Wall Street Journal,* 23 March 1992.

51. Quoted in Lally Weymouth, "Buchanan's Right Hook to Bush," *Washington Post National Weekly Edition,* 30 December 1991–5 January 1992, 23.

52. Based on the data in Federal Election Commission, *Reports on Financial Activity, 1987–1988, Final Report: Presidential Prenomination Campaigns* (Washington, D.C., August 1989), 42, table D.

53. Dan Balz, "California Moves Up '96 Primary to March," *Washington Post,* 6 October 1993.

54. Mark Shields, "High-Stakes Presidential Poker," *Washington Post National Weekly Edition,* 14–20 February 1994, 28.

55. Ibid.

56. Ibid.; and George Will, "Gramm Courts Iowans on Road to White House," *Des Moines Register,* 1 October 1994, 9A.

57. Gerald F. Seib, "GOP Presidential Hopefuls Use Leadership PACs to Get Early Start without Tossing Hats in Ring," *Wall Street Journal,* 5 April 1994, A20.

58. Thomas B. Edsall, "Conservative Republicans Join to Redefine Party," *Washington Post,* 13 January 1993, A4.

59. James A. Barnes, "Whoosh! There Goes Bob Dole!" *National Journal,* 6 February 1993, 351; and Timothy J. Burger and Glenn R. Simpson, "Dole's New Secret Weapon," *Roll Call,* 7 November 1994.

60. David Rogers, "At Empower America, Refuge for Conservatives, First Year Has Been a Tale of Money and Ego," *Wall Street Journal,* 6 January 1994, A14.

61. Burger and Simpson, "Dole's New Secret Weapon."

62. John King, "PACs Fuel Undeclared Candidates," *Memphis Commercial Appeal* 4 September 1994, A9.

63. Ibid.

64. Will, "Gramm Courts Iowans on Road to White House."

8

The Christian Right in the Presidential Nominating Process

With their sweeping congressional victory in the 1994 midterm elections, the Republicans are seemingly well positioned to take the White House in 1996. The GOP's 1996 presidential nomination therefore appears to be an extremely valuable prize. Does the Christian Right control the road to that nomination? As the preliminary stages of the 1996 campaign got under way, numerous signs pointed in that direction. Christian Right organizations experienced dramatic membership growth. In September 1994, the Christian Coalition claimed 1.4 million members, up from 250,000 two years earlier.[1] Christian Right activists took over state Republican parties in places as diverse as Virginia, Oregon, Minnesota, and Texas. A survey conducted by *Campaigns and Elections* magazine found the Christian Right to be a "dominant" force in eighteen state Republican parties and a "substantial" force in thirteen more.[2] The party's presidential hopefuls flocked to the conventions of the Christian Coalition and National Religious Broadcasters. Editorial writers and Democratic political leaders warned Americans about the growing power of the Christian Right.

We should, however, be cautious in interpreting these signs. Movement organizational strength is not easily translated into control of primary elections and caucus meetings. Takeover of state parties provides only limited control over the nominating process. And presidential hopefuls rarely hesitate to throw themselves before willing audiences.

To assess the power of the Christian Right in the presidential nominating process properly, we need to move beyond daily headlines and warnings leveled by the movement's opponents. Over the decade and a half of the Christian Right's existence, popular evaluations of its power have fluctuated wildly. Too often, coverage of the Christian Right has reached for sweeping, but false, conclusions. Movement successes lead to dire warnings about an impending evangelical theocracy. Movement setbacks bring proclamations that the movement has collapsed or is about to collapse. Neither collapse nor theocracy are imminent. To see why that is so, we need to dig deeper. This chapter analyzes the resources available to the Christian Right, the opportunities that the contemporary American nominating process provides to insurgent movements, and the history of Christian Right involvement in the nominating process. These analyses provide the basis for an overall assessment of the movement's influence.

I conclude that Christian Right "takeover" of the Republican nominating process—much less the imposition of theocracy on the nation—is unlikely. While the Christian Right boasts a powerful grassroots organization, it remains a minority movement within the party and the nation. Victory in primary elections is the key to presidential nomination, and this requires a base of support far broader than the Christian Right can provide on its own. But if the Christian Right cannot control the nominating process, possibilities for influence remain. In arenas such as caucuses, where participation rates are low, the movement's formidable organizational resources may compensate for a lack of wider support. Strategic alliance building may allow the movement to succeed where it could not on its own. The Christian Right can also influence the nominating process in less direct ways. As candidates devise their electoral strategies, they must consider the possibility that alienating the Christian Right could damage their chances in the general election.

Before continuing with analysis of Christian Right influence, however, we need a better understanding of the movement. It is to that task we now turn.

Who and What Is the Christian Right?

RELIGIOUS BASE

The Christian Right, as the name implies, is a religiously based movement. Christian Right leaders have, from the movement's early days, made claims to ecumenism. Jerry Falwell promoted his Moral Majority as a political and not a religious organization, one that could unite "moral" fundamentalists, evangelicals, Catholics, and Jews.[3] More recently, Pat Robertson's Christian Coalition has made significant efforts to reach out to conservative Catholics, orthodox Jews, and African-American Protestants. Nonetheless, the movement's primary base of support remains white evangelical Protestants. In order to understand the Christian Right, we need to know more about this base.

Roughly 20 percent of Americans can be classified as white evangelicals. Scholars of religion and politics arrive at figures somewhat above and below that percentage. Wade Clark Roof and William McKinney put 15.8 percent of Americans into their white "Conservative Protestant" category, while Kenneth Wald puts 22 percent into his white "Evangelical Protestant" grouping. Corwin Smidt draws on two different sets of surveys; these place either 18 percent or 26 percent of American whites in the evangelical category.[4] Different results are rooted in differing definitions and survey strategies. One approach is simply to ask respondents whether they consider themselves to be "evangelicals." More commonly, scholars label individuals as evangelical based on the denomination they belong to. (This then leads to controversy concerning the denominations that should properly be labeled evangelical.) Another approach is to classify individuals according to the religious beliefs they espouse: do they claim to be "born again," do they believe in a literal interpretation of the Bible, or have they attempted to convert others? Controversies arise here as well, concerning which questions best measure "evangelical" status. Each approach captures a slightly different evangelical population. Some members of evangelical denominations do not espouse evangelical religious beliefs. Some who do espouse such beliefs are members of liberal Protestant denominations or the Catholic church. Thus it is important to remember that while evangelicalism is a very real social phenomenon, its boundaries are not clearly delineated.

It is also important to remember that serious religious differences exist *within* the evangelical community. Particularly important are divisions between fundamentalists and charismatics. Fundamentalists are strict believers in the literal truth of the Bible. They are fierce opponents of evolution, theological liberalism, and cultural experimentation. Militancy is a defining characteristic. Jerry Falwell captures this quality with his definition: "A fundamentalist is an evangelical who is angry about something."[5] Fundamentalists have traditionally been wary of cooperating with the impure, and this has led to the development of innumerable small, independent sects. Independent Baptists are the largest contingent within the fundamentalist camp. Jerry Falwell has been their most visible spokesman in recent years.

Charismatics often share fundamentalists' attachment to biblical literalism, but, unlike their fundamentalist counterparts, they also hold that the believer today can be filled with the gifts of the Holy Spirit, gifts that most often manifest themselves in the form of glossolalia (speaking in tongues) and faith healing. Charismatics come in two main varieties. The first are members of charismatic *denominations* such as the Assemblies of God. These charismatics are also known as Pentecostalists. The second are members of charismatic movements within noncharismatic denominations, including liberal Protestant denominations and the Catholic church. Both the Pentecostalist denominations and the charismatic movement have experienced tremendous growth in recent decades.[6]

Fundamentalists have long been hostile toward charismatics, and conflict between these two groups plays an important role in the remainder of this chapter. A third group should be mentioned as well. Neo-evangelicals, or simply evangelicals,* are, in essence, more moderate fundamentalists. While they are believers in biblical authority, they show greater willingness to accommodate, and work within, the impure society that surrounds them. Billy Graham is the best known and most influential leader of the neo-evangelical movement.

What features characterize the members of the three religious groups (evangelicals) that form the Christian Right's base constituency? On average, they are slightly older than the population as a whole. There are more females than males in the groups. Evangelicals are more likely to live in the South and in rural areas than are nonevangelicals. While their levels of education and income are below the national average, the gap in these areas has been diminishing.[7] Drawing on this social base, the Christian Right has brought into the GOP a set of supporters quite different than the party's traditional upper-income, well-educated, mainline Protestant activist base.[8] The Christian Right thus broadens the party, but at the same time social and religious differences may inhibit alliance formation between its members and other elements of the party.

The religious base from which the Christian Right draws is difficult to measure, but by any measure it is sizable. Even the most modest measurement of its size leaves it significantly larger than the African-American, Hispanic, or Jewish communities. If mobilized, this base therefore has considerable political potential in presidential nominating processes—and elsewhere. For this potential to be realized, however, the group must be mobilized. The Christian Right has by no means managed to mobilize its entire religious base.[9] If it had, Jimmy Carter, Albert Gore, and Bill Clinton would be counted among its members. Nonetheless, the movement has made great strides over the past fifteen years.

MOBILIZATION
White evangelicals have been around for a long time, but their political mo-

---

* The reader will note here a problem of terminology. The word "evangelical" is commonly used in a variety of ways. Sometimes it is used specifically to apply to the moderate fundamentalists described in this paragraph. At other times, it is used as an umbrella term to cover fundamentalists, charismatics, and the moderate fundamentalist group. With the exception of this paragraph, I use the term evangelical in this second, broader sense.

bilization has been more sporadic. The Christian Right emerged in the late 1970s. Conservative leaders such as Richard Viguerie, Howard Phillips, and Paul Weyrich had by that time already developed a powerful "New Right" network of conservative groups built primarily on direct-mail appeals opposing gun control, the Panama Canal Treaty, and the Equal Rights Amendment (ERA). These New Right leaders were themselves Catholic and Jewish, but they looked out on the large, and largely unmobilized, evangelical Protestant constituency and saw great potential. Evangelicals were conservative on social issues important to the New Right, such as abortion, the ERA, and gay rights. After decades of political withdrawal, many evangelicals were ready to fight for control of the cultural institutions—schools, churches, the media, and, above all, the family—they believed were critical to passing on their values in a hostile world. Furthermore, in their local congregations, publishing houses, radio stations, and television networks, evangelicals possessed an array of religious institutions that could be extremely valuable if turned to political ends. In the late 1970s, New Right leaders reached out to recruit evangelical leaders such as Jerry Falwell and Pat Robertson. The Christian Right was born from those recruitment efforts.

Early Christian Right organizations included Religious Roundtable, Christian Voice, and the National Christian Action Coalition. But the group that dominated public perceptions of the movement was Jerry Falwell's Moral Majority. The movement garnered extensive media coverage and utilized religious networks to build a significant institutional presence in a short period of time. With the 1980 election of Ronald Reagan and a Republican Senate, the Christian Right turned its attention to Washington. Congress was bombarded with mail and a host of bills were introduced.[10] The movement met with mixed success, and by the mid-1980s activists began to question the movement's focus on Washington and the top-heavy nature of many of its organizations.

The mid-1980s saw the Christian Right begin a transformation that reshaped the movement and significantly improved its capabilities for action within the presidential nominating process.[11] Two changes were critical. First, the Christian Right deemphasized Washington and developed its grassroots capabilities. The movement's early organizations, built on direct mail and national publicity, often failed to develop vibrant local branches. While the major Christian Right organizations of today, such as the Christian Coalition, Concerned Women for America, and Focus on the Family, are national in scope, they nurture their local activists. Second, the religious base of the movement has broadened. The early Christian Right drew primarily on fundamentalist religious networks. Fundamentalist Jerry Falwell headed the Moral Majority; its board of directors and local chapters were overwhelmingly fundamentalist. A second, charismatic, wave of activists energized the Christian Right in the late 1980s.[12]

Both of these changes were linked, at least in part, to Pat Robertson's 1988 bid for the Republican presidential nomination. Many charismatics who had sat on the sidelines in the early 1980s were mobilized by their fellow charismatic Robertson. As Robertson activists attempted to build campaign organizations across the country and to take over local parties and caucuses, they augmented the Christian Right's grassroots strength and laid the foundation for future gains. Furthermore, the Robertson campaign focused the attention of movement activists on the Republican Party.

While a lull in Christian Right activity following the 1988 campaign led some observers to predict the movement's demise,[13] the early 1990s showed those predictions to be erroneous. The transformed Christian Right that emerged was stronger, better organized at the grassroots, and more religiously diverse than its earlier incarnations. It showed its strength at the 1992 GOP convention and has prospered under the Clinton presidency.

A wide array of Christian Right groups are prospering, but the most important for the purposes of this chapter is the Christian Coalition. Started by Pat Robertson in 1989, the Christian Coalition built on the foundation laid by Robertson's presidential campaign and has grown spectacularly since. By the fall of 1994, the group boasted over 1,000 chapters in all fifty states and 1.4 million members. The membership numbers should be approached with some caution; Christian Right groups have a history of inflating membership figures.[14] Nonetheless, it is clear that the group has developed an extremely powerful grassroots network. Furthermore, the Christian Coalition, more than other movement groups, focuses its attention on electoral politics. The coalition has been a major factor in the Christian Right takeover of an estimated eighteen state Republican parties. The Christian Coalition and the myriad local organizations that cooperate with it are now a force to be reckoned with in the Republican presidential nominating process.

Party Coalitions, Group Influence, and Changing Rules

American political parties have long been portrayed as loose coalitions of social groups. The famed New Deal Democratic coalition, tying together union workers, Catholics, big-city machine politicians, southern whites, and African Americans, provides the classic example. Social movements that grow out of these groups have often played a role in presidential nominations.[15] The influence of movements has been most noticeable within the Democratic Party. With varying levels of success, organized labor, the civil rights movement, the anti-Vietnam war movement, the women's movement, and, more recently, the gay and lesbian movements have all participated in Democratic nominating contests. In the process, these movements have brought in new waves of activists, transforming both the party and its image with the public at large. As we look at the Christian Right's attempts to influence Republican nominations, two things are important to keep in mind.

First, most accounts of movement influence within a party deal with the Democrats. The Republicans are different and this has consequences for the Christian Right. In the post–New Deal period, the Republicans have been a smaller but more homogeneous party. Jo Freeman argues convincingly that Republican political "culture" differs significantly from that of the Democrats.[16] Democrats, in keeping with the diverse, coalitional nature of their party, tend to grant considerable legitimacy to the groups and movements that make up their base of support. In the GOP, party loyalty is stressed, and group attachments are looked on with suspicion. The party is held together, in large part, by the social similarity of its members. As the Christian Right became involved in the party and its nominating process, it brought in a contingent of activists who did not fit the party's social profile and whose identification with their movement brought into question their loyalty to the party. Christian Right activists have repeatedly been called on to prove that they are loyal Republicans.

Second, the rules of the presidential nominating process have changed significantly in the last several decades, with important consequences for insurgent movements such as the Christian Right. Here, too, attention has focused on the Democrats. In the wake of the tumultuous 1968 Democratic National Convention, the party began a process of reform that significantly altered the rules of the nominating process. Democratic Party reform has alternately been characterized as a profound threat to good government and the party's electoral fortunes, as largely irrelevant given other long-term forces transforming the electoral process, and as a democratic opening of the party to long-excluded groups and movements.[17] The long-raging debate over Democratic Party reform is beyond the scope of this chapter, but several changes in the nominating process that grew out of the reform era are relevant here.

One important change was a proliferation of primaries. Reformed Democratic rules strictly regulated the operation of caucuses. Many state Democratic parties decided that the simplest course of action would be to switch to a primary. As Democratic state legislatures made this choice, their decisions often affected the Republicans as well. The result was a system in which primaries dominated the candidate selection process. In 1988, for example, 76.9 percent of Republican delegates were chosen in primaries.[18] If the Christian Right is to control the GOP's presidential nominating process, it will have to find an effective way to exert its influence in primary elections.

Another critical change in the presidential nominating process came about with the passage of the Federal Election Campaign Act (FECA) Amendments of 1974. In response to the financing scandals unearthed in the

Watergate investigations, the FECA amendments implemented rigorous reporting requirements, requiring disclosure of the names of major ($200 or more) contributors. They provided federal matching funds for candidates, but to qualify for those funds, candidates had to raise at least $5,000 in contributions in at least twenty states. The amendments limit individual contributions to $1,000 per candidate (only the first $250 qualify for matching funds) and PAC contributions to $5,000 per candidate.[19] The effect of the FECA amendments has been to favor candidates who can develop a nationwide base of small contributors. This would prove particularly important in the 1988 Robertson campaign.

Finally, a "nonchange" in the Republican nominating process is important as well. Whereas Democratic Party reforms imposed strict national regulations on the delegate selection procedures employed by states, the Republicans let state parties design their own procedures. The result has been a very wide variety of Republican nominating systems. Furthermore, because state parties can alter nominating rules, control of those parties becomes a valuable asset in the struggle between contending presidential factions. This encouraged the Christian Right to focus its attention on state parties, and the movement's control of a number of state parties may prove significant in future nominating contests.

Republican Party culture and nominating rules help shape the opportunities available for Christian Right influence, but how well has the movement made use of those opportunities? It is time to turn to an examination of the Christian Right's attempts to influence the GOP's nominating process.

The Christian Right Crashes the Party: Movement Influence in the Republican Nominating Process

EARLY YEARS

Prior to the 1988 campaign, the Christian Right played a very limited role in the Republican nominating process. Nonetheless, something very important was happening from 1976 to 1984: white evangelicals and the Christian Right were becoming firmly attached to the Republican Party. In 1976, attention was focused on an evangelical Democrat, Jimmy Carter. Eager to talk about his faith, Carter helped draw attention to evangelicals—*Time* and *Newsweek* labeled 1976 the "Year of the Evangelical"—and helped legitimate political involvement on their part. Carter received the public endorsement of televangelist Pat Robertson[20] and, in the general election, roughly half the votes cast by white evangelicals. This level of evangelical support, far above that obtained by the two previous Democratic nominees, helped propel Carter to the White House.[21] Many of his evangelical backers were quickly disappointed.

By the time the Christian Right was organized in the late 1970s, President Carter had already lost the support of the movement's leaders. Carter did not side with them on social issues such as abortion or the ERA. Nor, as some had expected, did he heed their pleas to appoint evangelicals to government offices. In any event, given the resolutely conservative rhetoric of Christian Right leaders and their New Right allies, cooperation with any but the most right-wing Democrat was unlikely.

As the 1980 nominating campaign began, Christian Right leaders were clearly leaning toward the Republicans, but there is little evidence that the organized movement played an active role in the nomination of Ronald Reagan. After all, the Moral Majority was only formed in September 1979; primaries and caucuses began just four months later. But if the movement did not select Reagan, it was nonetheless enthusiastic about the Republican nominee. Reagan was invited to—and attended—the Religious Roundtable's 10,000-strong "National Affairs Briefing." The Roundtable and Moral Majority conducted registration drives for the general election. Christian Voice distributed moral "report cards," ran anti-Carter ads, and attempted to mobilize ministers on behalf of Reagan.[22]

By 1984 the Christian Right had developed sufficient organization to be a force in nomination politics, but the Republican presidential nomination was not seriously contested that year. While some observers argued that the movement's social-issue concerns were being sacrificed to the Reagan administration's economic agenda, the Christian Right remained enthusiastic about the president and his party. By 1984, white evangelicals in general and the Christian Right in particular had become firmly attached to the GOP. In the 1983–84 period Republican identification among white evangelicals increased sharply, and in the 1984 election Reagan won an impressive 76 percent of the white evangelical vote (up from 67 percent in 1980).[23] Christian Right leaders were given prominent places at the 1984 Republican convention and, with funding from party sources, developed a massive voter registration drive for the general election.[24]

The shift to the Republicans among evangelicals and the Christian Right was fueled by two factors. First, the Democratic and Republican parties were, with each campaign, staking out more clearly opposed positions on the social issues of concern to these groups. The platforms and campaign rhetoric of the parties demonstrated that the Republicans had taken their stand with the Christian Right and the Democrats had taken theirs with the feminist movement and, to a lesser extent, the gay and lesbian movements. Second, the Republican Party was making a concerted effort to win over evangelical political and religious leaders. Robert Dugan, political director of the National Association of Evangelicals (NAE), described the parties' efforts as follows:

The NAE has been sought, wooed, approached by the Republican National Committee and by all of the Republican presidential candidates continuously, over more than recent months, going back a long time. On the other hand, the DNC has not approached us at all, nor has any other Democratic presidential candidate sought contact of *any* sort. . . .[25]

The Republicans' efforts paid off. As the 1988 campaign approached, the Christian Right was firmly within the party. The movement possessed the resources to have an impact, and with a contested race for the presidential nomination, it had an opportunity to use those resources.

1988

The Christian Right was a key participant in the battle for the GOP's 1988 presidential nomination. Not only did the party's front-runners actively compete for Christian Right support, the movement also produced a candidate of its own, televangelist Marion G. ("Pat") Robertson. The fate of Robertson's effort is instructive.

Robertson faced long odds. He was competing in a field that included the vice-president of the United States (George Bush), the former majority leader of the Senate (Robert Dole), a leading congressman (Jack Kemp), a former governor (Pete du Pont), and a former secretary of state and NATO commander-in-chief (Alexander Haig). Robertson had never held elected or appointed government office. Founder and chief executive officer of the Christian Broadcasting Network (CBN), he had the misfortune of running for president in the midst of a series of scandals that shook the world of televangelism. Robertson's third-place finish was thus quite respectable. Not only did Robertson win four states and match the spending of his strongest rivals, he also mobilized a powerful grassroots organization. That organization took over a number of state Republican parties and laid the groundwork for the future development of the Christian Coalition.

Under the current nominating system, campaigns start well before the election year; the Robertson campaign was no exception. In late 1984, Robertson began to give private consideration to a presidential bid.[26] Public speculation concerning a Robertson campaign grew in the following year. By 1986, pro-Robertson forces were contesting precinct-level caucuses in Michigan. In September of that year, Robertson announced a petition campaign. If 3 million Americans would sign petitions requesting him to run, Robertson declared, he would enter the race.

Robertson obtained, or at least claimed to obtain, his 3 million signatures and went on to demonstrate strength in a number of areas.[27] Fund raising was key among them. As noted earlier, the current nominating system favors candidates who can develop a large base of small contributors. Rob-

ertson had a tremendous advantage in this regard; when the campaign began, he had been raising large sums of money from small contributors for
over two decades. His Christian Broadcasting Network maintained a donor
list of over 900,000 names and in 1986 raised $230 million, much of it in
the form of small donations from viewers.[28] As the host of CBN's popular
700 Club, Robertson had established a personal connection with viewers
across the country. Utilizing the network of support developed at CBN,
Robertson garnered over $20 million in individual contributions for his
1988 campaign. That total was exceeded only by incumbent Vice-President
George Bush ($22 million). While Bush relied heavily on large contributions
($750–$1,000), Robertson relied on numerous small contributors. Eighty-
nine percent of the contributions to Robertson's campaign were under
$500.[29] The total number of Robertson contributors exceeded that of any of
his rivals, and because only the first $250 of a contribution is eligible for
matching funds, Robertson received more matching funds (just under $9
million) than any of his rivals. Thus Robertson, a candidate with no political
experience, was able to match or exceed the spending of his more experienced rivals.

Robertson was also able to utilize CBN resources—and local church networks—to mobilize an impressive grassroots volunteer force. The groundwork for Robertson's organizational effort was laid by a group called the
Freedom Council. Heavily supported by CBN, the Freedom Council was
formed in 1981 as a nonpartisan grassroots organization dedicated to pro-
moting political involvement on the part of evangelical Christians throughout the country. In 1985 its budget increased dramatically, and the council
began to look suspiciously like an arm of the Robertson campaign. It mobilized evangelicals to participate in the 1986 Michigan caucuses (the first
round of a complex process that would eventually select Michigan delegates
to the GOP's 1988 national convention). It also hired many of the individuals who were to go on to top positions in the Robertson campaign. Press
scrutiny and negative publicity led to the Freedom Council's disbandment in
late 1986, but not before it performed valuable work for the Robertson
campaign. Robertson was also able to tap into local evangelical (particularly
charismatic) congregations. The committed volunteers mobilized from these
churches formed the core of a formidable grassroots organization.[30] Outside
observers, focusing their attention on opinion polls and the traditional pool
of Republican activists, were repeatedly surprised by the strength of Robertson's "invisible army."

In arenas where the key to victory was turning out a few hundred, or a
few thousand, dedicated supporters, Robertson's invisible army met with
considerable success. State parties can, as discussed earlier, be a useful asset
in the Republican nominating process. State parties became battlegrounds in
a number of states as Robertson volunteers flooded into party meetings, tak-

ing over some and establishing themselves as a significant minority force in others. Robertson's organization also served him well in caucus states. The electoral season opened with a strong second-place Robertson showing in the Iowa caucuses, a dramatic setback for third-place finisher George Bush. Robertson's four victories all came in caucus states (Alaska, Hawaii, Nevada, and Washington) and he ran strongly in caucus states such as Michigan, Minnesota, and Virginia. Robertson's campaign ultimately failed, but it demonstrated considerable strengths and laid the groundwork for future Christian Right gains.

Nonetheless, for all Robertson's strengths, he still lost. Lavish funding and an effective grassroots network could only bring him to a third-place finish. Robertson failed to win a single primary and won only 128 of the 2,277 delegates at the 1988 convention.[31] What were Robertson's weaknesses, and what might those weaknesses tell us about the nature of Christian Right influence in the nominating process?

One problem was the candidate himself. While Robertson often reminded audiences that he was the son of a U.S. senator, a Yale Law School graduate, and a successful businessman, he could not hide the fact that he lacked the political experience Americans have come to expect in major-party candidates. Many who found Robertson and his message appealing still had doubts that he was qualified to be *president*. Robertson compounded these doubts with a series of damaging misstatements. Suggestions that he knew the location of American hostages in Lebanon, that Soviet missiles were still in Cuba, and that the Bush campaign was behind scandals that undermined televangelist Jimmy Swaggart all proved to be unfounded, undermining Robertson's credibility at critical stages in his campaign.

A second problem Robertson faced was vigorous competition for Christian Right support. His opponents fought hard for endorsements from Christian Right leaders and for the support of their followers. George Bush obtained an early endorsement from Moral Majority President Jerry Falwell. And Bush's campaign to win over evangelical leaders went far beyond Falwell. Bush attended their meetings, kept up personal correspondence, and, an internal campaign document boasts, "was photographed with over 1,000 evangelical leaders of influence."[32] The Bush campaign produced a biography and a campaign video discussing the candidate's faith, targeted evangelical audiences for selected mailings, and developed a network of informants within southern "superchurches." Jack Kemp entered the 1988 race as a champion of the party's conservative wing. While his primary appeal was economic, Kemp was solidly conservative on social issues. He won the support of New Right leaders such as direct-mail pioneer Richard Viguerie and anti-ERA crusader Phyllis Schlafly. Christian Right leaders came on board as well, including Robert Grant and Gary Jarmin (both affiliated with the organization Christian Voice), Tim LaHaye (widely selling author and one of the founders of the Moral Majority), and Beverly LaHaye (head of Concerned Women for America). Senator Robert Dole's ties to conservatives were weaker than those of Kemp, but he too reached out to the Christian Right. Dole recruited Robert Billings, the first executive director of the Moral Majority and the "evangelical coordinator" for Ronald Reagan's 1980 campaign.[33] Dole's openly evangelical wife, Elizabeth, provided a helpful bridge to the evangelical community. Senator Dole also won points with the Christian Right by defending local Robertson activists in their conflicts with state party hierarchies loyal to George Bush.

The competition for Christian Right support went beyond leadership recruitment and outreach efforts; Robertson's rivals also adopted positions likely to appeal to the movement's supporters. Admittedly, George Bush and Robert Dole were suspect in the eyes of the Christian Right. Before becoming Ronald Reagan's running mate in 1980, Bush had been pro-choice on abortion. Dole had originally backed the Equal Rights Amendment (ERA). By 1988, however, the major Republican candidates presented a uniform, conservative front on social, and most other, issues. Bush, Kemp, and Dole opposed abortion, supported prayer in schools, and opposed the ERA. Pat Robertson might offer greater fervor in the pursuit of a socially conservative agenda, but the candidates' official positions were remarkably similar, a fact that became clear in candidate debates. Robertson's campaign manager Marc Nuttle described the situation in the following manner:

> It is important to note—and I am not sure the press wrote about it—that the Republican candidates agreed on every single solitary issue.... The only discernible difference between the candidates during the debates was that George Bush was for the INF [Intermediate-range Nuclear Forces] treaty and the other candidates were leery of it. Ultimately the candidates all came around to the INF treaty and Robertson was no different.[34]

In a field of candidates taking similar stands, Robertson faced serious difficulties, for what set him apart from his rivals was precisely what he did not want to emphasize: his lack of political experience. Nevertheless, it should be emphasized that Robertson's *personal* weakness did not indicate weakness for the Christian Right as a whole. Indeed, the fact that the GOP's major candidates were reaching out to make connections with the movement's leaders and tailoring their messages to attract social conservatives was a sign of Christian Right strength.

A third problem the Robertson campaign faced grew from the religious divisions within the Christian Right described earlier in this chapter. In the early 1960s, Pat Robertson was ordained a Southern Baptist minister. One might be tempted, therefore, to link him to that denomination's fundamentalist and neo-evangelical traditions. Robertson, however, claims to have discovered the powers of the Holy Spirit and is firmly identified with the charismatic movement. His presidential campaign played a critical role in mobilizing charismatics, supplementing the primarily fundamentalist mobilization of the Christian Right's early years. Unfortunately for Robertson, he had serious difficulty moving beyond his charismatic base.

This difficulty manifested itself in a variety of ways, including the endorsements Robertson was able to obtain. While he won the early support of charismatic television evangelists such as Oral Roberts and Jimmy Swaggart, he had much less luck with fundamentalists Jerry Falwell, Robert Billings, Ed McAteer, and Tim LaHaye, who had led the first wave of Christian Right activism. Surveys show that Robertson's contributors and state convention delegates were very heavily charismatic.[35] The key test came at the polls, and there too doctrinal differences played a critical role. Clyde Wilcox's analysis of National Election Study Super Tuesday survey data leads him to conclude that support for Robertson was strongly associated with membership in charismatic (Pentecostal) denominations. Among members of Pentecostal churches, 43 percent rated Robertson more highly than any other Republican candidate. Among members of fundamentalist churches, zero percent gave Robertson such a rating. The large, and theologically divided, Southern Baptist constituency fell in the middle, with 8 percent rating Robertson more highly than any of his GOP rivals.[36] As these figures make clear, conservative Protestants were *not* united behind Robertson's crusade. The denominational differences so often ignored by outsiders had a profound impact on their political behavior.

Robertson's final and most serious problem was a lack of popularity with the general public. This problem was, of course, related to those mentioned earlier: Robertson's political inexperience, the competing appeals of his rivals, and religious divisions within his evangelical base. The problem reflected something deeper as well. The leaders and organizations of the Christian Right have, from the movement's beginning, been controversial and generally disliked. The movement's popularity has never matched its level of organization. In Robertson's case the poll numbers were striking. A November 1987 poll found only 13 percent of registered Republicans willing to give him a "favorable" rating; 50 percent responded "unfavorable." In another poll, 51 percent of Republicans responded that they "could not vote for" Robertson if he were to become their party's nominee (comparable figures for Kemp, Bush, and Dole were 13, 8, and 6 percent respectively).[37]

Robertson's low popularity doomed him in primary elections, and as we saw earlier, primaries have become the key to nomination. Table 8.1 illustrates the gap between Robertson's caucus and primary showings. While Robertson's organizational strength helped him do well in many caucus states, Robertson averaged only 9 percent of the vote in primary states, and in no primary state did he approach victory. His strongest primary state was

TABLE 8.1
ROBERTSON'S STRONGEST SHOWINGS

	Percentage of vote	Position
Caucus states		
Hawaii	81.3	1st
Alaska	46.8	1st
Washington	39.0	1st
Minnesota	28.2	2d
Iowa	24.6	2d
Primary states		
Oklahoma	21.1	3d
South Dakota	19.6	2d
South Carolina	19.1	3d
Arkansas	18.9	3d
Louisiana	18.2	2d

SOURCE: "1988 Republican Primary Results and 1988 First Round Caucus Results," *Congressional Quarterly Weekly Report,* 12 August 1988.
NOTE: The table actually understates Robertson's caucus strength. In Nevada, Robertson forces voted "uncommitted" in the first round, but Robertson went on to win the state.

Oklahoma, where he received 21 percent of the vote and finished a distant third.

Table 8.2 provides an even more striking demonstration of the gap between Robertson's caucus and primary results. Whereas Robertson won over 20 percent of the delegates selected in caucus states, he won just 1.2 percent of the delegates selected from primary states. These results can be explained, in large part, by differences in turnout. In the four caucus states won by Robertson, the *combined* turnout for first-round caucus meetings was under 30,000. In contrast, the Republican primary in the small state of New Hampshire drew over 150,000 voters.[38] In low-turnout caucus settings, a disciplined organization of several thousand motivated followers can prove decisive. Such an organization could prove helpful in a primary, but a much broader base of popular support is needed for victory.

While Pat Robertson's bid for the presidency failed, the Christian Right was not without influence in the 1988 campaign. The major Republican candidates courted its leaders and adopted many of its themes. The eventual winner, George Bush, supported a socially conservative platform, picked a running mate (Dan Quayle) very much to the movement's liking, and hired many top Robertson activists as part of his general election campaign team.[39] Furthermore, by mobilizing thousands of grassroots activists across the country, Robertson's campaign laid the groundwork for future Christian

TABLE 8.2
ROBERTSON DELEGATES

Delegates won	
In caucuses	106
In primaries	22
Percentage of total delegates	
Overall (128 of 2,277)	5.7
In caucus states	20.1
In primary states	1.2

SOURCE: Calculated from an Americans for Robertson press release, 12 August 1988. Aligned delegates—those pledged by law to other candidates but actually Robertson supporters—are not included in delegate totals. States with a nonbinding primary and a caucus are included as caucus states.

Right influence. Shortly after the 1988 election, Robertson assessed his achievement in the following manner:

> Could it be that the reason for my candidacy has been fulfilled in the activation of tens of thousands of evangelical Christians into government? ... For the first time in recent history, patriotic, pro-family Christians learned the simple techniques of effective party organizing and successful campaigning.
>
> Their presence as an active force in American politics may result ultimately in at least one of America's major political parties taking on a profoundly Christian outlook in its platform and party structure.[40]

The 1992 campaign provided a test of Robertson's predictions.

1992

With an incumbent Republican president in the running, the 1992 nomination campaign differed markedly from that of 1988. For much of 1991, it looked as if a repeat of 1984 was in store. In the wake of the Gulf War, George Bush's approval ratings were at astronomically high levels. Bush's nomination—and, for that matter, his success in the general election —seemed assured. But, as the glow of military victory wore off, concern about the state of the economy brought Bush's approval ratings down to earth and brought a challenge for the nomination from syndicated columnist and television commentator Patrick Buchanan.

Mixed Feelings. —The Christian Right faced difficult decisions in the 1992 campaign. These difficulties arose, in large part, from mixed feelings toward George Bush. Richard Land, director of the Southern Baptist Convention's Christian Life Commission, spoke for many within the movement when he declared himself "positively ambivalent" about the president.[41] George Bush had successfully reached out to movement leaders and evangelical voters in the 1988 campaign. Why, then, did he have trouble securing Christian Right support in 1992? The movement's ambivalence about Bush was rooted both in his background and in his actions as president.

George Herbert Walker Bush was always an unlikely champion for the causes of the Christian Right. An Episcopalian from a wealthy northeastern family, Bush was clearly uncomfortable with the Bible Belt enthusiasm of evangelicals. When he made his first bid for the presidency in 1980, he presented himself as the moderate alternative to the conservatism of Ronald Reagan. Significantly, he supported a woman's right to choose an abortion. Leaders of the then emerging Christian Right were not impressed. Jerry Falwell lobbied hard to keep Bush off the ticket. Bush reversed himself on abortion and even won Falwell's backing in his 1988 campaign. Nonetheless, many within the Christian Right felt that Bush was not "one of them" and that his professions of loyalty to their causes were of questionable sincerity.

From the perspective of the Christian Right, George Bush's record in office was a mixed one. On the issue of abortion, the president's past position was a source of concern. So too were statements by party chairman Lee Atwater and Vice-President Dan Quayle referring to the GOP as a "big tent," capable of accommodating conflicting views on the issue. Pro-life forces feared such language opened the way to significant weakening of the party's position on abortion; Phyllis Schlafly, in a joking remark with her supporters, referred to "tent" as a "four letter word."[42] On the other hand, the Christian Right was generally satisfied with the Bush administration's *actions* on the abortion issue. The Bush veto stood as a bulwark against prochoice legislation. The administration took a strong stand in its arguments before the Supreme Court, explicitly calling for a reversal of *Roe v. Wade*.[43]

The record was similarly mixed on other issues of concern to the Christian Right. Bush's selection of Clarence Thomas for a seat on the Supreme Court won the enthusiastic endorsement of the movement. While the general public was deeply divided over Thomas's nomination, Christian Right activists I have spoken to express uniform and very strong support. President Bush's handling of the National Endowment for the Arts (NEA) drew less support. Christian Right groups such as Pat Robertson's Christian Coalition were at the forefront of campaigns against the allegedly obscene and blasphemous art funded by the NEA under the leadership of John Frohnmayer.[44] Bush, a personal friend of Frohnmayer's, did not see the NEA as a high-priority issue and was slow to react.[45] Under pressure from the Christian Right and the Buchanan campaign, Bush eventually fired Frohnmayer, but the issue served to underline the movement's doubts about the president.

In the wake of the victory in the Persian Gulf, George Bush declared his intention to build a "New World Order." This, it turned out, caused considerable anxiety in Christian Right circles. For decades, conservative evangelical leaders had been warning against the coming danger of a "socialist, one-world order." Secular organizations of the far right, most notably the John Birch Society, had long promoted similar fears. Evangelical fears were rooted in a complex mix of nationalism and biblical prophecy (the emergence of the new world government was linked to the return of the anti-Christ). Both the secular and the religious far right argued that an "establishment" elite would sell out American interests in pursuit of a unified system of global domination. George Bush's embrace of the United Nations, his links to the foreign policy "establishment," and his use of the phrase "New World Order" provided fodder for a variety of right-wing conspiracy theories. While the general public heard little of the furor this issue raised, Leigh Ann Metzger, the Bush White House's outreach director for evangelicals, was kept busy reassuring the right that no sinister intentions lay behind the New World Order.[46]

It was on gay and lesbian issues, however, that the Bush administration's performance drew the sharpest and most public criticism from the Christian Right. Gay leaders had been invited to attend a White House signing of a hate-crimes bill. Bush campaign chair Robert Mosbacher met with leaders of gay and lesbian groups in early 1992. These actions certainly did not establish George Bush as a champion of gay and lesbian rights. They were, however, enough to outrage a number of Christian Right leaders.

The administration's mixed record provoked varying responses from Christian Right leaders. The loudest protests, interestingly, came from elements of the movement known in the past for their moderation. Richard Land and James Smith of the Southern Baptist Convention's Christian Life Commission joined the National Association of Evangelicals' political director, Robert Dugan, in scathing criticism of the president. These criticisms began in the wake of an April 1990 White House ceremony to which gay leaders were invited and continued through the 1992 primary season. Although other issues, most notably the NEA, drove criticism of the president, homosexuality remained the principal focus. The critics were not only concerned about Bush's past meetings, they also wanted him to come out with a strong public statement opposing gay and lesbian rights. In an attempt to deal with discontent, President Bush requested a meeting with fifteen evangelical leaders including Dugan, Jerry Falwell, and Beverly LaHaye. At the April 1992 meeting, Bush assured them that he opposed "special laws" to protect homosexual rights and affirmed his opposition to a District of Columbia domestic-partners law. While leaders of the Christian Right's more directly political organizations lined up behind Bush, NAE and Southern Baptist officials continued to express their dissatisfaction, publicly attacking Pat Robertson, Jerry Falwell, and Beverly LaHaye for supporting the president. Only after further reassurances from Bush—and the passage of a Republican platform with strong anti-gay rights planks—did the criticism die down.[47]

The Failure of the Buchanan Challenge.—Given the dissatisfaction with the president that existed among the Christian Right, Pat Buchanan's challenge might have been expected to have gained their enthusiastic support. Buchanan embraced the movement's social-issue agenda, attaining notoriety with his explicit ads attacking the National Endowment for the Arts. Gary Bauer of the Family Research Council and ex-Robertson campaign chair Marc Nuttle were among those in attendance at an early meeting where Buchanan explored the possibility of entering the race.[48] Buchanan also gained the support of some lower-level Christian Right activists. Pat Robertson's 1988 Michigan and Washington State campaign chairs enlisted in the Buchanan effort. The 1988 Washington chair, Bruce Hawkins, claims that many former Robertson activists were recruited to the Buchanan campaign but that, given a short lead time, Buchanan was unable to build the sort of grassroots organization Robertson had created in 1988.[49]

Overall, however, Buchanan's attempt to win over Christian Right leaders and their constituencies met with limited success. The movement's most visible figures, such as Jerry Falwell and Pat Robertson, remained firmly in the president's camp. On the eve of critical southern primary contests, the Bush campaign distributed a letter from Robertson reaffirming his support for the president.[50] A March 1992 poll taken at the National Association of Evangelicals' annual meeting showed Bush ahead by an 88 to 12 percent margin.[51] The Georgia primary illustrated the limits of Buchanan's evangelical appeal. Despite a series of advertisements attacking Bush's handling of the NEA, Bush prevailed over Buchanan by 60 percent to 40 percent among white born-again Christians. Buchanan's showing was slightly better than the 36 percent he received among the state's voters as a whole, but George Bush nonetheless won the majority of born-agains over to his side.[52]

Why did Buchanan fail to do better among Christian Right leaders and their constituencies? First, Buchanan's nativist and isolationist tendencies probably raised questions here, just as they did among the public at large. Second, the fact that Buchanan is a Catholic may have undercut his appeal to some evangelical Protestants. Third, and probably most important for Christian Right leaders, Buchanan stood little chance of winning. In the words of Christian Coalition chairman Ralph Reed, "We went through one suicide mission in 1988 and we won't do it again."[53]

Party Ties.—The Christian Right's unwillingness to undertake "suicide missions" reflected the fact that, by 1992, the movement had developed other, more effective, means of influence. The development of the movement's grassroots capabilities gave it the ability to exercise a powerful voice within the party. The Christian Coalition, in particular, was looking toward the long term, slowly building its legitimacy and power within the Republican Party. In addition, many Christian Right groups hoped to influence the struggle over the 1992 GOP platform. All these efforts might be undermined if the movement threw its support to a marginal candidate like Pat Buchanan.

Despite their misgivings, the major political leaders of the Christian Right therefore remained in the Bush camp. It was the leaders based in *religious* organizations, such as the Southern Baptist Convention's Richard Land and James Smith and the National Association of Evangelicals' Robert Dugan, who were most willing to break with the president. In Dugan's words, "We [the NAE] are not a partisan group and we can criticize both sides."[54] The Christian Coalition, on the other hand, is, for all practical purposes, a partisan group. Its officially nonpartisan nature notwithstanding, the coalition works almost exclusively on behalf of Republican candidates. Republican leaders flock to the podium at the group's annual conventions. A $64,000 grant from the National Republican Senatorial Committee represented the largest single contribution to the Christian Coalition in the course of the 1992 campaign.[55] These ties to the party may well be helpful to the Christian Coalition, but they do limit its freedom of movement. For an organization with such close party ties, turning against that party's incumbent president would be a costly course of action.[56]

The Christian Right, however, did not need to turn against the president to exercise influence in 1992. The movement became a powerful presence at the GOP convention and won a platform very much to its liking, largely by supporting George Bush. The Christian Coalition placed a high priority on getting its members selected as convention delegates. Though in most states primaries determine which presidential candidate delegates will be pledged to support, they often do not determine who will be the delegates. In many cases, the delegates are chosen in a separate process, in local caucuses or state party meetings. In 1988 the Robertson campaign used its strength at this level to send a number of their supporters to the convention as pledged "Bush" or "Dole" delegates. (While in most cases obligated by state law to vote for Bush or Dole on the first ballot, these delegates were free to side with Robertson on other issues.) The Christian Coalition, building on the foundation laid by the Robertson campaign, proved a powerful force in these narrow arenas in 1992. The organization worked hard to educate its members on the intricacies of the selection process and get them out to local meetings. The fact that Robertson had endorsed President Bush early on and reaffirmed his support during the primary process helped bolster the legitimacy of their requests for positions as Bush delegates. Christian Coalition leaders claim that 300 of the 2,209 delegates in Houston were members of their organization, a stronger delegate base than Robertson attained in 1988 when he was an active candidate for the nomination. With this base of delegates, the Christian Coalition played an active role as state delegate caucuses picked the members of the party's platform committee. Of the committee's 107 members, 20 were members of the Christian Coalition.[57]

The Christian Coalition was not alone in its organizing efforts. The Republican National Coalition for Life was started by conservative activist Phyllis Schlafly in October 1990 for the specific purpose of defending a pro-life platform. With a board of directors featuring Christian Right luminaries Beverly LaHaye and Gary Bauer (head of the Family Research Council) and long-time conservative activist Morton Blackwell, RNC for Life was active in mobilizing pro-lifers to become delegates and platform committee members. On the first day of full committee hearings, Schlafly held a press conference to demonstrate her group's grassroots strength, presenting the platform committee with nearly 100,000 "pledges" by individuals requesting that the party retain the antiabortion language of its 1984 and 1988 platforms.[58] Of the signatures, Schlafly says, 3,500 came from elected officials and individuals holding party titles. While Schlafly did not make specific claims as to how many on the platform committee were "members" of RNC for Life, she does contend that RNC for Life was on "very friendly" terms with 40 of the 107.[59]

The Christian Right's strength at the convention helped ensure the passage of a platform even more conservative than those of the 1980s. Attempts to weaken the platform's pro-life language were easily beaten back. More explicit language opposing gay and lesbian rights was added during the platform hearings.[60] Pat Robertson, speaking to a "God and Country" rally at the convention, celebrated the passage of "the most conservative platform in decades."

The Christian Right's presence was felt well beyond the platform. The prominence of movement delegates and speakers gave a distinct socially conservative cast to the convention as a whole. News coverage focused on the resurgent power of the Christian Right and the GOP's close ties to it. The identification of movement and party that emerged from the convention was of questionable value to George Bush's presidential campaign but, for good or ill, the 1992 convention pushed the Christian Right and its issue agenda into the national spotlight. That might not have happened without the movement's participation in the nominating process.

The general election brought defeat for George Bush, but not because of defections on the part of the Christian Right. Movement leaders loyally fell into step in the fall campaign, mobilizing their supporters on behalf of George Bush. White evangelicals remained faithful to the GOP, supporting Bush at high levels after other groups abandoned him. Of white evangelicals who attended church regularly, 70 percent voted for Bush; only 18 percent voted for Clinton.[61]

General Lessons: 1996 and Beyond

With formidable grassroots strength and control of state and local party organizations across the country, the Christian Right will certainly be a player in the 1996 presidential nominating process. Potential GOP candidates, flocking to the annual meetings of the Christian Coalition, show a keen awareness of this fact, as do the media that cover the process. What lessons does the story told thus far leave us with for 1996 and beyond?

THE CHRISTIAN RIGHT IS NOT A UNIFIED ENTITY

While it is convenient to speak of the Christian Right as a single entity (this chapter does so at numerous points), we need to remember that the organizations and individuals that make up the Christian Right do not always act in unison. Divisions between charismatics and fundamentalists remain a barrier to cooperation, as seen in Pat Robertson's 1988 presidential bid. Movement divisions go beyond religious differences. Most GOP figures have been willing to endorse a generally conservative line on the social issues dear to the heart of the movement. Therefore it should not be surprising that movement leaders and evangelical voters divide their support among a number of candidates. Personal ties, assessments of candidates' character, and judgments regarding electability can lead Christian Right leaders and sympathetic evangelical voters to divide their support. Thus in 1988, despite the presence of a candidate from the ranks of the Christian Right, all the major Republican candidates could boast significant support from movement leaders. Even in the less contested 1992 race, serious divisions between the movement's political and denominational leaders emerged.

With no Republican incumbent running, the 1996 race looks very much like that of 1988. One should therefore be suspicious of claims that a particular candidate is "the" choice of the Christian Right. Movement leaders are unlikely to support a candidate who takes positions directly contradictory to theirs on key issues such as abortion and gay rights, but all indications are that the Christian Right will have a wide array of acceptable candidates from which to choose. No one candidate is likely to obtain the unified backing of the movement.

THE SCOPE OF CONFLICT IS CRITICAL

E.E. Schattschneider wrote that "the outcome of all conflict is determined by the *scope* of its contagion. The number of people involved in any conflict determines what happens, every change in the number of participants ... affects the result."[62] This is, perhaps, the clearest message to emerge from our story. The Christian Right has been successful in arenas where the scope of conflict is narrow. The Christian Right's dedicated volunteers and organizational resources are a potent force where turnout is low. In 1988 Robertson showed his greatest strength in caucus states. In 1992 the Christian Coalition was a potent force in local meetings that selected convention delegates. The Christian Right has been encouraged to pursue influence within the state parties by Republican rules that make those parties a valuable prize in the struggle for the GOP's presidential nomination. Over the past decade, the movement has used its resources to make impressive gains within state and local Republican Party organizations. When the scope of conflict is broad, however, when more people are drawn into the conflict, the Christian Right fares poorly. Winning in primaries, or in the court of public opinion, requires more than good organization and a few hundred, or a few thousand, dedicated volunteers; it requires widespread support that the Christian Right has thus far been unable to generate. And, unfortunately, for the Christian Right, the current presidential nominating system is dominated by primaries. As you hear reports of Christian Right victories in narrow arenas (e.g., takeover of state parties), remember that such victories cannot easily be replicated where the scope of conflict is broader.

The Dilemmas of Coalition Building

While focusing on arenas where the scope of conflict is narrow can bring limited success, to be truly effective the movement must learn to prevail in broader arenas; for this, coalition building is necessary. Given the low approval ratings garnered by Christian Right organizations and leaders, the movement will have to reach beyond itself to develop coalitions capable of prevailing in primaries. The Robertson campaign illustrates the limitations of a candidacy based almost entirely within the Christian Right. Robertson failed to unite the entire movement behind him, but, even if he had, it is unlikely that this would have been sufficient. Broader coalitions are necessary for victory.

Ronald Reagan and George Bush won the GOP's nomination by putting together broad coalitions of which the Christian Right was only one element. As a part of those coalitions the Christian Right won platforms to their liking and significant policy concessions. But the Christian Right, particularly in the Bush administration, often felt it was not getting the attention it deserved. To strengthen its influence, the movement needs to do more than wait for a candidate outside its ranks to develop a socially conservative coalition; it needs to move toward producing such a coalition on its own.

The leadership of the Christian Coalition appears to have learned this lesson. In a recent series of high-profile moves, the organization has been reaching out to woo a variety of potential allies. In New York, the group cooperated with Cardinal John O'Connor in a joint effort to oppose school board policies and elect socially conservative members to the board. In California, the Christian Coalition specially targeted the African-American and Latino communities in its campaign on behalf of a school voucher initiative. Ralph Reed, the Christian Coalition's executive director, has also made efforts to reach out to other elements of the Republican Party. Insisting that his followers have concerns beyond a narrow social-issue agenda, Reed went on record in favor of traditional Republican economic issues, most notably by announcing his support of the NAFTA agreement. In an even more ambitious outreach effort, Reed invited the *Democratic* Party chair, David Wilhelm, to speak to the September 1993 convention of the Christian Coalition.

Unfortunately for the Christian Coalition, attempts to broaden the coalition have met with mixed results. Wilhelm's speech provoked a decidedly hostile response from the assembled delegates. The audience responded most enthusiastically to the sorts of provocative social-issue appeals director Reed was attempting to downplay.[63] Facing serious division within the movement, Reed backed away from his endorsement of NAFTA. The California school voucher plan lost badly at the polls; the results of the intervention in the New York school board races were mixed.

Any group that lacks a clear majority on its own must engage in coalition building, and that endeavor is rarely easy. The Christian Right faces a particularly severe problem. In a nutshell, the imperatives of coalition building are in direct contradiction with those of mobilizing its organizational base. To reach beyond its religious base, the Christian Right needs to present its arguments in broadly acceptable secular language, tolerate compromise, and move beyond a strict social-issue focus. Yet doing so could well undermine the movement's organizational resources that, from the Robertson campaign to the platform battles of 1992, have been the source of the movement's strength. The members of the Christian Coalition are active primarily for religious reasons; they are used to, and comfortable with, expressing their concerns in religious language. Nor will moving the Christian Right away from a preoccupation with social issues be easy. Movement leaders often attempt to do so, but rank-and-file movement members rarely follow. Grassroots activism is fueled by support for school prayer and opposition to sex education, abortion, and the civil rights of gays and lesbians. Anticommunist themes used to evoke some enthusiasm, but these are obviously of declining relevance in today's world.

As the 1996 election approaches, you will hear repeated claims about the broad-based nature of the Christian Right, its widened issue agenda, and its diverse allies. The Christian Coalition has taken the lead in this area, and its alliance building efforts are important. But you should remember the underlying dilemmas inherent in such efforts. Broad-based coalitions will be difficult for the Christian Right to construct, and, if constructed, they may come at the cost of undermining the enthusiasm and religiously based resources that have been the basis of the movement's strength.

THE THREAT OF EXIT
A hard-to-measure but nonetheless important Christian Right influence on

the presidential nominating process is derived from the movement's threat to leave the party in the general election. The fear that an unacceptable candidate might cause the Christian Right to bolt the party could affect the nominating process in two ways. First, party voters and activists might shy away from such "divisive" candidates on the presumption that they could be damaging to the party's fortunes. Second, candidates may alter their behavior to make sure that they are not perceived to be unacceptable. Ronald Reagan was clearly acceptable to the Christian Right; George Bush, through ardent courtship of the movement, made himself so. What will happen if an "unacceptable" candidate is nominated in 1996? Such candidates certainly exist. Robert Dugan of the NAE argues that any one of the "three Ws" (Governors William Weld, Christine Whitman, and Pete Wilson) will be very difficult for the movement to accept.[64] The crucial issue is abortion; the three Ws are all pro-choice. The potential for conflict with the Christian Right is quite real.

There are, however, several reasons to believe that conflict and the "exit" of the Christian Right are likely to be avoided. On the critical abortion issue, attempts at compromise language are already under way. If the emphasis can be shifted from an absolute ban on abortion to restrictions (parental notification, waiting periods) on abortion, compromise may become, if not easy, at least easier.[65] Exit is also rendered less likely due to the lack of palatable alternatives open to the movement. As the Democratic Party has more and more consistently embraced social liberalism, Christian Right defection to it has become implausible. Third parties face serious obstacles in the American electoral system. The most plausible option for the Christian Right might well be abstention.

Finally, exit is likely to be avoided because the Christian Right has developed a long-term stake in the party. Given the suspicion of group attachments characteristic of Republican Party culture, the Christian Right has, from the beginning of its involvement with the GOP, been open to charges of disloyalty. Over the years, Christian Right activists within the party have worked hard to prove that they are loyal Republicans. They have won positions within state parties across the country and the ears of the party's leaders. Just as backing Pat Buchanan in 1992 would have undermined the movement's role within the party, so too might threats to leave the party in 1996. The Christian Right has invested great energy in its efforts within the party. It will not throw those efforts away lightly.

Conclusion

The Christian Right is deeply rooted in the American social structure; it will not go away any time soon. It is also deeply rooted in the Republican Party. The dedicated activists mobilized by the movement are taking over state parties and commanding the attention of presidential contenders. The Christian Right is a force to be reckoned with in the presidential nominating process, particularly where the scope of conflict is narrow. Nonetheless, its strengths should not be exaggerated. The movement is divided and has yet to master the coalition building necessary for it to dominate arenas, such as primaries, where the scope of conflict is broad. Its developing ties to the party have given it influence but have also restricted its freedom to maneuver.

If the Christian Right has not taken over the Republican Party, it has taken up residence within it. In the process, it has pushed a new issue agenda to the fore and altered the electoral calculations of potential presidents. These are no small achievements for a movement still in its teens.

Notes

1. Michael Kranish, "Christian Coalition Again in Spotlight," *Boston Globe,* 17 September 1994.

2. John Persinos, "Has the Christian Right Taken Over the Republican Party?" *Campaigns and Elections* 15 (September 1994).

3. Jerry Falwell, *Strength for the Journey* (New York: Simon and Schuster, 1987), 359–65.

4. See Wade Clark Roof and William McKinney, *American Mainline Religion* (New Brunswick: Rutgers University Press, 1987); Kenneth Wald, *Religion and Politics in the United States,* 2d ed. (Washington, D.C.: CQ Press, 1992); and Corwin Smidt, "Evangelical Voting Patterns: 1976–1988," in *No Longer Exiles,* ed. Michael Cromartie (Washington, D.C.: Ethics and Public Policy Center, 1993).

5. George M. Marsden, *Understanding Fundamentalism and Evangelicalism* (Grand Rapids, Mich.: William B. Eerdmans, 1991), 1.

6. See Margaret Paloma, *The Charismatic Movement: Is There a New Pentecost?* (Boston: Twayne, 1982).

7. See Roof and McKinney, *American Mainline Religion,* chap. 4.

8. See Allen Hertzke, *Echoes of Discontent* (Washington, D.C.: CQ Press, 1993); and Duane Oldfield, *The Right and the Righteous* (Lanham, Md.: Rowman and Littlefield, 1995) on conflicts between Christian Right activists and party "regulars."

9. See Clyde Wilcox, *God's Warriors* (Baltimore: Johns Hopkins University Press, 1992), chaps. 5 and 9.

10. Matthew Moen, *The Christian Right and Congress* (Tuscaloosa: University of Alabama Press, 1989).

11. See Matthew Moen, *The Transformation of the Christian Right* (Tuscaloosa: University of Alabama Press, 1992).

12. See Robert Liebman, "Mobilizing the Moral Majority," in *The New Christian Right,* ed. Robert Liebman and Robert Wuthnow (New York: Aldine, 1983); and *God's Warriors,* chaps. 7–9.

13. Michael D'Antonio, *Fall from Grace* (New York: Farrar, Straus, & Giroux, 1989).

14. Leslie Kaufman, "Life Beyond God," *New York Times,* 16 October 1994, cites the 1.4 million figure, as does Kranish. But the figure given just a month ear-

lier in Persinos is 450,000. The truth probably lies somewhere in between.

15. See Denise Baer and David Bositis, *Elite Cadres and Party Coalitions* (Westport, Conn.: Greenwood Press, 1988).

16. Jo Freeman, "The Political Culture of the Democratic and Republican Parties," *Political Science Quarterly* 101 (1986).

17. See, respectively, Nelson W. Polsby, *Consequences of Party Reform* (New York: Oxford University Press, 1983); Howard Reiter, *Selecting the President* (Philadelphia: University of Pennsylvania Press, 1985); and Baer and Bositis, *Elite Cadres and Party Coalitions*.

18. Emmett H. Buell, Jr., and James W. Davis, "Win Early and Often: Candidates and the Strategic Environment of 1988," in *Nominating the President*, ed. Emmett H. Buell, Jr., and Lee Sigelman (Knoxville: University of Tennessee Press, 1991), 3.

19. Clyde Wilcox, "Financing the 1988 Campaign," in Emmett H. Buell, Jr., and Lee Sigelman, eds., *Nominating the President*.

20. There is some ambiguity as to Robertson's exact position. David Harrell, Jr., *Pat Robertson: A Personal, Political, and Religious Portrait* (San Francisco: Harper & Row, 1987) presents Robertson as an enthusiastic Carter supporter (176). John Donovan, *Pat Robertson: The Authorized Biography* (New York: Macmillan, 1988), contains Robertson's claim that he made a last-minute decision to vote for Ford (181), a claim I have heard Robertson make on the campaign trail.

21. Paul Lopatto, *Religion and the Presidential Election* (New York: Praeger, 1985).

22. Moen, *The Transformation of the Christian Right*, 75–76.

23. Smidt, "Evangelical Voting Patterns," 96–100.

24. Personal interview with Tim LaHaye, 28 March 1989; and Sara Diamond, *Spiritual Warfare: The Politics of the Christian Right* (Boston: South End Press, 1989), 66–68.

25. Dugan's comments are from a speech given as a member of a panel on "The Religious Factor in the 1988 Elections" at the 1988 National Religious Broadcasters Convention.

26. Pat Robertson, *The Plan* (Nashville: Thomas Nelson, 1989), 60–61.

27. See T.R. Reid, "Invisible Army Won Few Battles," *Washington Post*, 17 December 1988. This article questions the 3 million figure. Robertson's campaign manager, Marc Nuttle, defends its validity. Personal interview, 21 June 1989.

28. See Charles Babcock, "Robertson: Blending Charity and Politics," *Washington Post*, 2 November 1987; and Jeffrey Hadden and Anson Shupe, *Televangelism: Power and Politics on God's Frontier* (New York: Henry Holt, 1988), 254.

29. Wilcox, "Financing the 1988 Prenomination Campaigns," 96–101.

30. See Hertzke, *Echoes of Discontent*, chap. 4.

31. See Americans for Robertson, "Robertson Delegates Represent Broad Spectrum," press release, 12 August 1988.

32. Doug Wead, "The Republican Party and the Evangelicals" (twice abridged version), internal Bush campaign document, 31 July 1988.

33. Personal interviews with Schlafly, Jarmin, the LaHayes, and Billings.

34. Personal interview with Marc Nuttle, 21 June 1989.

35. See John Green and James Guth, "Robertson's Republicans: Christian Activists in Republican Politics," *Election Politics* 4, no. 4 (1987); and Corwin Smidt

and James Penning, "A House Divided: A Comparison of Robertson and Bush Delegates to the 1988 Michigan Republican State Convention," *Polity* 23 (1989).

36. See Wilcox, *God's Warriors,* chap 7.

37. Martin Plissner, "Campaign '88—A Year To Go," CBS News/*New York Times* Poll, for release 27 October 1987.

38. See *Congressional Quarterly Weekly Report,* 1988, 2254–55.

39. See Hertzke, *Echoes of Discontent,* chap. 5; and Oldfield, *The Right and the Righteous,* chap. 6.

40. Robertson, *The Plan,* 177.

41. "Evangelicals Offer Uneasy Support to Bush," *Christianity Today* 36 (6 April 1992).

42. Personal interview, 29 October 1992.

43. See "Bush Solidifies Support with Pro-Lifers," *Human Events* 52, no. 18 (1992).

44. Joe Conason, "The Religious Right's Quiet Revival," *The Nation* 254 (27 April 1992): 554.

45. Personal interview with Leigh Ann Metzger, 21 July 1994. In the Bush White House's Public Liaison office, Metzger was in charge of outreach to evangelicals.

46. Personal interview, 21 July 1994.

47. The information in this paragraph is based on a 22 July 1994 personal interview with Robert Dugan. On Bush, the Christian Right, and the gay rights issue, see also Thomas B. Edsall, "Gay Rights and the Religious Right," *Washington Post,* 10 August 1992; Ann Devroy, "Bush Faults Special Laws for Gays," *Washington Post,* 22 April 1992; and Kim A. Lawton, "A Republican God?" *Christianity Today* 36 (5 October 1992).

48. See "Why Buchanan Is Running," *Human Events* 51 (7 December 1991): 3. Note that attendance at the meeting did not necessarily imply an endorsement of Buchanan.

49. Personal interview with Bruce Hawkins, 14 August 1992.

50. Ronald Smothers, "Bush Less Than Loved among the Christian Right," *New York Times,* 10 March 1992.

51. Personal interview with Robert Dugan, 22 July 1994.

52. See Smothers, "Bush Less Than Loved."

53. Ibid.

54. Personal interview, 22 July 1994.

55. See Frederick Clarkson, "On the Road to Victory?" *Church and State* 45 (January 1992); and Donna Minkowitz, "Outlawing Gays," *The Nation* 255 (19 October 1992).

56. Bruce Hawkins suggested that a desire to build strength within the party and influence the platform lay behind Pat Robertson's decision to endorse Bush. Personal interview, 14 August 1992.

57. The figures for convention delegates and platform committee members are from a 14 August 1992 personal interview with Bruce Hawkins, the Christian Coalition press secretary at the convention. These numbers are difficult to confirm but I have not heard them challenged. During platform committee hearings, many members were using the rhetoric of the Christian Right. The members from several states were persons I was familiar with from my previous research on the Christian Right.

58. RNC for Life press release, 11 August 1992.

59. Personal interview with Phyllis Schlafly, 29 October 1992. Note that the forty members her group was on friendly terms with probably included many of the members claimed by the Christian Coalition.

60. I was at the 1992 platform hearings and the area of gay rights was the primary one in which I saw significant changes to the working draft with which the committee had started the hearings.

61. See Lyman Kellstedt, John Green, James Guth, and Corwin Smidt, "Religious Voting Blocs in the 1992 Election: The Year of the Evangelical?" Paper presented at the 1993 annual meeting of the American Political Science Association, Washington, D.C., 1–4 September.

62. E.E. Schattschneider, *The Semi-Sovereign People* (New York: Holt, Rinehart, and Winston, 1960), 2.

63. See Joseph Coon, "Detour on the Road to Victory?" *Church and State* 46 (October 1993).

64. Personal interview, 22 July 1994.

65. Republican strategist William Kristol, while admitting the dangers the abortion issue poses to the party, argues that such a compromise is possible and has, himself, been working to develop compromise abortion language. Personal interview, 22 July 1994.

9

Third-Party and Independent Candidates: How They Get on the Ballot, How They Get Nominated

EMMET T. FLOOD AND WILLIAM G. MAYER

As long as we restrict our attention to the two major-party candidates, little about the 1992 presidential election should strike us as especially surprising. As the fall campaign got under way, George Bush faced two overriding problems: the national economy was stagnant; and he himself had acquired an image of being out-of-touch, unconcerned, and ineffective, especially when it came to handling the country's most important domestic issues. A huge pile of political science writing, as well as common sense, indicates that incumbent presidents are usually voted out of office under such circumstances.[1] And so it was with George Bush. Nothing in the *two-party* presidential vote of 1992 requires political scientists, practitioners, or commentators to revise any of their long-settled ideas about the dynamics of presidential voting.

Unfortunately for the conventional wisdom, there was a third major candidate in the 1992 race, and on this score the results clearly *were* remarkable. For there is also a hefty literature in political science explaining why the United States has only two political parties and why third-party candidates rarely do very well in America, especially at the presidential level.[2] And, in general, this literature's predictions have been borne out quite well. As the figures in table 9.1 indicate, in the fifteen presidential elections

TABLE 9.1
STRONGEST SHOWING BY A THIRD-PARTY
OR INDEPENDENT PRESIDENTIAL
CANDIDATE, 1932–92

Year	Candidate	Party or Independent status	Total vote	Percentage
1932	Thomas	Socialist	884,649	2.23
1936	Lemke	Union	892,267	1.95
1940	Thomas	Socialist	116,410	0.23
1944	Thomas	Socialist	79,003	0.16
1948	Thurmond	States' Rights	1,176,125	2.41
1952	Hallinan	Progressive	140,023	0.23
1956	Andrews	States' Rights	111,178	0.18
1960	Hass	Socialist Labor	47,522	0.07
1964	Hass	Socialist Labor	45,219	0.06
1968	Wallace	American Independent	9,906,473	13.53
1972	Schmitz	American	1,099,482	1.41
1976	McCarthy	Independent	756,691	0.93
1980	Anderson	Independent	5,720,060	6.61
1984	Bergland	Libertarian	228,314	0.25
1988	Paul	Libertarian	432,179	0.47
1992	Perot	Independent	19,741,657	18.91

SOURCE: Computed from data in *America Votes*.

held between 1932 and 1988, the *strongest* third-party candidate in each election averaged a mere 2.0 percent of the total vote. Only two of these candidates—George Wallace in 1968 and John Anderson in 1980—managed to exceed 3 percent of the vote.

Against this background, it is hard to deny that the presidential candidacy of Ross Perot was one of the more extraordinary events in recent American politics. One may not like Perot or his approach to the issues or the way he has behaved since the election, but the fact of his success in 1992 seems difficult to avoid. In the end, the Texas billionaire received 18.9 percent of the votes cast on 3 November. This makes him, in popular vote terms, the most successful third-party candidate in the last eighty years and the third most successful in all of American history (the first and second most successful both being former presidents).

As we write this chapter, it is difficult to say what the future holds for Perot and his followers. Like other recent independent presidential campaigns, the "Perot phenomenon" depends on the decisions and actions of its leader; and if the past is any indication at all, predicting what Ross Perot will do next is not the sort of thing on which one would want to stake a lot of money (or one's academic reputation).

Regardless of Perot's own behavior, however, it seems likely that as the 1996 presidential election gets under way, one major topic of speculation will be the prospects of third-party and independent candidates.[3] Hence, in a book concerned primarily with the presidential nomination processes of the Democratic and Republican parties, it is a good idea to devote at least one chapter to an examination of what third parties do before the fall campaign. How do they spend their time and money when the Democrats and Republicans are engaging in primaries and caucuses, selecting delegates, and holding their national conventions?

Our discussion starts with a basic fact of American election law: While the Democratic and Republican presidential candidates are guaranteed a spot on the general election ballot in all fifty states, third-party and independent candidates generally are not. Hence, the first obstacle confronting third-party challengers—and the place where third-party candidates usually begin their preelection planning—is coming to grips with the imposing array of rules and procedures enacted by state governments to regulate ballot access. The next three sections of this chapter present an analysis of how these ballot-access laws work, their constitutional status, and the kind of effort that must be mounted by any candidate who hopes to get on the ballot in all fifty states. Next, we look at the decisions that come before the ballot petitions are circulated: how do third parties select their candidates? We conclude with an examination of the role of third parties in the American political system and their likely future prospects.

A Primer on Ballot Access

Any American who shows up at a polling place on election day and wishes to cast a vote for president must do so on a ballot printed by the government. This has not always been the case. For the first hundred years or so after the adoption of the U.S. Constitution, government merely provided a ballot box;[4] the actual ballots, the pieces of paper on which the voters indicated their preferences, were printed and distributed by political parties. In that highly partisan, patronage-rich era, workers for each local party handed out their own preprinted "tickets," containing the names of all party candidates running in that particular election. Prospective voters, it was hoped, would simply bring the party ticket with them into the precinct place and then deposit it, unaltered, in the ballot box. To encourage party loyalty further, parties often made their tickets a distinctive color or shape so that poll watchers could monitor who was voting for which party.

In the late 1800s, this system came under widespread attack on the grounds that it facilitated fraud and corruption. The result, between 1888 and 1910, was the universal adoption by state governments of the so-called Australian ballot. Under this system, each state now prepared an official ballot, listing all the offices at stake and the candidates running for them, which each voter then marked, in secret, at the polling place.[5]

Once state governments were in the business of printing official ballots, they were unavoidably faced with answering an important and difficult question: which candidates should get listed on the ballot? It should be clear, to begin with, that states must do *something* to limit ballot access. Every election cycle, as many as 150 individuals file forms with the Federal Election Commission announcing their intention to run for president.[6] If every such person could get his or her name printed on the ballot merely by requesting it, American election machinery would soon become impossibly complicated, expensive, and confusing to the voters. Almost no one, then, contests the point that state governments have some reasonable interest in restricting the ballot to "serious" candidates, who are capable of demonstrating some minimal level of popular support.

This argument alone probably justifies the kinds of rules and regulations that might restrict the ballot to 5 or 10 candidates, rather than 30 or 150. But many states have gone further and claimed that they have an interest in limiting the ballot to an even smaller number of candidates. One line of argument, for example, asserts that states "may validly promote a two-party system in order to encourage compromise and political stability." If three or more parties were on the ballot, another argument goes, "it is possible that no party would obtain 50 percent of the vote, and the runner-up might have been preferred to the plurality winner by a majority of [the] voters." Ballot-access restrictions have also been defended on the grounds that they inhibit "splintered parties and unrestrained factionalism" and discourage "independent candidates prompted by short-range political goals, pique, or personal quarrel."[7]

Merits and morality aside, access to the general election ballot has also been restricted simply because it is in the self-interest of the Democrats and Republicans and because the state legislatures that write such laws are populated overwhelmingly by members of these two parties. Though any particular third-party or independent candidacy might work to the short-term advantage of one major party or the other, over the long term the Democrats and Republicans have apparently seen more advantage in a system of oligopoly than in a regime of unrestrained competition.

Whatever the exact mixture of motivations, the incontestable fact is that all fifty states, plus the District of Columbia, have established their own highly detailed set of laws and regulations that determine how candidates can get their names printed on the general election ballot. In the next few pages, we attempt to present a broad overview of state ballot-access laws and the obstacles they present to third-party and independent candidates. It soon becomes clear, however, that one of the overriding themes of our account is that state election laws are remarkably diverse and highly resistant to any easy or concise generalizations. And this, in turn, reflects a fundamental feature of the American system of presidential elections: while the presidency is unquestionably an office of national power and provenance, the U.S. Constitution nevertheless vests substantial authority over its election process in *state* governments.

In general, the states have provided at least two, and sometimes three, avenues of access to their general election ballots. At the top of the pecking order, some parties get their candidates placed on the ballot *automatically, by achieving some minimum level of success in past elections.* The way this is generally done is as follows: Buried somewhere in hundreds of pages of dense prose, state election laws usually have a section that establishes a set of criteria that an electoral organization must achieve in order to qualify for what the laws generally describe as "major-party status." Appendix A shows several examples of the criteria that states currently employ for this purpose. In New Hampshire, for example, a group attains major-party status by having its gubernatorial candidate win at least 3 percent of the statewide vote in the last election. In Kentucky, major parties must receive 20 percent of the vote in the most recent presidential election. In Illinois, the test is whether the party's strongest candidate in the last election polled at least 5 percent of the total state vote.

Having established such criteria, states then make the reasonable assumption that any party that has attracted that much support in the recent past has thereby demonstrated that it is a serious and significant electoral competitor. Hence, in all fifty states, candidates who are nominated by major parties—for president and for almost every other office—are automatically placed on the general election ballot. In return for this privilege, it is only fair to add, major parties are generally required to submit to a detailed, frequently onerous regimen of other state laws that regulate their internal organization and procedures. Electoral organizations that are not major parties, for example, are generally allowed to nominate their candidates in any way they see fit. But the major parties are usually required to nominate their candidates via primary elections, in which they have traditionally had little or no say about who is allowed to participate.[8]

A close reading of appendix A indicates that the criteria for major-party status are usually defined in generic terms: that is, the laws set forth a set of performance measures that almost any party could theoretically achieve,[9] and do not specifically mention Republicans or Democrats by name. Nevertheless, as one can easily verify by comparing the standards in appendix A with any good compilation of recent election statistics, major-party status is generally defined so that both Democrats and Republicans will meet the qualification in all but the most exceptional circumstances. Perhaps an occasional Democratic or Republican nominee may fall short of receiving 20 percent of the vote, but it is difficult to envision a situation in which such a candidate could fail to win 3 or 5 percent of the votes cast. As a result, the Democratic and Republican parties rarely have to worry about ballot access for their presidential tickets. The most they are generally required to do is to choose a slate of presidential electors (this is usually done by the state committee or a state convention) and then send a letter of notification to state election officials.

Independent and third-party candidates do not fare quite so well. Depending on the quality of their organizations and candidates and on the particular criteria set forth in state law, a number of third parties do manage to cross the threshold into major-party status. As of late 1994, for example, the Libertarian Party had automatically qualified for the 1996 ballot in twenty-two states.[10] In general, however, third-party and independent presidential candidates do *not* receive automatic access to the ballot in most states.

For political organizations that are unable to qualify as major parties, many, though not all, states have created a second route of access to the ballot designed specifically for minor parties. In general, such provisions attempt to provide a way in which organized *parties,* as distinct from independent and unaffiliated contenders, can get their candidates listed on the general election ballot even though their past performance falls short of the standard for major parties. In many cases, the requirements for achieving "minor-party status" are no different from those faced by independent candidates, except that they allow the minor party to submit one set of petitions for its entire slate of candidates, rather than a separate set for each individual aspirant. But as indicated in appendix B, a few states do make a greater attempt to accommodate smaller parties.

In Maryland, New Mexico, and a number of other states, the petition requirements for minor parties are set substantially lower than those for independents. In Maryland, a third *party* will need only 10,000 signatures to gain access to the general election ballot in 1996; independents will need about 70,000 signatures. In Maryland and New Mexico essentially any organization that wants to call itself a party is allowed to do so. In 1992, for example, Ross Perot chose to get on the Maryland ballot as an independent, which required his supporters to collect about 63,000 signatures. But state law indicates (and state election officials confirm) that if Perot's Maryland organization had merely been willing to label itself as a party, it would have taken 53,000 fewer signatures to get the Texan's name on the ballot.

The election laws in Vermont and Delaware illustrate another common approach to the minor-party-access question, in which such parties can get on the general election ballot by demonstrating some minimum level of statewide organization. In Vermont, the threshold is having town committees organized in at least ten towns in the state. Arkansas and Mississippi are especially friendly to minor parties. In both states, current law allows essentially any organization that calls itself a party and registers with the secretary of state to have its presidential candidate listed on the general election ballot. In Connecticut, any organization whose candidate for any office receives at least 1 percent of the total vote becomes a party *for the purposes of that office* and is automatically placed on the ballot the next time that office comes before the voters. (Among other things, this means that in 1996, whichever presidential candidate is nominated by the Connecticut chapter of "Americans for Perot" is already guaranteed a spot on that state's general election ballot. The privilege would not extend to any other candidate nominated by this group.)

Candidates who fall short of both major- and minor-party standards—or who do not enjoy the option of minor-party-access provisions—have one final way of getting listed on the general election ballot: by petition. Unlike the arcane provisions that establish major- and minor-party status, the rudiments of the petition process are probably familiar to most politically attentive Americans. The supporters of an independent or third-party candidate must put together a document, usually on a form provided by state government, that lists the candidate, the office he or she is running for, and a number of other pertinent facts; supporters then must persuade a few hundred or several thousand registered voters in the state to sign the petition. Each state specifies in its election laws the number of signatures a candidate must collect in order to get on the ballot for any given office. (Often, the number is set as a percentage of the total number of registered voters or of the total votes cast in the last election.) And if the candidate does acquire the requisite number of valid signatures, his or her name gets added to the official ballot.

The three most successful independent presidential candidates of the last half century—Wallace, Anderson, and Perot—all managed to get on the ballot in all fifty states; in each case, they did so almost entirely through petitions. To say the least, however, it is not a simple undertaking. To begin with, there is the sheer number of signatures involved. Table 9.2 shows the number of valid petition signatures that each state requires before it will list a presidential candidate on its general election ballot. Again, one notices the enormous variation in state ballot-access laws. Any independent presidential aspirant who seeks to run in 1996 will need 200 signatures to get on the ballot in Washington State, 1,000 in Rhode Island, 5,000 in Ohio, 25,000 in Illinois, about 50,000 in North Carolina, and almost 150,000 in California. Though a few states may change their laws between now and the election year, currently a fifty-state ballot-access drive requires a candidate to collect slightly more than 700,000 petition signatures. The only consolation in these figures is that, over the past twenty-five years, ballot-access laws have actually become significantly *less* restrictive. As the second column in table 9.2 (p. 280) indicates, as of 1967, an independent candidate for the presidency needed to collect about 1.25 million signatures to get on the ballot in all fifty states.[11]

TABLE 9.2
SIGNATURE REQUIREMENTS FOR PRESIDENTIAL CANDIDATES
SEEKING TO GET ON STATE GENERAL ELECTION
BALLOTS BY PETITION

	Number required as of 1994	Number required in 1967
Alabama	5,000	300
Alaska	2,585	1,000
Arizona	7,813	3,783
Arkansas	0[a]	84,607
California	147,238	330,293[h]
Colorado	5,000	300
Connecticut	7,500	6,093
Delaware	3,600[b]	—[i]
District of Columbia	3,600[c]	10,097
Florida	65,596	7,500
Georgia	30,035	98,022
Hawaii	3,829	—[j]
Idaho	4,821	2,000[k]
Illinois	25,000	25,000
Indiana	29,858	8,320
Iowa	1,500	1,500[l]
Kansas	5,000	2,500[m]
Kentucky	5,000	1,000
Louisiana	5,000[d]	1,000
Maine	4,000	3,238
Maryland	10,000	5,000
Massachusetts	10,000	61,233
Michigan	30,891	13,371
Minnesota	2,000	2,000
Mississippi	0[e]	0[n]
Missouri	10,000	17,896
Montana	9,473	0[o]
Nebraska	2,500	—[p]
Nevada	3,761	6,393
New Hampshire	3,000	1,000
New Jersey	800	800
New Mexico	2,338	100
New York	15,000	12,000
North Carolina	51,904	10,000
North Dakota	4,000	15,000
Ohio	5,000	433,100
Oklahoma	41,711	5,000
Oregon	14,626	23,589
Pennsylvania	30,000[f]	10,522
Rhode Island	1,000	500

South Carolina	10,000	10,000
South Dakota	3,117	4,564
Tennessee	275	25
Texas	61,540	14,258
Utah	300	500
Vermont	1,000	1,362
Virginia	16,000[g]	1,000
Washington	200	100
West Virginia	6,837	7,920
Wisconsin	2,000	3,000
Wyoming	8,000	5,971
Total	719,248	1,252,257

SOURCE: 1967 figures are based on a synopsis of state ballot laws provided in *Congressional Quarterly Weekly Report*, 13 October 1967, 2068–73. 1994 figures are based on an analysis of current state election laws, supplemented by interviews with state election officials and a table printed in *Ballot Access News*, 15 November 1994.

NOTE: In general, the figure listed is the number of signatures that must be submitted by an independent presidential candidate. We have substituted the number required for a third-party candidate where (1) that number is lower than the number required for independents; and (2) essentially any group that wants to qualify as a party is allowed to do so.

a. State law allows any political group to nominate candidates for president, vice-president, and presidential elector by holding a convention, as long as a copy of the minutes and list of officers are filed with the secretary of state.

b. Estimate. The exact number is 1% of the total number of registered voters in the state as of 31 December 1995.

c. Estimate. The exact number is 1% of the total number of registered voters in the district as of 1 July 1996.

d. Independent candidates can also get on the Louisiana ballot by paying a qualifying fee of $500.

e. Mississippi law allows any organization registered as a party with the secretary of state to nominate candidates for the general election ballot.

f. Estimate. The exact number is 2% of the largest number of votes received by any candidate in the November 1995 judicial elections.

g. Estimate. The exact number is 0.5% of the number of voters registered in the state as of 1 January 1996.

h. A new party could also gain access to the California ballot by getting 66,059 voters to register under the party's name.

i. State law made no provision for petition candidates. A minor party could nominate candidates for the general election ballot if it represented at least 50 citizens in each of 19 state senatorial districts.

j. State law made no provision for petition candidates. New and minor parties were required only to show the existence of a general organization throughout the state.

k. State law also allowed new parties to nominate candidates at a convention attended by at least 200 delegates.

l. State law also allowed minor parties to nominate candidates at a convention attended by at least 50 voters.

m. State law also allowed minor-party slates to be nominated, via convention, by any political party having a national or statewide organization.

n. State law allowed any new or minor political party to nominate candidates for the general election ballot if it had previously filed a list of officers with the secretary of state.

o. Any new or minor political party could nominate a slate of presidential elector candidates for the general election ballot by convention.

p. State law made no provision for petition candidates. New and minor parties could nominate candidates at a convention attended by at least 750 voters.

In case gathering that many signatures does not seem daunting enough, most states impose a number of other procedural burdens and requirements. (We list a sampling of them in table 9.3.) In the first place, there are *filing fees*—small in most states, but cumulatively quite significant for a class of candidates whose campaigns are, in most cases, already underfunded.[12] Next, there are *filing deadlines*. As a matter of administrative necessity, state election officials have to set some sort of final date beyond which they will not accept any more petition candidates. As the entries in table 9.3 indicate, however, either state election boards operate with widely varying levels of efficiency or some states impose early deadlines as a further way of discouraging independent challengers. In 1992 one state set its filing deadline in May, three in June, ten in July, twenty-four in August, and thirteen in September.[13]

Many states also provide remarkably detailed regulations governing the collection and verification of petition signatures. Some read as if they were taken from an old Johnny Carson monologue:

- In North Carolina and Ohio, any one page of the nominating petition may contain signatures from only one county.
- In New Hampshire, Kentucky, and Washington, no voter may sign a petition for more than one candidate for the same office.
- In Kentucky, each voter signing a petition must also list his or her birth date or social security number.
- Of the 3,000 petition signatures needed in New Hampshire, 1,500 must come from each of the state's congressional districts.
- In Washington, petition signatures may be collected only at properly called conventions attended by at least 25 registered voters.
- In Nebraska and Texas, petitions may be signed only by people who did *not* vote in one of the major-party presidential primaries.

Finally, once the signatures are collected and submitted to the proper authorities in each state, third-party and independent candidates must also be prepared to fend off legal challenges (often brought by the Democrats or Republicans) either to the petition itself or to other alleged deficiencies in the qualifying procedure. According to one estimate, independent candidates generally need to collect about 30 percent more signatures than the number specified in state law, to make allowance for all the signatures that are likely to be declared invalid.[14] Many recent independent candidates—most prominently Wallace and Anderson—also needed to file their own lawsuits, to overturn state laws that seemed unduly restrictive.

And yet, almost every four years, some third-party or independent presidential candidate *does* manage to surmount all these obstacles and qualify for the ballot in all or most of the states. As table 9.4 (p. 296) indicates, it is

TABLE 9.3
OTHER PROCEDURAL REQUIREMENTS FOR PETITION
CANDIDATES: A SAMPLING OF STATE LAWS

State	Filing fee	Filing deadline in 1996[a]	Other conditions
Connecticut	None	7 August	1. No page of the petition may contain signatures from more than one town. 2. No voter may sign a petition for more than one candidate for the same office.
Illinois	None	6 August	1. Petitions must be of uniform size. 2. Petitions may be circulated only during the 90 days before the filing deadline.
Kentucky	None	29 August	1. All signers must include their birth date or social security number. 2. No voter may sign a petition for more than one candidate for the same office.
Nebraska	None	27 August	1. Petitions may not be circulated until after the primary. 2. No one may sign a petition who voted in a party primary in the same year.
New Hampshire	$250	7 August	1. 3,000 signatures must include 1,500 from each congressional district. 2. No voter may sign a petition for more than one candidate for the same office.
North Carolina	5 cents per signature	14 June	1. No page of the petition may contain signatures from more than one county.
Ohio	$100	20 August	1. No page of the petition may contain signatures from more than one county. 2. Petitions must be signed in ink or indelible pencil.
Texas	None	13 May	1. No one may sign a petition who voted in a presidential primary in the same year.

Continued . . .

TABLE 9.3 — CONTINUED

State	Filing fee	Filing deadline in 1996[a]	Other conditions
			2. No one may sign a petition before the date of the presidential primary.
			3. All signatures must include the signer's voter registration number.
Virginia	None	23 August	1. Petition must include at least 200 signatures from each congressional district.
			2. Each signature must be witnessed by a qualified voter from the same congressional district.
Washington	None	13 July	1. All signatures must be gathered at properly called conventions attended by at least 25 people.
			2. No voter may sign a petition for more than one candidate for the same office.

SOURCE: Compiled from state election statutes.
a. In some states, petitions must first be verified by town or county voter registration boards, then submitted to the state board of elections. The date listed here is the earliest deadline for submitting petitions to any government agency.

not just the Andersons and Perots who have accomplished this feat. Universal ballot access was also achieved by the Libertarian Party presidential ticket in both 1980 and 1992 and the New Alliance Party in 1988. Over the last five election cycles, nine other candidates have qualified for at least half of the state ballots.

The results in table 9.4 also reinforce the point made earlier that as complicated and treacherous as the current ballot-access regime may be, the *trend* is clearly in the direction of easier access. The 1968 election, in particular, emerges as a critical watershed. (As we see in the next section, 1968 was also the year in which the U.S. Supreme Court first ruled that excessively restrictive ballot-access laws were unconstitutional.) In the four elections prior to 1968, not one third-party or independent candidate managed to qualify for even thirty state ballots. In the six elections since that time, twelve different candidates have achieved ballot access in at least thirty states.

The Constitutional Status of State
Ballot-Access Laws

As the preceding discussion indicates, the obstacles confronting third-party and independent candidates fall into two distinct categories. On the one hand, a number of states—California, Florida, North Carolina, and Texas especially stand out—clearly have enacted laws that seem designed, intentionally or not, to make life difficult for any presidential candidate who is neither a Democrat nor a Republican. But the greater "culprit," one might argue, is the American system of federalism. As onerous and discouraging as the laws may be in any one state, the most daunting reality facing the independent contender is the necessity of coming to terms with fifty-one separate sets of regulations, requirements, and deadlines, where a tactic or procedure that works very well in one state may be ineffective or illegal in another. At a minimum, the enormous diversity in state election laws means that an ambitious third-party candidate requires not only money and manpower but a hefty supply of legal talent.

And this, in turn, raises a number of significant questions. How is it that state governments have come to play such an important role in regulating the procedures used to select America's only nationally elected official? Is there no way for Congress or the federal courts to restrain the worst excesses of state ballot-access laws, or at least to bring some measure of uniformity to the ballot qualification process?

Our answer to these questions begins, naturally enough, with the U.S. Constitution. That celebrated document, as is well known, took on its final form as a compromise between advocates of a strong national government and defenders of state power and prerogatives. And like many other American institutions, the presidential election system bears the clear imprint of that process. Though the presidency was the single most visible and powerful position in the new regime, the national government actually was given little role in supervising or regulating its election procedures. Article 2, section 1 of the Constitution provides for selection of the president through the mechanism of the Electoral College, but then specifically allows *state* governments to appoint these electors "in such Manner as the Legislature thereof may direct." The only role reserved for Congress in the original Constitution was the power to "determine the Time of chusing the Electors, and the Day on which they shall give their Votes."

Subsequent amendments have further limited state control over presidential elections in two major ways. First, a series of amendments have required states to extend the right to vote to blacks, women, and eighteen-year-olds and to eliminate the poll tax in federal elections.[15] Each of these has had important effects on American presidential elections in general, but none is implicated in the ballot-access issue.

TABLE 9.4
BALLOT-ACCESS RESULTS FOR MAJOR
THIRD-PARTY AND INDEPENDENT PRESIDENTIAL
CANDIDATES SINCE 1932

Year	Candidate	Party	Number of state ballots on which the candidate's name appeared[a]
1932	Thomas	Socialist	45
	Foster	Communist	39
1936	Thomas	Socialist	36
	Lemke	Union	35
	Browder	Communist	32
	Colvin	Prohibition	25
1940	Thomas	Socialist	30
	Babson	Prohibition	29
1944	Thomas	Socialist	28
	Watson	Prohibition	27
1948	Wallace	Progressive	45
	Thomas	Socialist	34
	Thurmond	States' Rights	16
1952	Hallinan	Progressive	28
	Hass	Socialist Labor	22
1956	Andrews	States' Rights	16
	Hass	Socialist Labor	15
1960	Hass	Socialist Labor	15
	Dobbs	Socialist Workers	12

Second, and of considerably more importance, the Fourteenth Amendment mandates that no state shall "deprive any person of life, liberty, or property, without due process of law; nor deny to any person within its jurisdiction the equal protection of the laws." While there has long been substantial disagreement as to what these clauses are or were supposed to mean, since the early 1900s the Supreme Court has repeatedly used the amendment's due process clause to require that state laws abide by the protections guaranteed in the Bill of Rights (which were originally applied only to the national government); and has invoked the equal protection clause to proscribe unreasonable discrimination generally. Thus, according to some interpretations, the First Amendment, as now incorporated against the states, can be read to secure the right to meaningful political association, possibly including protections for the right to vote; and the prohibition against unreasonable discrimination can be applied to candidates, voters, and political parties. On this foundation has gradually emerged a substantial body of constitutional law concerning ballot-access restrictions.

TABLE 9.4 — CONTINUED

Year	Candidate	Party	Number of state ballots on which the candidate's name appeared[a]
1964	Hass	Socialist Labor	16
	Dobbs	Socialist Workers	11
1968	Wallace	American Independent	50
	Halstead	Socialist Workers	19
1972	Schmitz	American	32
	Jenness/Reed[b]	Socialist Workers	23
1976	MacBride	Libertarian	32
	McCarthy	Independent	29
	Camejo	Socialist Workers	28
1980	Anderson	Independent	51
	Clark	Libertarian	51
	Commoner	Citizens	30
1984	Bergland	Libertarian	39
	Serrette	New Alliance	33
1988	Fulani	New Alliance	51
	Paul	Libertarian	46
1992	Perot	Independent	51
	Marrou	Libertarian	51
	Fulani	New Alliance	40
	Hagelin	Natural Law	29

SOURCE: Based on state election results reported in Alice V. McGillivray and Richard M. Scammon, *America at the Polls*, vols. 1 and 2 (Washington, D.C.: CQ Press, 1994). Especially in the elections of 1932–68, it is not clear how rigorous these volumes are in distinguishing between states where a candidate's name was listed on the ballot and states where the candidate received write-in votes. Some of the early figures in this table may, accordingly, be off by one or two states.

NOTE: Table includes the two independent or third-party candidates who qualified for the greatest number of ballots in each year and any other candidates who were on the ballot in at least half the states.

a. Includes Alaska and Hawaii after 1960 and the District of Columbia after 1964.

b. The official Socialist Workers nominee for president in 1972 was Linda Jenness, who was only 31 years old at the time, four years below the minimum age requirement specified in the U.S. Constitution. Election laws in a number of states do not allow a candidate's name to be listed on the ballot if that person is not legally eligible to serve in the office. Hence, in three states, the Socialist Workers candidate was Evelyn Reed.

The seminal ballot-access case is the Supreme Court's 1968 decision in *Williams v. Rhodes,* rendered in the heat of that year's presidential election campaign.[16] As of 1968, the Ohio ballot-access statute required new parties to obtain petitions signed by qualified voters totaling 15 percent of the number of ballots cast in the preceding gubernatorial election—about 433,000 signatures in 1968. Existing parties, on the other hand, were allowed automatic ballot position, provided their candidates had obtained 10 percent of the votes in the previous gubernatorial election. The Ohio American Independent Party, which had been formed under the aegis of presidential candidate George Wallace in January 1968, eventually obtained the requisite number of signatures; but under Ohio law, it was required to file them by 7 February 1968. The American Independent Party sued, claiming that the signature requirement, combined with the early-filing deadline and other statutorily imposed burdens, denied the party and Ohio voters the equal protection of the laws.

The Supreme Court sided with the American Independent Party.[17] The Court began by rejecting Ohio's claim that Article 2, section 1 of the U.S. Constitution gave it absolute authority to regulate the manner of choosing presidential electors. That provision, the Court insisted, did not give states the "power to impose burdens on the right to vote, where such burdens are expressly prohibited in other Constitutional provisions."[18] The Court then found that the challenged Ohio regime burdened two different constitutionally protected rights: the right of individuals to associate for the advancement of their political beliefs; and the right of qualified voters to cast their votes effectively regardless of political persuasion.

In analyzing the Ohio ballot restrictions, the Court applied what is known in equal protection clause jurisprudence as "strict scrutiny" review, the most stringent and plaintiff-friendly standard available in such cases. Under strict scrutiny, a challenged law or regulation will survive only if the government can establish that the restriction serves a "compelling state interest" and is narrowly tailored to achieve that purpose. And in this instance, the Court found that Ohio had proffered no such compelling interest. Ohio's claim that its regime protected the two-party system was met with the response that in fact it protected two particular parties at the expense of all others. The Court also rejected Ohio's assertion that the law could be justified by an interest in having the winner chosen by majority preference, and that relaxed ballot-access provisions would lead to numerous candidates and voter confusion. Concluding, the Court held that "taken as a whole," the Ohio regime imposed burdens on voting and associational rights sufficiently onerous to constitute invidious discrimination violative of the Fourteenth Amendment's equal protection clause.

Williams v. *Rhodes* stands for a number of still-viable principles of constitutional litigation: that ballot-access laws implicate and must not overburden fundamental voting and First Amendment associational rights, that these rights can sometimes be analyzed under the equal protection clause, and that a state's ballot-restricting laws may be challenged either in isolation or taken as part of a larger whole.

But *Williams* v. *Rhodes* has not survived in toto. In particular, the hard-to-satisfy "compelling state interest" test it imposed on the states to justify their ballot-access restrictions has not stood the test of time. As one commentator has rightly noted, subsequent Supreme Court treatment of ballot-access issues is a history of "retreat from the broad implications of *Williams*."[19] There have been sound constitutional reasons for this retrenchment. The compelling state interest requirement is strongly at odds with Article 2, section 1's explicit grant of power to state legislatures on the question of choosing presidential electors. The *Williams* Court plainly had difficulty specifying the precise nature and contours of the rights trammeled by Ohio's highly restrictive scheme. And the "compelling state interest" test is almost certainly too stringent, precisely because regulation of the ballot always involves not only some legitimate state interest but also state protection of the very same rights claimed by the challenging parties, namely, the right to associate and vote meaningfully for political candidates.

The next landmark Supreme Court ballot-access case was its 1983 decision in *Anderson v. Celebrezze,* another Ohio case growing out of another independent presidential candidacy.[20] The Ohio ballot-access regime in place for the 1980 presidential elections imposed filing-deadline restrictions requiring independent candidates to present petitions containing sufficient numbers of signatures to the secretary of state by 20 March 1980. John Anderson, having failed in his bid to obtain the Republican nomination, did not announce his independent candidacy until late April 1980, and his supporters tendered his nominating petition on 16 May. The secretary of state refused to accept the petition, stating that it was untimely. Anderson and three supporters brought suit alleging violations of the First Amendment, dilution of the value of votes in other states, and equal protection violations for failure to require comparable action by nominees of the major political parties.

The Court began by noting that the rights of candidates and the rights of voters cannot be neatly separated: laws affecting one will necessarily affect the other. Voting and associational rights are fundamental. Still, the Court acknowledged, state regulation is a practical necessity if elections are to be fair and orderly; a state's regulatory interests will justify reasonable, nondiscriminatory restrictions on ballot access. Because ballot-access laws implicate important interests on both sides, judicial assessment of such legislation calls for a three-pronged analysis. First, a court must consider the character and magnitude of injury to protected constitutional rights. Second, the court must identify and evaluate the state's interests asserted to justify the statutory burden imposed on protected rights. Finally, the court must weigh these competing interests to determine whether the challenged provisions survive constitutional challenge.[21]

Having set out the test, the Court then applied it to the question of the early filing deadline. Such a date, in the Court's view, deprives independent candidates of the flexibility enjoyed by the major parties, which are able to select nominees and adopt platforms at a later time, thereby enabling them to take greater advantage of changes in the public mood and political events.

In addition, those disaffected with the major parties' candidates and/or handling of the issues are denied the opportunity to react meaningfully. These factors reduce diversity and depress competition in the marketplace of ideas. Furthermore, the effects of one state's early-filing deadline extend beyond that state. Failure to obtain ballot access in Ohio deprives the candidate of access to a large bloc of electoral votes and reduces the pool from which voters and electors in other states may put together a majority coalition, thus placing "a significant state imposed restriction on a nationwide electoral process."

According to the Court, the asserted state interests underlying the restrictions—voter education, equal treatment,[22] political stability—did not outweigh these harms. Indeed, as Justice Stevens's opinion for a five-justice majority noted, an early filing deadline does not obviously serve the interests of the two-party system itself. The genius of the two-party system consists in large measure in its capacity to bring together and impose compromise on dissident and outlying party members and movements. Early filing deadlines diminish these prospects by forcing dissidents to exit the party before the need for compromise has become acute in the later stages of the presidential campaign.

Like *Williams* v. *Rhodes,* then, *Anderson* threw out what the Court saw as overly restrictive ballot-access provisions. But the decision bespeaks a quite different notion of how such restrictions are to be analyzed; and it sent quite different signals to states and would-be independents and third parties about the prospects for such suits in the future. The Court abandoned the stringent, equal protection analysis of *Williams,* which was more difficult for the states to satisfy, in favor of a due-process-style balancing test.[23] As significantly, the decision included a vigorous four-justice dissent, a dissent relying heavily on Article 2's broad delegation of elector-selecting power to the states.

The Supreme Court's most recent ballot-related decision was its 1992 decision in *Burdick* v. *Takushi.*[24] Although directed neither to the presidential nomination process nor to the precise issue of minor-party ballot access, the decision provides the most recent clues to the Court's direction and mode of analysis on the question of ballot access. At stake in *Burdick* was the constitutionality of a provision in Hawaii's state election law that, as interpreted by that state's supreme court, imposed a blanket prohibition on write-in voting.

Justice White's opinion for a six-justice majority began by rejecting Burdick's claim that strict scrutiny ought to be applied to *any* law burdening the right to vote.[25] The Court reaffirmed that challenges to state provisions burdening the right to vote would be assessed under the "more flexible" due-process-style balancing test developed in *Anderson.* It then noted that Hawaii provides three alternative paths for obtaining access to the ballot and concluded that in light of the general ease of access to the Hawaii ballot, any burden on the right to vote resulting from the ban on write-in voting was a very limited one. The Court then identified Hawaii's asserted interests in maintaining the ban: an avoidance of factionalism, averting sore-loser candidacies, and prevention of party raiding through organized switching of blocs of voters from one party to another so as to manipulate the outcome. Balancing the minimal burden on the right to vote against the state's legitimate interests, the Court held that the write-in voting ban, "considered as part of an electoral scheme that provides constitutionally sufficient ballot access, does not impose an unconstitutional burden upon the First and Fourteenth Amendment rights of the state's voters."[26]

What can be said overall, then, about the current constitutional status and likely future of state ballot-access laws? Four general points seem to us worth emphasizing. First, the Supreme Court has firmly established the principle that ballot-access laws do implicate fundamental constitutional rights and hence must conform to the demands of the First and Fourteenth amendments. Second, while the Court's willingness to invoke that principle has undoubtedly fallen short of what many third-party supporters might have wished, the Court has upheld the plaintiffs in a significant number of such cases.[27] In so doing, it has almost certainly played a major role in the trend documented earlier toward easier access for third-party and independent presidential contenders.

Third, the Court has plainly had trouble spelling out working principles for determining whether a particular ballot-access practice or regime is excessively restrictive. As the Court itself noted in *Storer* v. *Brown*, a case decided about halfway between *Williams* and *Anderson*:

> ... the rule fashioned by the Court to pass on constitutional challenges to specific provisions of election laws provides no litmus-paper test for separating those restrictions that are valid from those that are invidious under the Equal Protection Clause. The rule is not self-executing and is no substitute for the hard judgments that must be made. Decision in this context, as in others, is very much a matter of degree. . . .[28]

Indeed, the jurisprudential difficulty of formulating a consistent constitutional theory of ballot access is enormous. Such a theory would need to take account of a host of complications: that the rights of voters and candidates (and perhaps parties) are all involved; that the rights of voters are themselves bivalent, sometimes pointing to looser restrictions, other times to tighter ones; that the constitutional contours of the right to vote are not easily limned. Above all, there is the problem of integrating a coherent ballot-access jurisprudence into the already elaborate (and not always internally consistent) bodies of law surrounding the First and Fourteenth amendments.

Finally, the *Burdick* case, in particular, provides a fair guide as to what independent and third-party candidates may expect when seeking relief from the courts in the future. Such candidates must expect a reviewing court to apply a due-process-style balancing test, with considerable deference given to the state's asserted interests. Even with recent changes in the Court's personnel, would-be candidates should expect neither a return to the test outlined in *Williams* v. *Rhodes,* which was substantially more friendly to independents and minor parties, nor much else in the way of lesser changes. Given the obstacles just described, no constitutional decision of landmark significance, on the order of *Williams,* is remotely in sight. Except in demonstrably egregious cases, states will likely continue to enjoy substantial freedom in restricting access to their general election ballots.

Ballot Access and the Voting Decision

Given how difficult it is to get on the ballot in many states, a skeptic might reasonably ask if, in the end, the prize is really worth the effort. Third-party and independent candidates are almost always faced with a severe shortage of money and volunteers. Might it make more sense to wage a write-in campaign and reserve those scarce resources for other activities, such as communicating with the voters?

The answer is that getting on the ballot is worth the effort, in at least two distinct ways. To begin with, getting on state ballots has a number of important psychological benefits. One of the most severe obstacles in the path of third-party and independent candidates, no matter what office they aspire to, is the simple fact that most voters, political activists, and reporters do not take them very seriously. The "real election," in most people's minds, is between the Democrat and the Republican; other candidates are usually regarded as hopeless long-shots, if not as extremists, frivolous, or simply bizarre.

This problem is, to some degree, probably inescapable for third-party and independent candidates, which, of course, goes a long way toward explaining why such candidates win so few elections in the United States. But there are a few things that candidates can do to lessen this perception somewhat, and one of the most important, at the presidential level, is to try to get on as many state ballots as possible. Our review of national media coverage of third-party presidential efforts over the past twenty years suggests that reporters and editors often evaluate how "serious" a particular candidate is by noting on how many state ballots his or her name will appear. Whenever such candidates do get covered, this piece of information is almost always mentioned.[29] A candidate who qualifies for the ballot in thirty states is, accordingly, seen as more noteworthy and "respectable" than one who gets on the ballot in only five.

It is no accident, then, that when Ross Perot first indicated his willingness to run for president, he hinged his entry into the race on the condition that his supporters first get him qualified on the ballot in all fifty states. Indeed, Perot's comments on that occasion indicate not only that he understood how the press would use the ballot-access figures as a way of evaluating his candidacy; he himself intended to use the ballot qualification process as a way of seeing if his supporters were serious.[30] In a similar way, George Wallace's ability to get on the ballot in California for the 1968 election—which required persuading at least 66,000 voters to register as members of his new party—"started making believers of a number of people who earlier had shrugged Wallace off."[31]

But the benefits of getting on the ballot are not only psychological. Being on the ballot also pays off in the harder currency of votes. For candidates such as Wallace, Anderson, and Perot, who ultimately made it onto the ballot in all fifty states, it is impossible to offer anything more than speculation as to how their chances might have been hurt by not appearing on various state ballots. To see what difference ballot access really makes, we need to find candidates who were on the ballot in about half the states and not listed in the other half. Fortunately, two recent candidates in table 9.1 met this criterion. In 1972, John Schmitz, then a Republican representative from California, was the presidential candidate of the American Party, in which capacity his name appeared on thirty-two state ballots but was left off in eighteen other states and the District of Columbia. In 1976, former Democratic senator Eugene McCarthy, running as an independent candidate, made it on the ballot in twenty-nine states, while missing twenty-one states and the District. And as the figures in table 9.5 indicate, if the odds are already stacked strongly against third-party and independent candidates, they become even more hopeless when such candidates must depend on write-in votes.

In 1976, for example, McCarthy received an average vote of 1.45 percent in states where he was listed on the ballot, as compared to a 0.13 percent average in states where he was not listed. Put another way, McCarthy's average vote increased by a factor of eleven as a result of getting on a state ballot. For John Schmitz, the disproportion was even greater. Schmitz had an average vote of 2.71 percent when he was on the ballot, a mere 0.07 percent when he was not.

Indeed, though it seems not to be generally known, many states are reluctant to count write-in votes. Partly because of the inconvenience, partly because write-ins are often cast for entirely frivolous purposes, some states, in addition to their complex ballot-access laws, have established separate procedures that candidates must fulfill in order to run a valid write-in campaign. In Massachusetts, for example, anyone seeking presidential write-in votes must file, at least sixty days before the election, a list of candidates for

TABLE 9.5
EFFECT OF BALLOT ACCESS ON THIRD-PARTY
PRESIDENTIAL VOTE

	John Schmitz 1972	Eugene McCarthy 1976
Average percentage in states where candidate *was* listed on the ballot	2.71	1.45
Average percentage in states where candidate was *not* listed on the ballot	0.07	0.13
Actual vote	1,099,000	757,000
Estimated vote if candidate had been on the ballot in all 50 states and the District of Columbia	1,506,000	1,190,000
Actual percentage of the total presidential vote	1.41	0.93
Estimated percentage if candidate had been on the ballot in all 50 states and the District of Columbia	1.94	1.46
Percentage increase in candidate's vote due to being on all ballots	37	57

SOURCE: For details on how these results were derived, see note 34.

the Electoral College, all of whom pledge in writing to vote for that presidential candidate if elected. And only candidates who file such a form will actually get their write-in votes counted; any write-in vote for an uncertified candidate is put into an "All Others" category.[32] In Maine, a write-in candidate must receive at least 1 percent of the total vote in order for those votes to appear on the official tabulation. New Hampshire state law does require a write-in space for every office on the ballot; but according to a state election official, they "usually don't count" the write-ins.[33] The election laws in Hawaii, as we have seen, do not permit write-in voting at all. Legal requirements such as these help explain why, when McCarthy ran as an independent candidate in 1976, he was not credited with a single write-in vote in eight of the twenty-two states where his name did not appear on the ballot. Schmitz similarly received no write-in votes in twelve different states.

How well might McCarthy or Schmitz have done if their names *had* appeared on the ballot in all fifty states and the District of Columbia? In the lower half of table 9.5, we present an estimate of how universal ballot access would have affected the vote totals for these two candidates.[34] Had Schmitz been successful in getting on nineteen additional ballots, we estimate that his vote would have increased by about 40 percent, from 1.41 percent of the total votes cast to 1.94 percent. McCarthy's vote would have gone up by almost 60 percent, from 0.93 percent to 1.46 percent.[35]

It is important not to overstate what these results mean. Clearly, nothing in table 9.5 indicates that if ballot-access rules were significantly eased, third-party candidates would have a realistic shot at actually winning the next presidential election. Even their capacity to play the "spoiler" role—to help affect which major-party candidate wins—would not have changed much in these two instances. If one makes a fairly extreme assumption about where the new Schmitz and McCarthy votes would have come from —that all of the increase in Schmitz's vote would have been at Nixon's expense, and that all new McCarthy voters would otherwise have cast their ballots for Carter—the electoral votes of exactly one state would have been altered. Hawaii would have switched from the Democratic to the Republican column in 1976, lowering Carter's total from 297 to 293, but still leaving him well above the 270-vote level needed for victory.

But the results in table 9.5 do permit three more limited conclusions. The first is that third-party and independent candidates are right to be so concerned about ballot-access laws and to devote so much of their resources to getting on the ballot. Given that their potential vote is limited to begin with, it declines quite dramatically when they are not even listed on the ballot. Second, while the estimated vote totals shown in table 9.5 are paltry compared to those received by the two major-party candidates, there is reason to think that they might look very different to minor-party activists and supporters. Interviews with third-party and independent presidential candidates indicate that few, if any, of them are under any illusion that they have any real chance of winning.[36] They get into the race primarily for long-term educational purposes: to raise issues they think are being ignored by the Democrats and Republicans; to communicate an alternative perspective to the voters; to try to recruit new party members. But even hard-core ideologues who hope only for the eventual triumph of their ideas generally need some kind of short-term rewards to sustain them. To someone in this position, the difference between 750,000 votes and 1.2 million—or between 20,000 votes and 100,000—may be quite significant: the difference between feeling that there really is somebody out there listening and responding, and feeling that there are much more rewarding ways to spend every fourth autumn.

Finally, it is worth pointing out that a substantial change in ballot-access laws might significantly aid third-party and independent candidates another way that is not reflected in the estimates of table 9.5. As we have seen earlier, even when such candidates manage to get on most or all of the state ballots, it is never an easy undertaking. It usually requires a substantial investment of time and money—and money, in particular, is generally a very scarce commodity for third parties. Under the current system, a substantial portion of the funds that independent candidates manage to raise must be devoted to getting on the ballot, which leaves that much less available for advertising, travel, and the myriad other tasks of campaigning. In 1980, for example, John Anderson raised about $14 million for the independent phase of his presidential odyssey. But about $2 million of this total was spent dealing with ballot-access issues. By comparison, the campaign's *total* advertising budget—for television, radio, and newspapers—was only $2.3 million.[37]

Getting Nominated: Independent Candidates

Having looked at the complicated set of issues connected with getting on the ballot, we now take a step backward. How do third-party and independent candidates get to the point where ballot access becomes an active consideration? Of the many persons who belong to third parties or who might be contemplating a run for the White House, how are some pushed forward while others are "winnowed out"?

At this point, it is necessary to distinguish more clearly between two types of non-major-party challengers that are often grouped together: third-party candidates and independent candidates. These two terms are often used interchangeably (not only in the news media but in many state election laws); but strictly speaking, they do differ in one important respect, which relates precisely to the question of whether and how such candidates can be said to have been "nominated" for president.

Some of the presidential aspirants in table 9.1 were actually chosen by a *political party*: an organization that was independent of the ambitions and aspirations of any single person, that had been in existence before it got around to considering candidates for the presidency, that had relatively autonomous branches and affiliates in many states and localities, and that continued in operation after the presidential campaign was over. Throughout the nineteenth century, the most significant challenges to two-party presidential dominance almost all came from candidates actually nominated by a party in the sense just described.[38] The Anti-Masonics, the Free Soilers, the Know-Nothings, the Greenbacks, the Populists—all were parties with extensive grassroots operations, that held a national convention in order to choose one individual who would bear their standard in the fall campaign.

As we indicate shortly, there are still a sizable number of such minor parties in the United States, many of which nominate a presidential candidate every four years. But as a glance back at table 9.1 will confirm, the most successful non-major-party candidates of the past thirty years have generally *not* been connected with an actual party. George Wallace, John Anderson, and Ross Perot, in particular, were all "independent" candidates in a somewhat stricter sense of that term: men who got into the presidential race on their own initiative, without any ties to an ongoing political organization that was separate from their own ambitions. To the question, who nominates candidates like Wallace, Anderson, and Perot? the answer is: they nominate themselves, though often with a healthy assist from the news media.

John Anderson is a case in point. As is well known, Anderson started off the 1980 campaign season as an aspirant for the *Republican* presidential nomination. And during the first four months of 1980, the Illinois representative attracted a good deal of positive notice, initially from the press, later from many ordinary voters and political activists. But almost none of this enthusiasm came from members of his own party. On 24 April, after failing to win a single Republican primary, Anderson announced that he was striking out on his own.

A hundred and fifty years earlier, a politician in Anderson's position —ambitious but denied advancement within his own party—would probably have started to sound out the leaders of various third-party organizations to find out if there was any possibility of becoming their presidential nominee. (Two good examples are Presidents Martin Van Buren and Millard Fillmore, who, after being denied renomination by their own parties, later ran as third-party candidates, Van Buren with the Free Soil Party in 1848, Fillmore with the American or Know-Nothing Party in 1856.) But there is no evidence that Anderson even remotely considered such an option in 1980. Anderson did discuss his impending candidacy with a number of people, but the people he talked with, by all accounts, were distinguished only by their personal commitment to John Anderson. The discussants included campaign staff, paid consultants, prominent supporters, and members of his own family, but no one who represented an organized group or constituency. And with the possible exception of his family, these people could only offer advice and promises of support; the final decision about whether to run or not was made entirely by Anderson himself.[39]

Having made the fateful decision, Anderson lost no time in telling the press how he wanted his new campaign to be perceived and labeled. The first three sentences of his announcement speech read: "I have chosen, after careful deliberation, to pursue an independent course toward the Presidency of the United States. I will not run as a candidate of a third party. I will pursue an independent candidacy."[40] Indeed, Anderson said later in the same speech, though he was withdrawing from the Republican nomination race, he would continue his membership in the Republican Party. Anderson eventually did appear on a small number of state ballots as the candidate of the "Anderson Party" or the "National Unity Campaign," but this was only because, as we have seen, some state laws made it easier to get on the ballot that way.[41]

Not surprisingly, given this background, the fate of the Anderson "movement" was inextricably linked to the political fate of Anderson himself. For the first several years after 1980, the former representative did his best to stay in the news, giving speeches, writing a book, and frequently suggesting that he might try to create a new "party"—Anderson specifically used that term—that would nominate a presidential candidate in 1984. And in November 1983 Anderson actually announced the formation of the National Unity Party, saying that he would run again for the White House "if the party were to ask me to be a standard bearer."[42]

But this effort quickly ran into two major problems. First, Anderson did not qualify automatically for the 1984 general election ballot in as many states as he had apparently anticipated, raising the prospect of another series of long and expensive petition drives. Second, Anderson seems to have had trouble developing a compelling justification or a clear constituency for a second run at the presidency. In 1980 he had attacked the incumbent Democratic administration for its assorted failures—but he could plausibly argue that he also had major ideological disagreements with all of the other candidates in the Republican Party. In 1984, by contrast, his criticisms of the Reagan presidency were not very different from those being voiced by a small army of Democratic hopefuls. In April 1984 Anderson finally announced that he would not run for president that year; in late August he endorsed Walter Mondale.[43] Anderson continued at times to talk about creating a new party for the 1986 or 1988 campaigns, but by the middle of 1984, he says, "it was clear that we weren't going to succeed."[44] By 1985, the National Unity campaign had completely disappeared from the political landscape.

The media also played a central role in George Wallace's rise to national prominence. Wallace had been governor of Alabama for less than six months when, in June 1963, he made his defiant "stand in the schoolhouse door," in an attempt to prevent two black students from registering at the University of Alabama. His action was unsuccessful in policy terms—both students registered later the same day—but a dramatic political success, making Wallace a national symbol of resistance to racial integration and the growth of federal authority. Within three days of this nationally televised confrontation, he had received 40,000 letters and telegrams, the vast majority favorable and more than half from states outside the South.[45] In 1964, in an effort to prove that his message had appeal above the Mason-Dixon line, Wallace entered and did unexpectedly well in three northern Democratic presidential primaries. Early in 1967 he decided to make another foray into presidential politics, this time outside the confines of the Democratic Party.

Unlike Anderson, Wallace actually described himself as the candidate of a "third party"—specifically, the American Independent Party (AIP), whose label did accompany his name on most state ballots. But much like the National Unity campaign, the evidence makes it difficult to regard the AIP, at least in 1968, as anything more than a vehicle for Wallace's own candidacy and ambitions.

The creation of the American Independent Party was formally announced in June 1967, with the avowed intention of trying to get Wallace on the ballot in California and other states. Its nucleus was the substantial number of people who had earlier written or contacted Wallace to declare their support and urge him to run for higher office.[46] As one study described its operations:

> The AIP was not an integrated, functioning party.... [Wallace] issued a platform only when it appeared that he had to for the sake of legitimacy, and he named an official vice-presidential candidate only when it became apparent that several states would not be able to list him on their ballots unless he had a running mate.... In every state, even if a group had spontaneously decided that they wanted Wallace represented on their state's ballot, the people from [Wallace's national headquarters in] Montgomery came in to advise.... Local coordinators had no power in the Wallace organization; they were charged with little responsibility.... These people had to buy their campaign materials through Wallace headquarters, and the monies from sales and contributions received were forwarded directly to Montgomery.
> ... Since [Wallace] controlled the money and the manpower, he was also able to make certain that no one else was allowed to run on his ticket at the local and state levels, in all except one state—Oklahoma—where he had to make a compromise in order to get on the ballot.[47]

Indeed, at one point, a federal district court refused to order Wallace's name placed on the Ohio ballot on the grounds that the AIP was "a fictional party organized from the top down ... rather than ... from the bottom up."[48]

The American Independent Party differed from the National Unity campaign in only one salient way: having created a formal party structure, Wallace found the AIP somewhat more difficult to shut down after his campaign was over. Within six months after the 1968 election, two different groups of AIP members held national meetings for the purpose of creating a continuing party organization. And while both groups expressed support for Wallace and his views, one made it clear that the party "shouldn't belong to George Wallace; it should belong to the membership." Wallace ultimately sanctioned the less aggressive of these two groups, which had renamed itself the American Party, as the "official arm" of his third-party movement. But even then, Wallace maintained a careful distance from the new party: saying he would run under its banner *if* he ran as a third-party candidate in 1972 (but declining to commit himself to that strategy); urging the party's first national convention not to run too many candidates for state or local offices; and refusing to sever his ties with the Democratic Party. Eventually, Wallace chose to run in the *Democratic* primaries in 1972, though he apparently kept open the possibility of running again as a third-party candidate if the Democrats proved unresponsive.[49]

Any thoughts of a Democratic or third-party candidacy were dashed,

however, when Arthur Bremer shot Wallace five times on 15 May 1972, par-
alyzing him from the waist down for the rest of his life. The American Party,
which held its national nominating convention in early August, still clearly
wanted to draft Wallace for president, but decided against it after Wallace
himself informed them by telephone that his physical condition made another campaign impossible. The convention then nominated John Schmitz, a
lame-duck congressman from California with a fondness for conspiracy theories.[50]

Because of their past connections with Wallace, Schmitz and the American Party received considerably more press coverage in 1972 than third parties normally get. But without the compelling presence of Wallace himself on
the ticket, the American Party's vote declined drastically, from 13.5 percent
in 1968 to 1.4 percent in 1972. The American Party lingers on today—as
does the American Independent Party, a splinter group that broke off from
the American Party after the 1972 election and then resurrected the old
name from the 1968 campaign. But in none of the last four presidential elections has either group managed to win even one-tenth of one percent of the
total vote (see table 9.6). As one Wallace adviser accurately noted, "When
we left the American Party, we left an empty bag. It was a good vehicle
while it lasted, but when Wallace left, he took the voters with him."[51]

We recount the histories of the Wallace and Anderson campaigns in
some detail because of the obvious parallels they present to the political
movement led by Ross Perot. As with Wallace and Anderson, the media also
were a pivotal factor in Perot's emergence as a major national candidate.
Perot's quixotic run for the White House is usually said to have begun on a
television talk show, CNN's *Larry King Live,* on 20 February 1992.[52] That
initial announcement was largely ignored by the major national newspapers,
magazines, and network news programs; but it did get Perot interviews on a
host of other television shows, including *Donahue* and *60 Minutes.* By mid-
April, the mainstream press decided to make up for its earlier inattention,
according Perot a deluge of coverage over the next three months.[53]

As several accounts of the Perot phenomenon indicate, the Texas billionaire genuinely did have a lot of people urging him to run for president
and working to get his name on the ballot. In July, with Perot (temporarily)
out of the race, some of these enthusiasts formed an organization, called
United We Stand, America, in order to finish the ballot qualification process.
But much like the National Unity campaign and the American Independent
Party, the various Perot organizations were run in a "top down" rather than
"bottom up" fashion. Though the Texas billionaire always celebrated the
spontaneous, "from the people" character of his campaign, he also moved,
while the petition drive was still in its very early stages, to seize tight control
of the operation. Within weeks after his initial announcement, Perot was
pouring lots of his own money into the effort, sending key employees to

oversee the state campaigns, shutting down offices and committees that tried to remain independent, investigating and replacing local leaders who proved troublesome or embarrassing.[54]

Nor did that organization ever exercise much constraint on Perot's behavior. His withdrawal from the race in mid-July was clearly made against the expressed wishes of his many volunteers; and while he made a show of consulting some of these volunteers when he reentered the race in October, such consultations seem to have been no more than a cover for what Perot had already decided to do on his own. The Perot volunteers undoubtedly did do most of the hard labor involved in getting the Texan on the ballot in all fifty states. But once that phase was over, the Perot campaign seems to have been run in a remarkably centralized fashion, with most of its money going into media buys and other appearances by the candidate and relatively little into such "grassroots" activities as voter registration drives and literature drops. Through the end of the 1992 campaign, United We Stand endorsed not one other candidate for public office.[55]

Finally, like Wallace and Anderson, after the election was over, Perot was faced with the question of what to do next with his campaign organization and far-flung network of supporters. His solution, announced in mid-January 1993, was to turn United We Stand into a "not-for-profit watchdog group" that would organize in "every city, town, and neighborhood across the country" in order to continue fighting for the issues Perot had campaigned on. Much like George Wallace, however, Perot has apparently found it difficult to reconcile his personal ambitions and desire for control with an organization of individuals who are committed to grassroots democracy and participation. By June 1993, the *New York Times* was reporting that United We Stand was "in turmoil, riven by disputes that are beginning to cost it some of its most committed volunteers." In the short run, there seems little doubt that Perot will prevail in these disputes, not only because he is the organization's principal spokesperson but also because he is paying all its bills. In the longer run, Perot will almost certainly discover why it is so difficult to convert an independent presidential candidacy—even a very successful one —into a continuing "third force" in American politics.[56]

Quite clearly, a number of common themes run through the presidential candidacies of George Wallace, John Anderson, and Ross Perot. First, as we have noted, none of these candidates was *nominated* for president in any meaningful sense of that term. In particular, not one of them ever had to go before a nominating convention to seek formal ratification of either their own candidacy or their choice of a vice-presidential running mate. All three become general election candidates entirely on their own initiative, in each case claiming (with some validity) that they had a large contingent of ordinary Americans urging them to do so.

Second, in all three cases, the candidates' chances were given a significant boost by decisions the American media made about how and how much to cover them. Perhaps this is inevitable: there are, after all, thousands of Americans who think they would make a good president and who would love a platform from which to make highly publicized criticisms and analyses of American government. Any such individual, of course, can always *announce* that he or she is running for president, but most of them will be completely ignored by the media and ultimately, therefore, by the voters. For a variety of reasons—some defensible, others more questionable—Wallace, Anderson, and Perot were all taken more seriously. Media coverage decisions, in effect, "winnowed them into" the presidential campaigns of 1968, 1980, and 1992.

Third, each of these candidates ultimately developed an organizational apparatus to help carry out the various campaign-related tasks—in particular, getting on the ballot. But in each case, the organization was created and controlled by the candidate and existed primarily to serve his own ambitions. This arrangement worked relatively well for the Anderson organization, which never claimed (at least in 1980) to be doing anything more than trying to get Anderson elected president. Both the Wallace and Perot organizations, however, claimed at times to be something more: a party in the former case, a grassroots political movement in the latter. But an essential property of parties and grassroots movements, at least in democracies, is precisely that they attempt to exercise some measure of control over their leaders; and neither Wallace nor Perot was the sort of person who was willing to cede such control. This clash of expectations, not surprisingly, produced dissent and turmoil within the organization and led to feelings of disappointment and bitterness among many of the candidate's supporters.

Finally, after the election is over, the fate of an independent political "movement" is very closely tied to the decisions and behavior of its leader. When Wallace decided not to wage a third-party candidacy in 1972, the American Party presidential vote plummeted by almost 90 percent. If the National Unity organization ever had a serious prospect of becoming a real party, that chance evaporated once Anderson himself withdrew from the 1984 campaign. And whatever the future holds for United We Stand, America, it seems most unlikely that it will ever develop into anything more than a mechanism for the personal promotion of Ross Perot.

Getting Nominated: Third Parties

Though independent presidential hopefuls such as Perot and Anderson have garnered most of the publicity over the past several decades, the United States still has a large crop of actual third *parties*: ongoing organizations that are considerably more than vehicles for the promotion of one person's political aspirations. And precisely because they are parties, such groups as the Socialist Party and the Libertarian Party have clearly established rules and procedures for nominating candidates. One does not become the Libertarian candidate for president merely by holding a press conference or announcing one's availability on *Larry King Live.*

As anyone who has delved into the small but growing literature on this topic knows, American third parties are a remarkably diverse lot, ranging from the serious and thoughtful to the bizarre and paranoid, and coming in all sorts of sizes, styles, and ideological complexions.[57] While it is probably impossible to compile an exhaustive list of third-party presidential aspirants, table 9.6 presents detailed results for the *strongest* minor-party presidential candidates who ran between 1972 and 1992. To say the least, it is not an inspiring record. Of the forty-seven candidates shown, only two managed to get even one-half of one percent of the total presidential vote. None got 2 percent.

Of the parties shown in table 9.6, the only one that has even the slightest cause for optimism is the Libertarians, who definitely have established themselves in recent years as the largest third party in America. In the five presidential elections held between 1976 and 1992, the largest third-party vote was always received by the Libertarian candidate. And a number of state Libertarian parties have shown measurable signs of growth and vigor over the past few years. In New Hampshire, for example, the Libertarians have now achieved major-party status; in 1996, the state will even hold a Libertarian presidential primary on the same day as the fabled Democratic and Republican media spectaculars. In 1994, the New Hampshire Libertarians fielded 109 candidates for state office, up from just 4 in 1990 (only 2 of the 109 were elected, however); and their gubernatorial candidate was invited to all the major televised debates for that office. At the presidential level, however, there is little evidence to date that the Libertarians are catching on. The Libertarian presidential vote actually peaked in 1980 and has fallen off considerably since then.

Besides their lack of success, one other factor generally unites the current roster of American third parties and sharply distinguishes them from the Republicans and Democrats: they have a very different concept of what constitutes a party "member" and, consequently, of who may participate in internal party nomination processes.

Among those who study political parties from a comparative perspective, the Democrats and Republicans have often been seen as the archetypal examples of a kind of party organization known as a *cadre* party.[58] In a cadre party, those affiliated with the party can generally be divided into two distinct groups. On the one hand, there are a relatively small number of party leaders, consultants, and paid staff members, who run the party machinery, raise and spend its funds, and make decisions in its name. Outside this "inner circle," however, cadre parties generally do not have members in

TABLE 9.6

RESULTS FOR THIRD-PARTY PRESIDENTIAL CANDIDATES,

1972–92 (IN PERCENTAGES)

Party	1972	1976	1980	1984	1988	1992
Libertarian	*	0.21	1.06	0.25	0.47	0.28
Socialist and Marxist Parties						
Communist	0.03	0.07	0.05	0.04	—	—
Socialist	—	0.01	0.01	—	*	*
Socialist Labor	0.07	0.01	—	—	—	—
Socialist Workers	0.09	0.11	0.06	0.03	0.02	0.02
Other Left-Wing Parties						
Citizens	—	—	0.27	0.08	—	—
New Alliance	—	—	—	0.05	0.24	0.07
People's	0.10	0.06	—	—	—	—
Right-Wing Parties						
American	1.41	0.20	0.01	0.01	*	*
American Independent	—	0.21	0.05	—	0.03	—
Populist	—	—	—	0.07	0.05	0.10
Prohibition	0.02	0.02	0.01	*	0.01	*

SOURCE: Computed from data in *America Votes.*
"—" indicates that the party did not nominate a presidential candidate that year.
* indicates that the party did nominate a candidate but that he or she received less than 0.005 percent of the vote.

any formal or official sense. They may have lots of *supporters,* who like what the party stands for and vote for its candidates on election day; some of these supporters may also contribute money to the party or do volunteer work in its election campaigns. But one does not become a member of the Democratic or Republican Party in the same way that one can join a labor union, the Rotary, or the National Rifle Association. In a cadre party, the relation of party supporters to the party organization is much like that of football fans to their favorite team: they may feel a psychological tie and perform occasional acts of support, but they do not thereby become "members" of the Chicago Bears or the New England Patriots.

At the opposite end of the spectrum is the *mass* party, which does have formal members and a highly articulated organizational structure. Most textbooks on the subject use European socialists and communists as the prototypical examples of a mass party—but most American third parties also belong in this category. To become a member of the Socialist Party USA, for example, one must sign a membership application pledging commitment to "a new society based on democratic socialism" and then be inducted into its ranks by either the national party or one of its local affiliates. One must also pay party dues (currently set at $15 to $75 per year, depending on one's income), and anyone who falls six months behind in these payments is no longer considered a member in good standing. Roughly similar procedures and qualifications can be found in the bylaws of the Libertarian Party and the constitution of the Communist Party USA.[59]

The fact that American third parties are mass rather than cadre parties has several important implications for the way they nominate presidential candidates. In the end, almost all these parties select their tickets at a national party convention. But the delegates to these conventions are chosen at party meetings or state conventions in which only formal, dues-paying members may participate. Where the Democratic and Republican nomination systems have often been criticized for having removed the formal party organization and its leaders from any significant role in the process, most American third parties still select their national tickets through party-run procedures.

For a more detailed view of a third-party nomination process in action, we turn to the Libertarian Party, both because it is currently the largest and most active third party in the nation and because, unlike a number of other such parties, its internal rules and procedures are open and accessible to anyone who cares to study them.[60] The Libertarian presidential ticket is nominated at a national party convention that has traditionally been held about fourteen months before the general election. The Libertarian national candidates for 1988, for example, were nominated at a convention held in September 1987. The early date was necessary in order to give the party sufficient time to comply with state ballot-access laws, which generally require a group to have the name of a specific candidate before it is allowed to circulate petitions. As these laws have become somewhat less restrictive, and as the Libertarian Party has achieved major-party status in an increasing number of states, the Libertarian Party will hold its next national convention in July 1996, approximately the same time as the Democrats and Republicans.

The delegates to the Libertarian National Convention are selected by the affiliated state parties, all of which must be formally chartered by the party's national committee.[61] As of 1994, each affiliate party was entitled to select one delegate for every twenty persons in the state who were members of the national party, and one additional delegate for each 1 percent of the total state vote won by the party's last presidential candidate. Affiliate parties are given a substantial amount of latitude in deciding how to select these delegates (most use state conventions). But whatever method is chosen, it must be one in which only formal party members may participate; and all the delegates ultimately selected must be members of either the national party or an affiliated state party.

Though outside observers would probably rate their chances of victory at slim to none, the Libertarians have recently had a number of spirited contests for the spots on their national ticket.[62] Given its character as a mass party and the limited amount of press attention the party generally receives, Libertarian nomination campaigns are targeted almost entirely at an internal audience. Libertarian presidential hopefuls generally announce their campaigns by calling up influential party members and trying to obtain coverage in party newsletters. They seek support through mailings to party members and, especially, by addressing Libertarian Party state conventions.

How well have procedures like the one just described served American third parties? And more generally, what difference does it make for the American political system that some presidential candidates are formally nominated to run for the White House, while others get into the race entirely on their own initiative? Any attempt to answer such questions must begin, of course, with the recognition that most third parties have philosophies and perspectives that are different from those of the Republicans and Democrats and that their views as to what constitutes "a good candidate" are also distinctive. The standard list of traits and characteristics that have traditionally mattered to the major parties—a good family life, substantial previous governmental experience, being a white male Protestant or Catholic—are generally not very important to third parties. (In 1980, for example, the Socialist Party nominated a presidential candidate who was, by his own admission, a homosexual, Marxist, apostate Christian, recovering alcoholic, and pacifist who had been arrested for refusing induction during the Korean war; his running mate was a nun.[63]) What these parties *do* care about, given their current position in American politics, is finding someone who will be an articulate and attractive spokesperson for the party's principles. As far as we can tell from the small bits of press coverage they have received, most recent third-party standard-bearers stack up reasonably well on this dimension.

More important, we would argue, third-party nomination processes have served both their own members and the larger public interest by insisting on a commitment to the party ideology and thereby helping clarify the choices that voters will face on election day. Third-party nomination procedures, especially because they are generally closed to those who are not party members, guarantee that the party label actually stands for something. The Socialist Party presidential nominee may not have all the traits and qualities that Americans seem to desire in major party nominees, *but he or she will be a Socialist.* Several recent Libertarian candidates have not had any previous governmental experience, but they have been vigorously committed to the core values and ideas that animate that party.

To these and other third-party nominees, we may contrast the experience of Ross Perot in 1992, who built his campaign almost entirely around vague promises of "taking back the country" and "making America strong again" and never did stake out any clear or specific positions on a vast range of important issues. Had Perot been required to obtain a party endorsement, we think it most unlikely that he would have been able to run such a campaign. Going through a party nomination process, of almost any kind, would probably have contributed a great deal to defining and clarifying Perot's policy views.

The Future

What does the future hold for non-major-party candidates at the presidential level? If the past twenty-five years are any indication, we must offer separate judgments about the likely prospects of independents and third parties.

For actual third parties, as we have just seen, the recent past provides little cause for optimism. Over the past several decades, numerous third-party activists have expressed the hope that the American public's widespread dissatisfaction with the Democrats and Republicans would create an opportunity for one or more minor parties to fill the void—perhaps even to replace one of the majors altogether, just as the Republicans supplanted the Whigs in the 1850s. To judge by the results in table 9.6, however, the current antiparty mood is a rejection of *all* parties—of the very idea of parties—and not just the two leading ones. Whatever else one may think of it, John Anderson's claim that he was an independent *rather than* a third-party candidate seems to have embodied an accurate reading of American public opinion.

For independent presidential contenders, however, the past twenty-five years have been, at least in relative terms, quite fruitful ones. No independent candidate has come close to winning the presidency, of course, but as the figures in table 9.1 indicate, of the three best showings by an independent or third-party candidate in the past sixty years, all three were by independents and all three have occurred since 1968. Even Anderson, the weakest of the troika, scored a larger percentage of the vote in 1980 than the combined vote of the States' Rights and Progressive parties in 1948.

Four major trends in American politics have helped make the recent past a relatively propitious time for independent presidential candidacies. The first is the long-term decay of party allegiances within the national electorate, whether measured in terms of the growth of self-identified independents, the decline in the number of strong identifiers, or the increased willingness of all categories of partisans to split their tickets. Independent presidential candidates do best, not surprisingly, among voters who call themselves independents; hence, as the number of independents rises, the pool that might consider voting for someone other than the Democrat or Republican necessarily does as well.

Second, independent prospects go up as the voters become dissatisfied with *both* major-party nominees; and as several studies have shown, there has been, over the past three decades, a substantial and long-term decline in the popularity of major-party presidential nominees.[64] In the elections of 1952–60, the American public tended to have a generally favorable opinion of *both* presidential candidates: the one whom they intended to vote for, but also, frequently, the one they were not going to support. By the 1980s, it had become increasingly common for the voters to express an *unfavorable* opinion toward both contenders and to indicate that their vote was only a choice for the lesser of two evils. This trend does not necessarily mean that contemporary presidential candidates really are less objectively capable or qualified than the nominees of forty years ago. A more likely explanation for the decline in candidate popularity is the development of a culture, especially within the news media, that is substantially more suspicious and critical of *anyone* aspiring to hold a position of political power. However explained, it remains true that as voters become more dissatisfied with what the major parties are offering, they also become more likely to give serious consideration to the other contenders.

Third, as we indicated earlier, even though ballot-access laws still represent a significant hurdle for independent and third-party challengers, such regulations are considerably less onerous than they once were. Table 9.4, in particular, shows that more and more non-major-party candidates are managing to qualify for a substantial number of state ballots.

Fourth, changes in the mass media and campaign technology have made it substantially easier for an independent candidate to get his or her message to the voters. For the first century and a half of American politics, someone who wanted to run for president without a party endorsement would have needed to construct an *organization* in order to communicate with millions of voters scattered all over the United States, clearly a very difficult and time-consuming process. Mass media such as television and radio, by contrast, provide independent candidates with a preestablished channel of communication, available to anyone who is deemed sufficiently newsworthy or who has the money to purchase commercial time. Without such media, it is simply inconceivable that a person like Ross Perot, who was unknown to most Americans at the start of 1992, could have signaled his willingness to run in late February and then lead the opinion polls in June.

Against these four trends that favor independent presidential candidates, we must counterpose one that hurts them (as well as third parties): the passage of federal campaign finance laws in 1974, which has made it significantly more difficult for them to raise money. Under this law, major-party candidates have their fall campaigns financed entirely by the federal government. In 1980, for example, Jimmy Carter and Ronald Reagan both received a check for $29.4 million to pay for their general election expenses.

In 1992, the checks to Bush and Clinton were for $55.2 million. Minor-party and independent candidates do not receive such funds, though they may qualify for a far smaller, retroactive subsidy if they receive at least 5 percent of the final vote and agree to abide by a number of other restrictions in the law.[65] Yet, even though most independent challengers never see a dime in federal money, they are still required to abide by the contribution limits established in the 1974 law, under which no individual may contribute more than $1,000 to a presidential candidate, and no political action committee may give more than $5,000.

As Milton Friedman pointed out some years ago, radical and system-challenging movements have always depended, especially in their early stages, on the support of a few very wealthy benefactors.[66] Without large contributions, political groups that are unorthodox or "outside the mainstream" are usually caught in a vicious cycle in which they cannot raise money because they do not have enough supporters, and they cannot get more supporters because they do not have the money to propagate their ideas. Aside from changing the campaign finance laws, there are only two ways to break this cycle. One is to get the news media to take your candidacy seriously and thereby provide you with large amounts of free publicity. Wallace, Anderson, and Perot, as we have seen, all clearly benefited from such coverage; but the number of third-party or independent challengers who can possibly receive such extensive attention is always going to be limited. And in two of these three cases (Wallace and Anderson), the candidate was deemed newsworthy because of actions he had taken while still belonging to one of the major parties.

The second way to break the cycle is to take advantage of a loophole in the finance laws (actually carved out by a 1976 Supreme Court decision), that allows candidates to spend an unlimited amount of *their own* money on their campaigns. It was, of course, this latter option that Ross Perot took ample advantage of in 1992, enabling him to spend $65 million in the fall campaign, far more money than was available to either Bush or Clinton. But there are other examples. In 1980, for example, the Libertarian Party chose millionaire David Koch as their vice-presidential candidate primarily because he had promised in an open letter to the convention delegates that, if nominated, he would contribute $500,000 to the national campaign. In the end, Koch was better than his word: he gave $2.1 million to the party coffers (the party's total campaign budget that year was only $3.5 million), allowing the Libertarians to purchase forty-seven national network television spots.[67] It is probably no coincidence that 1980 was also, by a considerable margin, the best year ever for the Libertarian presidential ticket.

Absent a candidate who is personally very wealthy, however, any law that shuts off large contributions makes it that much more difficult for independents and third parties to run a competitive campaign. Even a candidate like John Anderson, who had a very effective direct-mail operation and got far more news coverage than independent candidates usually receive, was hurt by the fact that he had almost no money available for television or radio advertising in the fall campaign.[68]

Conclusion

In the end, Ross Perot fell well short of victory in the 1992 presidential elections. But the fact that he wound up with almost 20 percent of the popular vote—and that he led many national polls in May and June—suggests that the state of independents and third parties ought to be of some interest to all Americans concerned about the future of their political system, even those who may never vote for a non-major-party candidate. Even if the Democrats and Republicans continue to win, we think there is much validity in the view, expressed by a number of recent commentators, that third-party and independent candidates perform a variety of beneficial functions for the American political system. In particular, they help keep the major parties honest (or at least, more honest than they would be otherwise) by giving expression to discontented groups and individuals, by bringing up issues that the Democrats and Republicans might prefer not to discuss, by introducing a little more competition into the system and thereby motivating the major parties to aspire to a slightly higher standard of performance.[69]

For these reasons, two features of the present system strike us as especially troubling. The first is the operation of the campaign finance laws we have described. In retrospect, it is hard not to feel that the American political system has long been evolving in a way that provided a golden opportunity for a Perot-type candidate. On the one hand, there has been a significant growth in the potential constituency for independent and third-party candidates. Yet, most such candidates simply do not have the resources to run the kind of campaign that could mobilize that constituency. Under current federal law, the only sure way to overcome this dilemma is to find a candidate who is so enormously wealthy that he can finance his campaign entirely out of his own pocket. Put another way, we may have created a system where most significant third-party presidential campaigns will be run by the super-rich. If this scenario seems far-fetched, it is worth noting that, by taking advantage of the same loophole, a significant number of very wealthy individuals have already won election to the U.S. Senate, based on campaigns they paid for themselves.

We are also troubled by the long-term replacement of third-party presidential challengers by independent and unaffiliated candidates. Though candidates like Perot regularly deplore the existence of political parties, suggesting that they somehow create a barrier between the candidate and the people, we are more inclined to side with the large number of political scientists and social philosophers who have seen such intermediary groups as making a vital contribution to democratic governance and individual freedom. The Republican and Democratic nominating processes, whatever their other shortcomings, at least provide some sort of screening mechanism for presidential hopefuls, weeding out candidates who are seriously unqualified, exposing and testing their ideas on important policy questions, ensuring some measure of long-term continuity and accountability. Though third-party nomination processes are generally less concerned with their candidates' governing abilities—not surprisingly, since most such candidates have essentially no chance of actually becoming president—they at least demand ideological and programmatic loyalty from their nominees.

But the only agency that performs anything remotely like this for independent candidates is the press; and for a variety of reasons, the press is a poor substitute for political parties. Above all, the press helps "promote" an independent candidate, not because of his or her policy views or because he or she would make an effective officeholder, but because the candidate makes a "good story": because he or she fits such traditional criteria of newsworthiness as being colorful, controversial, and exciting. The American constitutional system was created by men who were generally skeptical of human nature and therefore sought to make up for individual shortcomings and frailties through properly designed institutions and governing processes. Unaffiliated candidates who are simply popular, who claim a "special relationship" with the people, are not an adequate substitute for a well-designed nomination *process*. But adequate or not, they seem to be the wave of the future.

APPENDIX A
CRITERIA FOR ACHIEVING AUTOMATIC
BALLOT ACCESS: A SAMPLING
OF STATE LAWS

ALABAMA: Have one candidate who received 20 percent of the total statewide vote at the last general election.

CONNECTICUT: Receive at least 20 percent of the vote for governor in the last gubernatorial election.

DISTRICT OF COLUMBIA: Automatic access to the presidential ballot is granted to any political party that has had its candidate elected president of the United States after 1 January 1950.

ILLINOIS: Have one candidate who polled more than 5 percent of the entire vote cast in the state at the last general election.

KENTUCKY: Receive at least 20 percent of the total vote cast in the last presidential election.

MASSACHUSETTS: (1) Have a candidate running for any statewide office at the last general election who received at least 3 percent of the total state vote; or (2) get 1 percent of the total number of registered voters in the state to register as members of the party.

NEW HAMPSHIRE: Receive at least 3 percent of the total number of votes cast for the office of governor.

NORTH CAROLINA: Receive at least 10 percent of the total state vote cast for governor or president at the last general election.

OHIO: Have a candidate for governor or president who polled at least 5 percent of the total state vote for that office at the last general election.

VIRGINIA: Have a candidate at either of the last two statewide general elections who received at least 10 percent of the total vote cast.

WASHINGTON: Have at least one nominee for president, vice-president, U.S. senator, or any statewide office who received at least 5 percent of the total state vote cast at the last general election held in an even-numbered year.

SOURCE: Compiled from state election statutes.

APPENDIX B
A SAMPLING OF STATE ELECTION LAWS PROVIDING
SPECIAL BALLOT ACCESS TO MINOR PARTIES

ARKANSAS: Any party holding a state convention is allowed to nominate candidates for president, vice-president, and presidential elector as long as it files a copy of the convention minutes and a list of the people attending with the secretary of state within two days after the convention adjourns.

CONNECTICUT: Any political party or organization whose candidate for any office receives at least 1 percent of the total number of votes cast for that office becomes a minor party with respect to that office. At the next similar election, it may nominate a candidate for that office in whatever manner is provided for in the party rules; that nominee will then be placed directly on the general election ballot, without filing petitions.

DELAWARE: Minor parties may get listed on the general election ballot if they can get five one-hundredths of 1 percent of the state's registered voters (about 180 voters in 1996) to register under the party's name.

MARYLAND: Any group can qualify as a political party and get its endorsed candidates listed on the general election ballot by filing a petition containing 10,000 signatures. Independent candidates, by contrast, are required to file a petition containing the signatures of 3 percent of the state's registered voters (about 72,000 signatures in 1996).

MISSISSIPPI: State law defines a party as any "association, committee, or organization" that nominates a candidate for any elective office whose name appears on the election ballot as the candidate of that association, committee, or organization. Any group that meets this definition and that registers with the secretary of state within 30 days after organizing is allowed to nominate candidates for the general election ballot without filing petitions.

NEW MEXICO: New and minor political parties may qualify for the general election ballot by filing a petition signed by one-half of 1 percent of the total votes cast for governor or president at the preceding general election (2,338 signatures in 1996). Independent candidates must file a petition signed by 3 percent of the total number of votes cast at the preceding gubernatorial election (14,571 signatures in 1996).

VERMONT: Any political party may nominate a candidate for statewide office if it has town committees organized in at least 10 towns in the state.

Acknowledgments

We would like to thank Robert Biersack, Michael Tolley, Amy Logan, and Karina Rinsky for their assistance in the preparation of this chapter.

Notes

1. Particularly relevant to this point are Angus Campbell, Philip E. Converse, Warren E. Miller, and Donald E. Stokes, *The American Voter* (New York: Wiley, 1960), esp. chaps. 3 and 4; Edward R. Tufte, *Political Control of the Economy* (Princeton: Princeton University Press, 1978); and Morris P. Fiorina, *Retrospective Voting in American National Elections* (New Haven: Yale University Press, 1981).

2. See, among others, Maurice Duverger, *Political Parties,* trans. Barbara and Robert North (New York: Wiley, 1954), 216–28; Steven J. Rosenstone, Roy L. Behr, and Edward H. Lazarus, *Third Parties in America: Citizen Response to Major Party Failure* (Princeton: Princeton University Press, 1984), chap. 1; William H. Riker, "The Two-party System and Duverger's Law: An Essay on the History of Political Science," *American Political Science Review* 76 (December 1982): 753–66; Leon D. Epstein, *Political Parties in the American Mold* (Madison: University of Wisconsin Press, 1986); and V.O. Key, Jr., *Politics, Parties, and Pressure Groups,* 5th ed. (New York: Crowell, 1964), 205–10.

3. For some early indications of this, see Dan Balz, "Independence a Trait Voters Find Attractive," *Washington Post,* 29 August 1994, A1; Richard L. Berke, "U.S. Voters Focus on Selves, Poll Says," *New York Times,* 21 September 1994, A21; Richard L. Berke, "From Not Quite Acceptable to Maybe Even Electable," *New York Times,* 3 October 1994, E4; and David M. Shribman, "Tsongas Suggests 3d Party, Sees Powell as a Candidate," *Boston Globe,* 13 December 1994, 1.

4. In some cases, indeed, government did not even provide a ballot box. As Ronald P. Formisano has noted, well into the nineteenth century, many states used *viva voce* voting or simply counted the number of persons standing at a public meeting. See *The Transformation of Political Culture: Massachusetts Parties, 1790s–1840s* (New York: Oxford University Press, 1983), 143–48.

5. For good accounts of this development, see, among others, Jerrold G. Rusk, "The Effect of the Australian Ballot Reform on Split Ticket Voting: 1876–1908," *American Political Science Review* 64 (December 1970): 1220–38; Austin Ranney, *Curing the Mischiefs of Faction: Party Reform in America* (Berkeley: University of California Press, 1975), 78–82; and Rosenstone, Behr, and Lazarus, *Third Parties,* 19–25.

6. See Nick Ravo, "But, Otherwise, This Candidate Is Still Running," *New York Times,* 9 August 1988, B1.

7. All these arguments are quoted from Supreme Court decisions, specifically *Williams* v. *Rhodes,* 393 U.S. 23, 31, 32 (1968); and *Storer* v. *Brown,* 415 U.S. 724, 736, 735 (1974). In some cases, it might be noted, the Court, while acknowledging the general validity of the argument, saw it as insufficient to justify the ballot-access restriction in question.

8. More recently, the U.S. Supreme Court has given political parties some right to determine the rules governing participation in their primaries. See *Tashjian* v. *Republican Party of Connecticut,* 479 U.S. 208 (1986).

9. The one exception is that a fair number of states still deny major-party sta-

tus to the Communist Party or any other organization advocating the overthrow of government by force.

10. The states are listed in *Ballot Access News,* 15 November 1994, 4.

11. As the figures in table 9.2 indicate, the petition requirements actually increased in twenty-eight states between 1967 and 1994, though in most cases by fairly small amounts. But there was a substantial decline in signature requirements in all five of the states that had imposed the largest burden in 1967.

12. Since the Supreme Court decisions in *Bullock* v. *Carter,* 405 U.S. 134 (1972), and *Lubin* v. *Panish,* 415 U.S. 709 (1974), states have been required to waive fees for indigent candidates and parties.

13. Based on information taken from a table in *New York Times,* 26 June 1992, A13.

14. Rhodes Cook, "High Hurdles for the Anderson Campaign," *Congressional Quarterly Weekly Report,* 17 May 1980, 1315.

15. The amendments referred to are the Fifteenth, Nineteenth, Twenty-Fourth, and Twenty-Sixth. None of these amendments, it should be noted, prevents a state legislature from selecting the electors themselves, without a popular vote. But whatever selection system is chosen, it must extend the same voting privileges to blacks, women, and eighteen-year-olds that it provides to all other citizens.

16. 393 U.S. 23 (1968).

17. Three justices dissented, including Chief Justice Warren, who lamented that the case, which reached the Court on the eve of the presidential election, was decided in the absence of "the unhurried deliberation which is essential to the formulation of sound constitutional principle." *Williams* v. *Rhodes,* [393 U.S. at 63]. This haste, as much as any other factor, accounts for the fact that the Court has been in flight from *Williams*'s broad pronouncements ever since.

18. 393 U.S. at 29.

19. Bradley A. Smith, "Judicial Protection of Ballot Access Rights: Third Parties Need Not Apply," *Harvard Journal on Legislation* 28 (Winter 1991): 181.

20. 460 U.S. 780 (1983). A number of cases decided between *Williams* and *Anderson* clearly show the Court recognizing the potential problems with the *Williams* framework and struggling to define a new standard of review. See, in particular, *Jenness* v. *Fortson,* 403 U.S. 431 (1971); and *Storer* v. *Brown,* 415 U.S. 724 (1974).

21. *Anderson* v. *Celebrezze,* 460 U.S. 780, 789 (1983).

22. Ohio law required any candidate in a major-party presidential primary to declare by that same March date.

23. In forgoing strict scrutiny, the Court certainly forfeited a certain analytic clarity (although *Williams* is no model of analytic rigor). Arguably, the loss of clarity was offset by the Court's employment of the more situation-specific balancing test, which provides greater sensitivity to the multiple interests affected by such legislation.

24. 112 S.Ct. 2059 (1992).

25. Burdick was asking, in effect, for a revival of the more searching review identified in *Williams* v. *Rhodes.*

26. *Burdick* v. *Takushi,* 112 S.Ct. 2059, 2067–68 (1992).

27. In addition to the *Williams* and *Anderson* cases, see also *Bullock* v. *Carter,* 405 U.S. 134 (1972); *American Party of Texas* v. *White,* 415 U.S. 767

(1974); and *Lubin* v. *Panish,* 415 U.S. 709 (1974).

28. *Storer* v. *Brown,* 415 U.S. at 731.

29. See, for example, "For Wallace's Old Party: A New Leader, A Brisk Bid for Votes," *U.S. News & World Report,* 25 September 1972, 22; Daniel Chu, "McCarthy on His Own," *Newsweek,* 1 November 1976, 24; "Will Gene Be the Spoiler?" *Time,* 25 October 1976, 17–18; Rhodes Cook, "High Hurdles for the Anderson Campaign," *Congressional Quarterly Weekly Report,* 17 May 1980, 1315–18; Kenneth T. Walsh, "Your Other Choices for the White House," *U.S. News & World Report,* 5 November 1984, 30; Rhodes Cook, "Third-Party Impact Is Small, But It Could Be Felt This Fall," *Congressional Quarterly Weekly Report,* 3 September 1988, 2485–86; Francis X. Clines, "He's on Every State Ballot, If Not on Every Voter's Lips," *New York Times,* 28 October 1992, A1; Adam Pertman, "Fringe Candidates Put Frustration on the Ballot," *Boston Globe,* 31 October 1992, A8; William Safire, "The Fourth Man," *New York Times,* 22 October 1992, A27.

30. For a detailed description of Perot's announcement, see Jack W. Germond and Jules Witcover, *Mad As Hell: Revolt at the Ballot Box, 1992* (New York: Warner Books, 1993), 218–23.

31. Stephan Lesher, *George Wallace: American Populist* (Reading, Mass.: Addison-Wesley, 1994), 400. The same point is made in Daniel A. Mazmanian, *Third Parties in Presidential Elections* (Washington, D.C.: Brookings Institution, 1974), 88.

32. In 1992, for example, in addition to eight presidential candidates listed on the Massachusetts state ballot, 13 write-in votes were cast for J. Quinn Brisben (of the Socialist Party), 2 votes for Earl Dodge (Prohibition Party)—and 1,990 write-ins were listed in the official tabulation only as "All Others," with no way to tell whose name was actually written in.

33. Interview with Karen Ladd, assistant secretary of state, 9 May 1994.

34. Data on the votes received by Schmitz and McCarthy, and on whether or not they were listed on a state's ballot, are taken from Richard M. Scammon and Alice V. McGillivray, *America at the Polls* 2 (Washington, D.C.: Elections Research Center, 1988).

To estimate how each candidate might have fared if he had been on the ballot in all fifty states, we began by estimating a regression equation for each candidate's vote in those states where they *were* listed on the ballot. For the Schmitz vote, the equation used the following independent variables: median family income, percentage living in metropolitan areas, a measure of state ideology, and a dummy variable for states in the West. (The measure of state ideology is taken from Gerald C. Wright, Robert S. Erikson, and John P. McIver, "Measuring State Partisanship and Ideology with Survey Data," *Journal of Politics* 47 [May 1985]: 469–89.) For McCarthy, the equation used percentage in metropolitan areas, state ideology, and separate dummy variables for the West and the South. Both equations accounted for at least 63 percent of the variance in the dependent variable; all independent variables were statistically significant at the .05 level.

We then used these equations to generate a predicted vote percentage for all states in which the candidates were *not* listed on the ballot, multiplied these percentages by the total vote cast in that state, and summed the results. This total was then added to the total vote each candidate received in the states where they were listed on the ballot.

35. Rosenstone, Behr, and Lazarus have estimated that McCarthy would have

polled 4.3 percent of the total vote if his name had been listed on the ballot in all fifty states. See *Third Parties,* 173–74. But this estimate seems excessive. McCarthy's best showing in the states where he *was* on the ballot was only 3.9 percent, and he achieved this level of support only in Oregon. In no other state did he receive even 3 percent of the total vote.

36. See, in particular, the fascinating series of interviews in Frank Smallwood, *The Other Candidates: Third Parties in Presidential Elections* (Hanover, N.H.: University Press of New England, 1983).

37. All figures are taken from Herbert E. Alexander, *Financing the 1980 Election* (Lexington, Mass.: Lexington Books, 1983), 341–56.

38. For a more extended development of this point, see Rosenstone, Behr, and Lazarus, *Third Parties,* chaps. 3 and 4.

39. For accounts of Anderson's decision to run as an independent, see Mark Bisnow, *Diary of a Dark Horse* (Carbondale: Southern Illinois University Press, 1983), chaps. 5 and 6; Jack W. Germond and Jules Witcover, *Blue Smoke and Mirrors* (New York: Viking Press, 1981), chap. 11; Clifford W. Brown, Jr., and Robert J. Walker, eds., *A Campaign of Ideas* (Westport, Conn.: Greenwood Press, 1984), xxx–xxxvi.

40. For the text of Anderson's announcement speech, see Gregory Bush, ed., *Campaign Speeches of American Presidential Candidates 1948–1984* (New York: Frederick Ungar, 1985), 299–304.

41. This possibility was noted in advance in the *Boston Globe,* 25 April 1980, 10.

42. See *New York Times,* 12 May 1981, B10; 23 November 1981, A20; 11 February 1982, 33; 22 June 1982, 18; 23 February 1983, A18; 11 June 1983, 8; and 9 November 1983, 25.

43. *New York Times,* 22 April 1984, 16; 27 April 1984, 12; 28 August 1984, 1; 29 August 1984, 1; and 19 September 1984, 8.

44. Interview with John B. Anderson, 24 October 1994.

45. Lesher, *George Wallace,* 238.

46. See Gladwin Hill, "Wallace Group on Coast Opens Campaign for 1968," *New York Times,* 21 June 1967, 28; "A Third Party in 1968? The George Wallace Story," *U.S. News & World Report,* 20 March 1967, 54–60; and Lesher, *George Wallace,* 387–93.

47. Jody Carlson, *George C. Wallace and the Politics of Powerlessness* (New Brunswick, N.J.: Transaction, 1981), 74, 76, 77.

48. *New York Times,* 30 August 1968, 15.

49. See *New York Times,* 17 November 1968, 66; 5 May 1969, 22; 27 May 1969, 17; 22 June 1969, 34; 20 July 1969, 44; 8 December 1969, 38. On Wallace's continuing interest in running a third-party campaign in 1972, see Lesher, *George Wallace,* 461–62; and Carlson, *George C. Wallace and the Politics of Powerlessness,* 142.

50. *New York Times,* 15 July 1972, 11; 30 July 1972, 38; 4 August 1972, 37; 5 August 1972, 12; 6 August 1972, 43.

51. Mickey Griffin, as quoted in Carlson, *George C. Wallace and the Politics of Powerlessness,* 153.

52. Several sources have since pointed out that Perot had already indicated his willingness to get in the race several weeks earlier, at a reception in Nashville. See Germond and Witcover, *Mad as Hell,* 215–16.

53. On the role of the media in Perot's rise to prominence, see John Zaller, "The Rise and Fall of Candidate Perot," IGS Working Paper 93–31, Institute of Governmental Studies, University of California at Berkeley, 1993.

54. This account of the Perot organization draws on Germond and Witcover, *Mad as Hell*, esp. chaps. 12, 17, 20, and 26; Timothy Noah, "Perot Waters His Grass Roots Heavily, Paying 'Volunteers' and Orchestrating Poll of Supporters," *Wall Street Journal*, 30 September 1992, A16; and *New York Times*, 17 April 1992, 1; 23 May 1992, 8; and 1 October 1992, 1.

55. Interview with Orson Swindle, former executive director of United We Stand, America, 27 January 1995.

56. See *New York Times*, 12 January 1993, 1; 17 January 1993, 1; 24 January 1993, 18; 8 February 1993, 13; 21 February 1993, 22; and 1 June 1993, 1.

57. The best overview of the diversity on the current third-party scene is J. David Gillespie, *Politics at the Periphery: Third Parties in Two-Party America* (Columbia: University of South Carolina Press, 1993).

58. The distinction between mass and cadre parties was originally developed in Duverger, *Political Parties*, 61–90. For a major reformulation and extension of the idea, see Leon D. Epstein, *Political Parties in Western Democracies* (New York: Praeger, 1967).

59. See "Constitution of the Socialist Party USA," Article 3; "Bylaws of the Libertarian Party," Article 7; and "Constitution of the Communist Party of the United States of America," Article 3.

60. Our account of the Libertarian Party's presidential nomination process draws on three principal sources:

(1) "The Bylaws and Convention Rules of the Libertarian Party," September 1993.

(2) Interviews with a number of Libertarian Party members, including Bill Winter, director of communications for the national Libertarian Party, 12 October 1994; Jeff Emery, chair, New Hampshire Libertarian Party, 18 October 1994; and Harry Browne, candidate for the 1996 Libertarian Party nomination, 19 October 1994.

(3) Press coverage of several recent Libertarian nomination contests, as detailed in note 62 below.

61. The Libertarian Party bylaws also make provision for a small number of ex-officio delegates, including its national officers, the members of its national committee, and all of its former presidential and vice-presidential candidates.

62. For accounts of some recent Libertarian presidential nomination contests, see *New York Times*, 30 August 1983, 14; 2 September 1983, 15; 4 September 1983, 30; 31 May 1987, 27; 4 September 1987, 10; and 6 September 1987, 35.

63. See the interview with David McReynolds in Smallwood, *The Other Candidates*, 56–78.

64. For evidence that voting for independents increases as voters become more dissatisfied with both major-party nominees, see Rosenstone, Behr, and Lazarus, *Third Parties*, 169–70. For evidence of the declining popularity of both major-party nominees, see *Gallup Opinion Index*, no. 177 (April-May 1980), 22; and Martin P. Wattenberg, *The Rise of Candidate-Centered Politics: Presidential Elections of the 1980s* (Cambridge, Mass.: Harvard University Press, 1991), chap. 4.

65. To date, John Anderson is the only non-major-party candidate to receive such funds in the general election. In a year when Reagan and Carter both got

checks for $29.4 million, Anderson received $4.2 million.

66. See Milton Friedman, *Capitalism and Freedom* (Chicago: University of Chicago Press, 1962), 15–21.

67. See *Dollar Politics,* 3d ed. (Washington, D.C.: CQ Press, 1982), 101. The figure of forty-seven network spots is cited in Richard Brookhiser, "The Party's Over," *National Review,* 21 October 1991, 33.

68. See Germond and Witcover, *Blue Smoke and Mirrors,* 236–37; and Bisnow, *Diary of a Dark Horse,* 316.

69. See, among others, Rosenstone, Behr, and Lazarus, *Third Parties;* Smallwood, *The Other Candidates;* Mazmanian, *Third Parties;* and Key, *Politics, Parties, and Pressure Groups,* chap. 10.

10

Does Party Reform
Have a Future?

ANDREW E. BUSCH AND JAMES W. CEASER

Reform means positive or constructive change. So it is hardly surprising that few wish to be considered enemies of reform. Better to capture the label of reform, even if it is to undo what the reformers have just done. The meaning of reform is always changing, and one generation's reforms become the next generation's orthodoxies.

Any concrete discussion of reform therefore requires that one adopt a specific frame of reference. For our purposes here, *reform* will refer to the changes in the presidential nominating process inspired by the 1968 New Politics movement inside the Democratic Party. That movement succeeded in transforming the basic system of presidential nomination in the United States for both political parties. The pre-1968 system was characterized by a process in which the majority of national convention delegates were selected in caucus/convention procedures and in which the state and local party organizations held a large part of the decision-making power. This system was supplanted after 1968 by a primary-centered process focusing on the national candidates in which the role played by the state and local party organizations was minimal. The scope of this transformation is demonstrated by the example of Hubert Humphrey's nomination in 1968. Humphrey became the Democratic Party's nominee that year without entering or winning a single state primary. This campaign strategy would have been inconceivable four years later. Since 1972, no candidate has been nominated without competing in the primaries and winning the largest share of primary delegates.

The most important changes of the reform era occurred at the outset, in the two years leading up to the election of 1972. But the full implementation of the reform agenda continued for more than a decade. Following every presidential election from 1968 through 1988, the Democratic Party established a national party commission to revise the party's nomination rules. This process amounted to an institutionalization of reform, in which prospective candidates and different groups in the party came to *expect* that the rules would be revised before the next election. As time went on, however, the link between these quadrennial exercises in change and the original reform impulse grew more tenuous. After 1976, some of the "reform" commissions sought modifications, amounting at times to rollbacks of the original reforms. The meaning of reform itself began to grow more obscure, as the conflicts focused on ever more arcane matters presupposing fluency in a new reform language ("thresholds," "front-loading," and "windows"). Yet at the end of the day in 1988, the essential reform system, modified slightly by certain counterreform measures, remained firmly intact.

The 1992 election brought that unusual kind of "event" that falls into the Holmesian (Sherlock) category of the dog that did not bark, that is, an occurrence whose significance is notable by virtue of the fact that it did not take place and so was never noticed. For the first time since 1968, no party commission was established to revisit the nomination rules. The whole process of institutionalized party reform ended, with neither a bang nor a whimper. To the extent there remained any public claimants to the label of reform in the electoral arena in 1992, they were to be found far from the Democratic Party in a grassroots movement to establish term limits for members of Congress.

This new situation prompts us to pose the obvious question: are there any imminent prospects for further revisions of the nominating system, or are we now entering a period of stability in the nominating process? Our argument in this chapter is twofold. First, following the line of analysis just sketched, the reform impulse of 1968 and the counterreform reaction of the early 1980s have indeed burned themselves out. In this sense, we have clearly entered a postreform period. Furthermore, an analysis of past historical cases indicates that a major system change such as the one that occurred after 1968 depends on the appearance of three factors: a broad popular movement, a specific electoral crisis, and the prospect of concrete political gain by a specific candidate or party. While no one can predict when a confluence of these three factors will reoccur (and with it the likelihood of another major change), for the moment there is no indication of any such development inside the major parties.

Nevertheless, and here we move to the second part of our argument, there are important changes in the nomination system already taking place as we approach the 1996 election; and there remains a reasonably strong prospect of revisions thereafter, perhaps even major ones. This paradoxical conclusion does not so much contradict as add to the first argument. Our argument here is that there are sources driving change in the system today that are different from those that produced previous system changes. Two such sources merit our attention.

First, within the current structure of the reform system, a significant, though unplanned, development has been taking place. Beginning in 1980, and with a huge leap since 1992, states have been rescheduling their primaries and delegate selection contests to take place in a five-week period at the beginning of the nomination season. If the timing of the delegate selection contests constitutes a major element of the system, this new "packed" arrangement already represents an important revision. When this change becomes apparent to the American people, as it surely will, a choice of a sort will be posed. Either the public and the parties will let this arrangement stand, effectively endorsing it, or they will insist on further revision, whether it is to "rationalize" this development or to reject it and seek a new relationship between the primaries and the party conventions. The final outcome may depend on how important parts of the population judge the specific results of the process in 1996 or 2000.

A second source of change, while it may be less likely, holds the potential for a far more dramatic transformation. The type of campaign waged in 1992 by Ross Perot may be seen as challenging the whole concept of party nominations. Perot presented himself for the presidency, not as a party candidate, but as an individual. He was nonetheless widely considered as being "presented" or "nominated." If, as many argue, a Perot-type candidacy is not a mere aberration but the harbinger of a new and viable method for seeking the presidency, we would then be witnessing an end to the long era of monopoly status of nomination by political parties and the advent of a personalist component in the presidential selection process. Personal nominations would accompany, if not finally replace, party nominations. The conflict between "personalism" and "partyism" in fact brings to the surface again one of the oldest and most vexing problems of presidential selection, and one which, incidentally, is confronting many other nations in the world with elected chief executives.

Pre-1968 Nominating Systems

The prospects for future revision of the nominating process cannot be weighed without first examining the circumstances and motivations that have accompanied major changes in the past. A brief survey of these changes should help identify some of the causal factors associated with past reforms.

The original system of presidential selection as envisaged by the Founders was predicated on the idea of individualism or personalism, in which the public and the electors would focus on the positions and the merits of the different contenders. Political parties of the type we now know were neither envisioned nor desired, and there would thus be no permanently organized nominating bodies. The selection system was to be institutionalized by the Constitution and supporting state laws. The functions of presentation (or nomination) and election were combined into a single constitutional process in the Electoral College.

This system did not survive the first decade of the Republic. By the end of Washington's second term, political parties had developed, growing out of the deep theoretical differences and repeated policy disputes between Alexander Hamilton and Thomas Jefferson. Each of the two parties (the Federalists and the Republicans) quickly saw the need from the standpoint of its own interests to establish a mechanism for designating a single presidential nominee; otherwise, the party would divide its strength among a number of contenders. Personal ambition had to be regulated in the name of the higher purpose of the party. The mechanism both parties adopted was the congressional caucus, a meeting of each party's adherents in Congress.

The congressional caucus functioned relatively effectively until the collapse of the Federalist Party after the election of 1816. The prospect of one-party rule made the Republican nomination tantamount to election. At the same time, however, it undercut much of the justification for having a nomination in the first place. If there was no real opposition party, if indeed parties themselves were undesirable (as most then believed), then why maintain a nominating mechanism? The caucus posed a threat to the principle of the separation of powers, as the Founders had explicitly rejected legislative selection of the president in order to ensure the president's independence from the Congress. And "King Caucus"—as the institution came to be known—was portrayed as an elitist system of secret decision making, hardly the kind of arrangement that could win public confidence in an increasingly democratic era.[1]

The death knell for the caucus was sounded in 1824 when four "defeated" candidates persisted in staying in the race for the presidency despite the caucus's designation of an official nominee, William Crawford. The election of 1824 marked more than a repudiation of the caucus, however. It represented a rejection of the entire idea of party competition, a development that had already been celebrated in the Monroe administration's proud proclamation of the existence of a nonpartisan "era of good feeling." The election of 1824 was a fully personalist campaign in which candidates ran as individuals and were "nominated" by makeshift bodies. The new personalism of 1824, operating in a context without any institutional mediation by the Electoral College, produced highly populist appeals directed at fomenting divisions among different sections and segments of the electorate. The result was a fracturing of the electoral vote that threw the election into the House of Representatives.[2]

Alarmed at the tendencies of this new system, Martin Van Buren took the lead in attempting to reverse it and reinstitute party competition. Working skillfully behind the scenes, Van Buren connected the rump of the old Jeffersonian party to Jackson's candidacy in 1828 and simultaneously encouraged the formation of an opposition party. A party, he realized, could not exist without multiple parties and hence a party system. He sought to lay the foundation for public acceptance of parties as legitimate parts of our political system and as the recognized instruments for the nomination of presidential candidates. His main objective was to control the genie of populist personalism in the pursuit of the presidency, which he was convinced would lead to a demagogic style of politics, to empty and short-term appeals, and to an increased factionalization of the electorate.[3]

When the parties publicly reappeared in the 1830s, they wisely jettisoned the discredited congressional caucus. Following the lead of the small Anti-Masonic Party, Jacksonian Democrats turned to a national convention to nominate presidential candidates. Originally a mass meeting of local party activists, the convention quickly evolved into a regularized representative assembly operating not under the aegis of federal or state law but under the "private" legal status of the parties. The parties established their own rules for delegate apportionment, for the writing and adoption of party platforms, and for the nomination of candidates. An indication of the parties' independent status can be seen in the Democrats' adoption, under insistence of southern members, of a rule requiring a two-thirds majority for nomination (which remained in effect until 1936), while the Whigs and later the Republicans proceeded by a simple majority. Notwithstanding this private legal status, the parties were now recognized as vital components of the political system, performing, among other things, the important function of nominating presidential candidates.

In contrast to the congressional caucus, the national convention system was a far more decentralized process. It depended for its vitality on state and local party organizations, which emerged as the real centers of power in this system. The nominating process consisted of a pyramid-style upward flow of power from local "primaries" (what we would call caucuses) to local conventions, state conventions, and ultimately the national convention. The party committees played the central role in the process; they maintained their position through a combination of organizational superiority, adroit use of the rules, sheer inertia, power over patronage, and, on occasion, fraud. The national convention itself was characterized by discretionary decision making by the delegates and bargaining among party leaders. The convention emerged as an important institution in its own right, insofar as it truly determined the nominee instead of merely ratifying a choice that had already been determined. It was at the convention that nominees were decided, and more often than not the results could not be known with any certainty before that meeting took place. Except for incumbent presidents, potential candidates generally avoided public campaigning before the convention. Such campaigning was considered a sign of dangerous ambition, and in any case a candidate could not win the nomination by such a strategy. Both symbolically and substantively, the party tended to come first, the candidate second.[4]

The United States had thus changed from a personalist regime in 1824 to a party, or semiparty, regime. Wearing a party label and receiving a party nomination were now requirements for election to the presidency, and the party label itself was a prime consideration in the voting decision of many citizens. Yet while parties came to be accepted, they could never fully eclipse consideration of the personal qualities and attributes of presidential candidates. An element of individualism remained a strong factor in the thinking of the public, and efforts by the parties to discount it too much provoked resistance and helped fuel a reaction against them.

By the end of the nineteenth century, the convention system itself began to come under sustained assault. Critics charged it with four flaws: it was too closed to popular influence; it was corrupt; it promoted mediocre candidates; and it depreciated and blurred matters of genuine principle. To some critics, these specific problems with the nomination mechanism were only manifestations of a still deeper problem. The American political system in their estimation had become too beholden to parties. Change was sought in one or both of two overlapping, but also partly contradictory, ideas: either the basis on which parties were put together had to be entirely changed from a motivation of interest to one of principle and/or candidates and individual leaders had to be set free altogether from the grips of party and permitted once again to operate on their own as individuals. The effort to navigate between these two ideas took the form of elevating dramatically the place of personalism *inside* the party; the character of the political party was modified from its nineteenth-century model, in which the party claimed to stand above the individual, to a new candidate or leader-centered conception. Woodrow Wilson best articulated this new idea, which he believed could be summed up in eight words: "No leaders, no principles; no principles, no parties." Wilson invented the modern idea of "leadership" in the presidency, which he argued could be secured only through a change in the nominating system. The convention system made it "impossible—or, at any rate, in the highest degree unlikely—that our presidents should ever be leaders again."[5] A new system was needed: nomination by direct primary.

The movement to curtail the influence of the nineteenth-century parties can be traced back as far as 1866, when self-styled "reformers" began to persuade some states to bring political parties under the jurisdiction of state law. Laws were adopted to regulate local party meetings and were eventually broadened to cover state conventions, party committees, and a host of other party affairs. Then, in the 1890s, another wave of change produced the first direct primaries—what we today simply call primaries—in which voters cast ballots directly for party nominees for state and local offices without the mediating influence of the party structure.[6] In the early part of this century, the Progressive movement seized on the direct primary as another tool in the arsenal of reform along with the initiative, referendum, and recall. The Progressives conceived of the primary as a means of bypassing existing party organizations and transforming the character of the parties.

It was not until 1912, however, that presidential preference primaries became a feature of the presidential nominating system. The shift to primaries in fourteen states in that year was driven in part by principle, but it was also clearly tied to practical political considerations in the Republican nomination campaign. Progressives believed that one of their own, Theodore Roosevelt or Robert LaFollette, would fare better in primaries than in the old party-centered processes, which would presumably favor incumbent William Howard Taft.[7] Events proved the Progressives right. Roosevelt dominated the primaries, but he was denied the nomination when Taft was able to hold the nonprimary delegates. Roosevelt then proceeded to bolt from the Republican Party, taking his nomination defeat as final proof of the corrupt and closed nature of the convention system.

Moved by Progressive ideas, President Woodrow Wilson in 1913 proposed the establishment of a national primary. While this idea made no headway in Congress, the general movement made headway in many of the states. By 1916, twenty-three states with 65 percent of the delegates had adopted presidential primaries. Yet with the political triumph of Progressive forces inside both political parties, and with the shift of national attention to foreign affairs with World War I, the reform impulse began to recede, falling far short of permanently achieving its objective. Instead of a national primary or a system dominated by state primaries, a new hybrid system emerged that came to be known as the "mixed system." This system represented an uneasy marriage between the ideas and the institutional arrangements of the nineteenth-century idea of the party and the new, Progressive conception. The older elements clearly held the upper hand. After 1920, caucus-convention procedures were in use in approximately two-thirds of the states, while the remaining third (from fifteen to eighteen states) held primaries. The process still culminated in a national convention, and the national convention remained the point of meaningful decision. Most delegates retained discretion, and the state and local party organizations remained the predominant force.

Even the component of the existing primaries did not operate entirely in the way Progressives had hoped. While candidates began openly campaigning before the convention, they usually seriously contested only a few primaries. Even when they did so, the predominance of winner-take-all rules and the frequency of primaries in which presidential preference and delegate selection votes were divorced meant that there was no guarantee that candidates would receive delegates in proportion to their votes. When combined with the fact that primaries produced only one-third of the delegates, these complexities produced a strategic environment in which candidates entered primaries more to prove electability to party leaders than to win delegates. The primaries served as an important outlet for public opinion, but public opinion did not directly control the process.[8]

The mixed system came crashing down after 1968. The New Politics movement, a combination of the left wing of the Democratic Party and the relatively moderate elements of the anti-Vietnam war movement, organized to deny Lyndon Johnson renomination. With Eugene McCarthy (and later Robert Kennedy) as its candidates, the movement forced Johnson out of the race. Yet when Hubert Humphrey took Johnson's place and opted for a campaign that avoided participation in all contested primaries, the New Politics forces proved unable to stop him. (Robert Kennedy, the more formidable opponent to Humphrey, had been assassinated after the California primary.) To the New Politics forces, Humphrey's nomination was illegitimate, the clear product of a corrupt and arbitrary system.[9] The New Politics movement had now also become a movement for party reform. As in 1912, there was confusion about whether reform meant a new kind of party organization that would continue to exercise many important prerogatives or an individualistic, candidate-centered nomination system operating under the loose umbrella of the party label. Initially, it was the latter idea that prevailed.

Presidential Nominations, 1968–92

Out of the chaos of the 1968 Chicago convention came the Commission on Delegate Selection and Party Structure, better known, after its two chairmen, as the McGovern-Fraser Commission. Seeking to promote the new virtue of "participation," the commission ultimately produced eighteen "guidelines," many of which were nevertheless often enforced as binding rules. Under these rules, caucuses were made less susceptible to influence by party regulars; primaries were made more plebiscitary (in the sense of selecting and tying delegates to a national candidate); and ex-officio delegates (party officials who became delegates automatically by virtue of their offices) were prohibited.[10]

Following the 1972 election, the Democrats established the Commission on Delegate Selection and Party Structure (or Mikulski Commission), which probably represented the zenith of reformism. It moderated a few of the McGovern-Fraser rules, but otherwise consolidated or expanded the reform impulse. In the view of political scientist David Price, "the Mikulski

Commission weakened the hand of party leaders even further."[11] Proportional representation (PR) requirements were toughened, as PR was mandated in caucus states, winner-take-all primaries were banned, and PR was preferred in primary states. (Plurality elections—so-called "loophole primaries"—were permitted as long as at least 75 percent of the delegates were chosen at the congressional district level or lower.) Caucus participants were required to declare a candidate preference, and slate-making procedures were modified to benefit candidate organizations.

The reforms of these two commissions produced what Byron Shafer would later call "the greatest systematic change in presidential nominating procedures in all of American history."[12] Overall, the party organizations had much less influence over the nomination, and the individual candidates (and, incidentally, committed interest groups and the media) had much more. In 1968, 96 percent of Democratic governors, 61 percent of senators, and 32 percent of representatives attended the Democratic National Convention as delegates; by 1976, only 44 percent of Democratic governors, 18 percent of senators, and 14 percent of representatives were delegates.[13] The number of states holding primaries doubled from 1968 to 1976, as some states attempted to conform to the new ethos of participatory democracy and others sought refuge from confusing or threatening elements of the new caucus rules by shifting to primaries.[14]

The Commission on Presidential Nomination and Party Structure (or Winograd Commission) of 1978 extended some of the original reforms even farther. For example, the commission moved back in the direction of demographic quotas, calling for "remedial action to overcome the effects of past discrimination," a decision bolstered by a subsequent Democratic National Committee ruling that states must equally divide their delegations among men and women. The Winograd Commission also completed the logical progression toward proportional representation by eliminating the option of the "loophole primary." And delegates were bound even more tightly to candidates. Yet in certain other respects, the Winograd Commission began to move away from reform, especially in instances where the rules might assist the incumbent President (Jimmy Carter) and make any challenges more difficult. The commission raised the thresholds necessary for candidates to receive delegates, lengthened filing deadlines for primary candidates, added pledged delegate slots for party leaders, and attempted to shorten the primary season and reduce the impact of small, early primary states by imposing an allowable primary period, or "window."[15]

In addition to changing the character of the nominating process, the reforms had opened up a new *method* by which to regulate the nominating system. This was the vehicle of centralized party rulemaking. The reformers' experience with the McGovern-Fraser Commission and later the Mikulski and Winograd commissions had convinced them that such national party commissions could serve as a kind of sovereign legislative instrument to alter the nation's nomination procedures. The commissions could pass rules; and because the Democrats held majorities in most state legislatures, the party would be able to impose its will on state law no less than on state party rules. Furthermore, the primacy of national party rules over state laws in this area had in some ways been recognized and endorsed in a series of Supreme Court decisions in the decade following the McGovern-Fraser reforms.[16] Yet it was just about this time, in 1981, that the reform impulse began to fade. After crushing defeats in 1972 and 1980, many Democrats began asking whether the new nominating system had not divorced the party too much from presidential nominations and strained party unity by providing too much encouragement to weaker candidates. Furthermore, the states began to react against the "legislative" pretensions of national Democratic reform commissions. True, the Democratic Party could ban delegates from the national convention who were not selected in accord with national party rules. But the Democratic Party could not force states to change their laws; and when states threatened to resist the national Democratic Party—as some of them now began to do—the national party faced the risk of securing compliance only at the politically self-defeating cost of alienating a large part of those states' voters. In short, in many cases, the mechanism of enforcement proved too severe and too impractical to contemplate using, and the commissions saw that there were clear limits in practice to their "legislative" authority over the nomination system.

The response to the growing doubts about reform was the Hunt Commission of 1982. This commission was the one great attempt under the banner of reform to rein in the reform impulse. In an effort to bring an element of the party back into the process, the Hunt Commission established, by national rules, a new category of unpledged "superdelegates," which, practically speaking, was another name for the ex-officio delegates excluded a decade previously. These unpledged superdelegates were primarily to be members of Congress and the Democratic National Committee who, it was hoped, would inject into the process a large element of mature deliberation by those having a stake in the well-being of the *party.* Comprising some 15 percent of all the delegates, the superdelegates were to be selected outside the plebiscitary system and without being bound to any particular candidate.[17] The Hunt Commission also restored the option of nonproportional primaries—an option many states exercised in 1984 and 1988—and suggested (though it did not mandate) that a marginal shift from primaries to caucuses might be in order.[18] As a consequence, the number of primaries in 1984 reached a post–1972 low of twenty-five, and a large number of them utilized nonproportional delegate allocation systems that gave an advantage to the winner.

Together, these changes—the addition of superdelegates, the resurgence of caucuses, and the importance of nonproportional primaries—were responsible for helping to put Walter Mondale over the top in 1984 against the insurgent-style candidacies of Gary Hart and Jesse Jackson.[19] Hart and particularly Jackson complained bitterly about the nomination system, denouncing it as "unfair." Evoking the old standard of reform, Jackson demanded an abolition of caucuses, the binding of the superdelegates, and the reimposition of proportional representation. No such radical result was forthcoming. The "Fairness Commission" that followed the 1984 election agreed to make minor changes in superdelegate selection procedures (they were to be selected later in the process) and once again to reduce the thresholds for proportional primaries.[20]

The events of 1988 virtually repeated those of 1984. Jesse Jackson, again a candidate, attacked nonproportional primaries and superdelegates. As in 1984, the superdelegates voted overwhelmingly for his opponent, this time Michael Dukakis. To mollify Jackson, Dukakis followed a tactic other nominees had previously employed: concessions on future party rules in exchange for political support during the campaign. Dukakis agreed to another set of rules changes, which would have reduced the number of superdelegates and eliminated nonproportional primaries. The Democratic National Committee balked at any plan to reduce the number of superdelegates, but ratified the decision on proportional representation.

We have said almost nothing about the Republicans in this discussion, largely because their stance on reform had little to do with the actual changes that took place. Republicans were in most important respects pulled along by the Democrats into the new system. This was truest of the growing ratio of primaries to caucus/convention states; the decision to adopt primaries was made by state governments and was generally applied to both parties. In certain other respects, where the procedures are controlled by internal party rules, such as the conduct of caucuses, or where the state primary laws differentiate between the parties, as on the degree of proportionality, the Republican process has not adopted many of the Democratic reform rules. (It should be noted, however, that some of the procedural abuses endemic to certain Democratic caucus systems before 1968 were not present in the Republican Party.) While there is much differentiation today in the details of delegate selection between the two parties, in broad outline both parties have operated under the same basic system in which primaries overshadow caucuses, candidates overshadow parties, and the national conventions no longer actually decide the nominees but ratify the choice of primary voters.[21]

The Causes of System Change

The preceding narrative can help identify some of the elements that have caused changes in the nominating system in the past and that, if present, would presumably do so again in the future. Three factors stand out as the most likely causes of transformations of the nominating system: a change-oriented movement; an electoral crisis; and an anticipated political gain by a movement, a candidate, or a party.

CHANGE-ORIENTED MOVEMENTS

One common factor propelling nominating reforms in the last century has been the presence of a powerful change-oriented political movement. The Populists of the 1890s argued for direct primaries and numerous other electoral reforms. They helped prepare the ground for the Progressive movement, which brought the direct primary into the presidential nominating process. Similarly, the New Politics movement drove the post–1968 reforms that were responsible for establishing the boundaries of the current system.

The connection between movements and nominating system changes is a complex one. Not all movements have brought nomination changes in their train (the conservative movement, for example, was able to gain success in the Republican Party in 1964 and 1980 by using the existing mechanisms of nomination); and not every change in the rules is driven by a movement. Movements nonetheless have been responsible for launching the major changes of this century in 1912 and in 1968. In these two instances, the philosophical orientation of the movements was in favor of a substantial reformation of society, in which the nominating changes were only part of a much broader agenda emphasizing democracy and participation and denigrating intermediate representative institutions, including the parties in their corporate capacity. The nominating reforms they proposed were part of a broader effort to bypass, control, and ultimately cleanse the forces of corruption. These movements also promoted nominating change out of a healthy sense of self-interest, in order to maximize their political strength against entrenched political forces. Thus, the Progressives tried to expand primaries because they calculated that Roosevelt and LaFollette (and, at lower levels, Progressive candidates in general) would do better in primaries than in caucus/convention proceedings, while the New Politics adherents believed that the old system had blocked their success in 1968 and that a reformed system would open the way to a New Politics nominee in 1972.

ELECTORAL CRISIS

A second factor common to many of the changes in the nomination system has been the occurrence of some sort of electoral crisis that has thrown the old system into disrepute. The clearest examples are 1824, 1912, and 1968. The debacle of 1824 exposed the factionalism and instability inherent in the congressional caucus in a one-party setting. Fewer than half the congressmen attended the caucus; five candidates ran, splitting the electoral vote sufficiently to require the contingency election to be held in the House, which was a method of presidential selection that virtually all agreed was unsatisfactory; and John Quincy Adams won, despite appearing to have had less popular support than Andrew Jackson. The congressional caucus was never used again.

The Taft credentials steamroller at the 1912 Republican National Convention likewise led to a short-term growth in the number of primaries. Progressives used the alleged unfairness of the convention and the organization's control over caucus state delegates, especially in the South where the Republican Party had only a tiny electoral base, as evidence of the undemocratic and corrupt character of the system. Finally, the riots and chaos of the 1968 Democratic National Convention in Chicago went far in delegitimizing the mixed system. Much was made of the fact that Hubert Humphrey was able to win the nomination without ever submitting himself to a test of the primary voters, but the scenes of violence that accompanied the convention were at least as powerful.

POLITICAL INTERESTS OF CANDIDATES AND PARTIES

A third factor that has hastened nomination changes along in specific cases has been the anticipation of an important political advantage by a movement, a candidate, or a party. The increased chance of winning the nomination and the presidency provides some of the energy needed to set in motion broader plans for change. Such was the case, as noted, for the Progressive and the New Politics movements, as well as for the candidacies of Andrew Jackson, Theodore Roosevelt, Eugene McCarthy, and George McGovern. The establishment of the precedent after 1972 of quadrennial commissions virtually invited further efforts at revision by the candidates, who naturally wished to see the rules written in a way that would protect or promote their interests. Thus, many of the recommendations of the Winograd Commission clearly sought to benefit President Carter, while some provisions of the Hunt Commission were promoted by those attached to the anticipated candidacies of Edward Kennedy and Walter Mondale. Likewise, some of the changes made after the 1984 and 1988 races were designed alternatively to soothe and to thwart Jesse Jackson.[22] What regularly started the process of revision were complaints by losing candidates that the rules were unfair. Such claims tend to gain credibility when the rules are new and different, for it is then that the rules stand out as an immediate and visible cause on which one may place blame.

The political parties, too, can on occasion drive the process of change to protect or realize the "interest" of the parties. We put "interest" here in quotations because it is an interest of a different kind than that of the candidates. The candidate's interest is to win, and the rules are seen as instrumental to this goal. The party's interest, at least as it has been conceived in many cases, has been to fashion rules for the long-term well-being of the party and the nomination process. The party's perspective is institutionalist or constitutionalist, not merely instrumental. Thus the election of 1824, while it was a general electoral crisis, was also a crisis for the old Jeffersonian Republican Party and for parties in general. The subsequent adoption of the national nominating convention was one part of the response to that crisis. Another example of party interest attempting to promote change is the Hunt Commission of 1982. Although this commission certainly interested prospective candidates seeking to enhance their political fortunes, it was nonetheless primarily a vehicle for party regulars to reassert the party's interest in the nominating system. Party leaders by 1980 had become convinced that the nominating system had contributed to the electoral defeats of 1972 and 1980 and that it was injurious to the party's well-being. These leaders undertook to help the party by strengthening the influence of the regular organizations and the moderate (and presumably more "electable") forces.[23]

Two points should be kept in mind regarding the factors that have led to past changes in the nominating system. First, it is clear that more than one factor may be operating at a time and that the more that are operating, the more likely it is that any revisions sought will lead to a long-lasting change. Thus in 1912 and 1968, powerful movements, an electoral crisis, and the interest of a particular candidate all coincided to produce a major system change. Second, the prospects for stability in the wake of a revision may depend on the coherence of the original plan and its degree of theoretical preparation. The transformation of the electoral system after 1824 was well thought out and aimed at certain clear objectives; it produced a remarkably stable nomination procedure that lasted for the rest of the century. By contrast, the reformers of 1968 paid more attention to what they opposed than to what, exactly, they were for. Some proponents of reform changed their minds as the reform process proceeded, and after a time many no longer seemed certain about what "reform" really intended to accomplish: a new kind of organization or an end to all organizational influence.

The End of the Reform Era

The preceding analysis of historical changes in the nominating system can help shed light on what has happened to the reform impulse of 1968. Democratic presidential politics in and immediately after 1968 saw all three of the key factors in play: a powerful, change-oriented movement; an electoral crisis of legitimacy replete with televised riots, tear gas, and blood; and the candidacies of Eugene McCarthy, whose supporters in 1968 considered themselves aggrieved by the results of the process, and George McGovern, whose supporters looked ahead in 1972 to the triumph of their candidate and their cause.

The electoral crisis of 1968 ended, and no similar crisis was repeated. Indeed, the New Politics movement had its way in 1972, both with the procedures of the nomination process and with the selection of the nominee, George McGovern. The existence of an electoral crisis having been removed as a motive, the impetus for reform was then left to the philosophical force of the movement and the interests of candidates and the party. The zeal for reform waned with time—first with its own obvious success in transforming the system and then with some confusion or embarrassment about its precise objectives. By 1980, the reform impulse was largely exhausted. The impetus for change then rested either with the party trying to recapture a role for itself or with the candidate seeking to win some temporary advantage. The various "reforms" after 1984 were entertained less in the spirit of general reform than of deal making to mollify important parts of the Democratic coalition. Yet interest by itself (especially candidate interest) is the most ephemeral of the factors, and the least capable of driving deep and long-lasting change.

Finally, in 1992, none of these three factors surfaced. There was no movement; there was no crisis; and there was no candidate's interest that was seriously compromised by the rules, nor did those in the Democratic Party, whose nominee won the election, feel that the party's interests had been ill served. Had the 1992 election turned out differently—had the Democrats with Bill Clinton lost the sixth of their last seven races—a consideration of party interest might well have led to a fundamental rethinking of the system. There were indications that such a process was under way in the spring of 1992, when party leaders such as Walter Mondale and former Virginia governor Gerald Baliles publicly expressed concern over the nominating process. (The problem, one should recall, was that most of the first-tier candidates—persons such as Mario Cuomo, Richard Gephardt, Al Gore, and Bill Bradley—had chosen not to run because of Bush's seemingly insurmountable lead; in the spring, all of the existing candidates in the field seemed to present huge liabilities because of political weakness or scandals.) In response to this situation, Baliles, for example, proposed to hold a closed convention for party activists and officials only, which would select a field of candidates from which the nominee would later be chosen in a national primary.[24] All this talk ended when Bill Clinton managed to overcome his earlier difficulties, gain credibility as a candidate, and win the presidency. Clinton's victory silenced the critics.

The Republicans also had an opportunity to think about changes in the system when they found themselves fastened to George Bush in the summer of 1992, despite Bush's "free-fall" after the Democratic convention. The lack of flexibility and discretion on the part of the delegates and the lack of influence by party leaders made it impossible to contemplate a change of nominees. There was a mini movement at the last hour by some Republicans to call on Bush to step aside, but there was no discussion about the arrangements that had led to the dilemma.[25]

System Change via the Primary Schedule

Thus far, we have looked at the standard, historical pattern for change of the nominating system. Yet, as noted, there are today two other possible sources for revision of the system. One derives from the schedule of the delegate selection contests. The impetus for this change derives, indirectly and unintentionally, from the reforms. Before the reforms, the advantage to be gained from positioning a state at an early point in the sequence was small because the nomination decision was made by the delegates and party leaders. After the reforms it quickly became clear that the primaries decided the nominee. The timing of a state in the sequence then became far more important. Legislators in many states began to think that their state would exercise more influence over the outcome if the state were positioned near the front of the process, when all the candidates were still in the race and when the election verdict could help establish momentum for the victor. Even more clearly, legislators from states with contests near the end of the process began to see that their states often had no influence at all on the final decision, as the nominee was already decided before the state held its primary; and as more states moved toward the front of the process, the problem for those that remained near the end became even more acute, as the probability grew that the decision would be made before their primary was held.

The "logic" of this situation began to work its effect in the 1980s. It was accelerated by a conscious plan of southern Democratic state legislators prior to 1984 and 1988 to create a kind of early regional primary, "Super Tuesday," in an effort to enhance the prospects for nominating a moderate Democratic candidate. Since 1992, the movement of states to the front has been driven again by the individual calculations of the states, now all the more conscious of the possibility of being simply frozen out of exercising any influence. California, Ohio, and New York have moved up their primary dates, and a number of other states are contemplating a change.[26] The result, of course, is that the "front" has lost most of its significance, for almost every other state is there. Most of the delegates will be chosen in a five-week period between mid-February and late March. Indeed, over 75 percent of the pledged delegates will be chosen before 1 April, and the nation's eight largest primaries will be held within a three-week period. No single state planned this new schedule, but neither is any state in a position to stop it. Each state acting rationally on its own has produced an overall arrangement that many states might have preferred to avoid.

The consequences of this new schedule, most analysts argue, are likely to be enormous, although there is little agreement on exactly what those consequences will be. The *Washington Post* has called the new system a "virtual national primary," which is an easy and tempting description.[27] But a more careful analysis of this system's possible effects suggests that it may be very different from a national primary (supposing, of course, one knows what those effects would be). For this reason, we prefer to call this schedule a "packed primary" arrangement.

One prediction often heard about the new arrangement is that it will increase the importance of early fund raising. The argument here is that once the primaries begin, there will not be sufficient time to capitalize on any successes through direct-mail fund raising. According to Mark Shields, the new calendar will make the process "virtually inaccessible for the underfinanced, overlooked long-shot."[28] Perhaps. But there is another possibility. If an underfunded and overlooked candidate should happen to make a breakthrough in Iowa or New Hampshire, he or she may now have a better chance than before to win the nomination. The momentum of the first victory might carry the candidate through the next few weeks, when most of the delegates will now be selected. The model here would be Gary Hart's campaign in 1984, when his victory in New Hampshire, far more than his subsequent fund-raising efforts, carried him to victory in the next round of primaries.

Another effect is that the citizenry will have less time in which to make a decision. Thomas Mann of the Brookings Institution argues that "what [the new calendar] doesn't do is allow you an opportunity to scrutinize a candidate over time and to rethink one's views of his suitability for high office."[29] And because the whole primary season will be radically condensed, candidates will have much less time to spend in each state. The much maligned "tarmac campaign" that characterized the 1988 Super Tuesday primaries, in which candidates frantically sped from one airport appearance to another, will be repeated on a national scale.[30] The ability of voters to form sound first judgments will be constrained, and their opportunity to make second judgments will be virtually eliminated. This general line of analysis is also, obviously, critical of the packed-primary arrangement. It is seen as a far less deliberative process than the previous arrangement, when the campaign unfolded over a long period and in which citizens could revisit the judgments of earlier primaries and assess candidates with more information at their disposal.

Beyond these points, there are two basic conflicting schools of thought about what the packed-primary arrangement may mean for the outcome of the nomination races. A "knockout" school holds that the candidate coming into the first contests with the greatest strength will have an insuperable advantage: "the New Hampshire winner could ride the momentum that a victory there often generates through the entire month of March," all the way to the nomination.[31] In this view, the new calendar "virtually guarantees an early end to the nomination fight."[32] The nominees will be decided by 1 April and will have the next three or four months to await their official coronations at the conventions.

An alternative "deadlock" or "bargaining" school argues that no candidate will likely be able to run effectively everywhere, so candidates will concentrate on regional or demographic pockets that hold for them the greatest promise; the likely result is that no one will be able to win outright a commanding majority of the delegates. The theory of momentum, after all, has so far depended for its operation on an early weeding out of weaker contenders, which leaves the field eventually to only one or two candidates; in the new calendar, there may be too little time to take full advantage of momentum.[33] In the words of one California Republican strategist, "If someone loses New Hampshire, loses Iowa, and comes in second or third on Super Tuesday but wins California, they're right back as the front-runner."[34] Under this scenario, the result of the new system may be that the nomination decision will rest once again with the delegates, perhaps at the convention or more likely in a bargaining process before it meets.[35] The probability of "deadlock" might vary between the Republican Party (which relies heavily on plurality primaries) and the Democratic Party (which uses proportional representation). To the extent that the appeal of the candidates is based more on issue differences than regional appeals, the Democratic Party's greater reliance on PR may produce more fractionalization among the candidates's delegate totals and thus offer a greater probability of "deadlock." In contrast, state Republican parties have shown more party discipline, and if the new arrangement encourages a slew of favorite-son candidacies the Republicans may find themselves with no clear winner emerging from the primaries.

The packed-primary arrangement is of course only one part of a system that includes many other features, not to mention the political factors that come into play in deciding the outcome of any particular campaign. Accordingly, only time and repeated occurrences will enable the social scientist to determine with any confidence what the general consequences of this arrangement might be, as distinct from the results in a particular race. Yet there is no guarantee that time will be forthcoming. It is at least as likely the parties or the American people will make further revisions in the system. For there is one "law," it seems, of change: it is always easiest to revise the rules just after they have been revised (and when social scientists know the least about them). It is when the rules seem new or different that they are most readily viewed as the immediate cause of the outcome. Moreover, if a large segment of the populace should consider the results of 1996 or 2000 unsatisfactory—perhaps the equivalent of an electoral crisis—they may find it easier than usual to attack the rules. After all, the packed arrangement is not a result that anyone has actively promoted. It has no constituency.

Options for Future Change

Within the party nominating system, there are two basic directions that future revisions could take: to consolidate and move farther toward a primary-centered, plebiscitary system; or to reject this system and seek new means for renewed party influence and for decision making by representative procedures. For each of these broad directions, there are in turn two possibilities: a radical and a marginal option.

MORE PLEBISCITARY: RADICAL

The radical plebiscitary option would be to formalize a national primary, eliminating the remaining caucuses and perhaps even eliminating the national convention. This possibility would fulfill the dream of Woodrow Wilson and would seek to "rationalize" the movement toward the packing that has been emerging on its own. The idea here would be very simple and no doubt appealing: since we have a "virtual national primary" now, why not eliminate all the inconveniences and difficulties of virtuality and adopt an actual national primary?

MORE PLEBISCITARY: MARGINAL

The moderate plebiscitary option would be to maintain the existing arrangement, but move the entire calendar back by two months. The nomination race would then end in June as it once did, but it would begin in April or May instead of February. This change might seem a sensible practical modification to the existing system, which most probably concur will now select the candidate too early in the year and not allow for any adjustments to new circumstances. A new starting date would not affect the current order and spacing of primaries, but simply require a two-month postponement, allowing the candidates to trudge together through the slush, rather than the snow, of New Hampshire. Of course, it is difficult to imagine taking such a step without also confronting the question of the logic of the entire schedule of primaries.

Another possibility, proposed by Morris Udall in the Winograd Commission deliberations, would be to have four evenly spaced primary dates within a specified period. In this case, the order of the states would be changed by a national party rule (or perhaps a congressional statute). In the 1980s, Democrats tried with only limited success to regulate the primary calendar by imposing a "window" of time within which primaries had to occur. Yet given the move to the front that has occurred since that time, the states might be less hostile to considering a proposal of this kind today.

LESS PLEBISCITARY: RADICAL

The antiplebiscitary option would be to reconstruct the system along the lines suggested by Gerald Baliles and political scientist Thomas Cronin. Primaries would be retained as the final step in the process, but the party conventions would be strengthened and made more deliberative. Party leaders would attend conventions that would serve as a screening mechanism for potential candidates before the primaries. Several states, including Massachusetts, Minnesota, and Colorado, have such a two-tiered system for state offices in which candidates must reach a specified threshold of support (usually 20 to 30 percent) in party activist-controlled conventions in order to be placed on the primary ballot.

LESS PLEBISCITARY: MARGINAL

The marginal antiplebiscitary option would be to move toward a few more caucuses and fewer primaries (and also perhaps toward more plurality and fewer proportional primaries). That this marginal shift is possible could be seen from what occurred in 1984, when there were just such shifts away from the plebiscitary system. A proposal made by *Congressional Quarterly* correspondent Rhodes Cook would attempt to reverse the "virtual national primary" by limiting primaries to three per week and by reversing the Democrats' rule against nonproportional primaries.[36] The changes here, while they would involve new national party rules, would ultimately rely on the states, acting in a decentralized fashion, to change their primary laws.[37]

An End of Partyism?

The possibilities for revisions of the nomination system discussed so far, no matter whether they were labeled radical or marginal, presuppose the existence of a party-dominated process. The prospect to which we now turn is more genuinely revolutionary in character. According to some analysts, the 1992 presidential campaign has called into question one of the most fundamental features of the presidential selection system: the dominance of the two-party system. The Perot candidacy prefigured the beginning of a transformation either to a multiparty system or, if we take what actually occurred in 1992, to a system in which presidential candidates may now bypass party nominations altogether and, much as they did in 1824, compete on their own as viable contenders. Stated differently, this last possibility holds that the United States is experiencing a breakdown in its system of party nomination and a return to a more personalist system in which individual candidates compete alongside the party nominees.

What is the likelihood of such a transformation? One should, of course, guard against superficial claims about the "unprecedented" character of the Perot campaign. It should be recalled that competition by candidates from outside the major parties is nothing new in American history; and it should also be remembered that the most important previous third-party candidacies in this century—those of Theodore Roosevelt in 1912, Robert M.

LaFollette in 1924, and George C. Wallace in 1968—were all strongly per-
sonalistic campaigns, in the sense that the strength of the party depended almost entirely on the individuals who were running.[38] Yet, even conceding
these points, there is still an argument that the Perot candidacy (along with
the 1980 candidacy of John Anderson, Perot's spiritual forerunner) prefig-
ures a major change in our electoral system. This view merits consideration,
even if we should judge it to be exaggerated.

One novel feature of the Anderson and Perot candidacies was that neither man presented himself as a party leader. For purposes of the electoral
laws in certain states, both in certain instances had to be classified as party
candidates, but this label was nothing more than an inconvenient legal fic-
tion. In Anderson's 1980 platform, which he issued himself, he claimed to
speak "for a patriotism greater than party" and declared that "America
needs an independent president."[39] Anderson held no convention and simply
named his own vice-presidential running mate. Similarly, while Perot from
time to time consulted his volunteers (and after 31 July met with the organization named "United We Stand"), he always offered himself as the people's
candidate. Both Anderson and Perot thus not only waged their campaigns
outside a party but in a sense against the idea of parties.

The possibility for a genuine revival of individualism or personalism,
some would argue, derives from a new environment that presents an opportunity for candidacies of a different kind. This argument points first to the
long-term decline in the strength of political parties. Fewer people today are
attached to the major political parties, and fewer are wedded to their nominees. Independent voters are not only independent of the major parties, but
independent of partyism. The logic of the Perot candidacy in this respect was
simple: if parties are really in decline, why not dispense with them altogether
and simply offer oneself as a "patriot servant"? One may be considered
"nominated" or "presented" in exactly the way that occurred in Perot's case
in 1992—when the candidate passed a certain threshold of support as measured in national public opinion polls.

Second, it is argued that parties are unnecessary in an age of modern
communications. Any viable candidacy must, of course, be able to communicate its message to the public. Yet, whereas once this capacity could be
supplied only by the parties—by their manpower, their ability to distribute
the candidate's message, and their influence or control over many newspapers—today the individual candidate can communicate to the public on
his own through the news media (especially by television news). If enough
journalists determine that a candidate should be covered, then that candidate is already "in" the race and can deliver his message; and if an independent manages to be invited to appear on the televised presidential debates
(as Perot was able to do in 1992), he will be that much closer to equality
with the major-party candidates.

It might even be said that an independent enjoys a certain communications advantage. News is a form of communication that emphasizes what is new, that is, what is dramatic and different or what looks to be a deviation from previous expectations. A personal campaign, for now at least, falls into this category. For this reason, Ross Perot in 1992 enjoyed extensive news coverage. As much as journalists detested Perot, they could not resist the story. Moreover, with the recent growth in the number of television channels, there are today a great number of shows that provide a forum for candidates to reach the public. The traditional gateway controlled by the major news journalists has been circumvented, with the effect being to equalize further the communications possibilities between a personal candidacy and the candidacies of the major parties.

Finally, it is argued that the extent of personalism that already exists in the current party nomination process has prepared the way for a completely personalist and independent candidacy. Modern candidates vying for their party's nomination sometimes run campaigns that are so "candidate centered" that the campaign of an independent does not appear anomalous to the American public. Pure personalism represents only a change in degree, not in kind, from the personalism already being practiced.

Conclusion

The future of the presidential nominating system depends on two fundamental questions: what processes will govern nominations within the parties, and to what extent will party nominations be rendered irrelevant by the rise of extraparty personalism?

Concerning the more conventional question of party process, several conclusions can be drawn. The impulse driving the reforms since 1968 is philosophically exhausted, the movement is extinct, and the crisis is long passed. The system has essentially stabilized for the time being, except for decentralized changes like primary "packing," which may prove to be quite significant but which are unconnected to any deliberate effort to change the system as a whole. Despite the exhaustion of the last set of major reforms, the interests of candidates and perhaps of parties will continue to drive marginal changes in the system. Major change will require the emergence of a coherent intellectual argument for change combined with a powerful political movement and/or an electoral crisis. It is impossible to predict, of course, when these things might happen. It is much less risky to predict that they will happen sometime and that when they do, the next wave of major systemic change will not be far behind.

What also cannot be predicted is what direction that revision will take. Thus far, almost all systemic changes have moved in the participatory and plebiscitary direction. Only the shift from the congressional caucus to the national convention system also moved in the direction of stronger parties. Much depends on the nature of the movement (which has thus far almost always been more participatory/plebiscitary in philosophy and interest) or the crisis (which could work in any direction), as well as the strength and nature of the opponents of change.

As for the second question, the conflict between partyism and personalism, the moment for a revival of a personalist regime has not yet arrived in American politics. The success that Ross Perot enjoyed in 1992, we have argued at length elsewhere, is attributable in the main to certain temporary factors, including a fascination with the outsider, the perceived weakness of the major-party candidates, and a series of political decisions by George Bush and Bill Clinton to give Perot what amounted to a free ride.[40] To be sure, the long-term factors cited by those predicting a system change are in operation, but they do not in our judgment add up to the certainty of more Perot-type candidacies. It is of course possible that our assessment is in error, and that the direction of the long-term trends points more toward personalism than we allow for. But in either event, it is a mistake to think that the character of the future nominating system is the product solely of trends that any analyst can foresee. Instead, the electoral system, within certain important constraints, is something that citizens and legislators can determine by the choices they make. These choices, one hopes, will be influenced by a careful judgment of the best institutional arrangements for the presidential selection system.

The history of presidential selection in the United States demonstrates that political parties are not "natural" or "inevitable" and that in a system with an elected chief executive, "personalism" (or self-nomination) is a possible alternative arrangement. Yet our history also suggests the wisdom of creating political parties as instruments for the presentation of presidential candidates. To be sure, parties, if they are to be consistent with the genius of our system, must find *within* their own conception and structure a way to balance the claims of the party and of the individual. Yet wrestling with the force of personalism within the parties is one thing; encouraging a personalist system beyond the parties is something quite different. Such a system would return us to the demagogic and factional politics that Martin Van Buren observed in 1824 and that we began to witness in many ways in 1992. It is with an eye to avoiding this danger that any future "reform" should be undertaken.

Notes

1. On the congressional caucus, see Frederick W. Whitridge, "Caucus System" (1883) reprinted in Leon Stein ed., *The Caucus System in American Politics* (New York: Arno Press, 1974); C.S. Thompson, "The Rise and Fall of the Con-

gressional Caucus as a Machine for Nominating Candidates for the Presidency," reprinted in Stein, *Caucus System;* Frederick A. Dallinger, *Nominations for Elective Office in the United States* (Cambridge, Mass.: Harvard University Press, 1897); Martin Van Buren, *Inquiry into the Origin and Course of Political Parties in the United States* (New York: Hurd and Houghton, 1867), 4–5; M. Ostrogorski, *Democracy and the Organization of Political Parties* (New York: Macmillan, 1908), 2:22.

2. The only other time that the House directly decided a presidential election was in 1800, when there was, by a kind of statistical accident, a tie between Jefferson and Aaron Burr. Jefferson and Burr were from the same party, with Jefferson known to be the presidential candidate and Burr the vice-presidential candidate. As a result of the problems with this election, the Twelfth Amendment was adopted to provide for a separate electoral vote for the president and the vice president.

3. James W. Ceaser, *Presidential Selection: Theory and Development* (Princeton: Princeton University Press, 1979), chap. 3.

4. On the convention system, see William J. Crotty, *Political Reform and the American Experiment* (New York: Crowell, 1977); Gerald Pomper, *Nominating the President* (Chicago: Northwestern University Press, 1963); Paul T. David et al., *The Politics of National Party Conventions* (New York: Vintage Books, 1964); Thomas R. Marshall, *Presidential Nominations in a Reform Age* (New York: Praeger, 1981); James Bryce, *The American Commonwealth* (London: Macmillan, 1889); and C. Edward Merriam, *Primary Elections: A Study of the History and Tendencies of Primary Election Legislation* (Chicago: University of Chicago Press, 1909).

5. Woodrow Wilson, "Cabinet Government in the United States" in *College and State,* ed. Ray Baker and William Dodd, 2 vols. (New York: Harper Brothers, 1925), 1:36–37; and "Leaderless Government," 1:344.

6. See Crotty, *Political Reform and the American Experiment;* Merriam, *Primary Elections;* Dallinger, *Nominations for Elective Office in the United States;* Austin Ranney, *Curing the Mischiefs of Faction* (Berkeley: University of California Press, 1975).

7. For a discussion of the drive to add primaries, see Louise Overacker, *The Presidential Primary* (New York: Macmillan, 1926); David et al., *Politics of National Party Conventions;* James W. Davis, *Presidential Primaries: Road to the White House* (New York: Crowell, 1967).

8. For the best descriptions of the mixed system, see David et al., *Politics of National Party Conventions;* Pomper, *Nominating the President;* Davis, *Presidential Primaries;* and John Geer, *Nominating Presidents* (Westport, Conn.: Greenwood Press, 1989).

9. New Politics forces were also genuinely convinced that they held a majority of support in the party and the nation, even though a Gallup poll taken two weeks before the convention showed that the convention accurately reflected the preferences of Democratic voters, who supported Humphrey over McCarthy by a margin of 53–39.

10. See the report of the commission, *Mandate for Reform* (Washington, D.C.: Democratic National Committee, April 1970). For the most detailed examinations of the McGovern-Fraser Commission, see Byron E. Shafer, *Quiet Revolution: The Struggle for the Democratic Party and the Shaping of Post-Reform Poli-*

tics (New York: Russell Sage Foundation, 1983); and William J. Crotty, *Decision for the Democrats: Reforming the Party Structure* (Baltimore: Johns Hopkins University Press, 1978).

11. David E. Price, *Bringing Back the Parties* (Washington, D.C.: CQ Press, 1984), 151.

12. Shafer, *Quiet Revolution,* 28.

13. Nelson W. Polsby, *Consequences of Party Reform* (New York: Oxford University Press, 1983).

14. Many reformers denied that an expansion of primaries was their objective, but it seemed to be a logical result of their efforts, intended or not. See Donald M. Fraser, "Democratizing the Democratic Party," in *Political Parties in the Eighties,* ed. Robert A. Goldwin (Washington, D.C.: American Enterprise Institute, 1980), 123; Ranney, *Curing the Mischiefs of Faction,* 205–6; Kenneth A. Bode and Carol F. Casey, "Party Reform: Revisionism Revised," in *Political Parties in the Eighties,* ed. Robert A. Goldwin (Washington, D.C.: American Enterprise Institute, 1980), 16–18; Polsby, *Consequences of Party Reform,* 59; Austin Ranney, *The Federalization of Presidential Primaries* (Washington, D.C.: American Enterprise Institute, 1978).

15. For a good discussion of the Winograd Commission, see Price, *Bringing Back the Parties,* 152–55.

16. See *Cousins v. Wigoda* 419 U. S. 477 (1975); and *Democratic Party of the United States v. LaFollette,* 450 U. S. 107 (1981). The effect of these decisions is discussed at greater length in James W. Ceaser, "Improving the Nominating Process," in *Elections American Style,* ed. A. James Reichley (Washington, D.C.: Brookings Institution, 1987), 29–52.

17. The superdelegates as we define them refer to delegates selected outside the state primary or caucus proceedings and who are unbound by the results of any of those contests. The rules also allowed for bound party officials to be added to the state delegations, but these are not considered superdelegates in the true sense. Later on, after 1984, other party officials have been added to the superdelegate category.

18. See Price, *Bringing Back the Parties,* 159–83.

19. See Priscilla L. Southwell, "The 1984 Democratic Nomination Process," *American Politics Quarterly,* January–April 1986, 75–88; " 'Back-Room' Party Caucuses Draw Fire from Mondale Foes," *Congressional Quarterly Weekly Report,* 2 June 1984, 1315; "1984 Democratic Party Rules Pad Mondale Delegate Lead," *Congressional Quarterly Weekly Report,* 23 June 1984, 1504–5.

20. See "1984 Democratic Party Rules Pad Mondale Delegate Lead," 1504–5; "Democratic Nominating Rules: Back to Drawing Board for 1988," *Congressional Quarterly Weekly Report,* 30 June 1984, 1568–69.

21. See Polsby, *Consequences of Party Reform,* 29; Marshall, *Presidential Nominations,* 42; Leon Epstein, *Political Parties in the American Mold* (Madison: University of Wisconsin Press, 1986), 103–4.

22. Jesse Jackson also had the support of a political movement in the "Rainbow Coalition." But it was a much weaker and more personalist movement than the earlier movements that drove reform, and its focal point was Jackson's candidacy rather than a change of the nomination process. Hence it makes more sense to consider the post-1984 and post-1988 rule changes to have been the result of candidate interest than movement agitation.

23. The Hunt Commission was preceded by several years of scholarly assault on the post-1968 reforms. See, for example, Polsby, *Consequences of Party Reform;* Jeane Kirkpatrick, *Dismantling the Parties* (Washington, D.C.: American Enterprise Institute, 1978); and James W. Ceaser, *Reforming the Reforms* (Cambridge, Mass.: Ballinger, 1982).

24. Walter F. Mondale, "Primaries Are No Test of Character," *New York Times,* 26 February 1992, A21; Gerald L. Baliles, " 'A Better Way to Pick a President' (Cont'd)," *Washington Post,* 19 April 1992, C7.

25. See for example George F. Will, "A Figure of Genuine Pathos," *Washington Post,* 29 July 1992, A23.

26. California legislators, for example, expressed their anger at the way in which California had become little more than a fund-raising stop for candidates because its June primary was usually irrelevant. Governor Mario Cuomo of New York and New York legislators likewise expressed hope that an earlier primary date would give New York more leverage in the process; some New York Republicans also admitted that they hoped an earlier primary date would give GOP presidential contenders more incentive to visit the state and raise money for Cuomo's challenger in 1994. See Richard L. Berke, "California Guarantees Warm Primary Season," *New York Times,* 23 September 1993, A16; Kevin Sack, "Albany Poised to Advance 1996 Primary," *New York Times,* 6 March 1994, A33.

27. Dan Balz, "California Moves Up '96 Primary to March," *Washington Post,* 6 October 1993, A3.

28. See Mark Shields, "High-Stakes Presidential Poker," *Washington Post,* 6 February 1994, C7.

29. Sack, "Albany Poised to Advance 1996 Primary."

30. For a discussion of this problem, see Rhodes Cook, "Primary Glut Leads to Hasty Judgment," *Congressional Quarterly Weekly Report,* 22 January 1994, 142.

31. Ibid.

32. Balz, "California Moves Up '96 Primary."

33. Sack, "Albany Poised to Advance 1996 Primary."

34. Berke, "California Guarantees Warm Primary Season," A16.

35. For a discussion of this possibility, see Wick Allison and William A. Rusher, "Let the Race Begin," *National Review,* 4 April 1994, 46.

36. See Cook, "Primary Glut Leads to Hasty Judgment," 142.

37. Ibid. Cook also proposes that the national parties use positive incentives to induce the states to change their laws. For example, he suggests that Democrats permit states that hold their primaries later in the process to use plurality elections.

38. For a discussion of the growing personalist character of third parties in this century, see Steven J. Rosenstone, Roy L. Behr, and Edward H. Lazarus, *Third Parties in America* (Princeton: Princeton University Press, 1984).

39. Donald Bruce Johnson, comp., *National Platforms of 1980* (Urbana: University of Illinois Press, 1982), 173, 102.

40. James W. Ceaser and Andrew Busch, *Upside Down and Inside Out: The 1992 Elections and American Politics* (Lanham, Md.: Rowman and Littlefield, 1993).

Index

About the Contributors

Emmett H. Buell, Jr., is a professor of political science at Denison University. He is the author of *School Desegregation and Defended Neighborhoods* and coeditor of *Nominating the President,* and he is currently researching negative campaigning in presidential elections. He received his Ph.D. from Vanderbilt University.

Andrew E. Busch is an assistant professor in the Department of Political Science at the University of Denver, where he specializes in American politics. He is coauthor of *Upside Down and Inside Out: The 1992 Elections and American Politics,* with James W. Ceaser. He received his Ph.D. in government from the University of Virginia.

James W. Ceaser is a professor in the Woodrow Wilson Department of Government and Foreign Affairs at the University of Virginia. He is most recently coauthor of *Upside Down and Inside Out: The 1992 Elections and American Politics,* with Andrew Busch. He is also the author of *Liberal Democracy and Political Science, Reforming the Reforms,* and *Presidential Selection: Theory and Development.* He received his Ph.D. in political science from Harvard University.

Anthony Corrado is an associate professor of government at Colby College. He is the author of *Creative Campaigning* and *Paying for Presidents,* as well as coauthor of *Financing the 1992 Election.* He has extensive experience in national politics, and in 1992 he served as national coordinator of the Kerrey for President campaign and as consultant to the Clinton for President committee. He holds a Ph.D. in political science from Boston College.

Emmet T. Flood has taught philosophy and the humanities at the University of Texas and Wesleyan University. He received a Ph.D. in philosophy from Texas and a law degree from Yale. His publications have addressed issues of interpretation in both philosophy and law. He has served as law clerk for Supreme Court Justice Antonin Scalia and is currently an associate in the law firm of Williams & Connolly in Washington, D.C.

Charles D. Hadley is a research professor in political science at the University of New Orleans, where he has taught since 1970. He earned his Ph.D. in political science at the University of Connecticut. He is coauthor, with Everett Carll Ladd, of *Transformations of the American Party System: Political Coalitions from the New Deal to the 1970s*, as well as coeditor of *Southern State Party Organizations and Activists* and *Political Parties in the Southern States: Party Activists in Partisan Coalitions*.

Michael G. Hagen is an associate professor of government at Harvard University. He holds a Ph.D. in political science from the University of California, Berkeley. He is coauthor of *Race and Inequality: A Study in American Values* and *Reasoning and Choice: Explorations in Political Psychology*, as well as a contributor to *The Iowa Caucuses and the Presidential Nominating Process*. His articles have appeared in a variety of academic journals.

James A. McCann is an assistant professor of political science at Purdue University in West Lafayette, Indiana. He received his Ph.D. at the University of Colorado and is the coauthor of *Democratizing Mexico: Public Opinion and Electoral Choices*. His research has appeared in several professional journals, including the *American Political Science Review* and the *Journal of Politics*.

William G. Mayer is an assistant professor of political science at Northeastern University, having received his Ph.D. from Harvard University. His first book, *The Changing American Mind*, is a comprehensive analysis of the change in American political opinion between 1960 and 1988. Mayer has published numerous articles on topics such as public opinion, voting behavior, political parties, and media and politics.

Duane M. Oldfield is assistant professor of political science at Boston College and will be a visiting assistant professor at Knox College in the 1995–96 academic year. He is the author of *The Right and the Righteous: The Christian Right Confronts the Republican Party*. He received his Ph.D. from the University of California, Berkeley.

Harold W. Stanley is an associate professor of political science at the University of Rochester. Holder of a Ph.D. in political science from Yale University, Stanley has published a number of articles and chapters on American politics and elections. Among his books are *Voter Mobilization and the Politics of Race* and *Vital Statistics on American Politics*, 5th edition, with Richard Niemi.